Modern Indian Responses to Religious Pluralism

Modern Indian Responses to Religious Pluralism

Edited by
Harold G. Coward

State University of New York Press

Published by
State University of New York Press, Albany

Printed in the United States of America

For information, address State University of New York Press, State University Plaza, Albany, N.Y., 12246

Library of Congress Cataloging in Publication Data

Modern Indian responses to religious pluralism.

Includes bibliographies and index.
1. Religious pluralism—India. 2. Religious pluralism—Hinduism. I. Coward, Harold G.
BL2015.R44M63 1987 291.1'72'0954 87-1943
ISBN O-88706-571-6
ISBN O-88706-572-4 (pbk.)

10 9 8 7 6 5 4 3 2 1

CONTENTS

Part II: Responses from Other Religions Within India

ACKNOWLEDGEMENTS

The preparation of this volume and the bringing together of the scholars involved was a project of the Calgary Institute for the Humanities. The Calgary Institute for the Humanities was established at the University of Calgary in 1976 for the purpose of fostering advanced study and research in a broad range of subject areas. It supports work in the traditional humanities disciplines such as languages and literatures, philosophy, history, and so forth, as well as the philosophical and historical aspects of the social sciences, sciences, arts and professional studies.

The Institute's programs in support of advanced study provide scholars with time and facilities to carry out their work. In addition, the Institute sponsors formal and informal gatherings to work on specific scholarly projects. In this event the Institute was able to bring senior scholars from Australia, England the United States and across Canada to study Modern Indian Responses to Religious Pluralism. The Institute also used its resources to prepare the final manuscript for publication.

The Calgary Institute for the Humanities is pleased to acknowledge the support of the following who helped to make this research project possible: The Department of Religious Studies, the Faculties of Humanities, General Studies, and Education at the University of Calgary. Generous funding was provided by the Social Science and Humanities Research Council of Canada and the University of Calgary Research Grants Committee. Financial and other assistance was provided by the Sikh Society of Calgary, and the Calgary Indian Community.

Special thanks are due to Robert Baird and Ron Neufeldt who helped to conceive and structure the project. Inder Kher almost single handedly organized the banquet of fine Indian food so thoroughly enjoyed by all. But the greatest debt is owed to the Institute's Administrative Assistant, Gerry Dyer, who handled all arrangements for bringing together such a far flung group of scholars, and organized all meals and rooms for the working sessions in such a pleasant way. The Calgary Institute for the Humanities has also been fortunate to find a publisher thoroughly committed to the topic and anxious to bring out the results of the research as quickly as possible. Working with William Eastman and his staff at SUNY has been a pleasure.

Harold Coward

INTRODUCTION

Religious experience has been defined as the quest for ultimate reality. Many religions exhibit an inner tendency in pursuing this quest to claim to be *the* true religion, to offer *the* true revelation as *the* true way of salvation or release. It would seem self-contradictory for such religions to accept any expression of ultimate reality other than their own.[1] Yet one of the things that characterizes today's world is religious plurality. In the past century the breaking of cultural, racial, linguistic and geographic boundaries is on a scale that the world has not previously seen. For the first time in recorded history we seem to be rapidly becoming a true world community. Today the West is no longer closed within itself. It can no longer regard itself as being the historical and cultural center of the world and as having a religion that is the sole valid way of worship. The same is true for the East. Today everyone is the next-door neighbor and spiritual neighbor of everyone else.

India has perhaps been living through this pluralistic challenge longer than the rest of us. Well before the advent of Christianity and Islam in the West, India was already experiencing the encounters of Hinduism, Buddhism and Jainism with one another. Other religions soon arrived to share India with the Hindus, Buddhists and Jainas. Christians seem to have been present in India early—perhaps as early as the arrival of Jesus' disciple Thomas in the first century C.E.[2] A small community of Jews also settled in India in Malabar, at Cochin, perhaps as early as the first century C.E. There is evidence of small Muslim communities in many of the coastal towns of the Indian Peninsula from the eighth century onwards.[3] But from about 1000 C.E. North-West India experienced increasing invasion and occupation from Muslim emperors in Afghanistan until Islam became the dominant religion of the region.[4] In the ninth century C.E. a group of Zorastrians left Persia to escape Muslim persecution and settled on the north-west coast of India. Their descendants still live there and today are known as Parsis. In the fifteenth century, in the midst of Hindu-Muslim turmoil yet another religion, the Sikh religion, was born with the aim of bringing peace to the conflicting encounter of religions.[5] Thus India, perhaps moreso than anywhere else, became a virtual "living laboratory" of religious pluralism with many of the world's religions living together in the same communities over several centuries.

What has been the result? The aim of this book is to examine the way in which the various religions are responding to the challenge of living side by side with one another in modern India. Since Hinduism, the dominant religion in India, considers itself, and is considered by many others, to be a very tolerant religion, the study of how religious pluralism actually functions in India is especially fascinating. The book is divided into two parts. Part One focuses on the dominant religion, Hinduism, and examines how it has responded to the challenge of having other religions living in its midst, and more recently, to the awareness that it is living in a global community side by side with other religions. The responses from within modern Hinduism are strongly shaped by the Hindu Renaissance movements of the Brahmo Samaj, the Arya Samaj, the Ramakrishna Mission, Aurobindo, Gandhi and Bhaktivedanta, and each of these is studied in a separate chapter. The chapter on Gandhi is presented first as a helpful way into the Indian experience for the Western reader. Responses of two mainline streams from within Hinduism, Vaiṣṇavism and Saivism, are examined. Finally the modern Indian philosophical response, which centers itself largely within Hinduism, is surveyed.

In Part Two the focus shifts from the dominant religion of Hinduism to the other religions within India and to their responses to the challenges of religious pluralism. Separate chapters are given to the Parsis, the Indian Muslims and the Sikhs. A particular Christian response—typical of the Calcutta area, but not of the many other communities of Indian Christians—is examined. Finally the dominant form of Buddhism now present in India, the Tibetan Buddhist community living in exile, is studied.

Because of space and other limitations not all religions living in India have been included in this book. Most notable by its absence is a consideration of the Jaina response. Although still an important religious minority in India, the Jaina community does not seem to have been much involved in the dynamics between religions in the recent past. Had the focus been on classical India, the omission of the Jainas would have been more serious, as their involvement with other religions was much greater than it now is. Some indication of the nature of the Jaina response can be gained, however, by studying the teaching of the Jaina Raychand to Gandhi summarized in Chapter Two. Still the omission of a chapter on the Jainas is a definite lack—one that it is hoped can be remedied by someone else's study in the near future. The other group that was not included was the Indian Jewish community. Its omission is serious for other, quite different reasons. In recent years the Malabar Jews have been leaving India for Israel in increasing numbers. Today the Cochin Jewish community numbers only a handful. Thus, study of its India experience is urgent if it is not to be altogether lost. Fortunately two American Fulbright scholars are currently hard at work in Cochin collecting interviews and materials that will provide the data for such a study.

It is recognized that the restriction of the Christian response to Bengal and the Calcutta area is a serious weakness. Especially in South India the Christian presence has been of much longer duration and has taken very different forms. We can but urge others to take up where we have left off and fill this gap. We must also acknowledge that the very subject matter studied has resulted in some flexibility of approach. In the case of the Hindu Renaissance responses, some chapters focus on founders and movements while other chapters keep the spotlight more narrowly on the founding figures themselves. This flexibility in approach seemed to highlight the essential character of the response in each case and so was retained.

The knowledge gained in the study is an important contribution to our understanding of how traditional Indian religion, especially Hinduism, is interacting with the other religions of the world. More than this, however, is the significant fact that this interaction between religions has been going on in India for centuries—that India is probably the world's oldest and most interesting "living laboratory" of religious pluralism.

NOTES

1. For an examination of how each world religion has handled this conflict of truth claims, see Harold Coward, *Pluralism: Challenge to World Religions*. Maryknoll, N.Y.: Orbis Books, 1985.

2. A.L. Basham, *The Wonder that was India*. New York: Grove Press, 1959, p. 342.

3. *Ibid*, p. 344.

4. *Ibid*, pp. 72–74 and 479–480.

5. Harbans Singh, *The Heritage of the Sikhs*. Columbia MO: South Asia Books, 1983, Cp. II.

Part I

RESPONSES FROM WITHIN HINDUISM

Chapter One

GANDHI AND RELIGIOUS PLURALISM

J.F.T. Jordens

The household in which Mohandas Gandhi grew up was one in which a young mind could experience religious pluralism in action. Whereas his father belonged to the famous Krishnaite sect of the Vallabhacharyas, his mother was an adherent of the Pranamis, an eclectic sect that sought to combine the best of Hinduism and Islam. Moreover, the Gandhi home was frequently visited by Jain monks, who provided religious counselling, and by Muslim friends. It was open to people of all faiths, and religious issues were often discussed in these gatherings. Religious pluralism was a living reality in young Mohandas' life: it was simply taken for granted and there was nothing disturbing about it. There was, however, one exception: the proseletyzing methods of the local Christian missionaries, which included vilification of Hinduism, filled him with a deep revulsion against Christianity.[1]

South Africa: religious pluralism becomes an issue

During his period in England Gandhi began his search for the meaning of Hinduism, and he met some Christians, but this did not produce any anxiety. It was in South Africa that religious pluralism became a pressing personal problem. Some of his closest friends and collaborators were fervent Christians, whom Gandhi admired and loved as much as they admired and loved him. These friends started to put great moral pressure on Gandhi to become a convert to Christianity. They claimed that it was the one true religion, that it was as such revealed by God in the Bible, and that the very content of the Bible proved its unique divine origin. This was a challenge of absolute superiority which Gandhi could not ignore. He decided that in order to clear his mind of doubts he needed to do two things: he should endeavor to know his own religion, and should investigate the meaning of the Bible in order to test the interpretation generally accepted by his Christian friends.[2]

In late 1884 Gandhi sent a list of questions about religion to his Jain friend Fajchandra Rajivbhai Mehta, whom he called Raychand. He had met Raychand on his return to India in 1881, and had been deeply impressed by his spiritual insight as expressed in his writings and evidenced in his life. Raychand's detailed answers[3] struck a chord in Gandhi as they clearly articulated ideas that had been vaguely present in his own mind and seemed in harmony with his own religious aspirations. It is important to set out the main principles of Raychand's thought, because, as will become clear later on, they exercised an enormous influence on Gandhi's developing conception of Hinduism, of religion in general, and of the essence of all religious aspiration.

Raychand categorically denied the existence of a God-Creator: ultimate reality to him, as a true Jain, consisted of two distinct, irreducible and imperishable orders: the order of the spirit, encompassing an infinite number of individual spirits (*ātman*, or in Jain terms *jīva*), and that of the material world composed of atoms.[4] These two orders had become entangled to the detriment of the spirit. Religion *(dharma)* referred to the process by which the individual spirits gradually free themselves from the bonds of matter (attachment and ignorance), and finally realize their true nature: that perfect state of complete liberation from all bonds of matter and from the cycle of transmigration itself is called *moksa*. Raychand wrote that the name Ishvara, which in Hinduism refers to the personal God, may be used only to indicate that *jīva* who has reached *moksa*. In very short compass, the above constituted for Raychand the essential doctrine of the one and eternal religion that has existed from the beginning of time.

That eternal religion had been revealed in the scriptures. The scriptures of the various religions, as books, are all by definition imperfect because they were composed by imperfect men, and not revealed by a personal God who does not exist. This applies as much to the Indian scriptures as to the Bible.

However, Raychand held that there was a great difference in value and depth between these scriptures. He considered the teachings of the Jain sages infinitely more profound than those contained in the *Vedas*, and he had a very low opinion of the doctrines of Christianity as compared with those originating in India. He accepted, therefore, that it was necessary to compare the various scriptures in order to find out not what elements were true or false, but which system 'had more power-truth.' In fact he indicated how this comparison should proceed:

> Only the test of proof can show what is the best and what is not. That religion alone is the best and is truly strong, which is most helpful in detroying the bondage of worldly life and can establish us in the state which is our essence.[5]

In other words, the comparative test consists of putting the various counsels into practice, and a religion proves its worth and truth by the degree of effectiveness of that practical application. As for the doctrines of the incarnation of Christ and of the Hindu *avatārs*, Raychand considered them to be concepts 'against reason', which at most could only have 'allegorical' value. Calling Krishna the perfect *avatār* of God, or God himself, was only the expression of the belief that Krishna's *jīva* had attained *moksa*, an achievement open to all *jīvas*.

As a scholarly Jain, Raychandra knew well the intricate Jain doctrines of *anekāntavāda*, the multifaceted plurality of all reality, and of *syādvāda*, the consequent relativity of all propositions. But as a poet and a writer of religious pamphlets, and a practitioner of the doctrines, he was able to express those abstruse doctrines in a practical, simple, and pithy way. No doubt it was that part of Raychandra's work that had most influence on Gandhi. A few examples are given here, which could well have been uttered by Gandhi himself.

> In essential reality there is no differentiation whatsoever; the difference is only in the eye of the beholder. Believe that, grasp the essence, and you will make progress in religion. Whatever

> religion you profess, I do not take sides for or against. Only this is worth saying: by whatever method, devotion, or dharma the contamination of the soul by this world is destroyed, that is the dharma, that is the discipline you should follow.
>
> This world has been unable to discover truth because it is shackled by the chains of doctrinal disputes.[6]

Gandhi realized how much he was influenced by Raychandra, and freely acknowledged this in his autobiography.[7] But his most telling account of that influence is to be found in his preface to the second edition of Raychandra's letters and writings. He stated there that Raychand was responsible for his peace of mind at the time of his religious doubts in South Africa. He summarized Raychand's religion as follows: "Dharma does not mean any particular creed or dogma. Dharma is a quality of the soul . . . " He praised Raychand's respect for other faiths and in his last paragraph he in fact presented his own view of religious tolerance as one that "followed Raychandbhai's point of view."[8]

While Gandhi was seeking help from Raychand for clarifying his ideas on Hinduism and on religion in general, he also explored another avenue. The Christian friends who were putting pressure on him were mostly "evangelicals". Very simply stated, their fundamental belief was that mankind had fallen into sin, and could only be saved by the atonement of Christ; faith in Christ was the only hope of salvation; the proof of that belief was contained in the Bible, which constituted the unique and final revelation of God and was to be interpreted in a fundamentalist way. Gandhi came to know that other Christians interpreted the Bible differently, and he wrote to Edward Maitland, founder of the Esoteric Christian Union, who sent him two of his books. The doctrines contained in these works seemed to Gandhi to provide an acceptable alternative interpretation of the Bible and to supplement and strengthen the ideas expressed by Raychand.[9]

Maitland believed that the sacred scriptures of various religions were but the recurring historical revelations of a basic universal revelation.[10] Consequently he categorically rejected a fundamentalist and historic interpretation of the Bible. To him the Christian scriptures did not primarily deal with historic events and persons, but rather with a deeper purely spiritual truth: their purpose was "to exhibit and illustrate processes and principles which are purely spiritual."[11] This approach led him to an interpretation of Christ very far removed from that of the evangelicals: "Christ Jesus, then, is no other than the hidden and true man of the Spirit, the Perfect Humanity, the Express Image of the Divine Glory."[12] Christ thus was the ideal of perfection, a perfection that was equally attainable by all men, because between them and Christ, "there was no difference whatever in kind . . . but only in the unfoldment of their common spiritual nature."[13] The similarities of these conceptions with some of Raychand's are obvious: religion is the process of the spiritualization of the individual; all individual spirits are able to achieve the final perfection; scriptures should not be understood literally, but as imperfect attempts at clarifying that process.

The ideas of Raychand and Maitland, reinforced by some ideas of Tolstoy,[14] and by further readings about various religions,[15] had given Gandhi a firm foundation in his approach to Hinduism and to other religions. His anxiety about the claims of Christianity disappeared. And during the remainder of the South African period the question of religious pluralism was raised no more.

Tolerance (1914–30)

"They are all rivers that meet in the same ocean."

From the time of his definitive return to India in 1914, Gandhi repeatedly made statements concerning religious pluralism. The reason for this was that he was frequently asked, even challenged, to clarify his ideas about Hinduism and other religions. These questions came from different quarters. Many Hindus were uneasy about what they considered Gandhi's radical and unorthodox stance in intouchability and Hindu-Muslim relations, and disliked what they considered his open flirtation with Christianity and Islam. On the other hand, Christian missionaries kept asking Gandhi questions about his attitude to Christianity, whereas Gandhi regularly took them to task for their conversion work, which he considered a misdirection of effort. All these issues touched upon the basic problem of religious pluralism, and during this period Gandhi's constant theme was that the various religions should "tolerate" each other's differences because they were all "rivers that meet in the same ocean,"[16] or in other words, "if we look to the aim, there is no difference among religions."[17]

Before analyzing what Gandhi's idea of tolerance meant, it needs to be stated that his concept of Hinduism was wider than that adopted by most: to him the term 'Hinduism' always included both Jainism and Buddhism under its wide umbrella. He stated, "I do not regard Jainism or Buddhism as separate from Hinduism"; and he often reiterated that strongly held opinion.[18]

The attitude of "tolerance" is mostly described by Gandhi in the context of his description of Hinduism. Hinduism is non-exclusive, or all-inclusive, accepts truth and revelation in all religions, gives room to the worship of all prophets, and admits that all religions are both perfect and imperfect and are able to lead man to his final goal, *moksa*, liberation from the cycle of transmigration and merger with the Absolute. Hinduism is "as broad as the Universe and takes in its fold all that is good in this world,"[19] and "what of substance is contained in any other religion is always to be found in it."[20] Not being exclusive, "it enables the followers of that faith not merely to respect all other religions, but also to admire and assimilate whatever may be good" in them.[21] However, Gandhi did not mean to say that Hinduism was but an eclectic amalgam; no, its inclusiveness stemmed from its very nature, from the fact that it was a faith based on the broadest possible toleration.[22]

A couple of times Gandhi indicated how that principle of toleration was formulated as a logical axiom in the "Hindu" tradition: he referred to the doctrines of *anekāntavāda* and *syād-vāda*, well-known categories of Jain philosophy. This is not surprising since to him they were part and parcel of the broad Hindu tradition, and since believing that Jainism had most rationally expressed the essence of religion, he considered it "the most logical of all faiths."[23] He stated: "I am an *anekātavādi*. This is the most important thing that I have learnt from Jain philosophy. It is implicit in Vedanta philosophy, while in Jain philosophy it is explicitly stated."[24] Elsewhere he declared that with the help of the *syādvāda* principle he "had established long ago the unity of all religions."[25] The *anekāntavāda* doctrine of Jainism is the doctrine of the many-ness of reality: reality is so complex that the many acceptable propositions about it may be very different, and even contradictory depending on the point of view of the observer. From there follows the *syādvāda* principle of logic: since all propositions essentially present only partial views, they should all be qualified by *syād*, or be prefaced by "from one point of view," thus leaving the door open for different statements which are equally true from other points of view.

> It has been my experience that I am always right from my point of view and am often wrong from the point of view of my honest critics. I know that we are both right from our respective points of view. And this knowledge saves me from attributing motives to my opponents or critics . . . I very much like this doctrine of the manyness of reality. It is this doctrine that has taught me to judge a Mussalman from his own standpoint and a Christian from his.[26]

However, for Gandhi there is beyond those ontological and logical categories an even deeper specifically religious justification why tolerance is of the very essence of Hinduism: "tolerance is also at the root of the dharma of truth."[27] Gandhi never tired of asserting that truth and non-violence constituted the essence of Hinduism:

> My correspondent accuses me of using the ambiguous middle in that I have confused truth and non-violence with the Hindu creed. The crime is deliberate. It is the good fortune or misfortune of Hinduism that it has no official creed. In order, therefore, to protect myself against any misunderstanding, I have said that truth and non-violence is my creed. If I were asked to define the Hindu creed, I should simply say: search for truth through non-violent means.[28]

It is evident that a search for truth respecting non-violence must be based on tolerance: tolerance, therefore, is "at the very root of the dharma of truth."

Thus Gandhi linked tolerance with the very essence of Hinduism. However, it is important to note that in defining the essence of Hinduism, Gandhi also intended to indicate what he considered to be the essence of religion in general. Whenever he specifically referred to the comparison of religions, or asked the question how one can detect the essence and root of all religions, his answer was the same as the one he gave when he spoke about the essence of Hinduism. For example, in answer to Dr. Crane's question, "But when you say that all religions are true, what do you do when there are conflicting counsels?", Gandhi answered:

> I have no difficulty in hitting upon the truth because I go by certain fundamental maxims. Truth is superior to everything and I reject what conflicts with it. Similarly that which is in conflict with non-violence should be rejected. And on matters which can be reasoned out, that which conflicts with Reason must also be rejected.[29]

Tolerance, therefore, was the proper attitude to all religions because of its intimate connection with the very essence of Hinduism and of all religions, and of Religion itself, namely truth and non-violence. On the other hand, Gandhi repeatedly stated that Hinduism was "the most tolerant of all religions."[30] Since Hinduism was the most tolerant of all religions, and since tolerance was of the very essence of religion, Gandhi drew the conclusion that it was preeminent among them, superior to them: "Hinduism is the most tolerant of all religions. Its creed is all embracing. But to claim that is to claim superiority for the Hindu creed above all the other creeds of the world."[31] That same idea is clearly implied in the following statements:

> What of substance is contained in any other religion is always to be found in Hinduism. And what is not contained in it is insubstantial or unnecessary.[32]

> I do not want you to become a Hindu. But I do want you to become a better Christian by absorbing all that may be good in Hinduism and that you may not find in the same measure or not at all in the Christian teaching.[33]

Equality (1930–48)

"They are all branches of the same tree."

It was precisely the realization that his doctrine of tolerance implied a suggestion of the superiority of Hinduism that made Gandhi alter his teaching. This deliberate change can be accurately dated: on 23 September 1930, he wrote to Narandas Gandhi as follows:

> Equality of Religions. This is the new name we have given to the Ashram observance which we know as 'Tolerance'. '*Sahishnuta*'

> is a translation of the English word 'Tolerance'. I did not like that word but could not think of a better one. Kakasaheb, too, did not like that word. He suggested 'Respect for all religions'. I did not like that phrase either. Tolerance may imply a gratuitous assumption of the inferiority of other faiths to one's own and respect suggests a sense of patronizing whereas ahimsa teaches us to entertain the same respect for the religious faiths of others as we accord to our own, thus admitting the imperfection of the latter:[34]

This was for Gandhi a deliberate and important change, to which he referred several times in the coming years. In a discussion with Krzenski on 2 January 1937, he answered the latter's observation that he had great respect for Gandhi's religion as follows:

> Not enough. I had that feeling myself one day, but I found that it was not enough. Unless I accept the position that all religions are equal, and I have as much regard for other religions as I have for my own, I would not be able to live in the boiling war around me.[35]

In answer to a question about his attitude to conversion, he said as follows in a discussion with Sarat Chandra Bose and others: "I have, of course, always believed in the principle of religious tolerance. But I have gone even further. I have advanced from tolerance to equal respect for all religions."[36] That this change was decisive for Gandhi is clearly demonstrated by the fact that in his writings after 1930 no single statement can be found affirming, or even suggesting, the superiority of Hinduism, which he did refer to before that date.

Another way in which the deliberate change of Gandhi's ideas is clearly indicated is the use of a new metaphor, which emerged in that most important letter to Narandas Gandhi previously referred to: "Even as a tree has a single trunk, but many branches and leaves, so is there one true and perfect religion, but it becomes many as it passes through the human medium."[37] Previously Gandhi's metaphor was that "religions are all rivers that meet in the same ocean."[38] That image does not necessarily suggest equality or identity in the essence of religions, but stresses the similarity of the final goal to which by their individual meandering ways they all eventually lead. The new metaphor concentrates on the sameness of essence: religions are equal because at the root, at the trunk they are really one; there is one true and perfect

Religion. Gandhi never went back to the metaphor of the river, but from 1930 onward he repeatedly used the one of the tree.[39]

Although on the one hand this was presented by Gandhi as a change of attitude and a new insight, on the other it does not seem to have been precipitated by a new discovery. In fact, Gandhi believed that he was simply drawing a conclusion that had always been implicit in his doctrine of tolerance, that he was making explicit what he had really believed and practiced before. He tried to explain this to Narandas Gandhi by recalling his experiences in South Africa:

> When I was turning over the pages of the sacred books of different faiths for my own satisfaction, I became sufficiently familiar for my purpose with Christianity, Islam, Zoroastrianism, Judaism and Hinduism. In reading these texts, I can say that I felt the same regard for all these faiths although, perhaps, I was not then conscious of it. Reviewing my memory of those days I do not find I ever had the slightest desire to criticize any of these religions merely because they were not my own, but read each sacred book in a spirit of reverence and found the same fundamental morality in each.[40]

If all religions are in final instance the same, but branches of one tree, then the question arises what exactly that "fundamental essence" consisted of. "The fact is that there are no irreconcilable differences between religions. If you were to probe the surface, you will find one and the same thing at the bottom."[41] Gandhi was pressed to explain how this could be reconciled with the fact that there were so many conflicting doctrines and counsels between the great religions. He held that the underlying unity could be discovered in the following manner:

> After a study of those religions to the extent that it was possible for me, I have come to the conclusion that, if it is proper and necessary to discover an underlying unity among all religions, a master-key is needed. That master-key is that of truth and non-violence. When I unlock the chest of a religion with this master-key, I do not find it difficult to discover its likeness with other religions.[42]

Truth and non-violence, therefore, were for Gandhi the supreme tests which in final instance decided what in any religion was fundamental and everlasting, what constituted the one Religion, the truth from which all branches grew. He wrote, "that one

Religion was beyond all speech. Imperfect men throughout the ages put it into such language as they could command, and their words continued to be interpreted by other men equally imperfect in scriptures and *shāstras*".[43] Whose interpretation was to be held to be right? Everybody was right from his own standpoint, but "it is not impossible that everybody may be wrong."[44] All scriptures, dogmatic structures, theological interpretations and moral codes are essentially imperfect, because they proceed from imperfect men: none should be considered to articulate ultimate answers. Gandhi's generous acceptance of the equal truth of all religions, including Hinduism, was based on the conviction that all their scriptures, teachings, and counsels were essentially of a relative nature. The rare pure gold of ultimacy could only be detected by the application of the acid tests of truth and non-violence; that Religion was one that "transcended Hinduism,— the basic truth that underlies all the religions of the world."[45] In fact, when accused of confusing truth and non-violence with the Hindu creed, Gandhi retorted," the crime is deliberate."[46]

Gandhi was, indeed, prepared to stand by his judgment, even if all Hindus rejected it: "My religion is a matter solely between my Maker and myself. If I am a Hindu, I cannot cease to be one even though I may be disowned by the whole of the Hindu population."[47] Elsewhere he wrote: "It has been whispered that by being so much with Musulman friends, I make myself unfit to know the Hindu mind. The Hindu mind is myself."[48] Gandhi was unrepentantly individualistic in his conception of Hinduism and of the essential Religion. In fact his ultimate criteria of truth and non-violence were not really criteria for sifting the true and the false propositions of scripture and dogma: the latter were by definition imperfect, relative and ultimately unimportant. They were criteria for deciding the right *action* because for Gandhi ultimately religion was not about credal or conceptual systems, but about moral action, right action to be undertaken by the individual here and now: "what cannot be followed out in day-to-day practice cannot be called religion."[49] That was the very essence of Gandhi's concept of religion, and that was the norm by which all had to be judged.

Conclusion

In fact, that concept of religion as self-purification in action, as the liberation of the individual spirit from the bonds of matter was the stance Gandhi took from very early days, and from which he never moved away. His explanation of Hinduism, his doctrine of tolerance, his doctrine of the equality of religions, his pronouncements about the one Religion, the trunk of which all religions were but branches, all these statements find their deepest explanation and justification in that fundamental Gandhian concept. To him religion was about self-realization, about the constant fight of spirit to conquer matter. Scripture, faith, dogmas and rituals were only imperfect human creations that may be a help or a hindrance in that struggle; as such they were all non-essential, interchangeable, dispensable, and, therefore, not worth quarelling over. Religion is essentially the individual's perpetual effort to realize perfect self-control in all his action, and it is precisely in that area of individual moral decision-making that the absolute criteria of truth and non-violence come into operation.

It is reasonably clear what the criterion of non-violence means in the sphere or moral action, but what does the criterion of truth mean in that context? Gandhi does not specifically answer that question at any one time, but one finds scattered fragments of the answer all along: truth-in-action means principles of conduct such as sexual abstinence, frugality, service, selflessness, fasting. Perhaps a more comprehensive answer may be indicated in the following way. According to Gandhi the *Bhagavadgītā* contained the essence of *dharma*,[50] and the essence of the *Gītā* was expressed in the last twenty stanzas of chapter Two.[51] What exactly is said in that vital passage? It spells out Krishna's definition of the *stithaprajna*, the person who has achieved complete mastery over inner and outer senses, over desires and dislikes, and has reached an attitude of total indifference to all that may please or displease: that total inner and outer control makes for peace. To Gandhi that constitutes the supreme religious achievement: such a person's every action has been and continues to be governed by "truth". That is the comprehensive answer of the meaning of truth as a criterion of action. In that context one understands why Gandhi, whose ideal was the *stithaprajna*, called his autobiography "The Story of My Experiments with Truth".

In the final analysis Gandhi's attitude to the multiplicity of religions stemmed from a basic normative stance: his own definition of religion, which was a very individualistic one, and which could not really be challenged because it was, to quote Gandhi himself, "a matter solely between him and his Maker". That is the normative dogmatism that lies at the root of his tolerance. Gandhi was able to accept the value of all the creeds, dogmatic structures, ritual systems and ethical codes because he considered none of them as ultimate, but all of them as having only relative and pragmatic value: they were imperfect means by which various cultures attempted to achieve the essential purpose of Religion: to shape the spiritual man who controls all his thoughts and actions by truth and non-violence.

How many Christians, Muslims, or even Hindus would be prepared to accept the religious "tolerance" or "equality" proposed by Gandhi with its full implications? Admittedly, Gandhi did not exalt Hinduism above any other religion in the last eighteen years of his life, a fact of which many Hindus were acutely and painfully aware. But what he did exalt above everything was his own individual concept of the essence of religion. No doubt, as we have indicated at the beginning, the influence of Jain ideas was very important in the emergence of the Gandhian concept of religion, and he did consider Jainism the most "rational" exposition of religion, but even the Jain believer would find it difficult to subscribe to Gandhi's radical relativism. In the final instance Gandhi's attitude of "tolerance" and "equality" towards religious pluralism is based on such an individualistic normative concept of the essence of religion that it is difficult to see how it could be accepted or countered outside that narrow framework.

Notes

1. Pyarelal, *Mahatma Gandhi*, vol. I, *The Early Phase*, Ahmedabad, 1965, pp. 213 ff. Besides Gandhi's Autobiography, Pyarelal's work and C.D.S. Devanesan's *The Making of the Mahatma*, London, 1969, are the best sources for the details of this paragraph.

2. Cf. Gandhi's autobiography, *The Story of My Experiments with Truth*, part II chh. X, XI, XV, and XXII.

3. A translation of Raychandra's replies is available in *The Collected Works of Mahatma Gandhi*, Navajivan Trust, Ahmedabad (henceforth quoted as CW), vol. XXXII, Appendix I, pp. 593–602. For an analysis of Jain influence on Gandhi, cf. S.N. Hay, "Jain influences on Gandhi's early thought", in S.N. Ray, *Gandhi, India and the World*, Melbourne, 1970, pp. 29–38.

4. This paragraph is based on the above, CW, XXXII, 593–602.

5. Ibid, p. 598.

6. Cf. Mallishena Suri's *Syādvādamanjarī*, ed. J.C. Jain, vol. 12 of the *Shrīmad Rāychandra Jain Shāstramālā*, Anand, 1970, Biographical Sketch of Raychandra, p. 9.

7. Autobiography, part II, ch. XV.

8. CW, XXXII, pp. 4, 11, 13.

9. Cf. Pyarelal, pp. 321–7. Gandhi not only "greatly liked" Maitland's works, he became a propagandist of the Esoteric Christian Union, and mentioned it on his letterhead. He regularly corresponded with Maitland until the latter's death in 1897, ordered many copies of his books, and defended the author in the *Natal Advertiser* (cf CW, 1, 139, 165).

10. Anna Kingsford and Edward Maitland, *The Perfect Way*, or *The Finding of Christ*, fourth ed., preface S.H. Hart, London, John M. Watkins, 1909, p. 28.

11. Ibid., pp. 225, 230.

12. Ibid., p. 112.

13. Ibid, p. 248.

14. Cf. Pyarelal, pp. 662 ff, and Naresh Guha, "Gandhi and Tolstoy, Brother Experimenters in Soul-Force", in C.D. Narasimhaiah, *Gandhi and the West*, Univ. of Mysore, 1970, p. 180.

15. Ibid, pp. 709 ff.

16. CW, VII, 338.

17. Ibid.

18. CW, XXXV, p. 167; cf also CW XIII, 220; XIV, 44; 27, 62; XXXIV, 24; XXV, 167; XL, 104 and 117.

19. CW, XXVII, 61.

20. CW, XXVIII, 194.

21. CW, XXXV, 166.

22. Ibid., 254.

23. CW, IV, 370.

24. CW, XXIII, 20.

25. CW, XXXIV, 24.

26. *Young India*, Jan 21, 1926, p. 30. Quoted in Pyarelal, p. 277.

27. CW, XXVI, 324.

28. CW, XXIII, 485, cf also XXVI, 131 and XXIII, 485.

29. CW, LXIV, 398; see also XII, 127; XXIII, 196; XXIV, 139; XXXII, 11; XLIV, 167; XLV, 223; LXXII, 254.

30. CW, XII, 220; XXXV, 166 and 254; XXXVI, 164.

31. CW, XXIII, 485.

32. CW, XXVIII, 194.

33. CW, XXXVII, 224.

34. CW, XLIV, 166.

35. CW, LXIV, 204.

36. CW, LXXXVI, 155.

37. CW, XLIV, 166.

38. CW, VII, 338.

39. CW, LVII, 17; LXIV, 203 and 420; LXXII, 254; LXXXV, 31; LXXXVI, 155.

40. CW, XLIV, 190.

41. CW, XLV, 223.

42. CW, LXXII, 254.

43. CW, XXV, 86; LXIV, 75.

44. CW, XLIV, 167.

45. CW, XXIII, 196.

46. CW, XXIII, 485.

47. CW, XXIV, 139.

48. CW, XXV, 202.

49. CW, XLI, 98; cf also XV, 317; XXIX, 444; XXXII, 228.

50. CW, XXVIII, 316; LI, 344; LVI, 341.

51. CW, XXVIII, 316; XXXII, 31 and 146; LXXI, 29.

Chapter Two

THE RESPONSE OF THE BRAHMO SAMAJ

J.N. Pankratz

In the Trust Deed signed by Rammohun Roy and seven of his associates in Calcutta on January 8, 1830, a plot of land and a building on Chitpore Road was set aside

> as and for a place of public meeting of all sorts and descriptions of people without distinction as shall behave and conduct themselves in an orderly and sober religious and devout manner for the worship and adoration of the Eternal Unsearchable and Immutable Being who is the Author and Preserver of the Universe but not under or by any other name designation or title peculiarly used for and applied to any particular Being or Beings by any men or set of men whatsoever and that no graven image statue or sculpture carving painting picture portrait or the likeness of anything shall be admitted within the said messuages building land tenements hereditaments and premises and that no sacrifice offering or oblation of any kind or thing shall ever be permitted therein . . . and that in conducting the said worship and adoration no object animate or inanimate that has been or is or shall hereafter become or be recognized as an object of worship by any man or set of men shall be reviled or slightingly or contemptuously spoken

of or alluded to either in preaching praying or in the hymns or other mode of worship that may be delivered or used in the said Messuage or building and that no sermon preaching discourse prayer or hymn be delivered made or used in such worship but such as have a tendency to the promotion of the contemplation of the Author and Preserver of the Universe to the promotion of charity morality piety benevolence virtue and the strengthening [of] the bonds of union Between men of all religious persuasions and creeds . . .[1]

The building was officially opened on January 23, 1830.[2] It became the home of the Brahmo Samaj,[3] and the Trust Deed has become known as the Trust Deed of the Brahmo Samaj.

For Rammohun Roy,[4] the dynamic force behind the Brahmo Samaj, this was not his first attempt to organize a forum for religious discussion and worship. In 1815, soon after he moved to Calcutta from Rangpur, he and several friends began the Atmiya Sabha, an association intended to provide a context for the free discussion of theological subjects. Membership and regular participation in the Atmiya Sabha appears to have been quite limited, but occasionally the group attracted considerable attention. One such occasion was the debate, in 1816, between Rammohun and Subramanya Sastri, a Brahmin from Madras, on the subject of image worship.[5] This debate was attended by many leading citizens of Calcutta, including Radhakanta Deb.[6] In this debate Rammohun challenged the usefulness, advisability, and legitimacy of image worship, insisting, as he already was beginning to do through his publications,[7] that the worship of the Universal Being through the medium of images was misleading and unnecessary.

But although the Atmiya Sabha provided a congenial context for theological discussion for Rammohun and his associates, it never became a context for systematic worship and religious devotion. By 1819 the meetings of the Sabha were irregular, and after that they were discontinued. Soon after this Rammohun began to focus his attention on another forum, and ths time the emphasis shifted somewhat from discussion and debate to worship.

In 1821 Rammohun helped to establish a Unitarian congregation in Calcutta. Rammohun's involvement in this venture began through his association with two Baptist missionaries, Mr. William Yates and Mr. William Adam, in the translation of the four Gospels into Bengali. Rammohun disagreed with Trinitarian theology, and as a result of the discussions about such questions during the translation work, Mr. Yates withdrew from the project, leaving Mr. Adam and Rammohun to continue. Subsequently Mr. Adam rejected Trinitarianism and announced that he was now a Unitarian. This change of theological position was dramatic and scandalous,[8] and the Baptist missionaries who had been Adam's colleagues until this time began to refer to him as "the second fallen Adam".[9] Adam's position in Calcutta was awkward and insecure; his status as a Baptist missionary was terminated.

Rammohun went to considerable lengths to assist Adam in establishing a new base for his presence in Calcutta. He, along with Adam, four other Bengalis and five British, established the Calcutta Unitarian Committee in September 1821,[10] and in January 1822, when Unitarian worship services were established in a house, Rammohun was one of the major supporters.[11]

Through his involvement with the Calcutta Unitarians Rammohun became involved in correspondence with Unitarians in England and the United States. In that correspondence he explained what attracted him to this interpretation of Christianity; but perhaps more importantly, he described his own interpretation of Unitarian Christianity. As he put it, in a letter to "a gentleman in Baltimore",[12]

> I wish to add . . . my view of Christianity is that in representing all mankind as the children of one eternal Father, it enjoins them to love one another, without making any distinction of country, caste, colour, or creed; notwithstanding they may be justified in the sight of the Creator in manifesting their respect towards each other, according to the propriety of their actions and the reasonableness of their religious opinions and differences.

In a small pamphlet, published under the title *Answer of A Hindoo,* Rammohun responded to the question, "Why do you frequent a Unitarian place of worship, instead of the numerously attended established Churches?" His answer:

> Because the prayers read, worship offered, and sermons preached in the Unitarian place of worship remind me of the infinitely wise Ruler of this infinite universe, without ascribing to him as Churchmen do, fellow-creators or co-operators equal in power and other attributes . . . Because Unitarians reject polytheism and idolatry under every sophisticated modification, and thereby discountenance all the evil consequences resulting from them . . . Because

> Unitarians believe, profess, and inculcate the doctrine of the divine unity—a doctrine which I find firmly maintained both by the Christian Scriptures and by our most ancient writings commonly called the Vedas.[13]

He actively supported Adam and the Unitarian projects in Calcutta until 1828, even though the church was losing rather than gaining support among both foreigners and Bengalis.[14] But much as he could identify with Unitarian Christianity theologically and promote it as an alternative to the established Christian churches, it was not finally to be his religious identify.

On August 20, 1828 Rammohun and many of his closest friends held the first meeting of the Brahmo Samaj. Accounts of the origins of the impetus for the Samaj vary; some suggest that William Adam encouraged the Hindu Unitarians in Calcutta to form an auxiliary association, one in which Christianity would have a less prominent role so that it was more acceptable to other Hindus. Other accounts suggest that some of Rammohun's friends who attended the Unitarian worship with him, expressed a strong preference for their own place of worship, and that Rammohun and a few others rented a house and organized a form of worship to make this possible.[15]

All contemporary accounts of the meetings of the Brahmo Samaj make it clear that while the congregational form which was used might partially owe its origins to Christian worship, all other aspects of the worship were Hindu in character.[16] The Vedas were recited by two Telegu Brahmins, seated in an adjoining room so that the texts would not be desecrated by being read in the immediate presence of common people. The Upanisads were read in Sanskrit and when explained in Bengali by Pandit Ram Chandra Vidyabagish. After this Pandit Vidyabagish preached a sermon. Hymns, based on Sanskrit texts or devotional themes were snug in Sanskrit or Bengali, and Vedic prayers were chanted in Sanskrit.

The dominant theological themes of this worship were the unity of God, the inadequacy of worship through images, the centrality of reason in understanding God, the importance of service to others as the authentication of true religion, the primacy of direct experience of God, and the tolerance of the true worshipper who recognized that all views of God were but partial.

The Brahmo Samaj was a logical institutional or organizational embodiment of the ideas Rammohun had expressed so frequently in his writings. He argued insistently that the true basis of all worship was the belief in and experience of the One God, the Universal Being.[17] This Being was known universally through reason and revelation.[18] Rammohun was grateful for the Christian revelation through which this Being was made known, and especially for the life and teachings of Jesus,[19] and willingly participated in worship with Christians within the framework of this revelation. But throughout his writings he insisted that this Being was also revealed through Hindu scriptures.[20] At times he went further and argued that Hindu scriptures, such as the Upanisads and the Vedanta, contained the most elevated texts and insights about the Supreme Being, and that by comparison, on these matters, Christian scriptures were inferior.[21] He was not opposed to Hindus becoming familiar with Christian scriptures, but he insisted that they should do so out of mutual religious interest and respect, not because of any inadequacy in Hindu scriptures. He did not intend this as a sectarian rejection of Christian revelation but simply as an affirmation of the truth already present within his own religious tradition; and for that matter, all other traditions.

There was more than cultural and national pride involved here, and this was more than a matter of generous tolerance; although Rammohun did try to foster national pride as well as to promote international tolerance and respect. This was an important theological issue for him, and it was central to his understanding of religious pluralism. He argued that the Universal Being was revealed and known in all nations, but that this knowledge, although universal, was expressed in specific forms within particular cultures.

In summary, there are five major motifs in Rammohun's writings and organizational activities which are especially relevant to understand his approach to religious pluralism, and these motifs are the legacy he left to the Brahmo Samaj. First, is an emphasis on the universal brotherhood of all those who worship the Author and Preserver of the Universe. Sometimes Rammohun expressed this principle even more broadly by stressing that all mankind were children under the common and shared Fatherhood of God, regardless of how they understood and worshipped God. The second motif is an explicit as well as an implicit critique of certain conceptions of God and forms of worship; specifically, Rammohun challenged polytheism, incarnation, and idolatry. Third, a vigorous advocacy of the unity of God and the worship of God by means of scripture, prayer, sermons, and hymns. Fourth, tolerance and generosity expressed toward those whose forms of worship are based on other religious traditions, and even toward those whose theology and worship is rejected by the worshippers of the one God. Fifth, the affirmation that since God is universally revealed, each nation or culture will have appropriate forms through which to express its understanding of God and to worship God.

Sivanath Sastri, the historian of the Brahmo Samaj, succinctly summarizes Rammohun's response to religious pluralism as follows:

> The sum total of the Raja's teachings, spread over many volumes of controversy, seems to be that the doctrine of the One True God is the universal element in all religions, and as such forms an article of faith of universal religion for mankind; but the practical applications of that universal religion are to be always local and national . . . [22]

Or, as Sastri puts it elsewhere, the foundation of the Brahmo Samaj was the "unsectarian worship of the One True God".[23] It was universal, but that universality was understood inclusively rather than exclusively; that is, the revelation was shared by people throughout the world and all participated in it together, albeit through their particular cultural and national form.

Certainly the need for an Indian expression of Unitarianism was the basic reason for formation of the Brahmo Samaj. And yet, when the Samaj came into being it was not simply an Indianized version of Unitarianism. Even the Unitarians, with whom Rammohun had such cordial relations, and William Adam, whom Rammohun had supported so generously, expressed disappointment when they saw that the Brahmo Samaj was not a transposition of Unitarianism into Indian form, but was a form of monotheistic worship which had its roots in Indian culture and religious history. As Adam expressed it in a letter in January 1829,

> There has accordingly been formed a Hindu Unitarian Association, the object of which is, however, strictly Hindu and not Christian, i.e., to teach and practise the worship of the One Only God on the basis of the divine authority of the Ved, and not of the Christian Scriptures. This is the basis of which I have distinctly informed Rammohun and my other native friends that I cannot approve.[24]

Adam and other English Unitarians were, after all, Christians; some of them were even Christian missionaries. Although they disagreed with the majority of Christians on Trinitarian theology, they still held Christian scriptures to have divine authority.[25] Although Adam was disappointed when he found that Rammohun was going to promote the worship of One God on the authority of the Vedic rather than the Christian scriptures, he expressed the hope that the Brahmo Samaj would prove to be a "step towards Christianity".[26]

His hope was not to be realized. In fact, during some of the first few years after the founding of the Brahmo Samaj it often seemed doubtful that the Samaj would even survive, let alone take a step toward Christianity. The Samaj had its first meetings in August 1828, and then was more formally established through the Trust Deed when it took occupacy of the building set aside for it in January 1830. Rammohun, the dynamic leader behind the Samaj, sailed for England in November of 1830, never to return. Those who had joined him in the Brahmo Samaj had varying commitments to its ideals and its theology. Dwarkanath Tagore, for example, was a major patron of the Samaj and Rammohun's close friend; yet it was well known that throughout the years of his association with Rammohun and the Samaj he continued to patronize and participate in the annual celebration of Durga Puja in his home,[27] and he later counselled his son Debendranath against becoming too involved in religious matters. On the other hand, Pandit Ram Chandra Vidyabagish, whom Rammohun brought to Calcutta from Rangpur District, continued to preside over the weekly worship of the Samaj during the years after Rammohun's departure. Often he was the only one present.[28] For seven years the Samaj went into a steady and serious decline. Its members, who were Hindus, did not find in the Samaj a significant alternative to the spectrum of religious alternatives already available to them.

The decline of the Samaj during the years immediately following Rammohun's departure from Calcutta, appears in large measure to have been the result of a diminution of the critique which was explicit in Rammohun's own life and writings. For all his emphasis on mutual respect between people of various nations and religions, much of Rammohun's public life was spent in polemical debates with Hindu and Christian opponents. His involvement in the Atmiya Sabha, the Unitarian Association, and the Brahmo Samaj was not based simply on a wish to add one or more religious options to an already adequate spectrum of options. His involvement was based on his vehement opposition to some of the central teachings and practices of popular Hinduism and Christianity. He rejected all forms of polytheism, incarnation and idolatry. His affirmation of religious pluralism was not a universal endorsement of religious belief and practice. His pluralism was a universalism which asserted that God had been revealed and experienced within each culture. The character of this Infinite God was now the reference point, the criterion by which all expressions of religious belief and practice were to be evaluated. This was both an affirmation and a negation, an endorsement and a critique.

It was the rediscovery of this critical component of the vision of the Brahmo Samaj which led to its revitalization. In 1838 Debendranath Tagore, son of Dwarkanath Tagore, experienced a spiritual reorientation. He became convinced of the inadequacy of the image worship which he and his family were practicing, and at about the same time became aware of the teachings of the Upanisads.[29] He sought the guidance of Pandit Ram Chandra Vidyabagish and began to take systematic instruction in the Upanisads. He established a society, the Tattvabodhini Sabha, for the study and dissemination of the religious texts which he was studying. He and his friends established weekly meetings for study and discussion as well as a monthly worship service. In 1841 the worship services of the Tattvabodhini Sabha and the Brahmo Samaj were combined.

Debendranath took the critical element of the Samaj seriously. He found that among those who attended the Samaj there were two fundamental contradictions to the vision of Rammohun: first, caste distinctions were fully maintained during worship, and second, members continued their polytheistic and idolatrous worship in their homes. Additionally, he found the worship service in disarray; the incarnation of Rama was being preached by one of the associate pandits, and prayer was not being taught and practiced as a form of religious devotion.

To correct these deficiencies Debendranath reorganized the worship and established a covenant for members of the Samaj.[30] This covenant included vows renouncing idolatry and affirming the worship of one God as taught in the Vedanta. Debendranath was the first to take these vows and was initiated into the Brahmo Samaj in December 1843. Others followed, and by 1847 the number of covenanted Brahmos was 767.

For several years the Samaj made the Upanisads its sole source of infallible revelation. In 1845, during a public controversy between the Brahmos and the Christians, the Brahmo newspaper, the *Tattvabodhini Patrika* declared, ". . . we consider the Vedas and the Vedas alone, as the authorized rule of Hindu theology. They are the sole foundation of all our beliefs and the truths of all other Shastras must be judged of according to their agreement with them."[31] But in 1848, after considerable controversy and debate, even the infallibility of the Upanisads was rejected as incompatible with universal reason. As Hem Chandra Sarkar puts it in his *The Religion of the Brahmo Samaj*, ". . . Vedantic Unitarianism came to be superseded by natural Universal Theism".[32] Even so, when Debendranath prepared a book entitled *Brahmo Dharma*, it was based on selections from the Upanisads.

The Brahmo Samaj became an active missionary organization, drawing adherents by and large from among educated Hindus, establishing branch Samajes in several towns in Bengal, and the Ved Samaj in Madras and the Prarthana Samaj in Bombay. It also challenged Christian missionary activity. Debendranath was one of the leaders of a large Hindu movement of opposition to the conversion of a young Hindu couple to Christianity in 1845.[33]

The next phase of the Samaj's response to religious pluralism centered around Keshub Chunder Sen.[34] He joined the Samaj in 1857 during Debendranath's extended absence from Calcutta. He was an active advocate of the changes introduced by Debendranath, but soon he and many of his young colleagues felt that the leaders of the Samaj were not following Brahmo principles consistently enough. They were especially perturbed to note that some of the worship leaders of the Samaj had retained their Hindu sacred thread, and with that their concern for caste status. These younger members of the Samaj pressed Debendranath, who had, at considerable damage to his reputation, refused to fully comply with the traditional Hindu *sraddha* ceremonies at his father's death in 1846, and who had also married his daughter according to Brahmo rites in 1861. Debendranath had discarded his own sacred thread, and he sympathized with the young reformers. He suspended the older, caste-conscious leaders. But this led to confusion and divisiveness within the Samaj. Soon after this the younger members celebrated an inter-caste widow remarriage, and this was farther than Debendranath and his generation of leaders wished to go. Debendranath reinstated the suspended leaders in October 1864, without insisting that they make any changes in their caste practices. There was a rupture between Debendranath and the young men associated with Sen, and this led to a split in the Samaj. The split widened until a new group was formed on November 11, 1866.[35] The new group became known as the Brahmo Samaj of India.

Most of the immediate issues which led to the rupture between the two factions and the eventual establishment of the Brahmo Samaj of India were social issues: the sacred thread, caste distinctions within the Samaj, intercaste marriages, widow remarriage, and the role of women. But other differences emerged which have immediate relevance to religious pluralism.

On May 5, 1866 Keshub Chunder Sen delivered a lecture in the Calcutta Medical College Theatre on "Jesus Christ: Europe and Asia,"[36] in which he acknowledged his identification with the life and teachings of Jesus, who was, as Sen emphasized, an Asiatic.

> Yes, and his disciples were Asiatics, and all the agencies primarily employed for the propagation of the Gospel were Asiatic. In fact, Christianity was founded and developed by Asiatics and in Asia. When I reflect on this, my love for Jesus becomes a hundredfold intensified; I feel him nearer my heart, deeper in my national sympathies.[37]

> Let my European brethren do all they can to establish and consolidate the moral kingdom of Christ in India. Let them preach from their pulpits, and exhibit in their daily life the great principles of charity and self-sacrifice. And on the basis of these principles, may brotherly intercourse and co-operation be established between them and my countrymen. May England and India, Europe and Asia, be indissolubly united in charity and love, and self-denying devotion to truth.[38]

For some of Sen's opponents in the Brahmo Samaj this declaration of identification and appreciation for Jesus was a confirmation that Sen and his associates had moved too far from the purpose and scope of the Brahmo Samaj. What had formerly been expressed as radical social reform was now being expressed for what it really was; a rejection of Hinduism and the prelude to conversion to Christianity.[39] Sen subsequently gave another lecture, entitled "Great Men", on September 28, 1866 at the Town Hall in Calcutta. In this lecture he attempted to widen the horizon beyond Jesus and to draw attention to the many great men who

". . . are sent by God into the world to benefit mankind."[40] But he was not able to allay the fears of his opponents, who remained convinced that he ws moving outside Hinduism and into Christianity.

Other actions seemed to reinforce these concerns. When Mary Carpenter, a Unitarian philanthropist from England, arrived in Calcutta in late 1866, Sen invited her and some European friends to his house for a worship service on Christmas Day. He preached on the biblical text from John 3:3, "Except a man be born again, he cannot see the kingdom of God."[41] Other Christian theological themes were given prominence in the new Samaj. The sense of personal sin and the need to repent from it by prayer was an emphasis adopted from Christianity. The missionary zeal and emphasis were also more typical of Christianity than Hinduism. And of course Sen and his followers were devoted to the character of Christ. It was not the historical Jesus who captivated them so much as an ideal or spiritual Christ who represented the perfection of the virtues which they aspired to: complete trust in God, self-sacrifice, and sympathy for the sinner.[42] Christian critics said this was largely a Christ of their own making, but Hindus, including members of the old leadership of the Brahmo Samaj, saw this as another confirmation of Sen's inclination to Christianity. In 1871, when Debendranath was invited to preach from the pulpit of Sen's Samaj he took the opportunity to speak strongly against the pro-Christian tendencies of the group.[43]

Actually the Brahmo Samaj of India drew its inspiration and resources even more broadly. During the last week of December 1866, a new book of scripture readings was published for use by the new organization, but this was a great change from the *Brahmo Dharma* published earlier by Debendranath; this book, entitled *Shloka Sangraha* was a compilation of theistic texts from Hindu, Muslim, Christian and other scriptures. The meeting on November 11, 1866, which gave formal birth to the Brahmo Samaj of India expressed the universalism of its vision in its second resolution, which declared, "Men and women of every nation and caste, who believe in the fundamental doctrines of the Brahma Dharma, shall be eligible as member[s] of the Brahma Samaj of India."[44]

When the new *mandir* (chapel) was consecrated on August 22, 1869, Sen read a declaration of the principles of the new organization. The declaration was strikingly like the Trust Deed of the Brahmo Samaj signed by Rammohun Roy and his associates in 1830. The section which dealt directly with religious pluralism stated:

> No created being or object that has been or may hereafter be worshipped by any sect shall be ridiculed or condemned in the course of the Divine Service to be conducted here. No book shall be acknowledged or revered as the infallible shall be ridiculed or condemned. No sect shall be vilified, ridiculed or hated. No prayer, hymn, sermon or discourse to be delivered or used here shall countenance or encourage any manner of idolatry, sectarianism or sin. Divine Service shall be conducted here in such spirit or manner as may enable all men and women, irrespective of distinctions of caste, colour, and condition, to unite in one family, eschew all manner of error and sin and advance in wisdom, faith, and righteousness.[45]

The declaration was read in Bengali, English, and Urdu.

Sen was also significantly influenced by Chaitanya and the Vaishnavism of Bengal, perhaps initially through his associate Bijoy Krishna Goswami, the Brahmo missionary. He adapted the *sankirtan*, the processional devotional singing, for use by the Samaj, especially on festive occasions. He also promoted *bhakti*, to the consternation of some Brahmos who regarded it as a concession to popular religion. He accused some of those who opposed him of being secularists and men of little faith.[46] At times he used explicitly Vaishnava imagry in his sermons.[47]

Other more explicit Hindu forms and theological positions emerged as well. In late 1876 Sen introduced a fourfold classification of devotees, to represent four different types of religious life: the *yogi*, the *Bhakta*, the *jnani*, and the *sevak*. He introduced special instruction for each type of discipline.[48] In late September, 1878, during the Durga Puja festival, Sen preached a sermon in the *mandir* encouraging his listeners to appreciate the spiritual significance of the goddess and the festival; in fact he used the names of the goddess when speaking about God.[49] Nearly two years later, on August 1, 1880, he returned to this issue in an article in the *Sunday Mirror*, entitled "The Philosophy of Idol Worship".

> Hindu idolatry is not to be altogether overlooked or rejected . . . it represents millions of broken fragments of God. Collect them and you get the indivisible Divinity . . . idolatry is nothing but the worship of a divine attribute materialized . . . We have found

out that every idol worshipped by the Hindus represents an attribute of God, and that each attribute is called by a particular name.

. . . Hence we should contemplate [God] with his numerous attributes. We should name one attribute Saraswati, another Lakshmi, another Mahadeva, another Jagaddhatri, etc., and worship God each day under a new name, that is to say, in a new aspect.[50]

Sen's friendship with the Bengali mystic Ramakrishna Paramahamsa reinforced this theological inclination.

Sen's attitude toward other religious traditions seems to have changed little during this lifetime, and this is best understood in reference to two of his publications. The first is his speech "The Future Church", delivered in Calcutta on January 23, 1869. In it he acknowledged that there were delusions and errors in the human search for God, but he insisted that there was also truth in all these human efforts. Eventually all human aspirations for God would be realized, and then ". . . instead of a hundred hostile churches, there shall be upreared, in the fulness of time, one vast cathedral, where all mankind shall worship with one heart the Supreme Creator".[51] Specifically, he added, the time would come when Islam and Hinduism would eliminate what was false within each of them and ". . . ultimately harmonize and form the future church of India".[52] Christianity would influence the growth and formation of that church, but the exact form of that church would be distinctively Indian. For, although "All mankind will unite in a universal church; at the same time it will be adapted to the peculiar circumstances of each nation, and assume a national form".[53]

Twelve years later, in an article in the *Sunday Mirror*, he expressed his position as follows:

Our position is not that truths are to be found in all religions, but that all the established religions of the world are true . . . Christianity and Hinduism are true; they are both dispensations of God . . . If there are untruths they are grafted on by men, they cannot be God's . . . All religions are dispensations of God, sent to the world at special times for the salvation of humanity.[54]

By the time Sen wrote these words in 1881, a new Samaj had already been in existence for three years. The Sadharan Brahmo Samaj was established on May 15, 1878 at a public meeting at the Town Hall in Calcutta.[55] Its members were former members of the Brahmo Samaj of India who had left Sen's group in protest over his continued authoritarian leadership and the scandal over the marriage of his daughter to the young Maharajah of Cooch Behar.[56] The new Samaj established a more structured organization, continued active missionary activity, maintained the tradition of active involvement in education and social service, and kept essentially the same theological perspective as the Brahmo Samaj of India, although without the highly personalized and devotional emphasis of Sen.

When the Sadharan Brahmo Samaj moved into its new *mandir* on January 22, 1881, the Declaration of Principles which was read demonstrated the essential continuity of purpose and theological orientation with Rammohun, Debendranath, and Sen, even though there was an implied critique of Sen's personality-centered leadership style.

> The catholicity of Brahmoism shall also be preserved here. No book or man shall ever be acknowledged as infallible and the only way to salvation; but nevertheless due respect shall be paid to all scriptures and the good and the great of all ages and of all countries. In the sermons, discourses, and prayers used in this Hall, no scripture or sect, or founder of a sect, shall ever be ridiculed, reviled, or spoken of contemptuously.[57]

The understanding of religious pluralism which was articulated consistently by the first generation of leaders of the new Samaj can be identified clearly.[58] First, God's revelation is universal. Second, the religious teachers and scriptures of all nations and ages are to be respected and, if possible, studied. Third, God is the Absolute and Infinite Creator who is also immanent. Fourth, because God is infinitely loving, and because man's sin is only finite, everyone will be brought to ultimate salvation or union with God. Fifth, this common universal religion will always be expressed in specific and local forms which may, superficially, vary substantially, but which are the same in essence. Sixth, the criterion by which all scriptures and teachers are evaluated is reason, which is universal.

Conclusion

Despite the turbulence of the first fifty years of the Brahmo Samaj, despite the variety of leaders and the changing social and religious environment, the understanding and attitude toward religious pluralism remained remarkably consistent:

1. There is one God who is Absolute, the Creator and Father[59] of all.
2. All people and nations are equally loved by God. All are equally children of God.
3. God has been revealed through nature and through people and scriptures in all nations and at all times.
4. Reason and conscience are the universal criteria for understanding the revelation of God and for evaluating and applying this revelation to life in society.
5. The knowledge of God and the response to God are always expressed in specific local forms, which should never be absolutized.
6. There are theological formulations as well as forms of worship which tend to detract from the unity and infinity of God, and the unity of humanity. These may be used provisionally, but should be replaced by forms which more adequately reflect the character of God.
7. There should be mutual respect among people for the revelations others have received.

There were noticeable differences in how leaders of the Brahmo Samaj actually responded to religious pluralism, even though their theological positions remained fundamentally identical. They differed, for example, in the way in which they used various religious traditions in their own writing. Rammohun used Christian terminology and scriptures when debating with Christians, and Hindu terminology and texts when debating with Hindus.[60] Debendranath used almost exclusively Hindu language and categories and had little interest in Christian scriptures and theology. Sen was much more eclectic, and used metaphors and scriptures from the Christian tradition very frequently when speaking to Hindus; in doing so he raised considerable suspicion about his own religious identity among many of his Hindu contemporaries. But these differences among Rammohun, Debendranath, and Sen were as much differences of familiarity with other religious traditions as they were differences of theological assumptions about the validity of these traditions.

These leaders, and the movements which they represented, also differed in their critique of those elements within religious traditions which they found misleading or in error. Rammohun granted image worship a minor provisional role in helping people to understand God, but the bulk of his efforts were directed at undermining and eradicating image worship. The covenant which Debendranath formulated and introduced when he joined the Samaj and then revised in 1850, was an attempt, in part, to eradicate the practice of image worship which was a common part of the private worship of most members of the Samaj. But it was only in the mid-1860s that he and other members of the Samaj began to formulate non-idolatrous domestic ceremonies so that there actually were alternatives available in practice. Sen was a strong advocate of non-idolatrous worship throughout the early years of his public career, but, as we have already noted, was willing, near the end of his life, to regard the worship of images with considerable tolerance.

There was also divergence in how the Samaj was understood in relation to other religious traditions. Although Debendranath was content to think of the Brahmo Samaj as the highest form of Hinduism, Sen, and perhaps Rammohun to some extent, hoped that the movement could be more, that it could be the beginning of a universal church. That hope has not been fulfilled. The movement has become a minority Hindu movement whose membership nowadays is mostly hereditary. Throughout the history of the Samaj there were always some Muslims and Christians who expressed interest and sympathy for its aspirations, but they did not become members. Today Hindus from non-Brahmo families rarely join either.

But its influence extends far beyond its membership. It has not led to as widespread reform in Hinduism as many of its members may have wished for, nor has it led to a new synthesis of religious traditions and identities on a national or international scale. But it has provided the basis for a rational critique of religious thought and practice, and has combined this with an inclusive and tolerant attitude toward the plurality of religious expressions which are part of human culture. Its simultaneous criticism and defense of Hindu religious pluralism has become widely accepted and adopted within Hinduism.

Notes

1. Sophia Dobson Collet, *The Life and Letters of Raja Rammohun Roy* (3rd ed.). Calcutta: Sadharan Brahmo Samaj, 1962, pp. 471–472.

2. Sivanath Sastri, *History of the Brahmo Samaj* (2nd ed.). Calcutta: Sadharan Brahmo Samaj, 1974, p. 27. Also Collet, pp. 277–278.

3. There is some debate about whether the Brahmo Samaj was originally named the Brahmo Sabha. Here the view of the editors of Collet, pp. 239–242 is followed, and Samaj is used throughout. Compare Sastri, pp. 25–26.

4. The spelling used here is the form he used to sign his name in English. His biographers traditionally date his life 1772–1833, but Ramesh Chandra Majumdar, *On Rammohun Roy*. Calcutta: The Asiatic Society, 1972, suggests that 1774 is a more probable birth date.

5. Collet, pp. 74–75.

6. Radhakanta Deb later became the leader of the Dharma Sabha, a society formed to counter the influences of the Brahmo Samaj.

7. Many of these works are collected in Kalidas Nag and Debajyoti Burman, eds., *The English Works of Raja Rammohun Roy*. Part II. Calcutta: Sadharan Brahmo Samaj, 1946.

8. See Collet, p. 124, and Sastri, p. 21.

9. Sastri, p. 21.

10. Collet, p. 131.

11. *Ibid.*, p. 132.

12. Quoted in Collet, p. 133.

13. Nag and Burman, Part II, pp. 193–194. It should be noted that when Rammohun used the term "Vedas" he meant the Upanisads.

14. Collet, pp. 217–219, and also Sastri, pp. 24–25.

15. Collet, pp. 220 ff.

16. The following summary is based on Collet, pp. 224–226, and Sastri, p. 25. Piyus Kanti Das, in his *Raja Rammohun Roy and Brahmoism*. Calcutta: Author, 1970, pp. 88, 104, asserts that the elements I refer to as Hindu were actually "universal".

17. See especially the publications collected in Nag and Burman, Part II.

18. See the summary and analysis of Rammohun's writings on this subject in James N. Pankratz, "The Religious Thought of Rammohun Roy", unpublished dissertation, McMaster University, 1975, pp. 41–72, 90–101.

19. See his introductory comments to *The Precepts of Jesus: The Guide to Peace and Happiness*, first published in 1820, now reprinted in

Kalidas Nag and Debajyoti Burman, *The English Works of Raja Rammohun Roy*. Part V. Calcutta: Sadharan Brahmo Samaj, 1948, pp. 3–4.

20. See particularly his defense of the Hindu tradition against attacks from missionaries in Nag and Burman, Part II. pp. 135–189.

21. This is found repeatedly in his writings directed to Christian criticisms of Hinduism in Nag and Burman, Parts IV–VI.

22. Sastri, p. 51.

23. *Ibid.*, p. 25.

24. Quoted in Collet, p. 222.

25. *Ibid.*, 227.

26. *Ibid.*, 247.

27. Amitaba Mukhopadhyay, *Unish Sataker Samaj O Samskriti*. Calcutta: General Printers and Publishers, Private, Ltd., 1971, p. 108. The information is based on a letter published in the *Samachar Darpan*, October 22, 1831.

28. Hem Chandra Sarkar, *The Religion of the Brahmo Samaj* (3rd ed.). Calcutta: Classic Press, 1931, p. 5. Also Sastri, pp. 52–56. In January 1985 the missionary-in-charge of the Samaj in Shaka, Bangladesh, Pranesh Samaddar, told me a similar story of conducting services alone in the now nearly deserted *mandir* in Old Dhaka.

29. Debendranath Tagore 1817–1905. For brief accounts of his spiritual reorientation see Sastri, pp. 53–56 and Sarkar, p. 5–6.

30. Sastri summarizes the covenant on p. 58, and reprints the revised 1850 version of the covenant on p. 558.

31. Sastri, pp. 63–64.

32. Sarkar, p. 9.

33. Sastri, p. 63.

34. Keshub Chunder Sen 1838–1884. His life is described extensively in Sastri, pp. 72–115, 129–276. Also see Prem Sundar Basu, compiler, *Life and Works of Brahmananda Keshav*. Calcutta: Navavidhan Publication Committee, 1940; David Kopf, *The Brahmo Samaj and the Shaping of the Modern India Mind*. Princeton: Princeton University Press, 1979.

35. Sastri, p. 113.

36. Reprinted in Basu, pp. 96–106.

37. *Ibid.*, p. 102.

38. *Ibid.*, p. 106.

39. Sastri, p. 11.

40. Basu, p. 111. The whole speech is in Basu, pp. 106–117.

41. *Ibid.*, pp. 117–118.

42. For example, in an essay printed in the *Indian Mirror* he commented, ". . . [theists] honour [Christ's] memory not because he shows,—for he cannot show,—what the Father is, but how the 'son' ought to be dutiful and obedient to the Father". The Brahmo Somaj, *Keshub Chunder Sen's Essays: Theological and Ethical* (4th ed.). Calcutta: Brahmo Tract Society, 1909, p. 13.

43. Sastri, 153. The differences between Debendranath and Sen on this issue are briefly analyzed in Sisir Kumar Das, *The Shadow of the Cross*. New Delhi: Munshiram Manoharlal, 1973, pp. 79–83.

44. Basu, p. 119.

45. *Ibid.*, p. 176. The full text is on pp. 175–176.

46. Sastri, p. 170.

47. On November 3, 1878, in a sermon preached at the *Mandir*, he used the *gopala* metaphor to speak about the relationship of the Deity to the devotee. See, Basu, p. 350.

48. Sastri, pp. 171–172.

49. *Ibid.*, pp. 196–197. Also Basu, pp. 349–350.

50. Sastri, pp. 197–198.

51. Basu, p. 169.

52. *Ibid.*, 172.

53. *Ibid.*, p. 173. See also the discussion of this motif in Das, pp. 84–88.

54. Basu, p. 572. This article was published on November 23, 1881.

55. Sastri, pp. 184–186. Also, Sarkar, pp. 16–17. For a helpful interpretive description of the differences leaeding to this split, see Spencer Lavan, "The Brahmo Samaj: India's First Modern Movement for Religious Reform", in *Religion in Modern India* ed. Robert D. Baird. New Delhi: Manohar, 1981, pp. 11–23.

56. Sastri, pp. 173–181 gives a full account and then adds, in the appendices, pp. 566–602, some of the correspondence which went on between various leaders within the Samaj, as well as the texts of some of the speeches made during the dispute. Basu, the compiler of Sen's speeches, refers to the dispute in one paragraph and dismisses it as

"innocuous", see p. 348. Kopf, pp. 327–329 discusses some of the consequences.

57. Sastri, p. 297. The full text in Sastri is on pp. 297–298.

58. The following points are summarized from Sivanath Sastri, *The Brahmo Samaj: Religious Principles and Brief History* (abridged ed.). Calcutta: Sadharan Brahmo Samaj, 1958, pp. 13–14; Sivanath Sastri, *Theistic Church in India*. Calcutta: Sadharan Brahmo Samaj, 1966, pp. 13–15; Sitanath Tattvabhusan, *Brahmaism: Principles and Practice*. Calcutta: Sadharan Brahmo Samaj, n.d., p. 13.; and Sarkar, *op. cit.*, pp. 60–64.

59. The word "Father" was used commonly to speak about God, but Brahmos understood that this was a metaphor to indicate the human relationship of trust and dependence on God.

60. See, Nag and Burman, Parts II, IV–VI.

Chapter Three

THE RESPONSE OF THE ARYA SAMAJ

H.G. Coward

The Arya Samaj is a modern Indian religious movement which can legitimately trace the impulse for its birth to Dayananda's encounter with the pluralism of his day. Before his four month stay in Calcutta in 1873, Dayananda was a naked Sanskrit-speaking reformer thoroughly immersed in the Hindu world on the banks of the Ganges. His visit to Calcutta, however, introduced him to a new world, a world of religious pluralism. No longer was it simply a case of reforming corrupt Hindu practices; now he was faced with the Christian claim to a revelation superior to the *Veda*. In addition to reforming Hinduism, he now had to take on this new pluralistic world which he encountered in the cities. Out of this encounter came the Arya Samaj, a movement which was to become the vanguard of the Hindu response to the challenge of other religions in the 20th century.

In this essay we will assess the nature of the Arya Samaj response by examining: I. Dayananda's Response to the Challenge of Religious Pluralism; and II. *Shuddhi* as a Response to Pluralism.

Dayananda's Response to the Challenge of Religious Pluralism

Dayananda Saraswati was one of the few Hindu reformers of the nineteenth century seriously to study and discuss other religions. Some twenty years before Vivekananda attended the Parliament of World Religions at Chicago in 1893, Dayananda organized a conference on the occasion of the Delhi Durbar and invited representatives of all religions.[1] Throughout Dayananda's public life two concerns were dominant. First, there was the study of Sanskrit and a turning back to the *Vedas* as the source of revealed truth. Second, Dayananda was always keen to widen his learning and his horizons—to other Hindu sects, to Jainism, Buddhism and finally to Christianity and Islam.[2] But although he educated himself on other religions, their teachings were always ruthlessly tested against the touchstone of Vedic truth.

In attempting to relate his own thinking to the wider world, including the other religions, Dayananda was well ahead of other thinkers of his day. Concern with the challenge of religious pluralism, which during the last decade has dominated the leading thinkers of all religions,[3] was Dayananda's focus as early as one hundred years ago. Dayananda also exhibited modern Religious Studies research methods in his refusal to depend on secondary sources. In his studies of other religions he took pains to study the original sources carefully, making notes to which he could refer while composing his commentaries and criticisms.[4] Since translations of other scriptures were not always available in languages used by Dayananda, he sometimes had to have a sacred text (e.g., the *Qur'ān*) translated privately so that he could study it.

Although Dayananda's insistence on working with original sources is to be commended, the same cannot be said for his ability sympathetically to enter into the spirit and content of the sacred scripture of another religion. Jordens observes that in his study and critique of other religions Dayananda made no effort "to grasp the deeper meaning of myth or symbol, or to probe the religious and historical rationale of a custom or rite."[5] Dayananda's *a priori* assumptions, based on his own perception of Vedic truth, made it impossible for him to gain much understanding of any religion which did not share the same assumptions.

Dayananda's a priori Assumptions

Dayananda's approach to the pluralism of religions and their various claims to truth was in many ways very modern. In line with the thinking of contemporary theologians like Karl Barth, Dayananda distinguishes between the Truth and the many institutional religions. Institutional religions such as Jainism, Buddhism, Christianity and Islam—as well as the various sectarian forms of Hinduism—are described in the *Satyarth Prakash* as "the product of ignorance."[6] Such religions are organized for the benefit of the priests, preachers or so-called *gurus* and serve only to lead the people into ignorance and superstition. In the midst of such selfish motivation from the priests, and conflicting truth claims from the competing pundits or theologians, how is one to find divine truth? Dayananda's answer is put in the mouth of the one he calls "the true teacher." The criterion for truth in the midst of the conflicting claims of the various religions is stated by the true teachers as follows: "In whatever they agree with each other, know that to be the *Vedic* religion worthy of being accepted, but in whatever they all disagree, know that to be wrong, false, sinful and unacceptable."[7] The points of agreement among all religions are described by Dayananda as including: speaking the truth, acquiring knowledge, controlling sensual passions, marrying in the full bloom of life, associating with the good, cultivating active habits and being honest in dealings with others. Irreligion shows itself by remaining ignorant, becoming a slave of the senses, committing adultery, keeping bad company, being dishonest, indulging in hypocrisy and doing harm to others.[8] In Dayananda's hypothetical discourse of the true teacher with the leaders of the various religions, the latter are portrayed as agreeing on the above points as a clear definition of true religion. The reason given by the pundits for not teaching this common truth to the people is that if they did so they would lose their disciples and their means of livelihood. In addition, argue the pundits, there can never be just one religion because people differ too much in their temperaments and characteristics.[9] But, maintains Dayananda, if all were educated alike in childhood, such differences would be negated and there would be one true religion.[10]

Jordens identifies four *a priori* assumptions as basic to Dayananda's interpretation of the *Vedas* and his approach to other religions.[11] First there was Dayananda's view of the *Vedas* as literally containing the eternal wisdom of God and therefore having the quality of universal truth. Consequently, Vedic statements could not possibly refer to historical or geographical data. Since the *Vedas* existed prior to all history, historical considerations, names of persons, places or particular events were explained by Dayananda as statements of principle or injunctions given dramatic form. Thus religions basing themselves on historic events, such as the life and teaching of Jesus Christ, were seen by Dayananda as having fallen away from the eternal truth.

Dayananda's second assumption was that the *Vedas* taught a pure monotheism. Names of gods appearing in the *Vedas* all signify the one Lord. Applied to the various sects of Hinduism and the other religions, this meant that there are not different gods but only the one Lord. As Dayananda put it, "The multitude of names like Indra signify not different Divine beings but different aspects of one Absolute Existence."[12] In line with other Hindu thinkers Dayananda assumed that the God spoken of by many names in the various Hindu sects and in the other religions was none other than the Lord revealed in the *Vedas* and for whom AUM is the highest name.[13] On this point Dayananda's major disagreement with some other interpreters of orthodox Hinduism was his monotheistic rather than monistic interpretation of the *Vedas*.

A third and very important assumption for Dayananda was that the revelation of eternal truth could not contain anything that would offend reason or morality. Most of the Swami's attacks on the Hindu sects and other religions are directed against their apparent irrationality or immorality. Miracles are irrational and therefore to be discredited. Myths sometimes suggest immoral acts. In Dayananda's view, neither irrationality nor immorality are found in the *Vedas* when correctly interpreted. Thus, as Rudolf Bultman has done for contemporary Christian interpretation of the New Testament,[14] Dayananda demythologized the *Vedas* on the assumption that in so doing the eternal Truth would be revealed.

A fourth assumption was that since the *Vedas* embody the totality of truth, therefore the truths of modern science must also be seen to be present in the *Vedas*. Jordens points out that since the Swami's own scientific knowledge was very limited, this aspect was only rarely elaborated.[15] Yet, as is the case with many modern Islamic writers, Dayananda saw it as a ground for appeal to the educated modern mind and as consistent with the Vedic claim to omniscience—even if only in seed form.

These four *a priori* assumptions can be seen to have guided Dayananda's response to other religions. Although he possessed a laudable desire to study other faiths, and although he commendably went to great lengths to work on primary texts, still these assumptions frequently prevented Dayananda from understanding the essential viewpoints of other religions. Of course Dayananda was not alone in this. Many of the Christian missionaries of this day were making exactly the same kind of arguments in attempting to demonstrate the truth of Christianity. They tried to demonstrate the irrationality and immorality of Hinduism and to prove that the *Bible* contained the absolute truth about God. As Jordens observes, "Dayananda accepted the Protestant premise that God has revealed himself in a book, and that the very content of the book proves its authenticity."[16] Thus, in any debate between religions only linguistic tools were appropriate since, in Dayananda's view, religious documents were of an eternal and not historical nature. In one way it may be said that Dayananda made Hinduism a religion of the book by adopting the Protestant principle of *sola scriptura* and applying it to the *Vedas*.

Dayananda and Eastern Religions

Dayananda's early religious life centered around the experience of a personal God manifested in the numinous figure of Siva.[17] This rather narrow religious base was widened with his exposure to Advaita Vedānta, Sāṅkhya-Yoga, Grammar, Nyāya-Vaiśeṣika and the *Brahmo Dharma*. Study of these various Hindu schools led him to a broader understanding of the *Veda* and God. This is formalized in Chapters I, VII, VIII and IX of his *Satyarth Prakash*, and in Chapter X is applied as a purifying critique of the various Hindu sects within India. Although Dayananda does turn his attention to similar examinations of Jainism, Buddhism, Islam and Christianity, it is with the purifying and renewing of Hinduism that his real interest lies. As is evident in his many attempts to establish schools, the education of the young into a true understanding of the *Vedas* and a life based on the practice of *dharma* were judged by Dayananda to be fundamental. According to the concluding pages of Chapter XI, the major obstacle to such a purification happening was corruption of the contemporary Hindu teachers and *sanyasis* who concern themselves only with a life of luxury and ease, and so lead the young astray.[18] Also, the Hindu pundits against whom Dayananda debated often did not know their texts and so resorted to corrupt means so as to appear to win. It was to purge such ignorance and corruption from Hinduism, and to establish a base from which the young could make a fresh beginning, that Dayananda devoted his life. Observing the problems of some of the other reformers of his day, e.g., Debendranath Tagore and Keshub Chunder Sen, Dayananda did not tie his reform of Hinduism to an institutional structure but attempted to base it upon the *Vedas* alone.

As he moved about India Dayananda met representatives of other Eastern religions, especially the Jains. His approach to Jainism followed pretty much the line taken in his critical examination of other Hindu sects. He set out to read the Jaina primary texts and then to criticize these texts from the basis of his four *a priori* assumptions. Dayananda's criticism of Jainism runs to over a hundred pages in the second edition of the *Satyarth Prakash* and contains many questions from Jaina sources. Dayananda focuses on what he judges to be the absurdities of Jaina doctrine. Against the Jaina doctrine of atheism Dayananda argues that without a God human beings could not have been created. Against the Jaina doctrine of the *jiva*, Dayananda said that since the human soul is circumscribed and limited, therefore it is impossible for it to achieve all knowledge, as the Jaina notion of Tirthankaras claims.[19] The Jaina definition of time or *Asankhyata*—described in terms of a pit six or eight miles square filled with the super fine hair of a *juguli* man (4,096 times finer than the hair of an ordinary man) with one *juguli* hair being removed each one hundred years until the pit is empty—is ridiculed by Dayananda as an example of novel and absurd Jaina beliefs.[20] He concludes that the Jainas are unacquainted with Geography and Astronomy and that their writings cannot be reconciled with the knowledge of modern science.[21] Thus, the beliefs of the Jainas are both absurd and, as their conception of the Tirthankaras as omniscient reveals, internally inconsistent. Dayananda also attempts to show the unacceptability of Jaina mythology when examined from the viewpoint of logic, common sense, and morality.

It must be said that for the most part Dayananda's criticism is of a scholastic kind which fails to perceive the deeper meanings behind the Jaina texts. Only the literal meaning is examined by Dayananda. His most bitter criticism is directed towards Jaina hostility toward other religions.[22] This, he argues, is a clear violation of the Jaina principle of non-violence *(ahimsa)*.

In the *Satyarth Prakash* Buddhism is treated very superficially. Buddhism did not seem to interest Dayananda, perhaps because as a living religion it was virtually absent from the India of his day. The careful reading of texts, which characterized Dayananda's approach to Jainism, seems lacking with respect to Buddhism. At times he lumped together Jainas, Buddhists and the Charvakas on the grounds of their common atheism. However, this was an error also made by some of the European Indologists of the day. Part of the problem here was that until the end of the nineteenth century the Jainas were very secretive about their scriptures. Published Jaina scriptures were simply not available for study. A twentieth century Arya Samaj scholar has gone some way toward rectifying this superficial treatment of Buddhism. Ganga Prasad Upadhyaya has written an excellent critical comparison of the teachings of Buddha and Dayananda.[23]

Dayananda and Western Religions

Both Christianity and Islam were active in the areas of India through which Dayananda travelled and taught. This was especially true of his time spent in the Punjab. Dayananda met both Christian and Islamic scholars, and held long discussions with them. Such meetings were followed up with private study of the *Bible* and the *Qur'ān*. There does not seem to be any evidence of meetings with Jews or study of Jewish sources. In the Introduction to Chapter thirteen of the *Satyarth Prakash*, Dayananda dismisses Judaism by saying that his criticism of the Christian Bible will hold good for Judaism as well. He also states that Judaism is only of secondary importance when compared with Christianity.

It was in Calcutta, particularly, that Dayananda's eyes were opened to the comparative study of religions. There he became better acquainted with Christianity and Islam, and learned to see Hinduism in the context of these religions. The result was not a weakening of his view of Hinduism but a strengthened affirmation of the superiority of Vedic truth. At Calcutta and thereafter he shifted his focus from villages, where usually everyone would be Hindu, to large towns and cities where Christians and Muslims would attend his lectures along with the Hindus. Dayananda responded to this wider audience by treating Christianity and Islam in much the same way as he had treated some of the Hindu sects. All were criticized against the touchstone of the *Vedas*. In Chapter seven of *Satyarth Prakash* three arguments are given to prove the truth of the Vedic revelation: (1)It is logically necessary due to God's infinite mercy; (2) The content of the *Vedas* proves their divine origin; and (3) The *Vedas* provide the criteria for all other books and religions. Dayananda's theory of creation assumes that humans were created in an innocent state with Sanskrit as the mother language. Thus Sanskrit as the language of the *Vedas* is the universal language (not the language of a particular country), and that very universal quality witnesses to its divine nature. By contrast the *Bible* and the *Qur'ān* are written in exclusive languages and scripts, and are thus seen to be inferior.[24]

Before going to Calcutta, Dayananda spent time in the Doab alongside the Ganges River. Here his early encounters with Christianity took place. Jordens notes that at Farrukhabad three missionaries and some Indian Christians held discussion with Dayananda. But his most significant discussions were with Reverend Scott and Dr. Hoernle. Both men expressed admiration for Dayananda and left records of his discussions with them. Scott presented Dayananda with a copy of the *New Testament*. They explained to him the Christian doctrine on various subjects. Dayananda mainly discussed the doctrine of God and the Christian notion of the forgiveness of sins, which he rejected because it did not square with the *karma* theory of personal responsibility for all actions. Dr. Hoernle observed that while Dayananda had read the Gospels, he did not seem to have read them carefully. These meetings came about because of the curiosity of the missionaries and totally lacked any mood of confrontation.[25]

Dayananda welcomed the lecture of the then President of the Adi Brahmos, Rajnarayan Bose, entitled, "The Superiority of Hinduism". But Dayananda was taken aback when the Brahmos rejected his own claim for the absolute uniqueness and superiority of the Vedic revelation. Dayananda wanted to prove his claim by demonstrating the complete truth of the *Vedas* and the failings of the *Bible*.

Dayananda criticized the Brahmos because they placed too much store in English and Christianity—to the neglect of the

Vedas. They spoke highly of holy men such as Moses and Jesus but forgot the ancient Vedic *Rishis*. In the face of the religious pluralism of the Brahmos of Calcutta, Dayananda's approach to other religions clarifies itself. Dayananda allowed that there could and would be many different religious groups so long as they all acknowledged the *Veda*—the many small rivers re-uniting in the ocean of Vedic wisdom.[26] At Bombay in 1875 Dayananda was involved with Christians and Muslims in public debate. Again Rev. Scott was the leading Christian representative. The discussion is reported to have centered on the issues of creation and salvation. It appears that this debate helped Dayananda to change his doctrine of creation from a position which argued for some sort of absolute beginning to the more orthodox Hindu view that the cosmos with its cycles is beginningless.[27]

Whereas in Calcutta the challenge to Hinduism had been essentially intellectual, in the Punjab the issue became intensely practical. "Missionaries were very active and effective in converting Hindus to an extent that the Panjabi Hindus felt that their community was seriously threatened."[28] In supporting the Punjab Hindus Dayananda strongly attacked Christianity in his public lectures, claiming that whatever power Christians experienced came from their practice of Vedic virtues. He criticized the Christian notion of "forgiveness of sins" maintaining in opposition a mechanical rebribution system of *karma*. The Swami also condemned the story of Adam, the concept of original sin, and the very idea of God becoming man. Every act must reap its appropriate individual rebribution; consequently, any notion of grace, forgiveness or vicarious atonement was unacceptable. God's justice via *karma* was absolute. For Dayananda any redeemer or grace-giving mediator, be it Christ or Krishna, was totally unacceptable. The only mode for interaction between man and God was *karma* as established in the *Vedas*.

Dayananda also took the lead to reconverting Indian Christians to Hinduism. He did this by extending the ancient doctrine of *shuddhi* (purification enabling one again to perform *dharma*) so as to cover the reinstatement of a lapsed Hindu.[29] This led Christian missionaries in the Punjab to consider him a threat.[30]

Dayananda's major writing on Christianity is Chapter thirteen of the *Satyarth Prakash*. He restricts his examination of Christianity to the *Bible* since the *Bible* is judged to be its source.[31] This, of course, parallels his approach in Hinduism, where all considerations are held to the *Vedas*. Jordens suggests that in writing his chapter Dayananda likely used a Sanskrit and a Hindi translation of the *Bible*.[32] Jordens effectively summarizes the method and result of Dayananda's examination of Christianity:

> The thesis presented in ths chapter is a very simple one: the claim of Christianity stands or falls with the Bible; the Bible is not the word of God; therefore, the Bible is not revelation and Christianity is not the true religion. To prove that the Bible is not God's word several arguments are used. The Bible is not universal, but particularistic and embedded in history. It contains a great number of statements that offend reason. By presenting a God who is limited by space and time, temperamental, deceitful, jealous, cruel, and a tawdry magician to boot, it contradicts the essential divine qualities. It also abounds in logical impossibilities, contradictions, and absurd miracles, and it displays a crude ignorance of scientific truth. Moreover, it contains many stories and precepts that are immoral, praising cruelty and deceit and encouraging sin. These are the basic arguments that are exemplified, page after page, in the many texts chosen from both Old and New Testaments.[33]

Dayananda's attack was clearly directed against the central tenets of Protestant evangelical thought dominant among the missionaries in India in the 1870s. The *Bible* was taken as the literal word of God and a logically consistent system of truth and morality. Dayananda's critique effectively challenged this theology of the *Bible* by focusing on its illogical and inconsistent assertions. Following the lead of the Christian missionaries, the approach adopted by Dayananda was that of "my scripture" against "your scripture" with the debate being carried on in a very scholastic and argumentative way.[34]

Jordens remarks that in his criticism of Christianity Dayananda has not really entered into the spirit of the *Bible*—thus going against his own request to the reader in the Introduction of the *Satyarth Prakash*. There he asks the reader to be aware of the intention of the author, of the total context, of the word meaning the author intends and any interpretation that gives rationality to the text.[35] Instead, what Dayananda offers is a literal reading of selected passages through the eyes of his *a priori* assumptions. Of course this procedure differs little from the approach taken by Christian missionaries of the day in their attempt to downgrade Hinduism—as for example in their attacks on the behavior of Krishna, the incest of Brahma, and cow-sacrifice in the *Vedas*.[36]

In the Introduction to Chapter fourteen of the *Satyarth Prakash* on Islam, Dayananda states that the text he is using is the *Qur'ān* translated from Arabic into Urdu and thence into Hindi.[37] Once again Dayananda follows his tried and true method for dealing with another religion. He offers a critical analysis of the sacred scripture of the religion showing how it deviates from the self-evident, reasonable and moral truths of the *Vedas*. Dayananda's commentary on the beginning *sura* of the *Qur'ān*, "In the name of God, the Compassionate, the Merciful" argues that "If (the Mohammedan) God be merciful, why has he sanctioned that men should inflict great suffering on other creatures by killing them for their food. Are not these animals innocent?"[38] To Dayananda it is clear that the Mohammedan God can never be called Merciful, because he shows no mercy towards those animals killed daily by the Muslim butchers. Nor can he be said to show mercy unto sinners because the *Qur'ān* directs that infidels are to be put to the sword.[39] Throughout his criticism Dayananda constantly returns to the observation that the *Qur'ān* teaches war, plunder and the killing of non-believers. Dayananda's fine eye for logical consistency is evident when he chides the Muslims, as the people of the book, for not also believing in the *Bible*. And if they do also believe in the *Bible*, observes Dayananda, then why was it necessary for the *Qur'ān* to be revealed as well? In his view there is so little difference between the two books that he finds it "reasonable to ask why the revelation was not sent down (once for all) in one (complete) book such as the *Veda*?[40] While Dayananda must be commended for his willingness to read the *Qur'ān* and enter into discussion with Muslim scholars, it was all done on the basis of his *a priori* assumptions and in a shallow scholastic fashion designed only to win debating points.

As a Hindu thinker of the late nineteenth century Dayananda showed a commendable interest in other religions. His approach was scholarly in that he insisted on studying the original source scriptures of the other religions, and in some cases (e.g., the *Qur'ān*) had translations made for him if none existed. However, his reading of the texts was always more polemic than scholarly in style. Passages would be selected for criticism where points of logical inconsistency or moral weakness could be shown. While he insisted on demythologizing the *Vedas* to overcome logical and moral difficulties, he refused this privilege to other scriptures.

Much of this was motivated towards the winning of public debates or private theological discussions, rather than the ideal he so often voiced of a common dispassionate search for truth.[41] But in this he was not unlike the best scholars of the other religions in late nineteenth century India.

Unlike most others of his day, however, Dayananda turned his criticism of the other religions also in upon his own religion. His overriding aim was to purify Hinduism of error and corruption so that modern Indians could take pride in their ancient heritage. His study of the other religions helped him to stand back and take a wide view of Hinduism, one that could overcome the petty squabbles that set Hindus against one another. Dayananda's vision of Vedic religion was of an eternal universal truth that could unify not just the many Hindu sects but also the other religions. In this Dayananda was at once modern and innovative and very traditional.

Shuddhi as a Response to Pluralism

If the guarding against sectarianism was Dayananda's key internal institutional response,[42] it was the orthodox Hindu notion of *shuddhi* or ritual purification that the Aryas used as their main external response to the threat of pluralism. In the hands of the Arya Samaj, *shuddhi* became a powerful tool for recovering lost Hindus, converting new Hindus and raising the status or reclaiming the low caste including the untouchables.[43] *Shuddhi* proved a powerful technique both for internal Hindu reform and for the forceful response to the converting activities of other religions—principally Christianity and Islam. Surprisingly, it was also a practice which, at times of communal stress, served to bring together the Arya Samaj and the orthodox Hindu leaders.

The concept of ritual purification, *shuddhi*, is an integral part of Hinduism. Its traditional purpose was to provide a means for restoring to purity and caste fellowship Hindus who had consciously or unconsciously broken caste taboos. *Shuddhi* (literally "purification"), traditionally took place through one or more ritual acts: bathing in a sacred river, pilgrimage, feeding Brahmins or *prayaschitta* (partaking of the five products of the cow.)[44] An ancient use of the rite was for the reinstatement of a "lapsed Hindu" who had been converted to another religion. The orthodox pandits had forgotten about the later law-books like the *Devalasmrti*, probably written after the Arab raids, which made provisions for the re-admission into Hinduism of people forcibly converted.[45] The Arya Samaj application of this traditional concept to meet the challenge of pluralism was intellectually imaginative and politically powerful. Its brilliance was such that it succeeded in evoking admiration and cooperation from some orthodox Hindu leaders who on most matters were solidly opposed to the Arya Samaj.[46]

It was on his visit to the Punjab in 1877 that Dayananda began to think about *shuddhi* as a way of counteracting the threat of Hindus being converted to Christianity. At Ludhiana some Hindus asked Dayananda to try to prevent the conversion of the Brahmin Ramsharan, a teacher at the mission school. Dayananda gave Ramsharan some instruction and the Brahmin decided not to go through with baptism. After thinking about the conversion threat he had encountered in the Punjab, Dayananda gave a lecture on *shuddhi* at Jullundur and himself performed the re-conversion of a Christian. Dayananda was actively involved in the reconversion to Hinduism of several Christians. He saw *shuddhi* as something right and appropriate for the specific Christian challenge to Hinduism which he encountered in the Punjab. But he did not develop the idea further.[47] However, the "seed idea" that had been planted gradually took root. As Jones notes,

> From mid-1884 onward, the Samaj sponsored and gradually came to perform ceremonies of readmission. Individuals and occasionally couples who had converted or otherwise lost their membership in the Hindu community turned to the Samaj for help in regaining their former communal identity . . . Samaj papers reported a continual stream of purifications; for Amritsar alone, thirty-nine in 1884 and fifty-five in 1885. Numerically of little importance, these cases marked the development of a new institution which would become a major element in Arya ideology, changing both the Samaj and the religious world around them.[48]

Punjabi Hindus who could look back on the loss of over half their community to Islam, and who were now under seige by Christian missions, began to see in the Arya Samaj formulation of *Shuddhi* a weapon with which they could defend themselves. No longer did Hindu religion need placidly to submit itself as a storehouse on which all the other religions could feed themselves.[49]

To begin with, orthodox Hindu rituals were used in the purification ceremony. "Candidates for reconversion were sent to

Hardwar for a bath in the sacred Ganges River, followed by the ritual of *prāyaschitta*, all under the supervision of orthodox Brahmins. Gradually Aryas developed their own set of ceremonies, consisting of tonsure, the fire or Hom sacrifice, investment of a sacred thread, and instruction in the *Gayātrī Mantra*."[50] During an interim period the Aryas employed both their own ceremonies and a trip to Hardwar for purification by an orthodox Brahmin. Eventually the trip to Hardwar was dropped off as too costly and unnecessary. For the reconverted person, however, it was the social acceptance following *Shuddhi* that proved most difficult. The Arya Samaj addressed this problem through a combination of persuasion and public ceremonies. After the purification ceremony a meeting of reconciliation was held in which the purified persons would distribute food and then all would eat together. A major flaw in the purification procedure, however, was that apparently no religious instruction was given beforehand so that those involved would have a clear idea as to the privileges and responsibilities their purification entailed. The biggest obstacle to the success of *Shuddhi* came from within the Arya Samaj's own ranks. Most of the Arya Samajists were apparently not willing to mix with the reconverted Muslims and Christians for fear of being ostracized by the orthodox Hindus. Such fear limited *Shuddhi* during this period to individual cases performed only by the most daring Arya Samaj branches.[51]

Shuddhi, the Sikhs and the Aryas

There were Arya attacks on Nanak and Sikhism as being "illiterate" and "hypocritical".[52] Dayananda had dismissed Nanak as having moble aims but no learning, since he knew neither Sanskrit nor the *Vedas*. As for his followers, they were as good as idolators since they worship the book *Granth Sāhib* and present gifts to it. But the Aryas of the Punjab found much in common with the Sikhs, who, like the Samaj, were attempting to establish a religion devoid of idolatry, caste and priestly domination.[53] During the early 1880's educated Sikhs took an active part in the Arya Samaj and on occasion rose to occupy executive positions in Samaj branches. But by 1885 Arya papers and speakers began to attack Sikhism as suffering from the same failings as Hindu orthodoxy. In 1888 several Arya leaders openly criticized the Sikh religion resulting in the cancellation by the leading Sikh Samajists of their memberships and an immediate crossing over to join the Singh Sabha.[54]

A renewed emphasis on *Shuddhi* within the Arya Samaj after 1893 established a new basis for cooperation between the Sikhs and the Samajists. In response to the growing threat from Islamic and Christian conversion campaigns, the Singh Sabha, like the Arya Samaj, established a major *Shuddhi* or reconversion thrust. In the mutual desire for self-protection, cooperation between the two groups with the focus on *Shuddhi* developed. Throughout the 1890's this Sikh-Arya co-operation centered on the common goal of *Shuddhi* continued. There was even a common newspaper, the *Shuddhi Pattai Khalsa Dharm Parkashak* published in Lahore to serve the needs of the joint *Shuddhi* effort. Until the issues of this paper are analyzed, however, we will not know the true nature and extent of the Arya-Sikh *Shuddhi* cooperation of this period.[55]

In 1896 the numbers undergoing *Shuddhi* suddenly increased as a result of a shift from individual to group reconversions. Several small groups were purified, culminating in the radical step of purifying a family of over two-hundred outcaste Sikhs. This final step added a new dimension to both the Sikh and Arya practice of *Shuddhi*—now it was a tool for social reform as well as conversion.[56] Because the outcasts were a prime target for Christian conversion, their social upgrading to full caste privileges as Hindus or Sikhs was a defensive measure against the missionaries. In the future it was this use of *Shuddhi* for the admittance of the outcaste to caste privileges that came to dominate.

In 1900 an event occurred which destroyed the Arya-Sikh cooperation for good. The Lahore Arya Samaj performed the *Suddhi* of a small group of Rahtias or Sikh untouchables.[57] As part of the ceremony the Aryas shaved their heads and beards, thus transforming them from Sikhs into caste Hindus. This action ruptured the cooperative Sikh-Arya *Shuddhi* venture and convinced many Sikhs that the Arya Hindu reconversion movement was potentially as dangerous to Sikhism as the Christian missionary threat. It helped to crystalize an already–forming Sikh identity quite separate from the Hindu community.[58] In this change of self-perception may be found some seeds for the Sikh-Hindu emnity which continues to the present.

Shuddhi, Islam and the Aryas

"The *Shuddhi* movement acted on relations between Hindus and Muslims, not to clarify overlapping identities, as with Sikhs and Hindus, but to reinforce existing communal separation."[59] There were more reconversions from Islam than from Christianity. As *Shuddhi* was turned to focus on outcastes, a large part of the Islamic community became available for reconversion. Pandit Lekh Ram led the charge of the Aryas against Islam. He wrote some thirty-two books and pamphlets against Islam. He argued that Islam was a religion of violence and tyranny, which engaged in holy war only as an excuse for the seizure of booty, women, children and slaves."[60] The violence of his verbal attacks so upset the Islamic community that when he could not be silenced through the courts, an assassin's bullet did him in. In the wake of his murder, rumors of violence against the Sikh and Arya *Shuddhi* leaders were spread, evoking counter threats of Hindu revenge. The legacy of Lekh Ram's murder has left a permanent anti-Muslim bias in the Arya Samaj. This Arya Samaj attitude has helped to feed the Hindu-Islamic communal hatred which has continued to flare into violence right up to the present day. Further aggravation with Islam occurred in the 1920s as a result of Swami Shraddhananda's *Shuddhi* drive for untouchables, and will be dealt with in the following discussion of "*Shuddhi* as upgrading within Hinduism".

Shuddhi Against Christianity[61]

Basing themselves on Dayananda's criticisms of Christianity for its practice of repugnant customs and for its superstitious and irrational theology, the Aryas during the 1880's mounted an aggressive offensive against the Christian missionaries. Munshiram (later Swami Shraddhananda) led the attack, employing *Shuddhi* as well as challenging missionaries in street debates, at fairs and in print. The growth of the Arya Samaj made it possible to send groups throughout the countryside to attend fairs and vigorously challenge the Christian missionaries whenever they attempted to preach the Gospel. At the same time a war of words went on through the publication by both sides of hundreds of tracts and pamphlets, the contents of which frequently sunk to the level of insult and insinuation. It was a period marked by reports of conversions and reconversions. The great temptation to convert to Christianity through attendance at the mission schools was lessened by the coming into existence of competing schools operated by the Arya Samaj. The Samajists realized that an essential tool for responding to the challenges of other religions and cultures was a high quality educational system in which the curriculum would be based in the *Veda* but also include modern science. By the end of this period in the Punjab, the efforts of the Aryas had succeeded to the point where few young upper caste Hindus were being converted by the Christians. But during this same period census figures continued to show huge increases through Christian conversions from the Hindu lower castes and the untouchables.

Eventually the Aryas came to realize that the best way to defend Hinduism against the Christian successes on the low caste Hindus was to change the emphasis of *Shuddhi* from reconversion to the upgrading of low caste and untouchable Hindus. By raising their status to full participation within Hinduism along with the provision of a Vedic based education, the prospect of conversion to Christianity would no longer attract them.

Shuddhi as Upgrading within Hinduism

In 1896 two events occurred which started the Aryas thinking of *Shuddhi* in a new way. First the Lahore *Shuddhi* Sabha purified a group of over two hundred Sikhs who had been outcasted years before. This was not a case of reconversion but of using *Shuddhi* to restore these Sikhs to full social and religious status. The second event resulted from a famine which in its wake had left a large number of orphans whom the Christians were beginning to look after. Realizing that here there was a danger of losing a large number of Hindu children to the Christians, the Arya Samaj, led by Lajpat Rai, initiated a rescue operation. Orphanages were established in the Punjab and by the end of 1897, nearly one thousand orphans had been resettled. Two years later Samaj members were sent to Bombay and the central provinces where there were many orphans needing care. Some 1700 were brought back to the Punjab and cared for. Thus the Aryas demonstrated to themselves and the Hindu community at large that they could compete with the Christians in caring for the unfortunate and at the same time prevent many potential conversions or losses to Christianity.[62]

Many years were to pass, however, before the Arya Samaj was to press into service the full power of *Shuddhi* as a means of upgrading low cste and untouchable Hindus. Like their founder, Dayananda, the members of the Arya Samaj wished to replace the many caste divisions of Hinduism with four *varnas* based on qualities of character rather than birth.[63] Reclaiming of the low caste and untouchables was an important first step in this direction, but a step to be taken with caution given the deep rootedness of caste tradition and practice in Hindu society. The Samaj leadership also realized that the lower castes would have to be educated, as well as formally purified, if any real or lasting changes in Hindu society were to be effected.[64] This, too, would take time and the development of a schooling system from the elementary level through University. Then too there were problems within the Samaj during the period 1900–1922 in getting the original and higher caste members to modify their own behavior in line with the stated ideals, and accept their newly purified brothers.[65] Part of the reason for the Arya's reluctance to move vigorously in the direction of *Shuddhi* was the fear that they would be outcasted by the orthodox Hindus.[66] Seeing the Aryas reclaim the depressed Hindu classes by admitting them to full Vedic privileges sent repeated shock waves through the orthodox community. Yet the orthodox leaders had to recognize the service of the Aryas in the defense of Hinduism, and realized that Hinduism needed the strength of the Aryas particularly in Northern India.[67]

It remained, however, for the 1923 leadership of Swami Shraddhananda to overcome the fears of the Arya Samaj, and to act in such a way as to receive some support from the orthodox Hindus. The central motivation of the Arya Samaj in this regard was not really religious in nature. *Shuddhi* was not clearly scripturally based, but was premised more on the fear that unless something like the *Shuddhi* of the low caste and untouchables was carried out, Hinduism in the future might dwindle in numbers and therefore in social and political importance.[68] This was a motivation to which the orthodox Hindus could subscribe or, at least, acquiesce. What the orthodox Hindus were not prepared to do was to accept purified ones from other religions or from the low caste and untouchable ranks into their social circle.[69] Thus the only home for these reclaimed ones was within the Arya Samaj circles. As Graham points out part of the problem here is that an isolated person converted from say Islam or Christianity is an anomaly in India. Such a person had the double problem of having been tainted by being a Christian or Muslim but also had to find a caste group to fit into. The purification of a whole caste or sub-caste group was much easier because only the taint of the other religion had to be removed. The *Shuddhi* group already had a caste home and so places did not have to be found for them within any of the higher caste brotherhoods.[70]

In 1923 Swami Shraddhananda pledged himself to save the untouchables.[71] Finding the Congress party unwilling to undertake an aggressive program to remove untouchability, which he judged to be the "anchor" of Muslims, Christians and the British Government, he set out to establish an Arya Samaj–based *Shuddhi* movement to accomplish that goal. But his appeal for support was to all Hindus:

> Noticing even the Congress powerless to absorb the so-called untouchables, I have made it the sole mission of my remaining life. I appeal to all Hindu Aryans, irrespective of religious or political differences, who do not like their six crores brethren to be cut away from their community, to help me with money and men.[72]

The first initiative under the Swami's leadership, but with support from orthodox Hindus, Sikhs and Jains, as well as a large contingent of Aryas, was directed at the reclaiming of the Malkana Rajputs. The aim was to conduct a *Shuddhi* campaign that would unite the low caste Malkanas with the Hindu Rajputs and thus prevent their absorbtion by missionizing Muslims. Within a year some thirty thousand Malkanas had been purified. Shraddhananda and his Arya supporters were the leaders of this successful *Shuddhi*. But the Muslims reacted strongly attacking the *Shuddhi* and the Swami as its leader. Congress leaders anxious to retain cooperative Muslim-Hindu support urged the dropping of the *Shuddhi*. But increasing support for the *Shuddhi* movement was being expressed by orthodox Hindu leaders. Even Orthodox pandits of Banaras gave their approval to the purification of the Malkana Rajputs.

Swami Shraddhananda and the Arya Samaj continued to provide leadership when the idea of organizing all Hindus into a national community for their mutual improvement was discussed at a 1923 Mahasabha meeting in Banaras. Arya ideas such as the common use of wells, full intermixing at public gatherings and ceremonies, the sharing of teaching by depressed class children with other Hindu children and the giving of full Hindu status to converts from Islam or Christianity, formed the agenda of the meeting although they were not approved.[73] Yet the Aryas were able to achieve some recognition from the orthodox Hindus on these points. On the matter of *Shuddhi*, the orthodox pandits were willing to receive a non-Hindu into Hinduism, but not into a caste. This left the Arya Samaj as the only place within Hinduism where such converts were welcome.

Swami Shraddhananda set out to carry the campaign of *Shuddhi* for untouchables to South India, where the tradition of untouchability was most deeply entrenched. The Swami's approach, which he situated squarely in the work of the Arya Samaj, argued that so long as untouchability continued in India there would be no grounds for arguing for self-government. *Shuddhi* of the untouchables was a prerequisite to Independence. Another reason for Hindu action, he argued, was that the Muslims, under the urging of the Aga Khan, were calling for the conversion of all untouchables to Islam so as to give them equal numbers to the Hindus.[74] Shraddhananda's citing of a Muslim conspiracy did not help to ease Hindu-Muslim tensions. It is not surprising, therefore, that Gandhi refused to support the untouchable purification campaign, with its anti-Muslim overtones. Instead, Gandhi criticized Shraddhananda and the Arya Samaj in print. For Gandhi, the Arya Samajists though dedicated and hard working were narrow, denominational and quarrelsome.[75] Swami Shraddhananda made several tours to aid the *Shuddhi* campaign for untouchables. He urged his Arya workers to continue to involve orthodox Hindus in the work as much as possible. At the 1926 meeting of the Mahasabha in Delhi the Swami and other Arya leaders (including Lajpat Rai and Shraddhanand's son Indra) finally managed to get more liberal resolutions accepted regarding the untouchables.[76]

Some indication of the success of this Arya Samaj drive to reclaim the untouchables may be seen in the free nature of their participation in the 1925 centenary celebrations of Dayananda's birth. A non-Arya journalist described the impressive way in which the untouchables joined in the event:

> I could mark no distinction between them and others . . . In the meetings, on the roads, in different functions they had accorded to them the elementary rights of human beings.[77]

To the untouchables *Shuddhi* gave the promise of the right to the full performance of *dharma*—access to all Vedic rites and the right to mix socially with caste Hindus. To Hinduism the Arya Samaj development of *Shuddhi* added a significant new dimension. Hinduism became a conversion religion. No longer were Hindus impotent in the face of attack on its numbers from other religions. *Shuddhi* gave to Hinduism the means for both defense and offense.[78] It also provided a foundation upon which the Aryas and the orthodox Hindus could work together. Arya Samaj scholars soon began producing publications arguing that far from being a new innovation *Shuddhi* had, for example, been practiced within Hinduism as early as 724 A.D. in Sind.[79] Whether or not it is a new innovation, it is evident that *Shuddhi* is a contribution of the Arya Samaj to Hinduism which enables it more effectively to cope with the challenge of the modern pluralistic context and, in addition, provides a means for social upgrading within Hinduism.

Conclusion

It could fairly be said that the whole of the Arya Samaj is a Hindu response to the challenge of modern religious pluralism. It was his encounter with Christianity and the syncretism of the Calcutta Brahmos that caused Dayananda to transform himself from a village Hindu reformer to a defender of Vedic truth before urban nineteenth Century British India. Aware of the self-destructive dangers of his reform movement becoming a sect, he built in safeguards which have enabled it to remain a dynamic force for reform within Hinduism. But his emphases on ritual purification, social reform and Vedic education depended upon the development of *Shuddhi* by his followers. In the hands of men like Lajpat Rai and Swami Shraddhananda *Shuddhi*, as a response to the challenge of Islam and Christianity, came to serve many creative roles. It provided a defense and counter-attack against the conversion of Hindus by other religions. In so doing it helped to create an identity and sense of self-confidence that Hindus found to be essential in modern pluralistic India. This even led the orthodox Hindus into a grudging admiration of the Aryas and a willingness to attempt to cooperate with them. Such cooperation opened the door for the Aryas to their larger goal of reforming orthodox Hinduism in its ritual and social practice.

The extension of *Shuddhi* as a mechanism to upgrade the low caste and take in the untouchables gave Hinduism a way to deal with the threat of losing one-half of their numbers to the aggressive missionizing of Christianity and Islam. Yet at the same time it required internal reform in matters of social acceptance for the purified within Hinduism. While the Arya Samaj found it difficult to actualize such caste reform even within its own ranks, it continues to work towards the ideal. The Aryas also realized that the provision of a good education for orphans and children of purified low caste or untouchable families is an important key to solving the problem. In India the Arya Samaj continues to be faithful to the ideas of Dayananda and to make solid contributions in the areas of education and publication. Internal organization within India remains strong with each state maintaining its own *sabha*.

To serve the diaspora of its followers Arya Samaj swamis are constantly traveling from India to attend gatherings all around the world. In itself the swami tradition, as developed by the Aryas, has been an important part of their successful response to modern pluralism. The worldwide activity of the swamis is given institutional support by the "umbrella organization" of the International Aryan League in Delhi.

With its more than two million adherents in India and spread round the world, and its continued thrust for caste and ritual reform within Hinduism, the Arya Samaj has to be judged as a successful modern Indian response to the challenge of pluralism.

Notes

1. Arvind Sharma, "Swami Dayananda Sarasvati and Vedic Authority" in *Religion in Modern India* edited by Robert D. Baird. New Delhi: Manohar, 1981. p. 188.

2. J.T.F. Jordens, *Dayananda Sarasvati: His Life and Ideas*. Delhi: Oxford University Press, 1978, Cp. XII.

3. See for example my recent book, *Pluralism: Challenge to World Religions*. Maryknoll: Orbis Books, 1985.

4. Jordens, *op. cit.*, pp. 247–248.

5. *Ibid.*, p. 266.

6. Dayananda Sarasvati, *Satyarth Prakash* (2nd edition). New Delhi: Arya Samaj Foundation, 1975, p. 479.

7. *Ibid.*

8. *Ibid.*

9. *Ibid.*, p. 482.

10. *Ibid.*, p. 483.

11. The following summary is taken from *Dayananda Sarasvati: His Life and Ideas*, *op. cit.*, pp. 271–272.

12. *Satyarth Prakash*, *op. cit.*, p. 2.

13. *Ibid.*

14. Rudolph Bultmann, *Jesus Christ and Mythology*. New York: Charles Scribner's Sons, 1958.

15. *Dayananda Sarasvati: His Life and Ideas*, *op. cit.*, p. 272.

16. *Ibid.*, p. 273.

17. *Ibid.*, p. 275.

18. *Satyarth Prakash*, *op. cit.*, pp. 483 ff.

19. *Ibid.*, p. 528.

20. *Ibid.*, p. 537.

21. *Ibid.*, p. 536.

22. *Ibid.*, pp. 547–559.

23. Ganga Prasad Upadhyaya, *Social Reconstruction by Buddha and Dayananda*. Allahabad: Ganga-Gyan-Mandir, 1956.

24. *Dayananda Sarasvati: His Life and Ideas*, *op. cit.*, pp. 103–104.

25. The above is summarized from Jordens, p. 72. See also J.T.F. Jordens, "Dayananda Sarasvati and Christianity," *Indian Church History Review*, *XV*, 1981, p. 34.

26. *Dayananda Sarasvati: His Life and Ideas*, *op. cit.*, p. 145.

27. *Ibid.*, p. 157.

28. "Dayananda Sarasvati and Christianity," *op. cit.*, p. 46.

29. *Dayananda Sarasvati: His Life and Ideas*, *op. cit.*, pp. 169–170.

30. "Dayanananda Sarasvati and Christianity," *op. cit.*, p. 41.

31. *Satyarth Prakash*, *op. cit.*, p. 587.

32. *Dayananda Sarasvati: His Life and Ideas, op. cit.*, p. 266.

33. *Ibid.*, p. 267.

34. "Dayananda Sarasvati and Christianity," *op. cit.*, p. 44. See also J.T.F. Jordens, "Dayananda Sarasvati's Interpretation of Christianity". To be published by Leiden in a volume edited by Arvind Sharma. In this article Jordens presents a detailed analysis of Dayananda's critique of the Christian doctrines of "the Bible as Revealed Scripture", "God and Creation," "Sin and its Atonement", "Christ, Son of God and Saviour", and "Faith in Christ". Jordens concludes that Dayananda's knowledge of Christianity was limited to one particular school, the Princeton school which focused on the inerrancy of Scripture, and which was dominant among the North India protestant ministers of that time. Although Dayananda grasped the bare basics of their beliefs about the fall of man, the mission of Christ and redemption through atonement and faith, he was never in a position to penetrate any distance into the complexities and subtleties of Christian theology. He did not read English so was restricted to sources in Hindi and Sanskrit, and often had to communicate with the missionaries through interpreters. See also, J. Jordens "Tradition and Modernity: Dayananda Sarasvati's Concept of the Vedic Golden Age". *Religious Traditions*, 1983, pp. 1–10.

35. *Dayananda Sarasvati: His Life and Ideas, op. cit.*, p. 267.

36. "Dayananda Sarasvati and Christianity," *op. cit.*, p. 43.

37. *Satyarth Prakash, op. cit.*, p. 649.

38. *Ibid.*, p. 651.

39. *Ibid.*, p. 652.

40. *Ibid.*, p. 654.

41. See, for example, his various "Introductions" in the *Satyarth Prakash*.

42. An aspect of Dayananda's response to the many religions and dominations that he encountered was his strong concern that the Arya Samaj not become yet another denomination or sect, but that it establish Vedic teaching as the basis on which all sectarian division, all pluralism would be overcome. See J.T.F. Jordens, "Sectarianism: The Case of the Arya Samaj." Unpublished paper read at the Asian Studies Association of Australia, Monash University, May 10, 1982, pp. 1–2.

43. Lajpat Rai, *The Arya Samaj*. London: Longmans, Green & Co., 1915, pp. 220–222.

44. Kenneth W. Jones. *Arya Dharm: Hindu Consciousness in 19th Century Punjab*. Berkeley: University of California Press, 1976, p. 129.

45. J.T.F. Jordens, *Dayananda Sarasvati, op. cit.*, pp. 169–170.

46. For a good description of the interaction between the Aryas and the Orthodox Hindu leaders on this point see J.T.F. Jordens, *Swami Shraddhananda: His Life and Causes*, Delhi: Oxford University Press, 1981, Cp. 6.

47. J.T.F. Jordens, *Dayananda Sarasvati, op. cit.*, pp. 170–1.

48. Kenneth W. Jones, *Arya Dharm, op. cit.*, p. 131.

49. *Ibid.*, p. 132.

50. *Ibid.*, p. 133.

51. *Ibid.*, p. 134.

52. Kenneth W. Jones "Communalism in the Punjab", *Journal of Asian Studies, XXVIII*, 1968, p. 47.

53. Kenneth W. Jones, *Arya Dharm, op. cit.*, p. 135.

54. *Ibid.*, p. 138.

55. A. Ph.D. student, Mr. Harjot Singh Oberoi, at the Faculty of Asian Studies, Australian National University is currently undertaking this task.

56. Kenneth W. Jones, "Communalism in the Punjab", *op. cit.*, p. 50.

57. J.T.F. Jordens, "Reconversion to Hinduism, the *Shuddhi* of the Arya Samaj", in G.A. Oddie (ed.), *Religion in South Asia*. Delhi: Manohar, 1977, p. 151.

58. Kenneth W. Jones, "Communalism in the Punjab", *op. cit.*, p. 50.

59. *Ibid.*

60. *Ibid.*, p. 51.

61. The following section is based upon Kenneth W. Jones, *Arya Dharm, op. cit.*, pp. 139–145.

62. The above paragraph is based on J.T.F. Jordens, "Reconversion to Hinduism, the *Shuddhi* of the Arya Samaj," *op. cit.*, pp. 150–1.

63. James R. Graham, *The Arya Samaj as a Reformation in Hinduism With Special Reference to Caste*. Ann Arbor: University Microfilms, 1943, p. 454.

64. *Ibid.*, p. 470. For an analysis of the considerable Arya Samaj educational achievements see Saraswati S. Pandit, *A Critical Study of*

the *Contribution of the Arya Samaj to Indian Education*. Baroda: University of Baroda, 1974.

65. *Ibid.*, p. 455.

66. *Ibid.*, p. 463.

67. Lajpat Rai, *The Arya Samaj*, *op. cit.*, pp. 229–231.

68. James R. Graham, *The Arya Samaj as a Reformation in Hinduism With Special Reference to Caste*, *op. cit.*, p. 517.

69. *Ibid.*, p. 519.

70. *Ibid.*, note 1.

71. J.T.F. Jordens. *Swami Shraddhananda*, *op. cit.* Most of the following discussion is based on Jordens' excellent analysis in Cp. 6, pp. 130–167.

72. As quoted by Jordens, *Ibid.*, p. 131.

73. *Ibid.*, p. 137.

74. *Ibid.*, pp. 143–144.

75. *Ibid.*, p. 145.

76. *Ibid.*, p. 156.

77. As quoted by Jordens, *Ibid.*, p. 159.

78. Kenneth W. Jones, "Communalism in the Punjab," *op. cit.*, p. 53.

79. Sri Ram Sharma, *Conversion and Reconversion to Hinduism*. Delhi: All India Shuddhi Sabha, n.d., p. 3.

Chapter Four

THE RESPONSE OF THE RAMAKRISHNA MISSION

R.W. Neufeldt

Introduction

Religious pluralism is a constantly recurring theme in the writings of the Ramakrishna Mission and in treatises on the Mission. The master himself, and the swamis who came after him seem always to have prided themselves with being able to cast an accepting eye on the religious traditions and practices of the world of faiths. Indeed, religious fanaticism of any sort receives harsh criticism and instant rejection in the writings of the mission. A personal experience underlines and illustrates this. I had occasion to ask a swami, visiting the University of Calgary, what he thought of the Hare Kṛṣṇa movement which was then growing in both popularity and notoriety. His response was typical. Short of condemning the movement he stated that the dogmatic fundamentalism of the movement was unhealthy, un-Hindu, and un-Indian. Hinduism, he said, has always been noted for its religious tolerance, but the Hare Kṛṣṇa movement deals in religious bigotry.

The centerpiece for the approach to religious pluralism is the statement, "many paths, one goal", which is frequently translated into the assertion that all religions are true, and, the so-called scientific religious experiments of Ramakrishna (1836–1888) which supposedly justify this statement. This is so from the sayings of Ramakrishna as recorded in the *Gospel of Sri Ramakrishna* down through the writings of the swamis to the present day. Whenever the issue of the many religious traditions is raised, resort is made to the statement, to the experiments, and to the many colorful illustrations Ramakrishna allegedly used in support of the statement. The statement is, of course, not new. By the Mission's own admission, it is at least as old as the Vedic assertion that the sages have given many names to that which is essentially one.[1] What may be relatively new, however, is the broad application of the statement to traditions and practices the world over.

The frequent nature of the repetition of the statement, the experiments, and the illustrations, gives one the impression of a programmed response. That is, for any serious question of a religious nature, one need only memorize the appropriate passages of the sayings of the master, in much the same way as fundamentalist Christians are taught to have a Bible verse ready for any and every occasion that might lead to the conversion of a lost soul. This penchant for repetition leads to the glib and superficial assertions that all religions are true and prevents a hard-headed examination of the views of the Mission on religious pluralism. This is true particularly of the writings emanating from the Mission itself and also of some of the writings about the Mission. The emphasis on repetition rather than critical examination, should not, I suppose be surprising, for according to Swami Nikhilananda, the *Gospel* is meant primarily for daily devotional study.[2]

The purpose of this study will be to attempt to flesh out in descriptive as well as critical fashion the views of the Ramakrishna Mission on religious pluralism. The main point of this analysis will be to argue that the stock phrases and illustrations used to support the assertion that all religions are true do not provide an adequate understanding of the Mission's stance on pluralism. Indeed, to allow the stock phrases and illustrations to stand alone is to tear the teachings of the Mission out of context. To use an old-fashioned principle of biblical criticism, one must interpret the scripture by the scripture. Once this is done in the case of the sayings of Ramakrishna and the writings of the swamis, one moves beyond the glib and superficial assertions that all religions are true and good. Indeed, what emerges is a position which is quite willing to criticize and judge religious beliefs and practices and even to speak of religious traditions as being unequal while affirming that all are true or good.

In this analysis I will spend some time on the sayings of Ramakrishna[3] and will follow this with some general observations about the writings of the swamis.[4] The justification for beginning with Ramakrishna should be obvious from the reference to the many repetitions by the swamis of pet phrases and illustrations taken from Ramakrishna. Whenever the issue of pluralism is raised, the swamis do defer to Ramakrishna or, at least to the *Gospel*. This should not be taken to suggest that nothing changes between the views of Ramakrishna and the swamis. Indeed, I shall attempt to show that there have been at least a few significant developments.

Ramakrishna according to the Gospel

Still the best and perhaps only source for the views of Ramakrishna is the *Gospel*, which covers a mere six or seven years of his life. Admittedly not a primary source since Ramakrishna did not keep journals or write memoirs, it nevertheless functions as a sort of bible or compendium of inspired sayings for adherents of the movement. Therefore, if reliable, the *Gospel* depicts not only Ramakrishna's response to pluralism, but also the official stance of the movement itself, a stance which one should expect to see repeated, at least to a point, in the writings of the swamis.

The *Gospel* depicts Ramakrishna as popularizing the idea of "many paths, one goal", through a number of images and illustrations which are immediately attractive because they are drawn from everyday life in India or from concepts familiar to Indian people. There is, for example, the illustration of travel.

> God can be realized through all paths. It is like your coming to Dakshineswar by carriage, by boat, by steamer or on foot. You have chosen the way according to your convenience and taste; but the destination is the same. Some of you have arrived earlier than others, but all have arrived.[5]

Or, there is the image of līlā.

> That which is Brahman is also Kali, the Adyasakti, who creates, preserves, and destroys the universe. He who is Krishna is the same as Kali. The root is one—all these are his sport and play.[6]

Or, there is the illustration of music.

> In the serenade we have here, one flutist plays a single note right along, while another plays various melodies. The Brahmos play one note, as it were; they hold to the formless aspect of God. But the Hindus bring out different melodies; that is to say they enjoy God in his various aspects.[7]

Or, there is the illustration of the rooftop.

> God can be realized through all paths. All religions are true. The important thing is to reach the roof. You can reach it by stone stairs or wooden stairs or by bamboo steps or by a rope. You can also climb up by a bamboo pole.[8]

These images and illustrations are used consistently, not only in the sayings of Ramakrishna, but also in the writings of the swamis, whenever discussion turns to religious pluralism or the many paths and faiths. The conclusion that is drawn is contained in the illustration of the rooftop—all religions are true. Supposedly this should be taken to mean that any path is equally as good as another to bring one to the rooftop, that all that matters in the choice of the path is the temperament and the inclinations or predispositions of the individual. According to Ramakrishna and the swamis,

> God Himself has provided different forms of worship. He who is the Lord of the Universe has arranged all these forms to suit different men in different stages of knowledge.[9]

Recognition of this fact supposedly has an important consequence for the relationship among practitioners of various paths. Having chosen a particular path, one should come to exercise a friendly attitude rather than animosity towards other faiths.[10] The paths are after all, all true, all equally good in that they will bring one to the same goal. Here the matter is usually left to rest.

But to leave it here, I would suggest, is to opt for a simplistic and uncritical reading of Ramakrishna and the swamis. And, however Ramakrishna and the swamis are content to leave it here, they opt for an uncritical self-assessment and perhaps, self-delusion, for, along with statements and illustrations which seem to place the variety of religious traditions on par with each other, one finds numerous statements which are both implicitly and explicitly critical and judgmental. In other words, the beliefs and practices of traditions do not escape criticism of judgment from either Ramakrishna or the swamis. This becomes evident if one takes care to look at the larger context of the statements and illustrations.

I begin with the example of Ramakrishna's illustration of reaching the rooftop. Following the illustration there is a lengthy explanation which has important implications for our understanding of religious tolerance in the Mission. He states:

> You may say that there are many errors and superstitions in another religion. I should reply: Suppose there are. Every religion has errors. Everyone thinks that his watch alone gives the correct time. It is enough to have a yearning for God. It is enough to love Him and feel attached to Him. Don't you know that God is the Inner Guide? He sees the longing of our hearts and the yearning of our soul. Suppose a man has several sons. The older boy addresses him distinctly as 'Baba' or 'Papa', but the babies can at best call him 'Ba' or 'Pa'. Now, will the father be angry with those who address him in this indistinct way? The father knows that they too are calling him, only they cannot pronounce his name well. All children are the same to the father. Likewise, the devotees call of God alone, though by different names. They call on one Person only. God is one but His names are many.[11]

Along with the ever present "many paths, one goal", one finds here two potentially significant elements. First, there is an attempt, at least in a small way, to define that which is necessary for anyone to reach the goal. We have here, the beginnings of what is regarded as essential for any path to be efficacious, or the essence of a truly religious path. Taken seriously, such definition will act as a critique on various paths or practices, putting some at a decided disadvantage and certainly, farther away from the goal than others. Secondly, there is the matter of focus best seen, perhaps, in the form of a question. Does the acceptability of people of various religious stripes have more to do with God, or the compassion of God, than it does with the devotee and his chosen path?

With reference to the first point, the definition of the truly religious path, one must ask in what sense all paths lead to the same goal. The answer seems to be that eventually they will all get you there, but only if they contain certain essentials. Apart from these, any chosen path can be misleading and even downright dangerous. The most obvious essential ingredient is *bhakti*, roughly defined as devotion or love. But, not just any devotion will do. When Narendra (Vivekananda) asked Ramakrishna about Tantra as a possible spiritual discipline, Ramakrishna reportedly answered that "it is extremely difficult to practice spiritual discipline looking on woman as one's mistress. To regard oneself as her child is a very pure attitude".[12] Thus the exercise of one form of *bhakti* is pure while another is downright dangerous, causing the downfall of many. Some paths then, have at least the potential to divert the mind from God.

For Ramakrishna, *bhakti* cannot be defined in a single word, rather, a cluster of words is necessary. On the one hand, it is loving devotion to God. He says, for example:

> The one essential thing is bhakti, loving devotion to God. Do the Theosophists seek bhakti? They are good if they do . . . A man should practice sadhana and pray to God with a longing heart for love of his Lotus Feet. He should direct his mind to God alone, withdrawing it from various objects of the world . . . You may speak of the scriptures, of philosophy, of Vedanta; but you will not find God in any of those. You will never succeed in realizing God unless your soul becomes restless for Him.[13]

On the other hand, this loving devotion, to be efficacious, must be sincere, earnest, and single-minded. A path will do only if it is characterized by sincerity, earnestness, and single-minded devotion. Only then will we find that all paths lead to God.[14]

> With sincerity and earnestness one can realize God through all religions. The Vaishnavas will realize God, and so will the Saktas, the Vedantists and the Brahmos. The Mussalmans and the Christians will realize Him too. All will certainly realize God if they are earnest and sincere.[15]

Rather pointed is the statement, "But if a man prays to Thee with a yearning heart, he can reach Thee, through Thy grace, by any path.[16] One finds here an echo of the words of God to Samuel in the choice of David as king of Israel.[17] It seems to be the inner attitude or feeling that counts. If that is right, any path will do; if it is not right, the chosen path will not do. "Verily, the Lord looks into a man's heart and does not judge him by what he does or where he lives. 'Krishna accepts a devotee's inner feelings of love.' "[18]

In addition to a longing which is sincere, earnest and single-minded, the path must also include renunciation. If it does not, it cannot lead to God. While required of everyone, renunciation is not to be pushed, but is to be taken up in the fullness of time, after one's craving for enjoyments has reached its limit.[19] A phrase one finds repeatedly in Ramakrishna and the swamis is renunciation of "woman and gold". One must come to the end of one's enjoyment of the world. But, renunciation of the world, to be efficacious, must not be characterized by false motivations. Correct renunciation is motivated by longing for God while "monkey renunciation" or false renunciation is motivated by loss of employment, poverty, and so forth.[20] Further, renunciation must be both inward and outward. That is, it is not enough to conduct one's worldly duties in a detached manner. At some point the ties to worldly duties must also be renounced.[21]

To speak of the essentials which are to characterize any path has significant implications for one's understanding of religious tolerance. Most important, perhaps, is the fact that it creates the possibility for entering into criticism and judgment of any and all paths. That Ramakrishna was willing to criticize and judge is clear at a number of points. While *bhakti* was regarded by him as the most important and efficacious path for his day, not all forms of devotion or love were to be countenanced, as is evident from him judgment of Tantra as a spiritual discipline. He freely criticized Hatha Yoga because of its concern for the body and approved of the Raja Yoga of Vedantists because it included *bhakti* aimed at god-realization.[22] In spite of his many assertions that the Brahmos were perfectly acceptable to him, he nevertheless criticized them rather severely.

> The Brahmajnanis of modern times sing of God as 'immutable, homogeneous'. It sounds very dry to me. It seems as if singers themselves don't enjoy the sweetness of God's Bliss. One doesn't want a refreshing drink made with sugar candy if one is satisfied with mere coarse treacle.
>
> Just see how happy you are, looking at this image of the Deity.

> But those who always cry after the formless Reality do not get anything. They realize nothing either inside or outside.[23]

Insistence on renunciation too, both inward and outward, has within it the potential for criticism and judgment, a potential which Ramakrishna on occasion realized. While God has supposedly provided various paths or forms of worship for diverse people, these forms are arranged to suit individuals at different stages of knowledge.[24] This means that as one progresses, certain forms of worship or spiritual discipline drop off or are renounced because one has now arrived at something more efficacious. Thus one can at a certain point dispense with *sandhya* devotions and other such rituals.[25] This amounts to an admission that there is among paths or disciplines a hierarchy, with some forms being more efficacious than others, with some forms having to be superseded if one wants to reach the goal.

Such hierarchization is applied even to the beliefs or experiences of devotees. They are not all of one piece. The inferior devotee says, "God exists, but He is very far of, up there in heaven". The mediocre one says, "God exists in all beings as life and consciousness, the Antaryamin or Inner Guide:. The superior one says, "It is God Himself who has become everything; whatever I see is only a form of God. It is He alone who has become maya, the universe, and all living beings. Nothing exists but God."[26]

It seems inescapable to me that we arrive finally at the prescription of a particular *sādhana*. It is a sādhana which admits of many paths provided that they contain certain essential ingredients. Only on this basis can one say that all paths are true, or that all paths lead to the same goal. A key term in Ramakrishna's vocabulary is that one must follow a chosen path *rightly*.[27] Only then will one reach the goal. The chosen path must include a devotion or longing which is sincere, earnest and single minded. Furthermore, it must include both inward and outward renunciation. At times Ramakrishna becomes quite detailed in his description of the austerities involved in outward renunciation.[28]

One might even go so far as to suggest that the *sādhana* to be genuine, must be informed by the belief that God is all, or all is God and must end in the direct vision or experience of this belief. In other words there must be the acquisition of a correct perception of reality. It is not enough to say that one must be devoted. Devotion should ultimately be informed by a certain view of things, a view which may begin as a belief but must at some point be experienced directly. I would suggest that this along with a particular *sādhana*, is what Ramakrishna means when he uses the term *Sanātana Dharma*. It is devotion characterized by sincerity, earnestness, and single-mindedness; it is renunciation of all attachments including woman, gold, and rituals; it is the practice of austerities; and, it is the belief–cum–experience that all is God.

This insistence on a direct vision leads Ramakrishna to be highly critical of disciplines so much prized by various traditions, including his own—scholarship, reasoning, study of scripture, etc. The direct vision has precious little to do with those. Just as one must leave off woman, gold and rituals, one must also cast off reasoning and scriptures. This is the sign of perfect knowledge.

> God cannot be realized through scholarship. He is beyond scriptures—the Vedas, Puranas, and Tantras. If I see a man with even one book in his hand, I call him a rajarshi, though he is a jnani. But the Brahmarshi has no outer sign whatsoever.[29]

Without such a direct vision one cannot claim to be truly religious. And, as has already been suggested, this vision has a particular shape.

> I do see God directly. What shall I reason about? I clearly see that He Himself has become everything; that He Himself has become the universe and all living beings.[30]

This direct vision becomes the vantage point from which one judges and criticizes, or, if one might be charitable, from which one interprets the true meaning of all scriptures. It is not the literal meaning of scriptual words that is important. Rather, it is the meaning behind the words, the occult knowledge, if you will, which can be had only through a direct vision which in turn is the result of a particular *sādhana*. This meaning behind the words results, of course, in curious interpretations of other traditions. The most well known are Ramakrishna's and the swamis' interpretations of Gautama and Buddha. "He was not an atheist. He simply could not express his inner experiences in words."[31] Or taking the Vaisnavite line, "This too is a Sport of God Himself, a new lila of God."[33]

The business of the direct vision brings me to the second point, the issue of focus. The direct vision is not entirely dependent on one's choosing a path and following it *rightly*. The explanation of the rooftop illustration suggests that reaching the goal may have more to do with God than it does with man. There is the adission that there are those who understand poorly, indeed that there is much error in man's religious traditions, but at the same time, there is the assertion that those who are in error are as dear to God as those who understand well. All will eventually reach the goal because God is compassionate and will draw them to Him, not because all understand and behave equally well. Indeed any chosen path or view is bound to be in error because God is infinite and cannot be comprehended in His totality. What we have, at least prior to the direct vision, are only partial glimpses.[33] Nevertheless, no matter how much in error the chosen path may be, God will after all honor the sincerity and longing evident in the choice of a path, because God loves all equally, and in the final analysis, because God is all.

One finds here echoes of Christian universalism—that all will eventually be saved because God is love, and it is simply inconceivable that a God of love will damn anyone to hell. But this universalism, too, allows for judgment and criticism, even while one is asserting that all religions are true. It allows one to say that all will eventually realize God, but it also allows one to say that there is a good deal of error and confusion in the paths and views represented by different traditions. Indeed, if one takes the hierarchization seriously, some traditions will have a good deal more error and confusion in them than others, and this will serve to slow down one's progress towards realization. To speed up that progress one must opt not only for engaging in a chosen path *rightly*, but also for subscribing to those views which most clearly express the nature of Reality.

The Swamis

On the issue of religious pluralism there is a good deal of sameness between the *Gospel* and the writings of the swamis. It is produced, of course, by the many repetitions, frequently word for word, of ideas, illustrations, and explanations found in the *Gospel*. Clearly the *Gospel* came to function as a kind of bible for the swamis, a text through which they could be schooled in and remain faithful to the ideas of the Master. Thus one finds the same emphasis on the path of devotion, on seeing all as God's *līlā*, on seeing all as paths to God-realization if these paths are pursued *rightly*, and on depending on the compassion of God to deliver one even while one embarks on a chosen path. There are, however, two important developments which require attention, because they raise the issue of the relationship of the teachings of swamis to the teachings of Ramakrishna as recorded in the *Gospel*.

First, there is the matter of hierarchization. Already in Ramakrishna, in spite of assertions that all religions are true, that all paths lead to one goal, there is a hierarchization which places devotees who see or experience reality in non-dual fashion, who see what everything is God, above other devotees whose vision is acceptable but not yet complete because one still has a way to go. There is also an implied hierarchization of traditions and spiritual disciplines. Otherwise it does not make sense to say that inevitably certain practices such as ritual or scriptual study will fall away or become superfluous. The implied image then is one of evolution in which all paths, all creeds, all understandings are helps or stepping stones toward the realization that God is all.

This hierarchization is made much more explicit, and indeed, carried much further in the writings of the swamis. In Vivekananda, for example, one finds the idea that the real spiritual object towards which we are all impelled is God. However, the journey takes us through a lot of mistakes and "little loves"[34] until we eventually find our true goal.

> Again and again we find our mistake. We grasp at something, and find it slips through our fingers, and then we grasp at something else. Thus on and on, and then comes light; we come to God, the only One Who Loves.[35]

Presumably those little loves or mistakes are the various paths and their ideals, all of which must at some point be transcended.

The same hierarchization comes through in Vivekananda's distinction between formal or ceremonial and supreme *bhakti* (*vaidhi* vs. *mukhyā*). *Bhakti*, he maintains, covers all worship seen in any country in the world.[36] Some of it is low and vulgar in that it is done for material things,[37] and much of it is simply *pratika*, worship that comes near to God but will not save man.[38] There is even an outright comparison of traditions in which India and Vedic religion are seen as clearly superior to other countries and their traditions. The *mukti* path he claims, is found only in

India.[39] Such problems as India has are to be laid at the feet of Buddhists and Jains for diverting attention away from *dharma*. They ruined India in the same way as Christ ruined the Romans.[40] Their aims might have been correct, but their means were faulty and need the corrective of the Vedic emphasis on *dharma*, which in ancient India went hand in hand with *mukti*.[41] This is, of course, all quite in keeping with Vivekananda's view that India is destined to be a missionary of spirituality to a spiritually poor West.

Similar ideas in heightened form are found in Swami Ghanananda. Here we find a clear evolutionary model in which all paths are viewed as preparatory for the real thing, that is, the true spiritual and cultural realism of India and the synthetic principles of Vedanta as expressed by Ramakrishna and Vivekananda.[42] Man is seen as moving in a spiritual pilgrimmage from dualism, which sees a "qualitative as well as a quantitative difference between his own self and God", to the truth of non-dualism which sees "that the part is to same as the whole, or rather that there is no such thing as a part, for Infinity cannot be divided:.[43] In other words, all is preparatory for the practice and realization of Advaita which is the apex to which all other traditions tend.

> Advaita regards the followers of all religions, irrespective of caste, creed or color, as pilgrims, more or less conscious, bound for the Temple of Truth, of which all religions of the world are so many roads. The flight of Ramakrishna's soul from the pinnacle of Advaita (non-dualism) to Islam was like the flight of a bird from the highest top of a tree to one of its branches.[44]

Religious traditions are therefore to be seen as a graduated series of steps suited to different minds in different stages of spiritual evolution. Each tradition or interpretation is seen to be true for its stage. Thus man progresses from truth to truth or from lower levels of experience to higher levels culminating in the vision of Advaita, which is to be found in India alone.

> India alone has preached that every church, every creed, is only travelling, a coming up, of different men and women through various conditions and circumstances to the same goal. No other country has furnished the basis of a universal religion which is all-embracing and all-inclusive.[45]

Similar messages are found in the writings of other swamis. Swami Ranganathananda asserts that one finds in India a more spiritual and less dogmatic view of religion than elsewhere.[46] Swami Brahmananda maintains that there are grades of worship all leading eventually and naturally to non-dualism.[47] In Swami Abhedananda we find the image of the ladder used to compare traditions. Advaita Vedānta is seen as the top rung for a number of reasons. While all religions teach the law of love, only the Vedas, Upanisads and Vedānta explain why one should love.[48] Vedānta was introduced to prove that the fundamental ideals and goals of all religions are the same.[49] Since Vedānta is the best commentary on the true religion of Christ, one should go to Vedānta, not the Church to understand what Christ taught.[50] On a comparative basis Hinduism is said to have provided a higher conception of man than has Christianity, and Christianity in turn has provided a higher conception of man than has Judaism.[51] In Swami Ashokananda one finds the assertion that Vedānta is superior to other traditions in that it is more scientific, indeed, it is the science and philosophy of all religions.[52]

If one takes this kind of hierarchization seriously one is led naturally to the second important development, the distinction between religion, or true spirituality, and the religions. Religion is made to be synonymous with Advaita Vedānta and is to be found in its best expressions only in India, in the texts of the *Vedas* and Upanisads. All else is to be classified as religions which are at best preparatory for the dawning of religion. The religions may contain religion but this is to be extracted from them through the eyes of Advaita. To use Vivekananda's phraseology, the religions comprise the "mistakes", "the little loves" through which we must pass in order to arrive at the real thing. "Reason, theories, dogmas, doctrines, books, religious ceremonies, are all *helps*; religion itself consists of *realization*.[53] They are grades of worship which are struggling toward the real thing, but are not the real thing itself.[54] This is vividly put in Vivekananda's criticism of churchianity.

> It is very good to be born in a church, but it is very bad to die in a church. To make it clearer, it is very good to be born in a certain training, a certain sect; it brings us out, but in the vast majority of cases we die in that little sect, we never come out or grow . . . If a young man does not go to church he ought to be condemned, but if an old man goes to a church he, also, ought to

> be condemned, he has no business with this child's play any more, the church should have been merely a preparation for something higher.[55]

The variety of images that have been presented also lead in the same direction. In the image of the wheel, religion or Advaita lies at the center, and the religions form the many radii moving towards the center. In the image of the tree, the highest top of the tree or the pinnacle is religion or Advaita, while the religions comprise the lower branches. In the image of the ladder, religion, or Advaita is the top ring, while the religions comprise the rungs underneath. As Swami Abhedananda says, Vedānta is its different phrases embraces all religions and provides the fundamental principles of all religions.[56]

Conclusion

If one takes seriously the picture presented here, one is left with two possibilities in the attempt to understand the view of religious pluralism in the Ramakrishna Mission. On the one hand, one can take the position that Ramakrishna and the swamis were blatantly contradictory or that the critical and judgmental statements either do not count or were not meant to be taken seriously. One is driven to this position, if one remains satisfied with the mere repetition of stock phrases like "many paths, one goal", and the rather simplistic and uncritical assertion that all religions are true. On the other hand one can, as I choose to do, take the position that Ramakrishna and the swamis meant the critical and judgmental statements to stand alongside the assertions that all paths are true and that both kinds of statements were meant to inform each other. However, the picture of the Mission's view of pluralism which then emerges is much more complex than it is usually made out to be. One is still left with an acceptance of all traditions, but it is an acceptance with certain limitations and qualifications.

It is, of course, true that Ramakrishna said, and the swamis continue to say, that all paths lead to the same goal and that all paths are true. But this is only so if the paths contain that which is essential. The religious experiments of Ramakrishna should also be understood in this sense. This insistence on essentials allows him and the swamis to enter into criticism of traditions to the extent that they do. Traditions can be judged as useful to the extent that they contain the ingredients essential for God–realization. In this respect some traditions are clearly better than others. I suspect that when Ramakrishna and the swamis say that all paths are true or that all paths lead to God, they simply meant to counter a dogmatism which says "my religion alone is true" rather than to suggest all paths are equal in the sense of containing equally good views and practices.

If one takes the hierarchization of devotees, practices, traditions and even countries seriously, one can still say all traditions are true or good without suggesting they are all equally true or good. They are true or good for the stage for which they were meant. Differences among traditions and perceptions are admitted with respect to the exact nature of the goal and methods employed in attaining the goal. These differences are to be understood in terms of different grades of experience in spiritual pilgrimages.[57] Further, one may say that all traditions are true and good, but in a preparatory sense only, that is, as leading on towards something higher and eventually to the dawning of the final realization or true religion. And, of course, this will only happen if one follows one's chosen path with sincerity and discipline. Although all are preparatory, some are clearly further away from true religion than others. One is reminded here of the model proposed by the founders of T'ien T'ai Buddhism. In order to harmonize the variety of Buddhist traditions, the various schools were set up in hierarchial fashion as leading up to the capstone, the truth of the *Lotus Sutra*. It is precisely at this point that the issue of the relationship between Ramakrishna and the teachings of the swamis becomes important; that is, to what extent is there continuity and change? One can argue, for example, that in the business of hierarchization there is continuity between Ramakrishna and the swamis. Ramakrishna, at least as depicted in the *Gospel*, was willing to engage in hierarchization of practices, beliefs, and devotees. In the swamis, of course, one sees this hierarchization both continued and carried much farther to apply to religious traditions and even to countries.

When such further application occurs one must ask whether there is a significant shift in the spirit of the teachings from Ramakrishna to the swamis. The answer, I think, must be, "yes". It is not just a case that the hierarchization is carried further than it is in the *Gospel*. There is also a considerable narrowing of vision vis-à-vis pluralism as one moves from Ramakrishna to the swamis. It could be argued that in Ramakrishna one has a "grab-bag' approach to the plurality of religions. While he is willing and able to criticize religious beliefs and practices from the standpoint of his own experience, he seems to be quite ready to let the wide variety of beliefs and practices stand, to be used as the occasion demands without any consistent need to reconceive these traditions and practices in terms of something higher. He seems to maintain a relatively open attitude to diverse beliefs and practices.[58]

This is not the case with the swamis. All traditions are to be understood as true or good because they point to Advaita and in pointing contain, at least implicitly, the truth of Advaita. But in order that we might see the Advaitin message in all traditions, they must be reconceived in terms of Advaita.[59] This is made abundantly clear in the Mission's traditional interpretation of Gautama the Buddha. I would see this as the most severe and problematic limitation in the Mission's response to pluralism. To understand traditions correctly they are to be seen as Advaitin, either explicitly or implicitly. This serves to make adherents of various traditions into either conscious or anonymous Advaitins. In the eyes of the Mission we are all okay, because, whether we realize it or not, we are all headed in the same direction. This is just as problematic as the use of the term "anonymous Christian", in that it makes people into something they may not want to be, and it refuses to see traditions in terms of their own self-characterization. Rather, from the vantage point of a higher wisdom or experience, all traditions are accepted and reconceived. One is still left with an acceptance of diverse beliefs and practices, but it is an acceptance with severe limitations in the sense that one is acceptable not on one's own terms, but only in terms of a reinterpretation favorable to Advaita. It is ultimately a position which says that the religious pluralism we see is not a real pluralism, but a pluralism in appearance only. And, it is appearance only because the truth to be experienced (i.e. religion) lies at the heart of all empirical religions, although in some it is buried more deeply than it is in others.

This is a position similar to the one sometimes taken on the comparative study of religions—that the task of the comparative study is to promote or bring to the light of day the unity of all religions. And, this is possible because underneath all of the historical accretions there is a real unity. The diversity is one of appearance only and is to be taken seriously on that level alone. Ultimately the diversity is not real, for beyond the diversity, there is a unity which the serious student of religion should be striving to uncover. There is, of course, a difference between this view and the view of the Mission. Spokesmen for the Mission *know* what that unity is, while comparativists who seek to uncover a unity are hopelessly divided on the nature of that unity.[60]

Notes

1. Rg Veda 1. 164.

2. Ramakrishna: *Prophet of New India*, tr. by Swami Nikhilananda. New York: Harper and Brothers Publishers, 1942, p. ix.

3. The translation used is Swami Nikhilananda's, *The Gospel of Sri Ramakrishna*, Madras: Sri Ramakrishna Math, 1969. This is a reprint of the American edition published by the Ramakrishna—Vivkananda Centre of New York. For a thorough discussion of the relative merits of this translation over against others, see Walter G. Neevel, "The Transformation of Sri Ramakrishna" in Bardwell L. Smith, *Hinduism: New Essays in the History of Religions*, Leiden: E.J. Brill, 1976, pp. 53–97.

4. For the sake of brevity I have chosen to treat Vivekananda together with other swamis, recognizing that this does not do justice to the importance of Vivekananda for the Mission. One can rightly argue that the mission begins with the genius of Vivekananda, and that the language of later swamis, used to express the ideals and concerns of the Mission, is, for all intensive purposes, established by Vivekananda. For a discussion of Vivekananda's place in the Mission see Cyrus P. Pangborn, "The Ramakrishna Math and Mission" in Bardwell L. Smith, *Hinduism: New Essays in the History of Religions*, pp. 105–119. For a complete discussion of Vivekananda see George M. Williams, *The Quest For Meaning of Suami Vivekananda*, Chico: New Horizons Press, 1974.

5. *The Gospel of Sri Ramakrishna*, p. 1008.

6. *Ibid.*, p. 1010.

7. *Ibid.*, p. 1023.

8. *Ibid.*, p. 39.

9. *Ibid.*, p. 5.

10. *Ibid.*, p. 158.

11. *Ibid.*, p. 39.

12. *Ibid.*, p. 51.

13. *Ibid.*, pp. 573–4.

14. *Ibid.*, p. 158.

15. *Ibid.*, p. 124.

16. *Ibid.*, p. 19.

17. I. Samuel 16:1–7.

18. *Gospel of Sri Ramakrishna*, p. 139.

19. *Ibid.*, p. 1012.

20. *Ibid.*

21. *Ibid.*, p. 150.

22. *Ibid.*, pp. 274–5.

23. *Ibid.*, p. 148.

24. *Ibid.*, p. 5.

25. *Ibid.*, p. 1.

26. *Ibid.*, pp. 205 and 901.

27. *Ibid.*, p. 322.

28. *Ibid.*, p. 842.

29. *Ibid.*, p. 871.

30. *Ibid.*, p. 709.

31. *Ibid.*, p. 940.

32. *Ibid.*, p. 941.

33. *Ibid.*, p. 701.

34. Swami Vivekananda, *Religion of Love*, Belur: Ramakrishna Math, 1927, p. 24.

35. *Ibid.*, p. 22.

36. *Ibid.*, p. 60.

37. *Ibid.*, p. 60.

38. *Ibid.*, p. 75.

39. Swami Vivekananda, *The East and The West*. Madras: The Brahmavadin Office, 1909, p. 9.

40. *Ibid.*, pp. 18–21.

41. *Ibid.*, pp. 23–3.

42. Swami Ghananda, *Sri Ramakrishna and His Unique Message*. London: Ramakrishna Vedanta Centre, 1970, third edition, p. 37.

43. *Ibid.*, pp. 120–21.

44. *Ibid.*, p. 88.

45. *Ibid.*, p. 165.

46. Swami Ranganathananda, *Science and Religion*. Calcutta Advaita Ashram, 1978, pp. 15–16.

47. Swami Brahmananda, *Spiritual Teachings*. Madras: Sri Ramakrishna Math, 1933, 2nd edition, pp. 130–31.

48. Swami Abhedananda, *Complete Works*. Madras: Sri Ramakrishna Math, 1924, p. 368.

49. *Ibid.*, p. 371.

50. *Ibid.*, p. 376.

51. *Ibid.*, pp. 240–41.

52. Swami Ashokananda, *The Influence of Indian Thought on the Thought of the West*. Mayavati: Almora Advaita Ashrama, 1931, p. 12.

53. Vivekananda, *Religion of Love*, p. 52.

54. Swami Vivekananda, *Addresses on Vedānta Philosophy, Vol. II, Bhakti Yoga*. London: Simpkin Marshall, Hamilton, Kent & Co., Ltd., 1896, p. 65.

55. *Ibid.*, p. 67.

56. Abhedananda, *Complete Works*, p. 377.

57. See for example, Swami Prabhavananda, *Vedic Religion and Philosophy*, Madras: Sri Ramakrishna Math, 1968, p. 10.

58. See Neevel's discussion in "The Transformation of Sri Ramakrishna".

59. If one wishes to argue that such reconception also takes place in Ramakrishna, it would not be reconception in terms of Sankara's Advaita. Rather, it would be reconception in terms of tantric thought. See Neevel, "The Transformation of Sri Ramakrishna", p. 76.

60. For a discussion of this development in comparative religion see Eric Sharpe's treatment in *Comparative Religion, a History*, New York: Charles Scribner's Sons, 1875, pp. 251–266.

Chapter Five

THE RESPONSE OF SRI AUROBINDO AND THE MOTHER

R.N. Minor

When the Indian political activist, Aurobindo Ghose (1872–1950) fled British India in 1910 for French Pondicherry in southeast India, he intended to concentrate on the development of a yoga which would bring in a new world. His yoga would, he believed, be an acceleration of the world's evolution, which he defined as the eternal Becoming of the Absolute.[1]

Within a decade he gathered around him a community of those who accepted his vision and the discipline which would further that evolutionary force in this world to higher levels of consciousness. At first four or five disciples joined him, but the number continued to grow and the need for maintenance and guidance began to tax Aurobindo's own yogic progress. On November 24, 1926, Aurobindo believed his yoga had resulted in the experience of the descent from higher levels of the Overmind consciousness, a level of consciousness above the ordinary human level of Mind, and intermediate to that of the higher Supermind. It was Aurobindo's "Day of Siddhi". As a result Aurobindo suspended his regular evening talks with the *sādhaks* and turned the management of the Ashram over to Mira Richard (1878–1973), whom he called the Mother.

Richard, the daughter of a French banker, was a student of the occult from an early age. She had begun a group for the purpose of "seeking the spiritual" in 1906. She later recalled in Aurobindian terms an early desire to found a retreat for seekers of spiritual things.

> I was very young at that time, and always I used to tell myself that if ever I could do it, I would try to create a little world—Oh! quite a small one, but still—a small world where people would be able to live without having to be preoccupied by problems of food and lodging and clothing and the imperious necessities of life, to see if all the energies freed by this certainty of an assured material living would spontaneously be turned towards the divine life and inner realisation.[2]

She met Aurobindo in March 1914 and returned to Pondicherry in April of 1920 to join the Ashram.

Aurobindo was convinced that she was an incarnation of the energy that was the evolutionary process, the *śakti* often traditionally pictured as a goddess, and even of Supermind consciousness itself.[3] Thus, her consciousness even exceeded his own. It was, therefore, most appropriate for her to lead the Ashram, which she did, while Aurobindo developed his yoga. She began the collective organization of the Ashram and expended its institutions and facilities as the number of its *sadhaks* grew. It now occupies over 400 buildings spread throughout Pondicherry, dominating the otherwise sleep town both socially and economically. On February 28, 1968, she founded what she hoped would become an international community five miles northeast of Pondicherry which would attempt to put Aurobindo's principles into practice, Auroville "City of Dawn". In 1960 she founded a central administrative agency to coordinate and manage the variety of international Aurobindo institutions, the Sri Aurobindo Society. She oversaw all of these activities until her death on November 17, 1973.

The Centrality of the Guru

From its beginning, the Ashram centered around a person, Sri Aurobindo. It was his vision, his "Integral Yoga" and its intuitive insights, which brought the disciples together. The yoga he practiced and spoke of in his voluminous writings was based upon the premise that there is a Divine diversity essential to human beings. Thus, he included no specific instructions for others to follow, nor did he describe his own practice specifically, "for the law of the Supermind is unity fulfilled in diversity."[4] Besides specific answers to the questions asked of him by his disciples, his "Letters" give as general requisites: the realization that one had a call, sincerity, persistence, aspiration, and faith in the Divine's guidance, "but the strongest, most central way is to found all such or other methods on a self-offering and surrender of ourselves and of our parts of nature to the Divine Being, the Ishwara. A strict obedience to the wise and intuitive leading of a Guide is also normal and necessary for all but a few specially gifted seekers."[5]

In practical terms this central requirement was an affirmation of the traditional *guruvada*, surrender to a guru, which for the movement meant application of the insights of Aurobindo and, later, the counsel and control of the Mother.[6] Though Aurobindo was the rallying point for the disciples, he proclaimed the Mother a greater guru: "Her embodiment is a chance for the earth-consciousness to receive the Supramental into it and to undergo first the transformation necessary for that to be possible."[7] At times *sādhaks* who held allegiance to Aurobindo questioned the Mother's authority and the nature of the Mother's consciousness, but Aurobindo always answered that their consciousnesses were harmonious. For example, in a 1934 letter he responded:

> The opposition between the Mother's consciousness and my consciousness was an invention of the old days . . . and emerged in a time when the Mother was not fully recognised or accepted by some of those who were here at the beginning. Even after they had recognised her they persisted in this meaningless opposition and did great harm to them and others. The Mother's consciousness is two, because that is necessary for the play. Nothing can be done without her knowledge and force, without her consciousness—if anybody really feels her consciousness, he should know that I am there behind it and if he feels me it is the same with hers. If a separation is made like that (I leave aside the turns which their minds so strongly put upon these things), how can the Truth establish itself from the Truth there is no such separation.[8]

So strong was the *guruvada* encompassing them both that Aurobindo recommended either a combination of their names or her name alone as the *mantra* to be used by his disciples. Usually it was "Sri Aurobindo Mira".[9]

Thus, the Aurobindo movement's response to religious pluralism must be seen in the light of the authority of Aurobindo and the Mother. It is not surprising that official spokespersons for the Ashram since the Mother's death have not been concerned to elaborate upon attitudes toward religious pluralism. The fragmentation and infighting which have taken place since her death and which have resulted in the intervention of the Indian government evidence the current vacumn due to the absence of its guru.

The Authoritative Ontology of Aurobindo's Experiences

From his experiences Aurobindo believed he had discovered a key to the universe and a system of thought and practice which he called Integral Yoga. He wrote as a yogi who was in a process of realization, not having finality but having discovered levels of consciousness which transcended those open to the methods of the ordinary mind. For the Ashram his authority as guru was based on the acceptance of the truth of his experiences.

The knowledge he believed he had realized in these experiences was "integral". Though it came from higher, more intuitive levels which were beyond reason, it was capable of integration with lower levels of consciousness such as that of Mind. "These truths present themselves to our conceptual cognition as the fundamental aspects in which we see and experience the omnipresent Reality."[10] Thus, the Ashram considers his conceptual system, though incomplete, as authoritative.

Central to his realizations and its system is the integral nature of his view of the Absolute. Using traditional Upanishadic terms, it is *saccidānanda*, (*sat*, "being, existence"; *cit*, "consciousness-force"; *ānanda*, "bliss, freedom"). Yet this Absolute transcends the limitations of the distinctions of the intellect, the level of consciousness he calls Mind. As such it is both eternal static Being and eternal dynamic Becoming. As this latter, it is the universe of phenomena in involution to lower levels of consciousness and evolution from lower levels of consciousness to higher levels. The evolution proceeds from the level of the least conscious, the physical, matter, to the greatest consciousness, the Supreme Saccidananda Unmanifest. It takes place through the activity of the level of consciousness known as Supermind, an eternal reality of the Divine which is a consciousness that sees both the Unity and the multiplicity.[11]

The world of phenomena is, therefore, real. It is not an illusion, but the Absolute in Becoming, and this level of Becoming is as real, as ultimate, as the Absolute as Being. Though these two may be logical opposites, based upon his experiences Aurobindo believes that the Absolute transcends such distinctions of that lower level of consciousness known as Mind.

> But the Absolute, obviously, finds no difficulty in world-manifestation and no difficulty either in a simultaneous transcendence of world-manifestation; the difficulty exists only for our mental limitations which prevent us from grasping the supramental rationality of the co-existence of infinite and the finite or seizing the nodus of the unconditioned with the conditioned. For our intellectual rationality these are opposites; for the absolute reason they are interrelated and not essentially conflicting expressions of one and the same reality.[12]

It was the reconciliation of the affirmation of the One and the Many as equally real which occupied "decades of spiritual effort" for Aurobindo. And his yogic experiences only became fully authoritative when they had affirmed both the One and the many as ultimate realities.[13] The world must be real and significant.

Though the inner human being is identical with Supermind, outwardly it is on the level of consciousness known as Mind. This level is "Nature become partially conscious of her own laws", and able to participate consciously in the process itself, beginning with the individual whose achievements both directly and indirectly effect the earth consciousness.

> The aim of the yoga is to open the consciousness to the Divine and to live in the inner consciousness more and more while acting from it on the external life, to bring the inmost psychic into the front and by the power of the psychic to purify and change the being so that it may become ready for transformation and be in union with the Divine Knowledge, Will and Love.[14]

Those who had attained this consciousness, the gnostic beings, would join with others to provide an atmosphere to further their evolution and prepare the environment to rise to higher consciousness. The collective spiritual influence of these communities would affect the world, much as traditionally it was believed that the *tejas* or splendor of a realized yogi would exude out to the world about him and bring observable change.

Aurobindo's Experiences and Other Religions

Aurobindo's response to other religions centered around the authority he gave to his own experiences. Applied to his evaluation of religion generally and to the religions, he asserted that the essence of religion was experience, not doctrines, creeds, or practices.

> The deepest heart, the inmost essence of religion, apart from its outward machinery of creed, cult, ceremony and symbol, is the search for God and finding of God. Its aspiration is to discover the Infinite, the Absolute, the One, the Divine, who is all these things and yet no abstraction but a Being . . . All this has nothing to do with the realm of reason or its normal activities; its aim, its sphere, its process is suprarational.[15]

The knowledge one gains in religious experience is intuitive rather than intellectual. On the basis of what he believed were his intuitive experiences of higher levels of consciousness, he criticized unenlightened reason as "out of its province and condemned to tread either diffidently or else with a stumbling presumptuousness in the realm of a power and a light higher than its own".[16]

He began by treating the variety of religious positions as reified entities, as "isms" (e.g., Christianity, Buddhism, Islam, Judaism). Unfamiliar with the variety included under each category, he treated each as a doctrinal monolith. Since doctrine was on the level of Mind, he criticized each for emphasizing that lower level of consciousness. The exception to this criticism was the traditions with which he had come most familiar, and which he treated under the category "Hinduism". Under this category he recognized the existence of a variety of doctrinal stands, he believed that its essential unity was not doctrinal stands, he believed that its essential unity was not doctrinal but experiential. As such, "Hinduism," unlike the other religions, placed the proper emphasis upon the essence of religion, religious experience.

> To the Indian mind the least important part of religion is its dogma; the religious spirit matters, not the theological credo. On the

> contrary, to the western mind a fixed intellectual belief is the most important part of a cult; it is its core of meaning, it is the thing that distinguishes it from others. For it is formulated beliefs that make it either a true or false religion, according as it agrees or does not agree with the credo of its critic. This notion, however foolish and shallow, is a necessary consequence of the western idea which falsely supposes that intellectual truth is the highest verity and, even, that there is no other. The Indian religious thinker knows that all the highest eternal verities are truths of the spirit. The supreme truths are neither the rigid conclusions of logical reasoning nor the affirmations of credal statement, but fruits of the soul's inner experience.[17]

Like other modern Indian religious figures such as Swami Vivekananda and Sarvepalli Radhakrishnan, the reified "Hinduism" was defined with its unity based upon religious experience. And also like these others, this was defined as the essence of all religions, though many who profess these religions foolishly do not recognize this fact.

When speaking of this experiential essence, Aurobindo identified it with his own understanding of his yogic experiences. Since they convinced him that the higher levels could integrate with the level of Mind, there were definite propositional, and some might say doctrinal, assertions about these experiences which were true. He applied these propositions in this evaluation of the religions as well as of other religious positions within the variety of understandings he recognized under the category "Hinduism", a variety non-essential to "Hinduism", whose essence is experience.

The essential religious experience which the religions and other Hindus should recognize as the essence of religion is an experience of Brahman as both Being and Becoming. As Being he believed that religions must affirm that the Highest Reality is the true Self, or, in traditional terms, that *ātman* is *brahman*. Thus the religions should emphasize "religion as it should be and is in its inner nature, its fundamental law of being, a seeking after God, the cult of spirituality, the opening of the deepest life of the soul to the indwelling Godhead, the eternal Omnipresence".[18] It is ignorance that hs caused religions to "suppose an extracosmic Deity who has created a world outside and apart from its own existence".[19] Thereby Aurobindo criticizes the western religions in particular. From his earliest writings as a student in England, in which he sought to develop an ethical system without reference to a God who is a lawgiver, he rejected the concept of the extracosmic Deity and, thereby, the religion of India's colonial rulers.[20] In contrast, he believed, Indian religions recognize the One Absolute which is the true Self as fundamental to religion.

> The fundamental idea of all Indian religion is one common to the highest human thinking everywhere. The supreme truth of all that it is a Being or an existence beyond the mental and physical appearances we contact here. Beyond mind, life and body there is a Spirit and Self containing all that is finite and infinite, surpassing all that is relative, a supreme Absolute, originating and supporting all that is transient, a one Eternal.[21]

The experience at the heart of all of the religions is not any experience about which one cannot speak, then, but one which is articulated first by the fact that the Highest Reality is not a separate Being, but identified with one's true Self. And religions which do not affirm this are in relative ignorance.

The experience of Saccidananda as Becoming, however, adds another dimension to Aurobindo's religious asertions about the Reality he experienced. As Becoming, the Absolute also eternally encompasses the concept of an ever-changing involution and evolution. It is not merely the One immutable state of consciousness of traditional Advaita Vedanta thought with the phenomena ultimately insignificant. Experienced and affirmed as Becoming, the phenomena have ultimate significance; the temporary is not merely temporary but an eternal movement of Saccidananda. Thus, religion must give a positive, Divine evaluation of this life.

On this basis Aurobindo criticized the religions in traditional, what he calls "orthodox", form because they treat the present life as merely a means of another life beyond the grave: "the orthodox religions looked with eyes of pious sorrow and gloom on the earthly life of man and were very ready to bid him bear peacefully and contentedly, even to welcome its crudities, cruelties, oppressions, tribulations as a means for learning to appreciate and for earning the better life which will be given us hereafter".[22] The evolution of the Supermind instead is the basis of the significance and ultimacy of this world.

Turning to his own tradition, Aurobindo believed that its negative valuation of the world is the responsibility of "Buddhism", and is therefore not essential to "Hinduism". Vedanta, which refers to Aurobindo's understanding of the teachings of the *Upanisads*, affirmed both the One and the Many as facts in the manner Aurobindo's vision does. But "Buddhism" entered to negate this teaching and to bring with it an interpretation of this world which saw karma and rebirth as a bondage from which to flee instead of a movement of the Divine to be affirmed and furthered.

> It is this revolt of Spirit against Matter that for two thousand years, since Buddhism disturbed the balance of the old Aryan world, has dominated increasingly the Indian mind . . . all [Indian philosophies] have lived in the shadow of the great Refusal and the final end of life for all is the garb of the ascetic. The general conception of existence has been permeated with the Buddhistic theory of the chain of Karma and with the consequent antinomy of bondage and liberation, bondage by birth, liberation by cessation from birth.[23]

Shankara in the eighth century took up and completed this negation which has weighted the tradition down with its "three great formulas, the chain of Karma, escape from the wheel of rebirth, Maya:.[24] Yet, these formulations, to the extent that they make the world anything less than Divine, are mistaken.

Within the Indian religious traditions Aurobindo is particularly critical of what he calls "Mayavada" or "Illusionism". In *The Life Divine* he took two lengthy chapters to critique their positions and further chapters to set forth his alternative vision and its understanding of the reality of the world. The Mayavadins begin, he said, in a sense of disappointment and frustration, but he argues that their "philosophy of world-negation" is still faulty.[25] He critiqued the analogies used by the position—dream, hallucination, mother of pearl, the optical illusion of two moons—and concluded that these are not helpful. "There is nothing in the operations of Mind-illusion that throws light upon this mystery; it is, as a stupendous cosmic Illusion of this kind must be, *sui generis*, without parallel.[26] The concept of cosmic illusion is, thus, a product of level of Mind. But Mind is of the nature of ignorance. So the very concept of Maya is a product of this ignorant Mind in conflict with the higher knowledge of religious vision. Shankara's version illustrates this.

> In the philosophy of Shankara one feels the presence of a conflict, an opposition which this powerful intellect has stated

> with full force and masterfully arranged rather than solved with any finality,—the conflict of an intuition intensely aware of an absolute transcendent and inmost Reality and a strong intellectual reason regarding the world with a keen and vigorous rational intelligence.[27]

Shankara solved this contradiction by recognizing the limits of reason "by dissolving the whole cosmic phenomenal and rational-practical edifice of things". Yet, this creates more difficulties than it solves. It ultimately fails to recognize both the nature of Mind ignorance and the fact that higher religious experience transcends the limits of Mind to affirm both the One and the Many as Real. "A diversity in oneness is the law of the manifestation; the supramental unification and integration must harmonize these diversities, but to abolish them is not the intention of the Spirit in Nature."[28] Ultimately falling back upon the authority of his own religious experiences, Aurobindo concluded that the experience of the Illustionists was on a lower level, for it affirmed only the One, leaving reason in its ignorance to determine the relationship of the One to the Many.

Just as Aurobindo's view of the Absolute as Becoming affirms the world, it provides for him the basis for its transforation: activity in that ultimately significant world which promotes its perfection. The *sādhak* is to raise the world-consciousness by bringing down the higher levels of consciousness the *sādhak* has experienced to transform lower levels. Aurobindo's writings are one example of the transformation, for he believed they integrated his intuitive insights into Mind and, thus, transformed that level of consciousness. In contrast to his confidence that his position can perfect the world, he criticized the religions for their failure to transform it. The religions have failed to attain the goals they themselves have set, much less those goals Aurobindo felt religion ought to accomplish. His criticism is universal and absolute, asserting not only that all religions have failed but that all non-religious attempts are failures as well.

> Altruism, philanthropy and service, Christian love or Buddhist compassion have not made the world a whit happier, they only give infinitesimal bits of momentary relief here and there, throw drops on the fire of the world's suffering. All aims are in the end transitory and futile, all achievements unsatisfying or evanescent; all works are so much labour of effort and success and failure which consummate nothing definitive: whatever changes are made

> in human life are of the form only and these forms pursue each other in a futile circle; for the essence of life, its general character remains the same for ever.[29]

Only this Integral Yoga can solve the world's problems.

In fact, rather than improving the world the religions have more often worked against the natural improvement inherent in the world's progress through the evolutionary movement of the Spirit: "Historically and as a matter of fact the accredited religions and their hierarchs and exponents have too often been a force for retardation, have too often thrown their weight on the side of darkness, oppression and ignorance . . ."[30] They have more often sown the seeds of discord than nurtured the ideal of human unity.[31] Though this is not true of the essential facts of religion which constitute Aurobindo's position these failures are inevitable in the religions in their "organized" form. They can provide a means for the inner growth of the individual, but they cannot change society, for they must compromise with the lower parts of societal life. "Religions so conceived can give a religio-ethical colour or surface tinge,—sometimes, if it maintains a strong kernel of inner experience, it can generalize to some extent an incomplete spiritual tendency; but it does not transform the race, it cannot create a new principle of the human existence."[32] Unlike Integral Yoga, which Aurobindo believed accomplished the preliminary step necessary for societal change, i.e., it changes the inner being, the religions "at best modify only the surface of the nature. Moreover, they degenerate very soon into a routine of ceremonial habitual worship and fixed dogmas.[33] They are, therefore, incapable of success unless they return to their essence, which is expressed in Aurobindo's position.

Since the Becoming is essential to Aurobindo's critique and since this Becoming is understood in terms of the evolutionary schema Aurobindo believed his experiences of higher levels of consciousness to have been authoritative, Aurobindo interpreted the cause of the inadequacies of the other religious positions in terms of his evolutionary scheme.[34] Higher and truer knowledge is that of higher levels of evolution, those above the level in which humanity currently finds itself, Mind. True religion, therefore, sees that reason is incapable of knowing Reality. Though reason is useful on the level of Mind to sharpen and order one's expression of Truth, it must find Truth in higher levels. Reason is not in error but in ignorance. It is a limited knowing. To truly understand, religions must recognize the limited nature of reason and its products: creeds, dogmas, forms.

Aurobindo credited the problems he saw with other Indian religious positions to their lack of intuitive vision of the levels of supramental consciousness he affirmed as authoritative. They emphasize Mind, giving it an exclusive status instead of recognizing, as he did, that the rational limits are not ultimate when speaking of the Being and Becoming which is Saccidananda. For example, Ganghi's commitment of *satyāgraha*, Aurobindo taught, was a commitment to limited mental theories. So inferior are viewpoints such as Gandhi's which are limited to the level of Mind that they are hardly worth attention.

> Gandhi's theories are like other mental theories built on a basis of one-sided reasoning and claiming for a limited truth (that of non-violence and passive resistance) a universality which it cannot have. Such theories will always exist so long as the mind is the main instrument of human truth-seeking. To spend energy trying to detroy such theories is of little use; if destroyed they are replaced by others equally limited and partial.[35]

Likewise, Aurobindo rejected Theosophical teachings as arising out of Mind or "raw imagination" rather than the higher supramental consciousness. "She [Madame Blavatsky] was an occultist, not a spiritual personality. What spiritual teaching she gave, seemed to be based on intellectual knowledge, not on realization.[36]

His approach to other Indian thinkers questioned even their commitment to true intuition. Instead of giving priority to intuition, Radhakrishnan and Joad took refuge in it only where their reasoning failed. "Can the issue be settled in so easy and trenchant a way? The fact is that the mystic depends on an inner knowledge, an inner experience, but if he philosophises, he must try to explain to the reason, though not necessary [*sic*] always by the reason alone, what he has seen to be the Truth."[37] What Ramatirtha thought were realizations "were more mental than anything else".[38] Though Aurobindo believed Ramathirta had intuitive experiences, they did not transform the lower levels of Mind and Vital and, thus, were not the result of higher knowledge. When Chaitanya believed he experienced the love and bliss of Krishna's consort Radha, this was also not of Supermind but "a logical conclusion which cannot be accepted wholly". The Mother also spoke of the inadequacy of the Buddha's experience in comparison with Aurobindo's. Though the Buddha experienced a partial spiritual experience, "his own theory of fleeing from *saṁsāra* kept him from a complete realization". Hence his experience was merely "an inner contact with something which, in comparison with the external life, was a non-existence . . ."[40] The authority of Aurobindo's experiences, therefore, resulted in a judgment by himself and the Mother of those whose experiences were not like Aurobindo's. They had not experienced the highest levels of truth but were most often working out of the level of Mind.

On the basis of the belief that his system is integral, other religions are understood to have partial understanding. It is not that they affirm what is completely unworthy of belief and practice in a particular space and time, but that they do not recognize that those beliefs and practices are only relative, partial. As a consequence they take these partial truths and non-essential elements as universal. The confrontations between religion and science, religion and philosophy, religion and ethics, or religion and aesthetics, and the disagreements between one religion and another, have been caused by this universalization of partial truths. In *The Human Cycle* he calls the emphasis upon these partial truths "religionism," and not the "true religion" which is that essence identical with his own affirmation.

> There are two aspects of religion, true religion and religionism. True religion is spiritual religion, that which seeks to live in the spirit, in what is beyond the intellect, beyond the aesthetic and ethical and practical being of man, and to inform and govern these members of our being by the higher light and law of the spirit. Religionism, on the contrary, entrenches itself in some narrow pietistic exaltation of the lower members or lays exclusive stress on intellectual dogmas, forms and ceremonies, on some fixed and rigid moral code, on some religio-political or religio-social system.[41]

Within "Hinduism" there are examples of this error. In *The Synthesis of Yoga*, Aurobindo presents Swami Vivekananda as an example of one who counterbalances the incorrect universalization of the desire for personal salvation by an emphasis upon the importance of service to others.[42] Yet, in his letters he criticizes Vivekananda too for making *sevā*, or service itself, into a universal requirement. No matter how essential it was to Vivekananda, Aurobindo saw this as making one relative side of truth absolute. "His ideal of *sevā* was a need of his nature and must have helped him—it does not follow that it must be accepted as a universal spiritual necessity or ideal".[43]

The other religions, however, go further by imposing these non-essential and partial elements upon others. They fail to recognize the variety of movements within the evolution of Supermind. "The ambition of a particular religious belief and form to universalize and impose itself is contrary to the variety of human nature and to at lest one essential character of the Spirit".[44] That essential character is the Spirit's principle of unity in diversity by which it allows the freedom for each individual being to grow according to its own nature.

In this universalization of relative and partial truths, the religions are opposed to the nature of Reality and the evolution of the Universe as Aurobindo envisioned them. Aurobindo's evaluation of the religions as guilty of egoistic universalizing and promoting these partial views is more than a declaration of their relative place in the evolutionary scheme. It is, as argued elsewhere, "an application of Aurobindo's belief that evil is the result of the egoistic tendency of principles that arise in the evolutionary process to extend themselves beyond their partial and temporary place in the Supermind's scheme".[45] Evil, for Aurobindo, is anything which retards the evolutionary process. "To the extent, then, that religions hinder or retard the evolutionary process, to that extent they are evil; as evil as anything can be in Aurobindo's view of reality".[46] Though they are built upon a good foundation, the experience which is essentially integral, they are egoistic hinderances to the Divine plan.

The Mother, however, often spoke of the religions more negatively. They are invariably distinguished by exclusivism, an attitude "natural to the religious mind," and fundamental to their very existence.

> The first and principal article of these established and formal religions runs always, "Mind is the supreme, the only truth, all others are in falsehood or inferior." For without this fundamental dogma, established credal religions could not have existed. If you do not believe and proclaim that you alone possess the one or the highest truth, you will not be able to impress people and make them flock to you.[47]

As such they are hindrances to the spiritual life from which a *sādhak* must be freed. Though she might encourage those outside the Ashram who hold a religion to continue in it, since they don't understand, to those in the Ashram she spoke more clearly: religions are based on ignorance and imposed on people through fear.[48] In fact they hinder spiritual progress.

> Note that I am telling you this because I know that here you are all liberated from religions. If I had before me someone having a religion he believed in, I would tell him: "It is very good, keep your religion, continue". Happily for all of you, you don't have one. And I hope you will never have one, for it means a door shut upon all progress.[49]

For the Mother, this is the very nature of the religions.

Evolution and Religious Pluralism

Aurobindo spoke of two responses to the variety of religions. In *The Ideal of Human Unity*, from September 1915 through July 1918 and which he revised slightly before World War II, Aurobindo wrote a chapter concerned with what he called a "religion of humanity:. This "spiritual religion" alone is the hope of future, not "what is ordinarily called a universal religion".[50] Though he spoke of it as based upon a realization and not a "universal religious system, one in mental creed and vital form," he defined it in terms which are propositional and, one might say, creedal, affirming his own ontological stance with its emphasis upon evolution and the oneness of the Divine and the universe.

> A religion of humanity means the growing realization that there is a secret Spirit, a divine Reality, in which we are all one, that humanity is its highest present vehicle on earth, that the human race and the human being are the means by which it will progressively reveal itself here. It implies a growing attempt to live out this knowledge and bring about a kingdom of this divine Spirit upon earth. By its growth within us oneness with out fellow-men will become the leading principle of all our life, not merely a principle of co-operation but a deeper brotherhood, a real and an inner sense of unity and equality and a common life. There must be a realization by the individual that only in the life of his fellow-men in his own life complete. There must be the realization by the race that only on the free and full life of the individual can its own perfection and permanent happiness be founded. There must be too a discipline and a way of salvation in accordance

> with this religion, that is to say, a means by which it can be developed by each man within himself, so that it may be developed in the life of the race.[51]

As true, he believed, and as based upon true realization, there would be no need for forceful promotion. Yet, its "creed and ideal" would be upheld "as a light and inspiration" to all.[52]

He spoke of "mechanical means" of doing this.[53] Hence, the various agencies of the Aurobindo movement have published his writings and those of the Mother and their disciples, in a variety of popular and library editions. They have established ashrams throughout India and around the world, attempting to bring realization to the elite and the masses. As a further means the Mother founded Auroville as "a center of accelerated evolution" which would raise the consciousness of all the earth to that envisioned by Aurobindo. As one goal of its Charter puts it: "Auroville will be a site of material and spiritual researches for a living embodiment of an actual human unity".[54] It would promote Aurobindo's understanding both directly as a model of environmental progress and through the power it collectively exudes. If a realized yogi is capable of exuding a force to change reality about him, much more would an entire community of integral yogins transform the world. Yet, since religions are a hindrance to spiritual progress, citizenship in Auroville assumes that one has given up the religions: "Auroville is for those who want to live a life essentially divine but who renounce all religions whether they be ancient, modern, new or future."[55]

Aurobindo's and the Mother's vision of the evolution of the Spirit provides the basis for the Ashram's attitude toward other religious positions. While the "religion of humanity" that is Integral Yoga makes itself "more explicit, insistent and categorically imperative,"[56] other religions should outwardly be treated as stages in the evolution which have become problematic by egoistically over-emphasizing the non-essential elements beyond their limited place in the evolutionary scheme. One must allow the existence of a variety of paths to the goal, as India has done.[57] Yet the process of upholding integral truth is understood as the integration of the essentials of these other positions which are Integral Yoga into Integral Yoga, affirming thereby their true insights. Beyond this, one need not worry about the ultimate fate of these views as separate positions. With confidence in the evolutionary process as set forth in Aurobindo's position comes confidence that this process in itself will result in the eventual elimination of the other positions as absolutes and the integration of spiritual seekers into that highest truth seen in Integral Yoga. Religion has evolved through stages in the past and will continue to evolve in the future. The Mother described this indifference toward other religions as: "A benevolent goodwill towards all worshippers. An enlightened indifference towards all religions. All religions are partial approximations of the one sole Truth that is far above them".[58] Someday humanity will without a doubt recognize this Higher Vision.[59] Science and philosophy will also come to affirm this stance.[60]

Ideally, then, for the Sri Aurobindo Ashram, pluralism is a recognition of the partial truths in all religions from the vantage point of Aurobindo's experiences and the resulting system in which these are integrated. In this Integral Yoga is found the true position which sees the relativity and error of others but does not consider itself a religion. The task of the Ashram is twofold: to make this position more explicit by direct promotion and yogic influence, and to recognize the relativity and temporary nature of other religious positions. The others are available as temporary paths for the less knowing, but the failures and temporary existence of religion itself, it is believed, point toward the Consciousness which Aurobindo envisions. "Whatever errors Religion has committed, this is her function and her great and indispensible utility and service—the holding up of this growing light of guidance on our way through the mind's ignorance towards the Spirit's complete consciousness and self-knowledge".[61] The Integral Yogi has work to do to promote the progress of the Divine evolution which the Ashram's gurus, Aurobindo and the Mother, believed only they alone, since the writers of the *Upanisads*, have seen clearly. Other religious positions, as temporary stages in the evolution of Becoming are unconsciously, even ignorantly, contributing to that work. Pluralism, then, for the Ashram, is rooted in the belief that given its view of the telos of Reality which transcends the religions one need not fear, for someday these others too will understand.

Notes

1. For a discussion of the development of Aurobindo's ontological theories, see Robert N. Minor, *Sri Aurobindo: The Perfect and the Good*

(Columbia, MO: South Asia Books, 1978). For discussions of his fully developed position also see Beatrice Bruteau, *Worthy is the World: The Hindu Philosophy of Sri Aurobindo* (Rutherford, NJ: Farleigh Dickinson University Press, 1971); Haridas Chaudhuri, *Sri Aurobindo: Prophet of the Life Divine* (San Francisco: Cultural Integration Fellowship, 1973) and L. Thomas O'Neil, *Towards the Life Divine: Sri Aurobindo's Vision* (Delhi; Manohar, 1979) among others. On his major works see Robert A. McDermott, ed. *Six Pillars: Introductions to the Major Works of Sri Aurobindo* (Chambersburg, PA: Wilson Books, 1974).

2. *Sri Aurobindo and His Ashram* (Pondicherry: Sri Aurobindo Ashram, 1981), 52.

3. See Minor, *Sri Aurobindo*, 113–115.

4. Sri Aurobindo, *Birth Centenary Library* (Pondicherry: Sri Aurobindo Ashram Trust, 1972) XIX, 971. Hereafter this set of his complete works is abbreviated *BCL*.

5. *Ibid.*, 907.

6. *BCL*, XXIII, 614–22.

7. *BCL*, XXV, 49.

8. *BCL*, XXVI, 455ff.

9. *Ibid.*, 511–2.

10. *BCL*, XVIII, 323.

11. *Ibid.*, 312.

12. *Ibid.*, 377. Cf. 78.

13. Robert N. Minor, "Sri Aurobindo and Experience: Yogic and Otherwise," in *Religion in Modern India*, ed. by Robert D. Baird (Delhi: Manohar, 1981), 277–304.

14. *BCL*, XXIII, 509.

15. *BCL*, XV, 122.

16. *Ibid.*, 127.

17. *BCL*, XIV, 123–4.

18. *BCL*, XV, 166.

19. *BCL*, XVIII, 397.

20. See his writing as a student in England in *BCL*, III, 7.

21. *BCL*, SIV, 125.

22. *BCL*, XV, 543.

23. *BCL*, XVIII, 23. Note the Mother's statement of this position in the Mother, *Collected Works* (Pondicherry: Sri Aurobindo Ashram Trust, 1978ff.), VII, 292–3. In XII, 212 she further says: "Sri Aurobindo has told us that this was a fundamental degradation of India. Buddhism, Jainism, Illusionism were sufficient to sap all energy out of the country."

24. *Ibid.*, 415–6.

25. *Ibid.*, 417.

26. *Ibid.*, 432.

27. *Ibid.*, 461.

28. *BCL*, XIX, 888.

29. *BCL*, XVIII, 416-17.

30. *BCL*, XV, 16.

31. *Ibid.*, 528.

32. *BCL*, XIX, 1058–9.

33. *BCL*, XXII, 139. Cf. XIX, 1022, 1023; XV, 339.

34. For an analysis see Robert N. Minor, "Sri Aurobino's Integral View of Other Religions," *Religious Studies* XV, 365–77.

35. *BCL*, XXII, 490-1.

36. *Ibid.*, 483, 447.

37. *Ibid.*, 187.

38. *Ibid.*, 117.

39. *Ibid.*, 92.

40. The Mother, *Collected Works*, VII, 292-3.

41. *BCL*, XV, 166–7.

42. *BCL*, XX, 257–8.

43. *BCL*, XXII, 150.

44. *BCL*, XV, 249. Cf. XIX, 863–4.

45. Minor, "Sri Aurobindo's Integral View," 373.

46. *Ibid.*, 377.

47. The Mother, *Collected Works*, III, 77. Cf. IX, 407–8; XV, 30.

48. *Ibid.*, III, 82.

49. *Ibid.*, V, 32. Cf. VIII, 148; IX, 198.

50. *BCL*, XV, 554. Chapter thirty-four of *The Ideal of Human Unity* is entitled "The Religion of Humanity".

51. *Ibid.*

52. *Ibid.*, 214.

53. *Ibid.*, 555.

54. The Mother, *Collected Works*, XIII, 200.

55. *Ibid.*, 212. Yet the Mother does answer a disciple's questions concerning whether one can retain either one's religion or one's atheism in Auroville with, "If one has not gone beyond that". (*Ibid.*, 195).

56. *BCL*, XV, 544.

57. *Ibid.*, XIX, 872–3.

58. The Mother, *Collected Works*, XV, 31–2.

59. *BCL*, XIX, 865–872.

60. *Ibid.*, XV, 215.

61. *Ibid.*, XIX, 874.

Chapter Six

THE RESPONSE OF SWAMI BHAKTIVEDANTA

R.D. Baird

By the time Swami Bhaktivedanta arrived in New York to engage in what would lead to the founding of the International Society for Krishna Consciousness, he was sixty-nine years of age.[1] Although he would encounter new ideas and practices in his remaining years, his Vaiṣṇava theology and the attitudes which provided the setting for his response to other religions had long since been fixed on Indian soil. He is particularly interesting since the general perception of his movement is that it engages in vigorous conversionism in a manner that contradicts the usual generalities about Hindu tolerance. Some of Bhaktivedanta's statements about adherents of other religions are indeed harsh, but his strongest condemnations are reserved for Advaita Vedānta, the system of thought that is commonly used to provide the structure for Western understandings of "Hinduism".

Ultimate Concern and Ultimate Reality

Swami Bhaktivedanta does not leave the content of his ultimate concern to chance. The "real purpose of life is to revive our dormant love for God."[2] This is not the only way it can be stated. "One's real desire should only be to achieve the state of living transcendental service to the Lord."[3]

What is the system and the analysis of the human condition that provides the basis for this statement of ultimacy? Vaiṣṇavism, *sanātana dharma*, *varnāśrama dharma* are ways that his system is designated. It is presented as a system that is as old as Kṛṣṇa himself, but has been passed on in disciplic succession (*paramparā*) down to and including Swami Bhaktivedanta. This system describes the highest principle as the Supreme Personality of Godhead. Unlike Advaita, which sees the personal god on the level of *vivarta* and only *nirguṇa brahman* as ultimate *sat*, Bhaktivedanta sees the truth in reverse order. There are three phrases to the realization of Absolute Truth: the impersonal Brahman, Paramatman, and Bhagavan.[4] Bhaktivedanta's view is a form of panentheism. Everything is contained in the Supreme Lord, but the Supreme Lord is not exhausted by everything that is in the world. All of these phases are really one and the same truth, but they constitute different features of it.[5]

> Brahman is the beginning of transcendental realization. Paramatma, the Supersoul, is the middle, the second stage in transcendental realization, and the Supreme Personality of Godhead is the ultimate realization of the Absolute Truth. Therefore, both Paramatman and the impersonal Brahman are within the Supreme Person.[6]

The Advaitin realization of the impersonal, therefore, is only a partial realization of the ultimate. It is the realization of the *sat* feature of the Supreme Personality of Godhead. The complete whole, however, is not formless. So Advaitin experience is true but incomplete.[7]

The human condition is that people are unaware of their position as part and parcel of God. This ignorance of one's position in Bhagavan is the cause not only of personal, but also of societal suffering and discontent. "Because of this lack of Kṛṣṇa consciousness in human society, people are suffering terribly, being merged in an ocean of nescience and sense gratification".[8]

The world is ultimately real. To designate it as *māyā* means that it is not the complete reality. *Māyā* points to "forgetfulness of one's relationship with Kṛṣṇa".[9] It is failure to realize that one is part and parcel of the Supreme Lord.

> Thus it is false to think that the living entity has no connection with the Supreme Lord. He may not believe in the existence of God, or he may think that he has no relationship with God, but these are all "illusions," or *māyā*. Due to absorption in this false conception of life, man is always fearful and full of anxieties. In other words, a godless concept of life is *māyā*.[10]

One's goal, then, is to return to Godhead, or as the ISKCON magazine is titled, come *Back to Godhead.*

True religion can only be given by the Supreme Personality of Godhead.[11] People have sought to produce imitation incarnations and have sought numerous human methods to search God. Such methods will not work and will ultimately side-track the individual so that the route to Kṛṣṇa consciousness is longer and more arduous than necessary. "If one actually wants to become religious, he must take up the chanting of the Hare Kṛṣṇa *mahāmantra*. . . .[13]

Historians and philosophers operate on the level on which no "truth" can be more than highly probable. But religious believers exude with a confidence and certainty that seems to leave no room for the possibility of error. This is true of Swami Bhaktivedanta. Anyone outside of the *paramparā* system is merely a "mental speculator," and it is that which leaves room for doubt. Bhaktivedanta never concedes, explicitly or implicitly, that there is any possibility that he might be wrong in his Vaiṣṇava theology, his assessment of the human condition, his proposed means to correct it and bring people "back to Godhead".

> Whatever one's position, *everyone* in this age of Kali needs to be enlightened in Kṛṣṇa consciousness. That is the greatest need of the day. *Everyone* is acutely feeling the pangs of material existence. Even in the ranks and files of the American Senate, the pinpricks of material existence are felt, so much so that April 30, 1974, was actually set aside as Prayer Day. Thus *everyone* is feeling the resultant pinpricks of Kali-yuga brought about by human society's indulging in illicit sex, meat-eating, gambling and intoxication . . . Kṛṣṇa consciousness should be distributed to *everyone* indiscriminately. In this way the *entire world* will be peaceful and happy, and *everyone* will glorify Śri Caitanya Mahāprabhu, as He desires.[14]

Pungent Judgment on Other Religions

In the light of the principles of *paramparā*, absolute certainty, and universal validity, it should not be a surprise to find that Bhaktivedanta has some harsh things to say about the numerous erroneous positions that stand outside his *paramparā* system. Some approaches to life are condemned outright. "The mammonist philosophy of work very hard and enjoy sense gratification is condemned by the Lord . . ."[15] Misguided descendents of Advaita and others who have no use for Kṛṣṇa worship are "like the dead branch of a tree".[16] Those who show Kṛṣṇa no respect and even despise him are asuras, demoniacs, and products of the Kali yuga.[17] According to Bhaktivedanta, Mayavadins hold that it is proper to worship any of the Indian deities, and that this is as good as worshipping Kṛṣṇa. Such "rascals" are actually leading people to atheism since they do not recognize the Supreme Personality of Godhead. "This philosophical hodge-podge exists under the name of the Hindu religion, but the Kṛṣṇa consciousness movement does not approve of it. Indeed, we strongly condemn it".[18] Advaitins who encourage this are "foolish".[19]

The Carvakas are, expectedly, atheists and ignorant.[20] But, the ". . . desire to merge in the impersonal Brahman is the subtlest type of atheissm. As soon as such atheism, disguised in the dress of liberation, is encouraged, one becomes completely unable to traverse the path of devotional service to the Supreme Personality of Godhead".[21] Even the young hippies in New York were not "offenders" as the Advaitins since they were attracted to Kṛṣṇa and joined the movement. Caitanya found that even "Mohammedans" were easier to convert than Advaitins. "We therefore conclude that the so-called *mlecchas* and *yavanas* of the Western countries are more purified than offensive Mayavadis or atheistic impersonalists".[22]

Since there is a gulf between approved practice within *paramparā* and human creativity, it is not surprising that the goal of Bhaktivedanta is most appropriately reached through conversion. Since there is only one approved system and it is for all human beings, Bhaktivedanta comfortably quotes from the *Bhagavadgītā* 18.66. "Abandon all varieties of religion and just surrender unto Me. I shall deliver you from all sinful reaction. Do not fear."[23]

The importance of Caitanya's example can hardly be overemphasized in this regard. "During his journey he had discussions with the Buddhists, the Jains and the Mayavadis in several places and converted his opponents to Vaiṣṇavism."[24] It is clear that Caitanya's preference was for conversion. Whether this is part of a hagiographical account is not important. For, as it stands it is a biographical model for Bhaktivedanta and those who would follow him.[25]

At certain points Bhaktivedanta appears to suggest a less vigorous opposition to other religions, but such statements are not permitted to stand without qualification. On the one hand, "In every system of religion, it is accepted that God is the supreme father of all living entities."[26] On the other hand, this statment is qualified by saying that "any religion that does not accept the Supreme Lord as the absolute father is called *kaitava-dharma*, or a cheating religion."[27] Again, "it does not matter whether one is a Christian, Mohammedan or whatever. He must simply accept the sublime position of the Supreme Personality of Godhead and render service to Him. It is not a question of being Christian, Mohammedan or Hindu. One should be purely religious and freed from all these material designations."[28] On the other hand it is because of this that "the Kṛṣṇa consciousness movement is gaining ground throughout the world."[29] To be part of the Bhagavatam movement is to be beyond the *guṇas* of *prakṛti*, while to be a member of another religion is to be bound by matter. In the end it is clear that there is no final acceptance of pluralism as a status quo.

> In this present day, man is very eager to have one scripture, one God, one religion, and one occupation. So let there by one common scripture for the whole world—*Bhagavad-gītā*. And let there be one God only for the whole world—Sri Kṛṣṇa Kṛṣṇa, Hare Hare/ Hare Rama, Hare Rama, Rama Rama, Hare Hare. And let there be one work only—the service of the Supreme Personality of Godhead.[30]

The Principle of Isolation

Another principle that helps to explain Bhaktivedanta's treatment of other religions is the principle of isolation. To begin with, a primary characteristic of a devotee's behavior is to avoid unholy association.

> Here the main point is that one should always stay aloof from unholy association. That is the sum and substance of a devotee's

> behaviour. And what is unholy association? It is association with one who is too much attached to women and with one who is not a devotee of Lord Kṛṣṇa. These are unholy persons. One is advised to associate with the holy devotees of the Lord and carefully avoid the association of unholy nondevotees.[31]

Moreover, the devotee is to be devoted totally in transcendental service to the Lord, thereby avoiding all speculative activities. One should listen to the recitation of the *Bhagavatam* and other Vaiṣṇava texts, but not from persons who are not in disciplic succession.[32] " 'No one should hear or take lessons from a person who is not a Vaiṣṇava. Even if he speaks about Kṛṣṇa, such a lesson should not be accepted, for it is like milk touched by the lips of a serpent.' "[33] If one is to read commentaries on accepted texts, they should be written by Vaiṣṇavas such as Ramanuja, Madhva, Visnusvami or Nimbarka.[34] Māyāvādī commentaries should be avoided. When one indulges in Māyāvādī philosophy one will gradually fall from devotional service. Since it is devotional service that is the means to the goal, such texts should be shunned.[35] Not only will unauthorized commentaries cause one to commit a great blunder, but as long as one persists, progress back to Godhead will be impossible.[36]

Moreover, Bhaktivedanta's translation of a verse in *Śrī Caitanya-caritāmṛta* has profound implications for his approach to other religions. "The devotee should not worship demigods nor should he disrespect them. Similarly, the devotee should not study or criticize other scriptures."[37] A careful reading of the many works and commentaries of Bhaktivedanta supports the view that he followed this advice himself. There is little to suggest that he read Māyāvādī commentaries (much less that he studied them), that he read the "Koran," the Christian scriptures or any philosophers or teologians in those traditions. While specific references are cited when he refers to the *Bhagavadgītā*, *Śrīad Bhagavatam*, or *Śrī Caitanya-caritāmṛta*, no such specificity is given in alien scriptures. What he knows about other religions comes largely from references to them in his own texts, from occasional personal contact and interviews with persons of other faiths, from information given by devotees converted from other faiths, and from hearsay. The point is that one cannot acquire real knowledge or make progress back to Godhead by reading the works of mental speculators. And, if one is not in disciplic succession, if one is not a devotee of the Lord, one is indeed a mental speculator. "One who disbelieves in this *śāstras* is an atheist, and we should not consult an atheist, however great he may be. A staunch believer in the *śāstras*, with all their diversities, is the right person from whom to gather real knowledge."[38] This principle will appear repeatedly in our discussion of specific religions.

Treatment of Other Religions

As we move to consider Bhaktivedanta's view of specific other religions, we will first pause to consider his assessment of religions in general and his view of how they arose.

Other Religions in General

One's original nature is to be transcendental to material nature. But when one forgets one's relationship to the Supreme Personality of Godhead, one comes into contact with material nature and generates faiths that are on the material platform. These faiths can be good, passionate or ignorant according to the *guṇa* that is dominant.[39] Bhaktivedanta believes that the entire world was originally under one culture that was Vedic.[40] Presently the earth is divided into many countries, religions and political parties. But these are all external divisions on the platform of matter. Some of them may have limited validity, but they can never provide the unity and Truth that is found on the transcendental level. Religions on the material level are able partially to satisfy the different bodies and minds that people have.[41] But the ultimate goal of human beings is reached only on the transcendental level.

We noted that one of the terms used to describe service to the Lord is *sanātana-dharma*. According to Bhaktivedanta, *sanātana-dharma* is, like the living entity itself, without beginning or end. In terms of reality, the rendering of service is the eternal religion of the living entity.[42] Hence, *sanātana-dharma* is, like the living entity itself, without beginning or end. In terms of reality, the rendering of service is the eternal religion of the living entity.[42] Hence, *sanātana-dharma* is not a sectarian religion on the platform of matter, and "when we mention the name Kṛṣṇa we do not refer to any sectarian name."[44] Ultimate unity is found only by transcending the plane on which religions exist. It is by becoming a vaiṣṇava, that is, engaging in devotional service to Kṛṣṇa and in effect by becoming part of the Kṛṣṇa consciousness movement that one reaches the transcendental level.[45] On the material level there are many religions, but they are *dharma kaitavah*, cheating religions. "None of these religions are actually genuine."[46]

Worship of Other Indian Deities

Swami Bhaktivedanta thinks that Christians and Muslims have a misconception about the "Hindu religion." They think that in Hinduism there are many gods. But there is only one god. There are many powerful entities called demigods who are delegated areas of responsibility and carry out the orders of the Supreme Lord.[47] But it is out of ignorance that people worship the demigods as though they are God. Bhaktivedanta does not deny that certain results come from such worship. Not only are there definite material benefits which accrue from worshipping the demigods, but such worship also determines the place of rebirth for the worshipper.[48] But while the worship of Kṛṣṇa is not sectarian, the worship of the demigods is. It is motivated by lust,[49] and is condemned by Kṛṣṇa and Caitanya.[50]

Demigods are merely "different energies of the Supreme Viṣṇu."[51] This means that ". . . directly or indirectly, all types of worship are more or less directed to the Supreme Personality of Godhead, Kṛṣṇa. In *Bhagavad-gītā* it is confirmed that one who worships the demigods is in fact only worshipping Kṛṣṇa because the demigods are but different parts of the body of Viṣṇu, or Kṛṣṇa."[52] The mistake made by such worshippers is that they mistakenly think they are worshipping God when they are merely worshipping one of his energies. Hence such worship is said to be *avidhi-purvakam*, improper. "One who worships demigods worships the Supreme Lord indirectly. One can worship Him directly."[53]

For this reason Bhaktivedanta makes even stronger statements about demigod worship. Since such worship is done in ignorance and improperly, it should not be done. Bhaktivedanta offers several texts to show that such worship should be avoided.[54] After all, all of the planets of the demigods such as Candraloka, Suryaloka, Indraloka, etc., are merely crations of Kṛṣṇa. As manifestations of Kṛṣṇa's energy they are on the level of matter, and can only be transcended through worship of Kṛṣṇa. "One should directly approach Kṛṣṇa, for that will save time and energy. For example, if there is a possibility of going to the top of a building by help of an elevator, why should one go by the staircase, step by step."[55]

Indian Philosophies

We have already noticed that Kṛṣṇa can be realized as Brahman, Paramatman, and as the Supreme Personality of Godhead. And these are realized through speculation *(jñāna)*, through the yoga system *(aāja)* and through devotional service *(bhakti)*.[56] This would suggest that the philosophies which emphasize one of the preliminary types of knowledge of Kṛṣṇa are correct and valid as far as they go. "But those who are attached to the impersonal Brahman or the localized Supersoul are also partially Kṛṣṇa conscious, because impersonal Brahman is the spiritual ray of Kṛṣṇa and Supersoul is the all-prevading partial expansion of K ṛṣṇa."[57] However, such systems are, like the worship of the demigods, only indirectly and hence imperfectly Kṛṣṇa conscious.[58] Since the so-called "orthodox" schools of Indian philosophy do not affirm the supremacy of the Supreme Personality of Godhead, they are all the result of mundane philosophy.[59] Hence they will never take one beyond the *guṇas* to the transcendental realm.

> Impersonal speculation, monism (merging into the existence of the Supreme), speculative knowledge, mystical yoga and meditation are all compared to grains of sand. They simply cause irritation to the heart. No one can satisfy the Supreme Personality of Godhead by such activities, nor do we give the Lord the chance to sit in our hearts peacefully. Rather, the Lord is disturbed by them.[60]

Bhaktivedanta seems to accept the Sāṇkhya philosophy's analysis of the twenty-four elements of the material universe.[61] But what the Sāṇkhya philosophers do not realize is that these elements are "originally offshoots from Kṛṣṇa's energies and are separated from Him."[62] The Sāṇkhya philosophers are atheistic since they "do not know Kṛṣṇa as the cause of all causes."[63] It is not possible to attain Absolute Truth by following Sāṇkhya or by practicing Patanjali's yoga. Since they do not follow Kṛṣṇa as the Supreme Personality of Godhead, their ambition will never be fulfilled. If this is true of philosophies that have a spiritual goal, how much more would it be true for the Lokayata's who are classed with modern "materialistic scientists and anthropologists."[64] Those who do not believe in the existence of the soul are even further from the truth than those who do without recognizing the Lord there.

While there may be some truth in other Indian philosophies and some of them at least may be an indirect worship of Kṛṣṇa, in the end all kinds of yogis (*karma, jñana, hatha,* etc.), have to move on to *bhakti* and Kṛṣṇa consciousness to reach devotional perfection. None of them are therefore approved means of reaching back to Godhead.

Advaita Vedānta

Advaita receives more attention from Bhaktivedanta than any other Indian philosophical system. It is also inescapable that the harshest statements made with incredible frequency are reserved for the "impersonalists," "Māyāvādīs," "followers of Śaṅkara's Advaita," and "monists." While it might seem strange that Advaitins would be more harshly censured than Muslims or Christians, several things must be kept in mind. The attitude of Swami Bhaktivedanta is molded by what he finds in his accepted scriptures, and it is clear that some of Caitanya's most serious disagreements came with Advaitins. He had more difficulty in converting them than in converting Muslims, and they sometimes vigorously attacked his position. It is a general principle that those who attack the Vaiṣṇava position are worse off than those who are merely ignorant of it. Furthermore, of primary importance to Bhaktivedanta is the Supreme Personality of Godhead, Kṛṣṇa. Hence those positions which deny the ultimate supremacy and reality of the personal God are more harshly condemned than those who affirm the ultimate reality of the personal deity as do Muslims and Christians.

Māyāvādīs consider themselves Vedantists. But according to Baktivedanta, the Vedānta philosophy is found in the *Bhagavadgītā* and its compiler is Kṛṣṇa, not Śaṅkara. There is also the tendency to be less harsh with the founder of a movement than with the tradition itself. In the present case, "Śaṅkarācārya preached Māyāvādī philosophy in order to bewilder a certain type of atheist. Actually he never considered the Supreme Lord, the Personality of Godhead, to be impersonal or to have no body or form."[65] But this concession to Śaṅkara is not consistently followed, and usually he is associated with the impersonalists who followed him.

Those who direct the masses of people to the impersonal rather than to the Personality of Godhead are "scholarly demons".[66] After a tirade against the *prakṛta-sahajiyās*, because they do not consult the Vedic scriptures and because they are "debauchees, woman hunters and smokers of Ganja,"[67] Bhaktivedanta goes on to say that they are, nevertheless, "more favorable than the impersonalists, who are hopelessly atheistic. The impersonalists have no idea of the Supreme Personality of Godhead."[68] To support their atheistic theory, "the Māyāvādīs cite false scriptures, which make people bereft of transcendental knowledge and addicted to fruitive activities and mental speculation."[69] Because they do not accept the Supreme Person they are "atheistic rascals."[70] Bhaktivedanta's quarrel with the impersonalists is particularly striking since he alludes to them even when the text on which he is commenting seems not to be addressing the issue. He deals with them whenever his flow of thought brings them to mind.[71]

Nevertheless, Advaitins are not without truth and what they experience is real. But they do not go far enough, often denying there is something beyond their experience of the impersonal absolute. The impersonalist has only achieved the first stage in the realization of the Lord. But as we have seen, there is the experience of Brahman, Paramatman and Bhagavan.

> These three aspects can be explained by the example of the sun, which also has three different aspects, namely the sunshine, the sun's surface and the sun planet itself. One who studies the sunshine is only the preliminary student. One who understands the sun's surface is further advanced. And one who can enter into the sun planet is the highest. Ordinary students who are satisfied by simply understanding the sunshine—its universal pervasiveness and the glaring effulgence of its impersonal nature—may be compared to those who can realize only the Brahman feature of the Absolute Truth.[72]

At what points, then, does Bhaktivedanta differ from the impersonalists? If the Māyāvādīs take the designation of Brahman as *nirguṇa* to mean that the ultimate is without qualities, Bhaktivedanta holds this to mean that the Absolute Truth is without material qualities, certainly not without spiritual ones.[73] Their respective views of the world also affect the way they perceive temple worship. The Māyāvādī sees the image of the deity as an imaginary form since the ultimate is without form. But the Vaiṣṇava sees the image as being both one and different simultaneously according to Caitanya's *acintya bhedābheda* philosophy. "Yogurt is nothing but milk, but at the same time it is not milk."[74] The Māyāvādīs even deride temple worship, saying "that since God is everywhere, why should one restrict himself to temple worship."[75] Bhaktivedanta retorts that if God is everywhere that includes the temple deity!

There is also a difference over the use of the *mantra*. Śankara sees *tat tvam asi* rather than the Hare Kṛṣṇa mantra as the primary vibration. Actually, *tat tvam asi* is a warning to people not to mistake the body for the self. Therefore, it is meant for the conditioned soul, while the Hare Kṛṣṇa *mantra* is meant for the liberated soul.[76] The Māyāvādīs see devotional service as suitable only prior to liberation. But for Bhaktivedanta, devotional service continues even after liberation. Since liberation does not do away with distinctions one is continually engaged in serving the Lord. It is the liberated one who can truly chant the *mahāmantra*.[77] In the end it is unfortunate that they do not know that "there is no conflict between personalism and impersonalism" which is reconciled in Caitanya's doctrine of *acintya bhedābheda*.[78]

Buddhism

I have noted the tendency to be more charitable toward the founder of a religious tradition than toward the subsequent tradition itself. The Buddha is a case in point. He was an incarnation of Kṛṣṇa whose intention was to stop the atheists from killing animals. The Buddha did not speak of God because the people were unable to understand that and so he limited himself to speaking against killing.[79] On the other hand, Buddhists are teachers of "voidism" which is hardly distinguishable from Advaita.[80]

In the *Śri Caitanya-caritāmṛta*, it is stated that Caitanya had an encounter with the leader of a Buddhist cult who attempted to establish his "nine philosophical conclusions" by logic.[81] Bhaktivedanta lists them along with his refutation. This is instructive for several reasons. In the first place it indicates the validity of the principle that he acquires knowledge of other religions either through personal encounter (as did Caitanya here) or through material internal to his own tradition. It also reveals that although the Buddha is purportedly an *avatar* of Kṛṣṇa, some of the doctrines attributed to him by followers are deficient and erroneous. Finally, it is the philosophy of an unnamed cult leader whose views are unacceptable.

Briefly, then, the nine principles are as follows. First, "the creation is eternal; therefore there is no need to accept a creator." But if annihilation or dissolution is the highest truth, as the Buddhists say, then one cannot say that the creation exists eternally. For his part, Bhaktivedanta accepts the beginning of creation and a creator who existed before creation. Second, "the Buddhists argue that the world is false . . ." This is wrong since the world is temporary, but not false. The suffering and pleasures of sentient existence are factual. Third, "the Buddhists maintain that the principle 'I am' is the Ultimate Truth, but this excludes the individuality of 'I' and 'you.' " He seems to mean that the Buddhist excludes the Supreme Personality of Godhead from reality. But if there is no duality, the individual soul and Supersoul, there can be no argument since argument rests on duality. This constitutes a refutation of Buddhism since it tries to rest its case on logic but undercuts what is necessary to make a logical argument. Fourth, "there is repetition of birth and death." Fortunately, the Buddhists accept transmigration, but they do not properly explain the next birth. According to Bhaktivedanta there are 8,400,000 species of life and the next life may not be human.[82] Fifth, "Lord Buddha is the only source for the attainment of knowledge." This is necessary since the Buddha did not accept the authority of the Vedas. But, "if everyone is an authority, or if everyone accepts his own intelligence as the ultimate criterion—as is presently fashionable—the scriptures will be interpreted in many different ways, and everyone will claim his own philosophy supreme." The only adequate solution is disciplic succession. Six, "the Buddhists theorize that annihilation, or *nirvaṇa*, is the ultimate goal." According to Bhaktivedanta, it is true that annihilation applies to the body, but not to the soul. If all physical bodies were to be annihilated, then the soul would have to obtain a nonmaterial or spiritual body if there is to be another birth. And this is the case. If the soul is to return to Godhead, it does not become void or zero, but accepts a spiritual body. Seven, Bhaktivedanta cannot accept the view "that the Buddhist philosophy is the only way" for it contains too many defects. Only Vedānta philosophy, that is, the Vaiṣṇava system taught by Kṛṣṇa is without defect. Eight, "according to the Buddhist cult, the *Vedas* are compiled by ordinary human beings." This does not square with Bhaktivedanta's understanding of the matter. In the creation, Brahma did not create the *Vedas*, but after the creation, "the Supreme Person imparted Vedic knowledge within the heart of Brahma." The only conclusion, then, is that the *Vedas* are not the work of a human being. Even Śaṅkara accepts this fact. Finally, "it is stated that mercy is one of the qualities of the Buddha, but mercy is a relative thing." Mercy can only be shown from a superior to an inferior. Hence without the Supreme Being, Buddhist mercy is ultimately defective. Also, one must know what true mercy is. It is to preach Kṛṣṇa consciousness so as to revive "the lost consciousness of human beings."

It is not clear what sect the "Buddhist leader" might have represented. Bhaktivedanta is aware of the "Hinayana" and "Mahayana" philosophies. But some of the above principles do not fall clearly within either camp, while others would appear to be inferences made by the Vaiṣṇava school from other assertions that can be located more clearly. That the creation is eternal in the type of speculation avoided by the Pali canon. That *nirvaṇa* is annihilation is also going further than that body of texts would permit. The third principle of "I am" is probably an inference made by vaiṣṇavas from the "Buddhists'" denial of the reality of the Supreme Person.

Islam and Christianity

Bhaktivedanta's references to Islam are few. Muslims are not criticized for their doctrines since they hold that the Supreme Lord is personal. However, Muslims (Bhaktivedanta refers to them as Mohammedans) are the objects of conversion by Caitanya. They are persons of low cultural practices since they are meat-eaters.[83] Bhaktivedanta advised avoiding contact with such abominable persons who eat meat. Thus, although he had ample opportunity to understand them as the largest religious minority in

India, he learned about them from his own texts and presumably avoided contact with them himself. There is virtually no discussion of their theology or law.

Bhaktivedanta's knowledge of and contact with Christians seems to have been nonexistent until he arrived in New York in 1965 at age 69. As before, the principle of isolation comes to play. It is pointless to read Christian books or to study Christian scriptures. Referring to "some Bishop in Boston" who wants to change "Thou shalt not kill" into "Thou shalt not murder" in order to preserve animal slaughter, he writes, "We have all respect for these great preachers, but we do not require to study books save and accept for some reference."[84] In the same letter he advises, "So these Christian and Buddhist scriptures were delivered for a different class of men, and we needn't spend our time in studying their doctrines. You should read our own books over and over again and as far as possible do not try to enter into controversy. We do not concern outselves with any other religion. Our religion is to become the servant of the servant of the servant of Kṛṣṇa." Again, it would seem that he followed his own advice. In a letter to a disciple Tosan Kṛṣṇa, he says, "Regarding New Testament, we can simply agree that the New Testament accepts God is great and the creation came into existence by His Word. I do not know the details of New Testament, but I do so fat *(sic)* that it is stated there that all creation is made by God."[85]

In a letter to disciple Dasarha, he encourages the disciple to avoid arguments with Christians since they are predominantly sentimentalists and have no philosophy. But he advises,

> Regarding your other question, you should not read such nonsense books, nor allow your mind to dwell on such subject matter. Instead utilize your time for advancing Krishna consciousness by reading our books. We have got sufficient stock, and if you simply go on reading them, chanting regularly 16 rounds, engaging yourself 24 hours in Krishna's business, then all your questions will be answered automatically, because Krishna promises to his sincere devotee that He will give him the intelligence to understand Him.[86]

Bhaktivedanta's repeated criticism of Christianity has to do with meat-eating. He holds that the command "thou shalt not kill" has to do not only with murder but with killing animal life for consumption. He holds that those who read it as a prescription against murder have changed the text. Bhaktivedanta is convinced that the *Bible* teaches "thou shalt not kill" but is not sure where to locate the statement. He repeatedly attributes it to Jesus. It is difficult to trace the development of Bhaktivedanta's thought on this issue. This is partly a difficulty in dating. Some of his interviews in *Back to Godhead* can be dated, while others can only be assigned a publication date rather than an interview date. Likewise the distinction between the interview date and publication date creates another problem. In a selection from *Science of Self-Realization* in the December 1977 issue of *Back to Godhead* (12.12), Jesus is designated as the source of this teaching when he says, "A preacher of God consciousness is a friend to all living beings. Lord Jesus Christ exemplified this teaching, 'Thou shalt not kill.' "[87] In an undated interview published in November of 1977, he says, "Jesus Christ said, 'Thou shalt not kill.' So why is it that the Christian people are engaged in animal killing?"[88] In a conversation with some disciples in Hyderabad in April of 1974, but published in January of 1982, he still attributes the statement to Jesus Christ when he says, "Jesus Christ says, 'Thou shalt not kill.' "[89] In a conversation with some disciples in Dallas in March 1975, and published in 1983, he identifies the source correctly as the Ten Commandments when he says, "In the Ten Commandments the Bible clearly says, 'Thou shalt not kill.' But they'll not obey. That is sinful.[90] One might think that the clarification was made sometime between April of 1974 and March of 1975. However, in a letter dated March 2, 1969 to a disciple Shivananda, it is clear that Bhaktivedanta thinks that it is Jesus Christ who gave the Ten Commandments. "If we wish to criticize Christian faith we can do so, and we can prove that hardly there are any sincere Christians. In the Ten Commandments we see Lord Jesus Christ advised 'Thou shalt not kill.' "[91] This would pose no problem for development since it is an early letter. However, in an interview with a journalist published in *Back to Godhead* in 1979 but given in late 1968 (hence prior to the 1969 letter) Bhaktivedanta is quoted as locating the statement with some precision. "For instance, in the Old Testament there are the Ten Commandments, and one commandment is 'Thou shalt not kill.' "[92] It is possible that the 1968 interview was edited in line with his later understanding.

However one settles the issue, it would seem clear that Bhaktivedanta has no acquintance with the texts of which he speaks. This should not make us lose sight of his argument, however, which remains constant throughout. It is that Christians have changed the words and intent of Jesus so as to enable them to eat meat. Hence they are to be faulted not because of error in the teaching but because of their unwillingness to obey it.

Not only did he believe that Jesus was teaching the truth in this regard, but that he also taught *saṅkīrtana*. He must have been told that Jesus Christ approved of his activities. He responds, "Perhaps you have marked it in my preaching work that I love Lord Jesus Christ as good as Krishna; because he rendered the greatest service to Krishna according to time, circumstances and society in which he appeared."[93] In the same letter he continues with advise that Kirtananda should prepare a small book on *saṅkīrtana* in the Bible. "And because it is approved by Lord Chriest *(sic)* at least the Christian world will accept our Kirtan procedure. I have seen in the Bible that Lord Jesus Chreist *(sic)* recommended this Kirtan performances in the Bible. You know better than me and I would request you to write a small book on SANKIRTAN MOVEMENT IN THE BIBLE."

He also discovered a book titled *Aquarian Gospel* which led him to believe that Jesus lived for some time in the Jagannath temple in Puri. Since non-devotees would not have been allowed to live there, Jesus must have been a devotee of Kṛṣṇa.

> There is a book called *Aquarian Gospel* in which it is stated that Lord Jesus Christ lived in the temple of Jagannath. Without being His devotee, how could he live there and how the authorities could allow a non-devotee to live there? From that book it appears that Lord Jesus Christ lived in intimate relations with the priest order. So far as possible, you should prepare yourself for future writings that our movement is not against the philosophy of Jesus Christ, but it is in complete collaboration with his line of religiosity.[94]

By November of 1969 he wrote disciple Hansadutta that he would not accept a book like *Aquarian Gospel* as authoritative since sometimes it contains words not actually spoken by Christ.

While Bhaktivedanta's knowledge of Christianity is limited and his judgments on Christians are sometimes harsh, there are also ameliorating dimensions. For example, he says on a number of occasions that he is not seeking to convert Christians to Hinduism. "Yes, I don't say that Christians should become Hindu. I simply say, 'Please obey your commandments.' I'll make you a better Christian. That is my mission. I don't say, 'God is not in your tradition—God is only here in ours.' I simply say, 'Obey God.' I don't say, 'You have to accept that God's name is Kṛṣṇa and no other.' No. I say, 'Please obey God. Please try to love God.' "[95] In that same interview he states that comparing his approach with that of Christianity, the end and the methods are the same. The difference is that he is teaching people practically how to follow it. Any religious scripture one follows might give you enlightenment. However, the inference drawn from this is not that Bhaktivedanta will cooperate to enhance the institutional forms of these other religions or encourage people to stay therein. Rather, he says, "Similarly, any religious scripture you may follow will give you enlightenment. But if you find more in this Kṛṣṇa consciousness movement, then why should you not accept it?"[96]

Likewise, Bhaktivedanta argues that Christ is merely a form of Kṛṣṇa. The name is the same.

> *Christ* comes from the Greek word *Christos*, and *Christos* is the Greek version of the word Kṛṣṭa. When an Indian person calls on Kṛṣṇa, he often says Kṛṣṭa. Kṛṣṭa is a Sanskrit word meaning 'the object of attraction.' So when we address God as 'Christ,' 'Kṛṣṭa,' or 'Kṛṣṇa,' we indicate the same all-attractive Supreme Personality of Godhead.[97]

But again, the inference of this identity is not only to eliminate unnecessary conflict but also to enlist support for his movement. "Therefore, the Christian clergymen should cooperate with the Kṛṣṇa consciousness movement. They should chant the name Christ or Christos and should stop condoning the slaughter of animals. This is not some philosophy I have fabricated; it is taught in the Bible."[98] Since the names are the same, he can counsel his disciple Jadunandan that he can chant any name of God, but Kṛṣṇa is to be preferred.[99]

Finally, although Bhaktivedanta says that it is not his intention to make Christians into Hindus, that does not mean that he does not expect them to associate with the Kṛṣṇa consciousness movement. For,

> The religion of the *Bhagavad-gītā* is not Hindu religion or Christian religion or Mohammedan religion. It is the essence of religion—the reciprocation, the exchange of dealings, between God and the Soul, the Supreme and the subordinate living entity. To accept

> Kṛṣṇa as our Lord, to surrender to the lotus feet of Kṛṣṇa—this is bhakti, or real religion.[100]

If one accepts the *sanātana dharma*, the essence of all religion, one accepts devotion to Kṛṣṇa. The completion of this would be to associate with devotees, and lend support to the Kṛṣṇa consciousness movement by becoming part of it. In a letter to his disciple Jadunandan, Bhaktivedanta indicates that "So we are teaching love of Godhead, not any particular type of religion. Our Kṛṣṇa conscious movement is not a religious movement; it is a movement for purifying the heart."[101] It is not a religion, it is not Hinduism, but it is a movement with which one should align oneself. For above the quotation just made, Bhaktivedanta discusses a strategy for converting Christians. ". . . When you want to convert Christians into Krishna Consciousness, you should understand first of all the philosophy of Krishna Consciousness. Without understanding the philosophy of Krishna Consciousness, if we try to convert Christians into Krishna Consciousness, it will be utter failure."

Conclusion

There is no place in the corpus of Bhaktivedanta's writings where one can go for a systematic treatment of his approach to other religions. However, scattered through his writings one can find principles stated and judgments made which enable one to weave together a coherent account. There is truth in all religions. But they are inevitably incomplete, and if one is to return to Godhead, one must finally resort to *bhakti*, which alone raises one above the mundane plane to the transcendental level. While one's goal is not to convert people to "Hinduism," Kṛṣṇa consciousness is not "Hinduism" but *sanātana dharma* or the eternal religion. On balance there is more criticism of religions than praise. His principle of isolation makes it unlikely that one will acquire accurate factual knowledge of traditions other than one's own. But Bhaktivedanta has passed on. As the movement moves from sect to denomination, there is evidence to suggest that Bhaktivedanta's more ameliorating statements will be held up and his more characteristic harshness will be tempered.

Notes

1. The author wishes to express his appreciation to Subhananda dasa, Senior Editor of Bhaktivedanta Book Trust, who made available unpublished letters of Swami Bhaktivedanta dealing with other religions.

2. A.C. Bhaktivedanta Swami Prabhupada, *Teachings of Lord Caitanya* (Bhaktivedanta Book Trust, 1974), p. 242.

3. *Ibid.*, p. 61.

4. A.C. Bhaktivedanta Swami Prabhupada, *Śrī Caitanya-caritāmṛta* (hereafter referred to as *CC* (Bhaktivedanta Book Trust, 1975) *Madhya-lila*, VI, p. 144.

5. *Ibid.*

6. A.C. Bhaktivedanta Swami Prabhupada, *Bhagavad-gītā As It Is* (Collier Books, 1972), p. 690.

7. A.C. Bhaktivedanta Swami Prabhupada, *Śrī Iśopaniṣad* (Bhaktivedanta Book Trust, 1972), pp. 1–2.

8. *CC*, *Ādi-līlā*, III, p. 89.

9. *Teaching of Lord Caitanya*, p. 60.

10. *Ibid.*

11. *CC*, *Madhya-līlā*, VIII, p. 199.

12. *CC*, *Madhya-līlā*, VI, p. 262.

13. *Ibid.*

14. *CC*, *Madhya-līlā*, IV, p. 20 (*emphasis mine*)

15. *Bhagavad-gītā As It Is*, p. 181.

16. *CC*, *Ādi-līlā*, III, p. 41.

17. *CC*, *Ādi-līlā*, II, p. 165.

18. *Ibid.*, p. 257.

19. *Ibid.*, p. 256.

20. *Ibid.*, p. 111.

21. *CC*, *Ādi-līlā*, I, p. 79.

22. *CC*, *Madhya-līlā*, VII, p. 80.

23. *CC*, *Madhya-līlā*, IX, p. 223.

24. *The Teachings of Lord Caitanya*, p. xx.
25. *Ibid.*
26. *CC, Madhya-līlā*, VIII, p. 155.
27. *Ibid.*
28. *CC, Madhya-līlā*, IX, p. 306.
29. *Ibid.*
30. *Bhagavad-gītā As It Is*, p. 28.
31. *The Teachings of Lord Caitanya*, p. 122.
32. *CC, Madhya-līlā*, VIII, pp. 404–405.
33. *CC, Antya-līlā*, IV, p. 171.
34. *CC, Antya-līlā*, I, p. 169.
35. *CC, Madhya-līlā*, IV, p. 163.
36. *Bhagavad-gītā As It Is*, p. xii.
37. *CC, Madhya-līlā*, VIII, pp. 397–398.
38. *CC, Ādi-līlā,*, I, p. 380.
39. *Bhagavad-gītā As It Is*, p. 754.
40. *CC, Madhya-līlā,*, IX, pp. 403–404.
41. *CC, Madhya-līlā*, VII, p. 100.
42. *Bhagavad-gītā As It Is*, p. 16.
43. *Ibid.*, p. 18.
44. *Ibid.*, pp. 17–18.
45. *CC, Madhya-līlā*, IX, p. 363.
46. *CC, Madhya-līlā*, VII, p. 99.
47. *CC, Ādi-līlā*, III, p. 157.
48. *CC, Ādi-līlā*, II, p. 241.
49. *Bhagavad-gītā As It Is*, p. 18.
50. *CC, Ādi-līlā*, III, p. 158.
51. *Teachings of Lord Caitanya*, p. 66.
52. *Ibid.*
53. *CC, Madhya-līlā*, VIII, p. 98.

54. *CC, Madhya-līlā,* IX, p. 272.

55. *Bhagavad-gītā As It Is,* p. 470.

56. *Teachings of Lord Caitanya,* p. 69.

57. *Bhagavad-gītā As It Is,* p. 318.

58. *Ibid.*

59. *CC, Madhya-līlā,* IX, pp. 326–328.

60. *CC, Madhya-līlā,* V, p. 66.

61. *Bhagavad-gītā As It Is,* p. 13.

62. *Ibid.,* p. 368.

63. *Ibid.*

64. *Ibid.,* p. 107.

65. *Teachings of Lord Caitanya,* p. 214.

66. *Ibid.,* pp. viii–ix.

67. *CC, Madhya-līlā,* I, pp. 18–19.

68. *Ibid.*

69. *CC, Madhya-līlā,* II, p. 304.

70. *CC, Madhya-līlā,* IX, pp. 52–53.

71. See the author's "Swami Bhaktivedanta and the *Bhagavad-gītā* "As It Is" in *Modern Indian Interpreters of the Gita,* edited by Robert N. Monor (State University of New York Press, 1986).

72. *Bhagavad-gītā As It Is,* pp. 73–74.

73. *Teachings of Lord Caitanya,* p. 34.

74. *CC, Madhya-līlā,* IV, p. 103.

75. *Bhagavad-gītā As It Is,* p. 461.

76. *CC, Madhya-līlā,* II, p. 269.

77. *Bhagavad-gītā As It Is,* p. 447.

78. *Ibid.,* p. 374.

79. *CC, Madhya-līlā,* IX, p. 320.

80. *Teachings of Lord Caitanya,* p. 22.

81. *CC, Madhya-līlā,* III, p. 314.

82. For a complete discussion of Bhaktivedanta's views on *karma*

and rebirth see the author's "Swami Bhaktivedanta: Karma, Rebirth and the Personal God," in *Post-Classical Indian Views of Karma and Rebirth*, edited by Ronald Neufeldt (State University of New York Press, 1985).

83. *CC, Madhya-līlā*, VIII, p. 33.

84. Letter to Hansadutta, November, 1969, copy on file.

85. Letter to Tosan Kṛṣṇa, June 23, 1970, copy on file.

86. Letter to Dasarha, March 4, 1972, copy on file.

87. *Back go Godhead*, 12/12 (December 1977), p. 16.

88. *Back to Godhead*, 12/11 (November 1977), p. 12.

89. *Back to Godhead*, 17/1 (January 1982), p. 14.

90. *Back to Godhead*, 18/6 (June 1983), p. 14.

91. Letter to Shivananda, March 2, 1969, copy on file.

92. *Back go Godhead*, 14/2–3 (February/March 1979).

93. Letter to Kirtananda, April 7, 1967, copy on file.

94. Letter to Hayagriva, July 31, 1969, copy on file.

95. *Back to Godhead*, 14/2–3 (February/March 1979), p. 5.

96. *Ibid.*

97. *Back to Godhead*, 12/12 (December 1977), p. 16.

98. *Ibid.*

99. Letter to Jadunandan, April 13, 1968, copy on file.

100. *Back to Godhead*, 19/4 (April 1984), p. 22.

101. Letter to Jadunandan, April 13, 1968, copy on file.

Chapter Seven

THE RESPONSE OF MODERN VAIṢṆAVISM

K.K. Klostermaier

I. Introduction: What is modern Vaiṣṇavism?

Vaiṣṇavism constitutes the numerically largest segment of Hinduism. Speaking of Vaiṣṇavism, then, does not mean to speak of an obscure little sect in some corner of India, but of mainstream traditional Hinduism, the living religion of several hundred million people, concentrated mainly in northern and central India, with a history going back thousands of years.

1. In modern scholarly handbooks[1] Vaiṣṇavism, or Bhāgavatism, is described as consisting of four major constituencies *(catuḥsaṁpradāya)* differentiated from each other by their founder's particular version of Vedānta:

a. The Śrīvaisnava-saṁpradāya follows Viśiṣṭādvaita. Its best known and most important *ācāya* teacher is Rāmānuja (1050-1137) and its most important center is Śrīrangam in today's Tamilnadu.

b. The Brahma-saṁpradāya, also called Madhva-saṁpradāya after its founder Madhva (1197–1276), follows Dvaita or

Svatantra-asvatantra-vāda, has its most important center in Melkote in today's Kaṇṇāḍa.

c. The Kumāra-saṁpradāya, supposedly founded by Nārada, the son of Sanat Kumāra, also called Haṁsa-saṁpradāya or Nimbārka-saṁpradāya, according to its most prominent representative Nimbārka (1125–1162), who advocated Dvaitādvaita, has its headquarters in Vrindaban, Uttar Pradesh.

d. The Rudra-saṁpradāya, founded by Viṣṇu Swāmī (ca. 1200–1250) also called Vallabha-saṁpradāya after Vallabha (1479–1531), who advocated Śuddhādvaita or *puṣṭimārga* has its main center in Vrindaban, Uttar Pradesh.

Two other major saṁpradāyas—sometimes listed separately—are usually affiliated with one of the four above mentioned.

e. The Caitanya-saṁpradāya, named according to its founder (1485–1533), which terms its teachings Acintyabhedābheda, with its main-center in Nāvadvīp (today's West-) Bengal is often (and today officially) associated with the Madhva-saṁpradāya.[2]

f. The Śrī-saṁpradāya, founded by Rāmānanda (1400–1470) with its main center in Ayodhyā (today's Bihar) is usually associated with the Vallabha-saṁpradāya.

This division and the affiliation of many smaller sects to one of the *catuhsaṁpradāyas* goes back to the 14th century.[3] Vaiṣṇavism, however, is a very ancient Indian tradition and it has today in many ways outgrown this schema, which reflects a stage in the development of Indian religions when Vedānta was predominant and scholars vied with each other producing ever new variations of it.

2. Authoritative contemporary descriptions of Vaiṣṇavism tend to emphasize both the great antiquity of this tradition and the features common to all its branches. They also put much greater emphasis on Vaiṣṇava practice than on Vedāntic teachings.[4]

Thus Swāmī Śrī Rāghavācāryajī Mahārāj, the Adhipati of the Ācārya Pīṭha (Śrīraġam) provides a summary of a modern view of Vaiṣṇavism under the title *Vaiṣṇava sadācara*,[5] explaining that according to Yajñavalkya, besides *śruti* (scripture) and *smṛti* (authoritative tradition) *sadācara* (correct mode of life) functions as *dharma-pramāṇa* (means to establish *dharma* or as proof for orthodoxy).

The author refers to the Vedic roots of Vaiṣṇavism: in the Vedas Viṣṇu is identified with sacrifice. Jaimini recognized

Viṣṇu as supreme deity: everything is pervaded and designed by Him.

Vaiṣṇava practice is inseparable from Vaiṣṇava religion: *upāsana* (ritual worship) and *śaranāgati* (taking refuge of Viṣṇu) are constitutive of Vaiṣṇavism.

The *sādhana* or practice of a Vaiṣṇava encompasses 'pure food', 'avoidance of religious acts not enjoined by *śāstras*', '*virtues' (such as kindness and humility), and finally, 'not being depressed by sorrows and not being elated by good fortune'.*

Further the Vaiṣṇava is to study śruti and *smṛti* and to fulfill his duties as commandments of God. He begins each religious act with the formula: "by the instruction of the Lord, for the delight of the Lord, in service of the Lord . . ."

Pūjā (ritual worship of an image) is the distinguishing mark of Vaiṣṇavism through which the Vaiṣṇava realizes the four stages of consciousness as described in the Upanisads and offers up to the Lord the three *āradhanas* (entertainments) and eight *puṣpas* (flowers). The three *āradhanas* consists of a heart free from hatred, a mind free from falsehood, and a body free from violence.

The eight *puṣpas* are *ahiṁsā*, sense-control, comparrion with all beings, forbearance, equanimity, meditation, contemplation and truth. By way of conclusion the author emphasizes the advantages of the Vaiṣṇava path over the path of the *ātmadārśana*: the life of the Vaiṣṇava is *bhagavadīya*, consecrated to the Lord.

Brāgavat Ācārya Prabhupāda Śrīman Prāṇakiśor Goswāmi Maharaj M.A., Vidyabhūsana, Sahityaratna, traces in another contribution under the title *Vaiṣṇava dharma*[6] the (common) history of Vaiṣṇavism: Beginning with the Rgveda all *śruti* and *smṛti* texts, the *itihāsas* and the Purāṇas give witness to the recognition of Viṣṇu as supreme God. He singles out the *Pāñcaratra* as the best and most mature articulation of this tradition.

Vaiṣṇavism is comprehensive: it includes Smārtas, Vaidikas, Vedāntins, Tantrikas and Paurāṇikas. They all remember the holy name of Viṣṇu—Viṣṇu is omnipresent. Vaiṣṇavism is God's gift to humanity, the descent of the deity into the world of mortals.

The qualities of a Vaiṣṇava are detailed with reference to Viṣṇu: there is religious egalitarianism among Vaiṣṇavas, because every Vaiṣṇava's heart is Viṣṇu's throne, each of his limbs is Viṣṇu's temple, his walking a circumambulation of Viṣṇu, his speaking an utterance of the Name, his seeing an act of Love, his daily activity Worship.

Vaiṣṇavism is universal: it knows no boundaries of time and space. All humans are qualified and obliged to worship the Supreme One. One is made a Vaiṣṇava by 'taking the name of the Lord'. Vaiṣṇavism promises rich rewards for small efforts.

Referring to the *Bhāgavatam Purāṇam* (XI, ii, 29–31) the author enumerates the virtues of a Vaiṣṇava: mercy and friendliness towards all creatures, truthfulness and readiness to help others, freedom from passions and desires, peacefulness and seriousness.

Śrī Kṛṣna Datta Bhatta's paper *vaiṣṇav jan to tene kahiye*[7] begins with the question: "Who is a 'Vaiṣṇava'? Why is one called a 'Vaiṣṇava'?" And he continues: "It is a simple, easy question which has a simple answer: 'A Vaiṣṇava is a person who accepts Viṣṇu, whose support Viṣṇu is, who has faith in Viṣṇu, who has surrendered himself to the lotus-feet of Viṣṇu'." His external signs are: *japa* (repetition of the name), *māla* (rosary), *chāpā* (imprint on body) and *tilaka* (sign on the forehead). His internal signs are, according to Narsi Mehta: giving help to those in need, being compassionate and full of love. This is exemplified by Mahātma Gandhi—the model Vaiṣṇava! A Vaiṣṇava is free from evil desires, he is leading a pure life, he is not appropriating what is not his, he is beyond all "mine-ism". The author concludes by saying: "A Vaiṣṇava is an image *(putlā)* of love *(prema)*, of compassion *(karuṇa)*, of truthfulness *(satya)*. His characteristic is service *(sevā)*; purity of soul *(ātmasamśodhana)* is his way; passionlessness constitutes his provisions. He complains that "nowadays our words are very high-sounding, but our actual behavior is very mean". But he is confident that we too can become true Vaiṣṇavas if we make the necessary efforts.

3. Vaiṣṇavism does not speak with one voice. Apart from a solid scriptural and liturgical/practical tradition it is today represented by articulate individuals who succeed in blending their own new ideas with the received body of teachings. While one would not be able to say—on the basis of a survey of the contemporary Vaiṣṇava literature and a familiarity with the actual Vaiṣṇava milieu—that religious pluralism was a major concern of Vaiṣṇavism, it is a concern for some individual Vaiṣṇavas who have a voice within their community. Thus the major part of the following essay will be devoted to a fairly detailed description of three individual responses.

II. A variety of Vaiṣṇava responses to religious pluralism

A Courageous Vaiṣṇava's attempt to provide a scholarly home to religious pluralism

Born Narendra Nath Mukherjea on March 23, 1901 the late Swāmi Bon Mahārāj was one of the most widely known Vaiṣṇavas of our time, whose relevance to our topic is quite unique.[8] He grew up in what is today Bangladesh and had some of his secondary schooling in the English Mission school at Ranchi. At age 23 he joined the Neo-Caitanyite movement of Bhakti Siddhānta Saraswatī Goswāmi Mahārāja and accepted the name of Tridaṇdi Swāmi Bhakti Hridaya Bon Mahārāj. He preached the gospel of Caitanya in many parts of India and succeeded in being invited to lecture (in English) in a number of important institutions throughout the country. He was instrumental in founding several Caitanya centers in India and in organizing several spectacular exhibitions. After about ten years of active missionary service in India on behalf of the Neo-Caitanya Mission he was sent to Europe. With recommendations to persons of high rank and position he addressed many audiences and eventually founded a small temple in London. He was well received by high-ranking representatives of major Christian denominations and was approached by quite a few young people who wanted to return with him to India to lead a Hindu religious life. He was triumphantly welcomed back to Calcutta in late 1935. On January 1, 1937, the founder of the Gauḍīa mission died and the group could not decide on a successor. Swami Bon left the mission. He spent some time in Ayodyā, then in Benares, went on a lecture tour to the U.S.A., Japan, Burma. He stayed for another two years at Varāṇāsī. In contact with Pandit Madan Mohan Malaviya, the first Vice-Chancellor of Benaras Hindu University, the idea of founding a "Vaiṣṇava Theological University" seems to have grown. After several years of intense religious practices and preparations in Vrindaban Swami Bon went ahead with the foundation of the Vaiṣṇava Viśvavidyālaya. He contacted influential and prosperous acquaintances, bought a large tract of land and began to build. In 1949 Dr. Sampurnananda, then education minister of U.P. inaugurated the Vaiṣṇava Theological University. Many great names became associated with the enterprise: Dr. K.M. Munshi performed Vana-Mahotsava in 1950, Dr. S. Radhakrishnan, then

Vice-president of India, addressed the first convocation in 1952, Dr. Katju, then Union Home Minister, addressed the second convocation in 1954. A number of Doctor of Theology degrees were conferred on established scholars as well as on some research students. Meanwhile Swāmi Bon had been elected President of all four Vaiṣṇava sampradāyas at the *Kumbha Mela* in Hardwar in 1950, and again in Allahabad in 1954. He campaigned as a candidate for the Lok Sabhā in 1952 on behalf of the Rām Rājya Pariṣad, founded by a fellow-religious, Swāmi Karpatrijī Mahārāj.[9] He lost and never again tried. In 1956 the University Grants Commission Act was passed and the Union Education Ministry, to whom Swāmi Bon had applied for recognition suggested to rename the Vaiṣṇava Theological University into Institute of Oriental Philosophy. It was to function as an Advanced Research Centre and to seek affiliation with a recognized University. The memorandum prepared by Swāmi Bon and submitted to Dr. C.D. Seshmukhn, the Chairman of the University Grants Commission, proposed to replace the Vaiṣṇava Theological University by an Institute of Oriental Philosophy, specializing in advanced research in different schools of Oriental Philosophy and a Vrindaban Teaching University, comprising five faculties.

For the Institute of Oriental Philosophy the establishment of eighteen Chairs was proposed, amongst which all the major philosophico-religious schools were to be represented. Equally, the program of the Vrindaban Teaching University was quite pluralistic in its conception. The single most important drawback was the lack of finances: Swami Bon had no property or income of his own; the generosity of his donors had its limits; the scheme was so grandiose that after another five years most of the buildings started were only partly finished and only a fraction of the scheme was realized. Nevertheless Swami Bon persisted: he contacted state-governments and foreign legations for endowments of chairs, he founded the Indian Association for the History of Religions, he held on the premises of his institution of All India Symposium on Spiritual Values East and West, at which besides more than one hundred Indian academics, also some Christian clergy participated. Swami Bon attended the Xth International Congress of the International Association for the History of Religions at Marburg in 1960 and utilized the months after this congress to canvass among academics and higher clergy in Europe and U.S.A. for his scheme.

The "aims and objectives" as articulated in the printed Scheme and Report of 1962 certainly were pluralistic. The scheme itself was no less so: out of the eighteen chairs proposed (the sequence, interestingly changed) five were considered "already established" and seven more "in the process of being established". "Our aim", read a statement printed in 1962,

> "is to establish an indigenous residential Institute on the lines of the Universities of Taxila and Nalanda as a real Seat of Learning and Culture, where advanced scholars and earnest seekers of Absolute Knowledge may congregate from every corner of India and also from all Foreign Countries amidst congenial, serene and sacred environments, free from the bustle of worldliness, with modern amenities, and sit around the table with their great Professors, to study, understand, assimilate and be engaged in drinking deep the eternal nectar of the truly inner concepts of Indian Philosophy and Indian Spiritual Culture—the highest contributions made by the self-realized Ṛṣis and Acharyas of ancient times."

The 'Chairs', comprising modest stipends for research-guides and for one or two Ph.D. candidates each, were funded by state governments on an annual basis. Some business people, whom Swami Bon had met as a preacher on behalf of the Gaudīya Mission had made donations whch had gone into the plot and the buildings—not enough to complete them. Locally the Swami had to contend with a great deal of opposition. He had been able to establish his Institute only against a very strong orthodox Hindu (largely Vaiṣṇava) opposition, which found his whole idea outrageous: what had Buddhist, Christian and Islamic studies to do with the holy city of Kṛṣṇa?

The Institute also published a Quarterly: *Indian Philosophy and Culture*. While it, again, largely served as a vehicle to propagate the Vaiṣṇava, and especially the Caitanya standpoint, it did accept occasionally also articles dealing with other traditions.[10] In the late sixties Swāmi Bon was persuaded to develop the greater part of his educational institution into a local Arts and Science College. Generous donations enabled him to complete the buildings and to hire teachers for B.A. and M.A. courses in a variety of general subjects. The Institute of Oriental Philosophy slowly ceased to function and with it the ideas of fostering religious studies in a spirit of religious pluralism faded. Swāmi Bon became again elected president of all four Vaiṣṇava saṁpradāyas at the Kumbhamela in Allahabad. He witnessed with some resentment the success of his Gurubhāī Swāmi Bhaktivedānta in founding the Hare Krishna Movement in the West and the establishment of the movement in a separate institution in Vrindaban. He died, a highly respected senior Vaiṣṇava monk, in late 1983, without leaving a successor to continue the work of fostering religious pluralism.

A scholarly Vaiṣṇava's theory of religious pluralism

Bibhuti S. Yadav, a member of the religion department of Temple University, comes from a Vallabha background and has shown himself an able as well as spirited exponent of the *pūstimārga.* In an address read at Bangalore, and later published in *Religion and Society,*[11] he develops over against Hans Küng's theory of the relationship of Christianity and the other religions as Vaiṣṇava (Vallabha) Theology of Religious Pluralism. After highlighting and criticizing Hans Kn̈g's theology of religions as it had appeared in *Being Christian,* he offers his own theology of religions.

Yadav is not kind towards Hans Küng. By hitting out at Hans Küng,however, who in most matters of doctrine maintains a fairly traditional Catholic position, Yadav rejects some widely entertained tenets of contemporary Christianity: "(Hans Küng) represents a special revelation and a 'chosen people', a people the *a priori* necessity of whose will to love is, that they be committed to the moral obligation of 'freeing' the religions, of liberating them from their function, values, and ultimately the reasons to exist. The exclusivity of this will-to-love demands that world religions be so conceived *a priori* that they call for their redemptive correction by Christianity." (p. 39) After quoting a reference to Hinduism in Küng's book—admittedly one which is objectionable—Yadav lashes out again:

> Hans Küng is under moral obligation to misunderstand religions by using second-hand data. He can say that the son of Joseph and Mary was the only Son of God, not an anthropomorphic projection but the flesh of the trinitarian God. This son of Joseph and Mary arose from the grave. His resurrection was the eschatological fulfillment of all history; it is a historical fact, not a myth . . . Krishna was born to Vasudeva and Devakī as mysteriously and with as much commitment to moral justice as Jesus to Joseph and Mary.

> But Hans Küng is authorized to say that Krishna's birth was not a case of Logos becoming flesh, that Vaiṣṇavism is based on popular superstition, and is unhistorical and mythical. (p. 60)

Yadav chides Hans Küng's theology as "a methodology of perceiving fantasies as facts, theological space as history". (ibid.) He charges that he espouses a "theology that does not kill God, only lets him live a life of thousand qualifications", (ibid.) "Hans Küng does not let God be God. Driven by the will to become God in history, he makes God in his own image and then claims to have been made in the image of God. The collective wish of a people that they be unique and special is unconsciously transcendentalized in the garb of 'special revelation.'" (p. 41) Summing up his critique Yadav states: "Hans Küng's theology of religion is an unfortunate mythology in support of a missionology that has fortunately failed. . . . Hans Küng performs conversion by conducting dialogue with the Buddha, whose *a priori* destiny is to say what new Israel wishes to hear. Dialogue thus becomes a technique of converting forms of thinking of a people, it is the recent way of handling *depositum fidei.*" (pp. 43f) His own statement of a Vaiṣṇava (Vallabha) Theology of Religious Pluralism is prefaced by "methodological clarifications". Here he states that he builds his case on a radically pluralist vision of religion: he not only rejects Küng's claim of representing a historical religion over against which all others are "non-X", but also Radhakrishnan's thesis that Hinduism is a "synthetic unity". The various forms of Hinduism may have common scriptures.

> "But they made absolute and exclusive claims on all fronts, viz. the genesis and validity of scriptures, theories of language and methodology of interpreting texts, epistemology and metaphysics, myths and rituals. The so called Hinduism is a rolling conference of conceptual spaces, all of them facing all, and all of them requiring all. Each claims loyalty to the *śrutis*, each showing how its claims are decisively true, and charging the rival schools with perpetuating the confusion of tongues in the *dharmakṣetra*. They are not out to achieve 'synthetic unity' between themselves, but to creatively continue their contrasting identities through dialogue (*vādavidhi).* A lay Hindu, however, thinks and lives in time, and not in a conceptual space. He subscribes to most of these schools in daily life and is therefore a living contradiction, unsynthetic and logically incomplete to any and to all." (p. 45)

Quite categorically he states after writing off a great deal of modern Hinduism as the creation of an aloof brahmin elite—that the "history of modern Hinduism is a history of giving Western answers for Western questions." (p. 46) Over against this declared aversion against neo-Brahminism he accepts Gandhi as an "ecumenist in thought, language and social action" and "a Vaiṣṇava as well". (p. 47)

He then develops his Vaiṣṇava theology of religious pluralism under four headings: Scriptural Realism—God as *co-incidentia oppositorum*—Religious Democracy—Dialogue. Although well read in Western thought and Christian theology and —while responding to Hans Küng—using *topoi* of this particular tradition, he succeeds in developing a Vallabhite standpoint which is authentic, and being so, adds important dimensions to the debate on religious pluralism.

Yadav stresses the point that Vallabha takes the Word of God seriously: God really communicates himself through words, words have real meaning with regard to God, God being the primary meaning of all words. Reacting against the modern Christian theologian's distinction between a 'special' (Biblical) and an "ordinary" (extra-Biblical) revelation he asserts that "all Words are 'special' to Him because they are His words, and He gives Himself to all peoples in a special way." (p. 57) Thus the particularity of all religions is grounded in their special revelations, which does not imply inferiority or superiority. To absolutize one such historic revelation "makes Him subservient to His Word". (p. 58) Yadav insists that "God has become equally immanent in all religions, just as He is equally transcendent to all of them." (p. 59) God's own freedom is expressed in the freedom of religions: "To deny redemptive value to religions by giving exclusive redemptive value to one's own religion is atheism. In Vallabha's theology of religious democracy all history is sacred history; it is inhabited by many Israels, each of them distinct, parallelly universal, and mutually linked but equally relative to one absolute Person, God." (ibid.) In a quite striking formulation he sums it up by saying: "History is a moving conference of sacred histories, a dialogical circle of Israels through which God is saying 'This I am'." (ibid.)

Speaking of dialogue Yadav declares it to be "God's mode of being in time and not a concession to the needs of time." (p. 60) He castigates the failure of Christian theologians to recognize that the *logos* has become flesh in many forms. Explaining the meaning of the Vallabhite teaching of God's *avirbhavatirobhava līlā* he writes: "God gives Himself as Krishna to Hindus, and he conceals Himself as Christ from the Hindus. In giving Himself to Christians as Christ, He conceals Himself as Krishna from the Christians. The world is a revealment-concealment *(avirbhava-tirobhava)* dialectic of sacred histories, a dialogical situation *(kṣetra)* wherein a Word as God is out to discover all other Words as God. Dialogue therefore is not *in* history; dialogue itself *is* history." (p. 61)

Yadav develops this dialectic further to postulate an onto-theological (and therefore irreducible) difference between the religions, which are as much constituted by that through which they differ from one another as by their own being what they are. Vallabha's insistence that God reveals himself in his hiddenness to the seeker provides another relevant insight: "Dialogue . . . gives a Vaiṣṇava the delightful experience of belonging to Krishna. It also gives him a redeeming agony caused by the immediacy between him and the distant God as Christ. To say that God has only one word is to kill God, it is to be dishonest to history, as well. To say that a people or person can belong to all the religions is to say that man is God; it is to be dishonest with being man." (p. 62)

Yadav has learned from Vallabha that reaching God is not as important as attempting to reach out for him. "What is called for is Vṛndavana, the process of man chasing God, God escaping man, and then the two meeting for the sake of meeting." (p. 62) Yadav takes this to be the paradigm of dialogue which he calls a "non-redemptive kind of relationship between the religions." (ibid.) He also sees in dialogue an "argument against reductionism: against reducing God to His Words, against reducing all the Words of God to one Word, and against reducing one Word to any or all other Words. Dialogue is a request to outgrow the either/or logic . . ." (ibid.) Over against Vallabha's insistence that God is larger than His words, that God is infinite and His words are infinite *(Hari ananta Hari kathā ananta)* and the realization that "no religion, no revelation, or Word of God is as final as God" (p. 56) he draws attention to "Christian subjectivity which absolutizes what it wishes to hear and does not let God go against its own will; in absolutizing the form *in* which it had been elected, Christianity enslaves God by not letting Him elect Himself otherwise than his election of Himself in Jesus." (p. 57) And: "God indeed is one; only that He has several Sons, including a few daughters, whose company in history the generous Son of God in the Gospels need not mind." (ibid.)

Śrī Kṛṣṇaprem Vairāgī:[12] a Christian convert to Vaiṣṇavism

Genuine religious pluralism implies the possibility of choice: instead of remaining within the tradition into which one had been born or which by virtue of circumstances beyond one's control one came to consider one's own, individuals as well as communities should be able to choose among the various religions recognized as authentic by those who accept religious pluralism.

Choosing another tradition can be motivated by many different reasons: it need not necessarily involve a decision for Truth over against Falsehood, for Salvation over against Condemnation, for or against God.

Modern Vaiṣṇavism has been found so attractive by a number of Westerners, who had grown up in Judaism, Christianity or no religion at all, as to become the religion of choice for a fair number of our contemporaries. Leaving the 'Hare Krishna Movement' for a separate contribution, I wish to briefly deal with an Englishman who became a well-known Vaiṣṇava guru, attracting Indians as well as non-Indians to the fold.

Born Ronald Nixon on May 10, 1898 in Cheltenham/U.K., he studied classics and science at Cambridge, was a flyer in the Royal Flying Corps in World War I, where he saw action in France. He often mentioned a "miracle" which saved his life in one particular mission—for him a firm proof for the existence of a "higher power". After the war he went back to Cambridge but switched over to "Mental and Moral Science". In Cambridge he came into touch with Theosophy and felt attracted to Buddhism and to India, the birthplace of Buddha. So he grasped the opportunity after graduation in 1921 to take up a teaching position (in English) in India.

After a very brief period at Canning College (Bengal) he was invited to Lucknow University by its then Vice Chancellor J.N. Cakravarti, a prominent Theosophist who had attended the 1893 Chicago Parliament of Religions. He stayed in Cakravarti's spacious guesthouse and became soon a member of the family. His siding with the Indian independence movement (he also refused to join the local Anglo-Indian Society) could have been risky for him had it not been for the protection of the Vice-Chancellor who happened to be a personal friend of the Governor, Sir Harcourt Butler. The young Professor Nixon soon came under the influence of the Vice-Chancellor's wife, Monica Cakravarti, who eventually became his guru. Monica was the daughter of Raybahadur Gaganachandra Ray of Ghazipur, in whose home Swāmi Vivekānanda had stayed for some time. During this time Vivekānanda had performed *Kumārī-pūjā* with young Monica, who later accepted *dīkṣa* from her husband.

When Professor Nixon accompanied the Cakravartis for their summer holidays to Almora he studied Hindī with the help of a paraphrase of the *Bhāgavatam* provided by Monica Cakravarti. He visualized *Kṛṣṇa and* asked *Monica* for *dīkṣa.*

In 1926 Dr. J.N. Cakravarti was invited to become Vice-Chancellor of Benares Hindu University. In spite of a reduction by more than fifty percent in his salary, Ronald Nixon moved there too and two years later followed Monica Cakravarti, who had decided to retire to Almora and lead the life of a religious. She accepted *saṁnyāsa* from the hands of a Goswāmi from Vrindaban (who continued to stay on as priest for the Kṛṣṇa shrine) and was known from then as Yaśodā Māī. A little later Ronald Nixon took *saṁnyāsa* from Yaśodā Māī and became Krishnaprem. He lead the austere life of a very orthodox Vaiṣṇava *vairāgi.*

In 1931 Āśram was completed: situated about eighteen miles away from Almora, near a hamlet called Mirtola, it comprised besides a temple and simple accommodation for its inhabitants, a library and a classroom as well as a dispensary. Yaśodā Māī, who had been a schoolteacher before her marriage, taught basic skills and hygiene to the village-children, Krishnaprem was in charge of the library and later took over as cook as well as temple-priest. A former friend from Cambridge, who had become a reputable surgeon in Lucknow, Major R.D. Alexander joined as Ánandaprīya and operated the dispensary. He was later to take *saṁnyāsa* and became known as Haridās. Monica's only daughter Motī also joined the group.

Krishnaprem's friends in Almora and others who saw him on his travels remarked what a model Vaiṣṇava *vairāgi* he had become: he scrupulously observed all regulations concerning food and worship and was fully accepted by Hindus as teacher and guide. He became fluent in Hindī and Bengalī, he studied Sanskrit and Palī and wrote several works which were received well by scholars and seekers.[13] He also learned Bengalī *kīrtan* and after the death of Yaśodā Māī in 1944 he was administrator of the Centre for more than twenty years. He died after a long illness on November 15, 1965. Hundreds of villagers took turns to carry his body up to the āśram-area for cremation.

Krishnaprem's standing as a Vaiṣṇava was recognized by all: his identification with Vaiṣṇavism was his free choice and remained firm throughout his life. Dilip Kumar Roy, one of his closest friends, reports how an Anglo-Indian lady once berated Krishnaprem (whose blue eyes and fair skin gave him easily away) for "throwing everything away"—his culture, religion and country. When she asked: "What have you gained?" Krishnaprem "calmly produced his beloved Image of the Lord and answered, with his radiant smile: 'I have got Him, madam: my Krishna!' "[14]

He is not on record as at any time attacking any other religion or entering into any exchange with anyone on the issue of religious pluralism. In a letter he expressed his reaction to the reading of some of Dr. Stanley Jones' books.

> "Dr. Stanly Jones' books not only have no appeal for me at all—but they actually leave a very bad impression on my mind. He 'loves and respects Buddha'?—very kind of him I am sure! But he 'cannot respect Krishna'? Dear, dear! That is too bad—hadn't we better shut up the Krishna cult altogether . . . if Dr. Jones really had experience of Christ he would know quite certainly that Christ and Krishna are the same. He would know quite certainly that certain sayings and doings of Krishna are either symbols whose meaning he has not understood, or else interpolations. He would know this for the same reason that I know that certain sayings of Christ, as recorded in the Gospels, are interpolations or have been misunderstood by those who wrote them down. Do not think I have any prejudice against Christ. The Christ of the fourth Gospel is the same as Krishna. But it seems to be useless to attempt a *human* biography of Krishna such as can with difficulty be written of Christ or Buddha. Why is Christianity tottering so—at least among the educated? Primarily because the Christians have pinned their faith on historical events and a historical person. Modern knowledge has shown that we cannot be certain of those events or that Person (again I say: do not mistake me or suppose that I am sceptical myself) and therefore the bottom is falling out of the whole thing. In my opinion the Gnostic Christ, even the Christ of the Fourth Gospel is far more important than any historical human figure. The human figure was important just because he manifested that Eternal Christ and so with Krishna. Certainly I agree that a vivid presentation of the human can do much to awaken a love and devotion that may carry the bhakta to what is within and above his self but it will do so only if the devotee is free from sectarianism even of the sympathetic modern sort and makes no distinctions between the

> various 'Sons of God'. Otherwise it may give a pleasant warmth of feeling, or it may even inspire a decent moral life but it will not give that immortality which can only be achieved by the knowledge of the One who 'takes without hands, travels without feet, hears without ears and sees without eyes'. That One is in all beings—even the very meanest. Know Him through Christ, through Krishna or through Buddha, but *know Him somehow or other*."[15]

There is also a fascinating account of Krishnaprem's meeting with Rāmaṇa Mahārsi, who is reported to have called Krishnaprem "a *bhakta* and a *jñāni* in one, a rare combination."[16]

Vaiṣṇava universalists

Besides the voices which advocate the superiority of Vaiṣṇavism over all other religions and the need faithfully to fulfill all details of Vaiṣṇava worship and discipline there are also those who emphasize the fundamental unity of all religions and the universal nature of true worship. Thus Swāmī Rāmdās asserts[17] that the many different religions, sects and theologies have basically one and the same orientation: they convey a notion of the spiritual, transcendental reality and thus promote the universal brotherhood/sisterhood of humankind and the universal father/motherhood of God. He deplores the fact that instead of fostering unity, love and understanding, religions have acted as divisive forces in history and have antagonized each other in the name of God.

The great masters, however, who made the divine light reach the hearts of humans, did not belong to any one particular religion or Church: the whole world is their temple, for them the Lord reveals himself in all creatures. They are over and above all sects and divisions. Their love is universal like wind and sun.

True service of the Lord is grounded upon the equality of all men and the principle of peace. Thus the true servant of the Lord exhibits features which can be realized by everyone: he realizes God in his heart and serves the family of mankind as one of its members, he sees God in all.

Swāmī Rāmdās concludes with the exhortation that we should forget our petty differences and realize the truth of unity and universality. God's own omnipresence, omnipotence, grace and love should become visible in all of us. We should prove ourselves true children of the Lord by exhibiting his qualities.

He ends his contribution by a poetic "message/mission of the Supreme Soul" which, like the *Veni Creator Spiritus*, passionately pleads for a universal renewal, a new birth, a new beginning in unity and love, in peace and understanding.

Less openly speaking of 'religious unity' but promoting it in his own way is Kṛṣṇadatta Bhaṭṭa, the author/editor of a series of twelve booklets with the title ". . . *dharma kyā kahāta hai?*" devoted to a simple exposition of the basic history and teachings of all the major religions.[18] Besides four such booklets devoted to Hinduism there are booklets on Buddhism, Taoism, Confucianism, Islam, Zoroastrianism, Sikhism, Christianity and Judaism. The description is simple, making use of translations of extracts from the sacred literatures of these religions, emphasizing the appealing and edifying elements in their doctrines and histories. All booklets are free from polemics or from critical remarks.

Similarly universalist is the approach of Bankey Bihari, a learned Vaiṣṇava recluse in Vrindaban, who in his several volumes on saints of different traditions freely draws on many traditions without discriminating against any.[19]

The *Santāṅk* special volume of *Kalyāṇa* is quite catholic too:[20] it contains an article on *Mahātma Isāmasih* by Śrī Gopināth Joshi.[21] After a brief summary of the Gospel narrative of the life of Jesus the author offers a translation of, and commentary on, the Sermon on the Mount, which many Hindus consider to be the quintessence of Christianity. In the same volume there are essays on Jain and Buddhist saints, on Sikh gurus and on major Advaitins, as well as short sketches of the life and the poetry of several Sūfis.

There surely are many contemporary Vaiṣṇavas who are deeply committed to Vaiṣṇavism as well as open to all other expressions of genuine religiosity. Professor M. Yamunacarya (1899–1971), for many years a professor of philosophy at Mysore University, author of a valuable anthology of Rāmānuja[22] was one of the participants at a 'dialogue meeting' in Ootacamund (Nilgiris) which was organized by Dr. D. Steere (World fellowship of Friends) bringing together some Hindus and Christians from different backgrounds.[23] His account of the 'Inward Journey"—the umbrella-theme of the meeting—was touching in its emphasis of the great role which his maternal grandfather had played in it. Alkondavilli Govindacharya was a quite well known Śrīvaiṣṇava sage and the author of several books.[24] In *The Divine Wisdom of the Dravida*

Saints, the author makes numerous explicit sympathetic references to Christian writings and Christian saints. Jadunath Sinha, a prolific writer on Indian Philosophy, coming from a Vaiṣṇava background (without being an exponent of a specific *saṁpradāya*) has made a quite unique contribution to religious pluralism in his *Unity of Living Faiths, Humanism and World Peace.*[25] Dealing topically/systematically with the central concepts and issues of religion, he quotes side by side from Hindu, Buddhist, Jewish, Christian, Zoroastrain, Sikh, Taoist, Confucian, Islamic (primary) sources, evidencing thus the basic agreement of the major religious traditions on major issues. Manilal C. Parekh, during the lst phase of his work associated with the Śrī Bhāgavata Dharma Mission in Bājkot, might be considered (among other things) a Vaiṣṇava. A Christian convert during his early life, he not only wrote books on Vallabhāchārya, on Keshub Chander Sen and Ram Mohan Roy but also a History of the Christian Church, a Commentary on the Gospel of St. John, and translations of some minor works by St. Berrard and Brother Lawrence's "Practice of the Presence of God". He became very critical of Christian Missions in India and wrote a quite hostile book entitled *Christian Proselytism in India: a Great and Growing Menace.*[26] He finally crowned his quite pluralistic literary work by *A Hindu's Portrait of Jesus Christ*[27] subtitled "A Gospel of God's free gift of His sonship".

III. Conclusion

For the majority of Vaiṣṇava "religious pluralism" is not a major concern. In fact, one can notice that it is today less of a concern than it had been fifty years ago.[28] Then, under the British Rāj, many institutions of higher education operated under Christian Church auspices and all students in these were exposed to some teaching of Bible and Christian doctrine. Then, too, the missionary movement of the Christian Churches was quite aggressive in some parts of India. Most educated Hindus were aware of the existence of other traditions and reacted in some way or other to these, either incorporating them into their own thinking or rejecting them as alien.

The Indian Independence movement politicized Hinduism to a considerable degree. Its success was seen by many as a success of Hinduism over other faiths. Being a Hindu became more important than being a Vaiṣṇava or a Śaiva or a Śākta. Those Hindus, who with the extreme right consider the independence gained from British rule in 1948 as an incomplete liberation from foreign domination, attempt to transform the many heterogenous sects and traditions termed "Hinduism" into a unified religion along the lines of (pre-reformation) Christianity. The Hindu Mahāsbhā with its offsprings the Rāṣṭrīa Svayamsekvak Sangh and the Viśva Hindu Pariṣad have been busy distilling from the immense and varied traditions a basic Hindu mythology and a set of doctrines as well as practices which should become the basis of the identity of the new Hinduism.[29] Many Vaiṣṇavas are working within these organizations, considering their All-Hindu identity more important than their sectarian family background. The socio-political concerns of these new Hindu movements override the traditional doctrinal and liturgical concerns which led to the formation of the various *saṁpradāyas* Many modern active Vaiṣṇavas are of the opinion that the divisions of the *saṁpradāyas* have outlived their meaning and that a unified and centrally organized Hinduism should replace all sects. It is quite interesting to note that His Holiness Jagadguru Rāmānujācārya Swāmī Rāghavācārya Mahārāj of the Śrī Ācarya Pītha in his message to the Hindu Viśva Pari ṣad entitled *What is Hinduism?* does not mention Vaiṣṇavism at all but only speaks of *dharma* in a contribution to the same publication under the title *Hindutva kī rakṣa meñ vaiṣṇava sa mpradāya kī anupama dena* subordinates Vaiṣṇavism to "Hindutva".[31] It may be of some interest in this context to point out that Vīr Savarkar, one of the great ideologues of the Hindu Mahāsbhā, defined *Hindutva* (Hindudom) as a cultural tradition over against *Hindu dharma* (Hinduism) in the religious and sectarian sense.[32] It is quite evident that for the Vaiṣṇavas who are active under the banner of *Hindutva* the traditional characteristics of piety and doctrine have become largely irrelevant. Whether by design or by coincidence, certain issues like cowslaughter, celeration of religious festivals, marriage laws, and so forth, have become all-Hindu concerns irrespective of sectarian affiliation.

Vaiṣṇavas consider their own tradition as *sanātana dharma*, i.e., as *the* religion of mankind, divinely ordained from the beginning of the world. It has considerable latitude in many ways it admits a multitude of gods and goddesses, a variety of cults and customs, a choice of holy places and of holy books. But it insists on its own inerrancy and ultimacy: the acceptability of other schools of thought and other religion depends on their accepting/rejecting central parts of the Vaiṣṇava tradition. Thus

Śaivism and Śāktism, the worship of Sūrya and Ganeṣa have—on the whole—been accepted by Vaiṣṇavas as part of the *sanātana dharma*, whereas Buddhism, Jainism and the Advaita of Śaṅkara have been shunned and condemned as heretical. Similarly, certain forms of Christianity (especially Catholic and Eastern Orthodox) have found acceptance—even so much so, that examples from the Gospels and from the lives of Christian saints are part of the contemporary teaching of Vaiṣṇava *gurus*. Islam, however, remains an outsider and many modern philosophies are rejected as incompatible with Vaiṣṇavism.

Vaiṣṇavism's attitude to pluralism seems to know mainly two alternatives: inclusivism and exclusivism. The former allows Vaiṣṇavas to consider other religions as part of their own (more often than not as imperfect, not fully developed forms of their own religion); the latter dispenses them from the need to examine and analyze other religions (because of their fundamental errors). Inclusivism is peculiarly close to the Vaiṣṇava mentality: not only is Viṣṇu the "all-including-one", but Vaiṣṇavism itself has grown from an inclusion of many different deities under one Lord, as the great number of *avatāras* of Viṣṇu demonstrates.[33]

In such a context the theology of religious pluralism developed by B. Yadav is quite an original venture. It remains to be seen what kind of response it finds within the traditional Vaiṣṇava community. It seems to advocate an equality of—in this case—Vaiṣṇavism and Christianity.

Neither inclusivism nor exclusivism represent genuine religious pluralism. Much effort and time has gone, over the centuries, into emphasizing exclusivity, special status, difference and superiority of the in-group to which one happened to belong, and this effort has been crowned with vast success, as is evident all over the world. It will not be easy for most adherents of any such group to shift gears and to convince the members of the many small and large groups that differences can be good, that to consider oneself chosen in an exclusive sense is presumptuous and that there is no religiously valid reason to feel oneself superior to others. Pluralism, obviously, is not a term which would describe the actual situation in the world, but a program which some exponents of religion try to realize.

Notes

1. Rāmdās Gaur, *Hindutva* (Hindī) Viśvaprasād Gupta: Kāśī 1995 (samvat) pp. 640–687.

2. O.B.L. Kapoor, in a very well-documented article "The Saṁpradāya of Śrī Caitanya" in: *Indian Philosophy and Culture* (Vrindaban) Vol. XVIII/3 (Sept. 1973) points out significant differences in the doctrines of Madhva and Caitanya and suggests that the *Caitanya-saṁpradāya* is a quite separate *saṁpradaya*. Caitanya himself appears to have received his *dīkṣā* from a *saṁnyāsī* in the Śaṅkara tradition.

3. G.S. Ghurye, *Indian Sadhus*, Popular Prakashan: Bombay, 1964 pp. 160 f.

4. See the contributions to *Kalyāna: Śrī Viṣṇu-aṅgka*, Gītā-Press: Gorakhpur Śrī Kṛṣṇa Samvat 5198 (A.D. 1973).

5. *Kalyāna: Bhaktiaṅgka*, Gītā-Press: Gorakhpur Saura 2014 (A.D. 1958) pp. 12–15.

6. Ibid. pp. 28–33.

7. Ibid. pp. 447–451.

8. The account is based on personal communications as well as on some printed material such as Swāmi Bon Mahārāja's autobiographical Preface to the first Volume of his translation of Śrī Rūpa Goswāmi's *Bhakti-Rasāmrta-Sindhuh*, Institute of Oriental Philosophy: Vrindaban, U.P. 1964, pp. IX ff; several papers in Shri Tamalkrishna Das, M.A. (ed.) *Swami Bon Maharaj* (On the occasion of his Fifty-fifth Advent Anniversary) V.T. University, Vrindaban U.P. 1955 and *The Founder of Institute of Oriental Philosophy*: His Holiness Tridandi Swami Bhakti Hṛdaya Bon Baharaj, Vrindaban, U.P., n.d. The name *Bon* is the Bengali form of Vana, one of the names traditionally associated with Śaṇkara's Daśanāmi *sa mnyāsis*.

9. Swāmi Kārpatrījī Mahārāj is the author of the quite unique *Marks-vād aur Rāmrājya* (Marxism and the Kingdom of God) Gītāpress: Gorakhpur samvat 2019 pp. 885.

10. Typically, the first issue of the first volume (March 15, 1956) contains an article by Dr. R. Naga Raja Sharma: "Vaiṣṇava Theology: Its Place in the Sun" (pp. 9–17). It ends with the following para: "That is the message of Vaishnava Theology to modern mankind, erring, struggling and stumbling in intellectual and spiritual darkness: LIGHT WOULD BE SHED ONLY BY VAISHNAVA THEOLOGY. It must have its place in the Sun. H.H. Swami Bon Maharaj working under divine guidance and

inspiration is sure to preserve and protect Vaishnava-Theology in its pure, pristine, unalloyed and unsullied form."

11. Bibhuti S. Yadav, "Vaiṣṇavism on Hans Küng: A Hindu Theology of Religious Pluralism", in: *Religion and Society* (Bangalore) XXVII/2 (June 1980), pp. 32–64.

12. Śrī Mādav Āśis, "Śrī Kṛṣṇaprem Vairāgi" in *Kalyāṇa* 40/2 (February 1966) pp. 745–749.

13. *The Yoga of the Bhagavadgītā* and *The Yoga of the Kaṭhopaniṣad.*

14. Dilip Kumar Roy, *Yogi Śrī Krishnaprem*, Bharatiya Vidya Bhavan: Bombay, 1968 (with an introduction by Gertrude Emerson Sen). p. 108.

15. Ibid., pp. 153 f.

16. Ibid., pp. 104 ff.

17. Swāmijī Śrī Rāmadāsajī Mahārāja, "dharmik ektā" in *Kalyāṇa: Bhaktiāngka* (see note 5) pp. 33–34.

18. Published by the Sarva Seva Sangh, Rājghāt, Vāranāsī 1963 (several reprints).

19. E.G. *Minstrels of God* (2 vols.) Bharatiya Vidya Bhavan: Bombay 1956 (reprints); *Sufis, Mystics and Yogis of India*, ibid. 1962 (reprints), *Bhakta Mīra*, ibid. 1961.

20. Vol. 12/1 (A.D. 1937).

21. pp. 456–58.

22. M. Yamunacharya, *Rāmānuja's Teachings in His Own Words*, Bharatiya Vidya Bhavan: Bombay 1963 (reprints).

23. See the report in: *Kairos* IX/2 (1967) pp. 142–44.

24. *The Holy Lives of the Āẓhvārs: The Divine Wisdom of the Dravida Saints*, English translation of Rāmānuja's *Gītābhāṣya.*

25. 2 volumes, Sinha Publishing House, Calcutta, 1974/75.

26. Published in 1947 by Harmony House, Rajkot.

27. Published in 1953 from Harmony House as Volume 8 of the Śrī Bhāgavata Dharma Mission Series.

28. Comparing the volumes of *Kalyāṇa* from the 30s to the 70s, one finds much less material on other traditions in the later volumes as compared to the earlier ones.

29. Cf. *Hindu Viśva Viśeṣāṅka, January 1966.*

30. *op. cit.*, pp. 53 f (English Section).

31. *ibid.* pp. 53–55 (Hindī Section).

32. *Samagra Savarkar Wangmaya:* Hindu Rashtra Darshan, Maharashtra Prantik Hindusabha, Poona, 1964 Vol. VI: "Essentials of Hindutva" pp. 1–91.

33. Thus one finds in *Back go Godhead* frequent reference to Jesus Christ as Son of Kṛṣṇa.

Chapter Eight

ŚAIVA SIDDHĀNTA AND RELIGIOUS PLURALISM

K. Sivaraman

I am the servant of the servants of the devotees drawn to His feet, also of all regions and climes *beyond here* and of the vast times yet to come *beyond now* and in the past.[1]

Tēvāram 7, 39, 10.

He of the Shrine of Gangaikondacoleśvaram takes whatever forms that his worshippers visualize.

Tiruvisaippā 131,5.

The Great City is but one (and the same destination) though six (and more) are its routes (that stretch out) to reach it. Similar is with religions six (and more). 'This one (alone) is true, the other religions are false' thus cavil those that resemble but a dog that barks (without ceasing) at the yonder hill that stands (in serene indifference).

Tirumantiram, 1558.

Claim and the contest of all religious creeds, ways which bewilder the warring religions He takes, none guessing his greatness.[2]

Tāyumānavar, 1,1.

In the expression "modern Saivism", which represents the perspective from which the writer is asked to reflect on the issue of religious pluralism, Saivism will stand for *Śaiva Siddhānta*, a historically and geographically defined and even socially determined expression of Hinduism: its faith finds expression in "community", comprising a large section of Tamil-speaking "Hindus" of South India, Sri Lanka, Singapore and Malaysia, Indonesia and South Africa.[3] While a vast proportion of Hindus may be worshippers of Siva and thus entitled to be described as Saivites, the expression Saivite is used here as a proper name to refer to those who "belong to" the specific Hindu religious tradition called *Saiva Siddhanta*. Needless to say, incidentally, re-ifications like "religion", "Hinduism", "Saivisim" and the conceptualization of belongingness to what is thus re-ified are extrinsic to the vocabulary of the tradition itself. They are appropriated under the pressure of historical circumstances in imitation of Christian-Western ways of regarding religious traditions and the relation in which the adherent stands to them.

Śaiva Siddhānta, as in the case of Hinduism in its generality, has no ecclesiastical organization, no church, chapel or congregational system. Not even in the sense in which a whole society based on well-demarcated caste duties may be said to form a governing body representing a binding religious form of the kind characteristics of "orthodox" Hinduism that, one may consider, obligatory on its adherents. *Śaiva Siddhanta* does not repudiate the sacramental ordering of society under caste as the *Vīira Śaiva* tradition[4] does but instead, views, if one looks at the matter through the focus of its most significant canonical text (eleventh century), every function in a functional heirarchy from that of the priest and the king down to that of the potter and the fisherman, including even the so-called untouchable, as literally, a priesthood, and every operation as if it were a sacred rite *provided it entails love for and worship of Śivam.*[5] Śivam, literally, the Benign, is the proper name by which the Godhead is spoken of and by reference to which the tradition sect-labels itself. A medieval Saiva commentator on *Brahmasutras* cites as Mundaka upanisadic text the following:

> Even if one were a candala if he but were to utter the name sivam talk to him, dwell with him and dine with him *(tena sahasamvada, tena saha samvasa tena saha bunjīta)*.[6]

a sentiment that is repeated almost in identical words in the Tamil devotional poems that the tradition has come to acclaim as "revelation".

In this paper, however, no attempt will be made to present the case on behalf of "community proclaiming the faith". The writer has no other method of structuring the response save as part of thinking the tradition and its textual repertoire, as an "insider". For the writer the insider/outsider distinction is not one of "belonging" or "not-belonging" so much as the distinction as between one who thinks and is open to learn *from* and one who would only think and learn *about* a religious tradition. One that thus thinks a tradition does not have to be a traditionalist and the writer, in any case, does not disclaim that his perspective, even as an avowed "insider" to the problem, is shaped by an understanding which is, frankly and unapologetically, "modern". Surely it is not that only as a modern that one take seriously the truth-claims of other religions, that one becomes exercised to respond to religious pluralism. Still one cannot gainsay that there is something modern about this preoccupation coupled also, as it is, with a concomittant sense of urgency. There is today a general awareness of the historically changing and culturally specific character of particular religious traditions including one's own.[7] There is also a corresponding widespreadness, largely through increased communication and research, in the appreciation of the richness and plausibility of other religions and a consequent gain in the apperception of what religion in the singular means as shedding light on religion in the plural.

The writer hails the vantage point of modernity even while recognizing that the premises on which rests its coming to be, in principle, mark an emphatic "no" to religion as such. It compels religion, in an unprecedented way, to pass through self-understanding, self-searching and self-criticism and makes one see that if religion is viable there is not only no opposition between religion and cooperation among religions at all levels, theological, cultural, social-moral, global-spiritual,[8] but that, indeed, there is a greater need for it today for the very survival of the planet. From attention being confined to the issue of religious pluralism in terms of dialogue, we are painfully reminded of the urgency to move to attend to the issue of the very condition that makes dialogue, among other things, at all possible.

Not much needs to be said about *Śaiva Siddhānta* for purposes of this paper. Students of Hindu religious history know of it as a *bhakti* movement (cognate with *Vaisnavism*), with roots stretching into dim antiquity but which grew strong in the middle and later half of the first millenium principally in Tamil India but also in other centers of India like Karnataka and Kashmir and produced among other things, a considerable body of very eloquent devotional and doctrinal literature. The general tone of their writings is distinctively mono-theistic *(ekānta bhakti)* and their theology one of unequivocal exaltation of the reality of Godhead *(Isvarādvayam)* whether understood "dualistically" in cognate terms with man and the world or non-dualistically in terms of the One.[9] A circumstance which greatly contributed to their popularity is their liberal tone in regard to caste and class distinctions, where the emphasis was not on high birth and learning but on character and sincerity and more on devotion to God in relation to where all stood on equal footing. In these respects the literary expression of the movement differed from the genre of earlier brahminical literature, notably of the re-collected "tradition" *(smṛti)* which claimed its authority on an original "revelation" *(śruti)*.

To the extent the Saiva bhakti movement represented a continuity with the earlier stratus of Vedic Hinduism one may understand the continuity more as a case of "re-incarnation" than one that may be discerned between two stages in a single life time. This remark may be seen to be justified by the historical circumstance that the growth of Saivism at least in Tamil India at the hands of its illustrious founders was accomplished in the name of a resurgence of the "Vedic way of life" (not the same as Vedic "orthodoxy").[10] The "Tamil aglow with the *Veda*" was the description given at once to refer to the new discourse received as "revelation" ("In my word did He speak:[11] as He spoke the *Veda*) and to the new way of life in which all stood united in their love of Śivam. The newly spoken "word" succeeded, in a manner the unspoken word of the *Veda* did not quite succeed, in communicating, in building "community" between and among persons, regardless of class, caste, color and sex distinctions, Vedic theocentricism came to have an after-life coming steadily to prevail against the Śrāmanic movements which recruited large numbers of mendicant and lay followers and enlisted royal patronage, thus constituting a significant force not merely as a spiritual idea but as a social political and economic force. *Śaiva Siddhānta*, in its specific sense, almost was born as it were, in the process of this clash and confrontation between ways of life and thinking, one of which affirmed and the other denied the "givenness" of saving knowledge (*gnosis*).[12] A *sramana* is one who espouses the way of toil and rejects an eternally accomplished perfection as God or Being and its self-disclosure of which another name is *gnosis*. The founders of *Śaiva Siddhānta*, whose corpus of hymns constitute the *Veda* for the tradition demonstrated through "miracles" like bringing the dead back to life, etc., not a show of their supernormal accomplishments or —the *sramana* is no stranger to a concept of *siddhi* acquirable through austerity power /but the reality of the power ever accessible within man and gives itself to an attitude of surrender of subjectivity. "When one is rid of a sense of 'I do' and also thereby of a sense of I, then the deed (thus disowned) becomes His deed, He verily discloses himself thereby".[13]

It is not quite by accident that the earliest Western interpreters of the tradition were Christian missionaries (e.g., G. V. Pope, Schomerus).[14] To a theologically biased historian of religions like Zaehner, Saiva Siddhanta is a "crowning achievement of Indian spirituality", if for no other reason than that it approximates most closely to Christianity, ("All that is lacking is the Incarnation")[15] in refreshing contrast, as he views it, to "non-dualist Vedānta:. It is easy to exaggerate the divide between what may be termed the personalistic and trans-personalistic elements of Hindu religious thinking, especially as the two are verbalized—one may say 'theologized' in opposition to each other in later developments. *Śaiva Siddhānta* tradition understands itself not in opposition to Vedanta but as indeed representing for the discerning the heart and soul, the cream and quintessence of Vedānta and claims to provide the indepth answers to the question of Vedānta as well. The experiential dimension embodied in the scriptures and sought to be uncovered by these interpreted traditions—Vedānta and Siddhanta, provides witness to the distinction between the two experiences that the author of one of the canonical Saiva works verbalizes respectively, as "*becoming* Oneself" and as simply "letting *be* of oneself",[16] and the built-in creative tension in their self-articulation.

The Christian perception of *Śaiva Siddhānta* as an atypical form of Hinduism, nevertheless, is not entirely unfounded. Much has been written about how incompatible the conceptualization "Hinduism: is with the religious outlook of the Hindus themselves. The mass of phenomena sheltered under the term is, on Hindu self-understanding (*pace*, the Neo-Hindu advocate) not a unity, nor indeed does it aspire to be a unity deserving the label of a proper name. It is well-known that Hindus, despite impression to the contrary, glorify in diversity and celebrate a plurality of religious forms. The characteristic Hindu affirmation is that truth though one has many aspects, as many as there are persons to perceive it. This may seem banal to a creedal religionist like the Christian to whom there is one Christianity, no matter how diversified and truncated it is in actual practice. How to be a Christian is a unifying concern that overrides schism and sectarian allegiances and surfaces, as it does in recent times, in the form of a concern for ecumenism.

In this respect the tradition of *Śaiva Siddhānta* may be seen to resemble Christianity. Unlike "Hinduism", the name *Śaiva Siddhānta* is not the one given by others to identify. Both as a term and as a concept it figures in the vocabulary of the classical tradition. Not only was it used self-consciously as a term of self-reference, but it was significantly employed to define its position in relation to other religions. The distinctness, the self-conscious reality of a religious community seemed to have been present almost from the moment of its inception. When it originated as a movement, it coincided in time and content, however, with the establishment and spread, anachronistically, though it may seem, of a strong Tamil national feeling and with the cultural expression of this fact. Buddhism and Jainism were regarded as "outer" or alien to its self-identity and to the national self-identificaton of the Tamil speaking "Hindus", Tamil here being veiwed as sacred language, and interestingly enough, not so much as theological "heresies" to be condemned.

In the remaining pages an attempt will be made briefly to evoke the new sensitivity to the problem of religious pluralism that is tacitly present in the heart of this important strand of spirituality which is a typical and incertain interesting ways also an atypical expression of the spirit of Hinduism[17] *Śaiva Siddhānta* is "philosophy" in the precise sense in which one may use the term in the context of higher Indian philosophy, not meaning a closed system where opposites are mutually exclusive and things are either so or not so irrespective of the level or point of view from which one perceives them. Very much as in the case of Vedanta it is philosophy in the sense of a hermeneutic of the revealed word and a consistent doctrine which is also at once (not an ancillary but) itself a discipline of self-realization (*ātma lābham*). But unlike Vedanta in its generalized and abstract form, it is not 'metaphysics' but religion primarily and self-consciously. If Vedanta is religion, it is so in an inverted sense.

Metaphysical knowledge is concerned only with universal possibility that can be realized at all times and at no time in particular. Possibilities of concrete manifestation are only admitted in a metaphysical philosophy in the sense that they are not apriori excluded. For *Śaiva Siddhānta* in its primordial sense (as the label for Saivāgama), Ultimate Truth is surely a universal possibility but it cannot exist unless it is incarnated or rather it "incarnates" itself in specific forms here or there, now or then expressed mythically symbolizing history and geography. (Truth's incarnation, incidentally, is interpreted in Saivism not in a cosmological setting as in Vaiṣnaivism but in the context of salvific knowledge (gnosis) descending from above (*āgama*), not as incarnation literally (*avatāra*) in a public sense with reference to a given age or aeon,[19] but as a free manifestation (*āvirbhāva*), private, local and episodic of which there can only be a hagiological account. Perhaps it is too strong an expression when it is said that "it cannot exist". One may emend it to mean that it cannot exist in a significant way.

The difference, nevertheless, are not divergences or deviations so that each may view the other as a "heresy". They are significant distinctions—significant as illuminating the sense or purport that lies obscured when viewed by themselves. The ultimate reality of metaphysics or religion eventually is supreme identity in which the opposition of all opposites, the duality of the "two" becomes resolved, where I and you do not remain "over against" each other. Vedanta and brahmanical Hinduism express the metaphysical (or the sapiential) and the cosmological aspect of the doctrine and Saivism the operative and the existential dimensions of the tradition.

Consistent with its "existential" orientation in which mediation, descent or immanence becomes the very essence of the Highest (*Śakti*, the creative Logos, the very apotheosis of Gnosis is the *dharma*, of which Siva, the Transcendent *Sat* itself is the *dharmin*)[20] *Śaiva Siddhānta* exhibits an understanding of the Truth of upanisadic Hinduism percisely as truth but also as wed to love and faith. Grace, which in the words of an early Tamil text is the child begotten of love, is the very interior dimension of truth and is implicitly present in every authentic claim to "true conclusion" in the name of religion. "However men approach me even so do I come I with my consort who is but my very side:[21]

is the important refrain of the texts, not only implying that the deity "chosen" *(ista)* in any cultic path is only an operative presencing of the One to receive and reward the act of invokation in the very mode of its "how", but also the good aimed at as the goal of every religious endeavor, the "reality" sought to be realized as a state of being. Men standing at different points on the path are all *intrinsically* partaking in the Highest.[22]

In claiming its label as a proper name *(siddhāgṅta)*, parodoxically, rests upon its acknowledging of the presence of these elements in all "religious" orientations, even those describable as atheistic, agnostic, anti-theistic, as well as the theistic of all shades.[23] All partake of the illumination from one Spiritual Sun and its radiance, through minds in *incommensurably* different degrees of spiritual maturity apprehending reality *differently*. The claim to ultimacy and estimation of positions at variance with one's own as non-ultimate is a parodoxical expression of the very essence of religion.

Every religious tradition which believes that in its revelation the ultimate Truth is known is, in a sense, an exclusive and enclosed world representing a whole sphere of life and meaning, isolated and, therefore, almost a kind of infinity. But in another, profounder sense, the one which directly concerns the issue of religious pluralism, isolated though religious traditions stand, they have a positive relation to each other. Each tries to integrate the other. The perspectives and points of view of those that say "yea" and of those that demur and say "nay" may appear hopelessly incommensurable and yet the "believer's" position in relation to the "unbeliever" is one of inclusion. It overflows and integrates it. This is pre-eminently the case with any authentic faith.

The world of a man of light overflows in all directions and integrates the world of blindmen. The story of the blindmen and the elephant is one of the recurring themes of the religio-philosophical traditions of India, and is applied in a hundred ways. Buddha narrates the parable, how several blindmen commissioned to describe an elephant responded by saying that the elephant was a pillar, a wall, a snake or a rope. The interpretation of the parable, one can only guess, from the words with which Buddha closes: "Just so are these sectarians who are wanderers, blind unseeing, knowing not the truth but maintaining it is thus and thus."[24] One can see here an attitude to religious pluralism based on a pronounced anti-theological, anti-metaphysical stand. There is an implicit concern for the state of ignorance and the attachment that it generates to one's view about reality to the extent of equating it with the real itself, but there is no suggestion of toleration even as a modest posture of enduring or putting up with (which the term etymologically suggests.)

The Jaina religious tradition, which almost seems to have a patent on this parable, uses it in support of what may be described as a willful "non-unequivocal" orientation to knowledge and reality purporting to relativize all standpoints of doctrine that religious traditions represent as a kind of exercise of intellectual or spiritual non-violence *(anekāntavāda)*. There is here a manifest "toleration" of pluralism very much in the spirit of science today: all theories are partly true; diverse modes of existence are possessed by a thing at one time or other and statements can be asserted of anything in some way or other. Combined with this is also a concern for the divisive character that seems to be almost built into religions and for which the true answer is "syncretism", replacing "and" for "either-or" of dogmatism.[25]

The *Śaiva Siddhānta* understanding and use of this parable consistent with its acknowledgement of ultimate reality as the condition which renders possible the being and the knowing of what is, is more positive and less positivistic. The real elephant can be known only by seeing it and so one who is "blind" simply does not know even if he touches all its parts. The purposes of this parable in Buddha's meta-physical agnosticism and in Jaina "non-absolutism" are only *prima facie* acceptable to the siddhantin who understands them in effect to mean that our cognitive concern is not with ultimate reality but rather with the empirical world and understanding its structures. When the blind men gain their sight, there is "recognition" of the elephant at least in a negative sense as "what was not previously unexperienced" *(nānānubhūtam)*.[26] It is in this sense it may be said that for a man of sight his world overflows and integrates the world of the blind. "Recognition" which dawns when the "dogmatic" scales of one's eye falls (or to change the metaphor, when one wakes up from his dogmatic slumber), should enhance one's sensitivity to religious pluralism, making it possible to view in a new light one's own religious tradition as well as the religion of the other on other's own term of incommunicable otherness.

The Saiva tradition, in the eloquent opening words of its principal text, describes Godhead *(Śivam)* as the very substance of the respective insights revealed to the six kinds of religion (which spanned the entire religious landscape of the times).[27]

Keeping in mind what was acknowledged at the outset as distinctive of any modern responses to religious truth and pluralism in a context where one is forced to be aware of the historically changing character of particular religious traditions, one's own as well as "others", the writer wants to say in conclusion that the modern Saivite stands under special obligation to encounter afresh the "six" modern counterparts of the Six Religions of his classical past. Buddhism in its post Indian and specially Sri Lankan forms, Jainism in the light of its new global resurgence as a force for peace, Judaism, Christianity and Islam as worlds in themselves with their own centers axis and structure representing ways of thinking and feeling that he simply cannot assimilate into his own, and finally and also most inescapably, the "religion" that threatens in its global form to displace all religions, not by aggrandisement and imperialism, but by voluntary acceptance, viz., modernity itself and its offshoot of secularity or secularism. The example of past history may not always be helpful and may sometimes even hinder one's coming to terms with what is new in this endeavor. The challenge of pluralism in the modern world to religious traditions, and this is posed with a particular urgency by the demand of a secular substitition of religion, is how they overcome their built-in divisive character and transcend their limited loyalties in favor of a recognition of religious faith as a global human characteristic which makes man more truly human and therefore, also, divine.

For, in the final analysis, what else is true religious faith other than attempts at being truly human? Imitating the words of Professor Wilfred Cantwell Smith,[28] one may say that "a person is not a human being and then also a Hindu (or a Saivite Hindu), but, One is a human being by being a Hindu (or a Saivite Hindu)".

So much for a personal response as a "modern" and as a "Saivite" to the issue of religious pluralism. As it was stated earlier, the writer has no other method of effectively representing the case on behalf of what may be called modern Saivism save to interiorize it and respond in the first person. In all his experiences as participant in dialogue with Western religions, whether "unilaterally" as with Christianity, Christian life and thought or "multi-laterally" taking his place in the midst of representatives of multiple world religious traditions,[29] he was doing nothing else than to respond to the very issue of there being a pluralism of religions from a position or point of view determined by his involvement and identification with and some in-depth awareness (of which he can claim, by virtue of study and learning, a modest share), of the tradition of *Śaiva Siddhānta*.

Dialogue for him is not simply a matter of discovering what is already there, although in a sense it is true and there perhaps can be no other truly valid way of ascertaining the ultimately true. However, what is meant in the context of a "dialogue between religions" is that it is not an issue resolvable by appeal to more incisive scholarship but one pertaining to the creative dimension of thought and sensitivity. Dialogue between religions, consequently, should, in a spirit typical of the age in which religions are called upon to respond to multi-religionism, involve openness to face criticism directed against one's own religious basis, but also acknowledgement of a certain unforeseeableness of the outcome, whether the two in a dialogue will fertilize each other resulting in reciprocal transformation (as zealous futurists dream) or rather gain in sharper self-definition that earlier did not allow a scope to emerge in sharpness before confrontation with the "other" (the vision and hope of progressive conservatists). There may be a sharper "self-definition" by a growing recognition of the immense difference between them—one's own and the "other"—as rooted in a two-foldness of awareness and involvement as Western, i.e., Hellenic Judaeo-Christian and as Eastern, i.e., Hindu, Buddhist and Jaina. Within each complex again there may be differences in respect of particular religious traditions themselves. In the case of the "Eastern", for example, are differences between *Śaiva Siddhānta* and other Hindu or Indian religious forms, expressed, humanly speaking almost as "perennial alternatives" in respect of truth. To become aware of differences between religions as entailing different orientations of spirit can also prove a cohesive instead of a divisive force. To become really alive to the reality of pluralism can also mean, no less than a liberal syncretism, recognizing creatively the absolute common bond between them, paradoxical though it may sound.[30]

Just to set the record straight to merit the description of Response to Religious Pluralism by modern Saivism, two modern Saivite's accounts are presented here, one who wrote in a global setting in the beginning of this century and the other a contemporary *Śaiva Siddhāntin* who is also a great academic scholar and has most extensively written on the meaning of the tradition for the modern man.

Sir Ponnambalam Ramanthan, a Sri Lankan Tamil who played a decisive role in the public life of the nation as the Attorney-

General, "propagated" (in the words of H. W. Schomerus, the Lutheran Missionary from Germany who like G. U. Pope lived and worked in South India and published his *Der caiva Siddhanta* in 1912) *Śaiva Siddhānta* in the United States and published commentaries on the gosepl of St. Mathew and St. John and one the Psalms based on the standpoint of *Śaiva Siddhānta*.[31] Moreover he presents *Śaiva Siddhānta* in his book *The Culture of the Soul among Western Nations*.[32] As to why he chose to interpret the Christian Gosepls, the answer is provided in a section of the last-mentioned work, captioned "The True Missionary Spirit". He conceived his role as a *Śaiva Siddhāntin* in effect to be that of a missionary, but in a reverse gear, if one may use that expression. There is only one God to preach and his own role was to make God intelligible to each religionist "by means of the very religion in which he was born and bred". An Australian disciple who came to study with him, and whom he exhorted to begin with the study of the Bible, said, "What is there in the Bible? I have given that up many years ago. I want something better". Ramanthan's reply was, one may say the true spirit of *Saiva Siddhanta* at least as he perceived it: "If you know your Bible well you would not want much more. . . . After you have learned something of it we shall see whether you still think 'there is nothing in it'."[33] After reading the Gosepls of St. Mathew and St. John with Ramanathan, it is reported, all her doubts were removed and she became an ardent preacher of the Gosepls in Australia.[34]

Of Ramanthan's writings his pamphlet bearing the title *The Mystery of Godlinness* stands out as a testament of experience of the "sanctified in Spirit". The editor of the now deceased *Śaiva Siddhānta* Journal, *Siddhānta Dipika* ("The Light of Truth"), who published this as an article in the issue dated May 1903 observed: "The expression 'Mystery of Godliness' which occurs in St. Paul's First Epistle to Timothy, Chap. 3, v. 16, corresponds to our term *Siva Rahasyam*", the paper carries as its title quote citations from Tiruvacakam, Mathew's Gosepl, Epistles, Psalms and First Corinthians and discourses on how modern material science had failed to solve the fundamental problem of life and refers to the "Masters of Spiritual Science":

> In India the masters of Science are called *jnanis* or men of Light or Wisdom, and the Light, Wisdom or knowledge they possess is *jnanam*. Other men are not of the Light. Being attached to the false shows and pleasures of the world they are *ajanis*, unwiseman,

> men in darkness whose knowledge is foolishness because it makes them. . . . mistake the world for the goal to which it is the appointed way. . . . Europeans in India know something of the exoteric side or spiritual India as exemplified in the objective worship carried on in the temples but also nothing of its esoteric side. . . . The earnest seekers who fail to find satisfaction in the objective method, soon discover that the exoteric system, which no longer appeals to them, is really intended as a stepping stone to the esoteric and that the key of the latter is in the hands of the *jnana*-guru or Teacher of Godly Wisdom. Those thirsting for the sanctification of the Spirit leave their home in quest of him, crying to him now, as in the days of yore 'thou art my way, thou art my way'. (quoting Maitrayana Brahmana Upanisad)
>
> Of the teachers, the *jnana* guru is acknowledged to be the greatest. Unlike the *vidya* guru who imparts knowledge on any given secular subject, unlike the *samaya* guru who imparts knowledge on any given religion, the *jnana* guru is concerned with the very foundations of knowledge, with truth eternal, unchangeable. He is therefore, a teacher of teachers, a guru in the real sense of the term and hence called a *jagat* guru or *Loka* guru, a Preceptor or Light of the World.[35]

Ramanathan elucidates these ideas in a language which is clearly Christian with due awareness based as it is on his conviction of the *philosophia perrenis* of the availability of sanctified spirituality in the name of Christianity or Hinduism. In the above context for example, talking of guru as the "light", he cites "our God is a consuming *fire:* Hebrew, XII, 49, "god is Light", John 1,5. "I am come to send *fire* on earth: Luke XII, 49. "I have overcome the world", John XVI, 33. "I am the Light of the World", John IX, 6.[36]

G. V. Pope, it is reported, brought this pamphlet to the notice of Dean Inge, who quotes Ramanthan in his book on *Christian Mysticism* with the prefatory remarks "I shall take the liberty of quoting a few sentences from a pamphlet written by a native judge *(sic)* who I believe is still living. His object is to explain and command to Western readers the mystical philosophy of his own country."[37] The quotation that follows these remarks bears to be repeated for our purposes, as it shows how a *Śaiva Siddhāntin* could interiorize Christian terms and concepts in verbalizing the basic principles of *Śiava Siddhānta* with an implicit avowal of a perennial tradition of sanctification of spirit behind the phenomenon of a plurality of religions:

> He who is perfect rest rises from the body and attains the highest light, comes forth in his own proper form. This is the immortal soul. The ascent is by the ladder of one's thoughts. To know God, one must first know one's own Spirit in its purity, unspotted by thought. The soul is hidden behind the veil of thought, and only when thought is worn off, becomes visible to itself. This stage is called knowledge of the soul. This is the end of progress; differentiation between self and others had ceased. All the world of thought and senses is melted into an ocean without waves or current. This dissolution of the world is also known as the death of the sinful or worldly 'I', which veils the true Ego. Then the formless Being of the Deity is seen in the regions of pure consciousness beyond the veil of thought. Consciousness is wholly distinct from thought and senses; it knows them; they do not know it. The only proof is an appeal to spiritual experience.

Dr. V. A. Devasenapathi is the other exemplar whose writings typify the approach of what may be called "modern Saivism" to the question of Religious Pluralism. He has been the editor of *Śaiva Siddhānta* a quarterly journal devoted to the exposition of Siddhānta Philosophy, Religion, Literature and Comparative Understanding, in vogue now for some two decades and published as the official organ of *Śaiva Siddhānta Mahāsamājam* (recently reristened as *Śaiva Siddhānta Perumaṉṟam*, meaning the Great Forum of *Śaiva Siddhānta*). Among other writings, the one which concerns us is a serial of articles that he wrote under the caption: Hinduism and other Religions: (Vol. XIII, Nos. 3 & 4, Vol. XIV, No. 1). Turning to the issue of features of other religions which Hinduism (by which the author means *Śaiva Siddhānta*) may find it difficult to accommodate or assimilate, Devasenapathy observes: "Because Hinduism welcomes truths from all sides, the Hindu may take for granted that he understands all of them in their true significance." He then proceeds to ask, "The concept of a suffering God, the doctrine of vicarious suffering, the passion and death of Jesus Christ—do these mean to the Hindu exactly what they mean to the Christian?" In order to get a true insight into the matter is the only way of coming close to the heart of Christianity and so he cites references to the idea of a suffering God in Hinduism. Of these, the one relevant to *Śaiva Siddhānta* needs to be underlined.

Citing the farthest expression of a suffering God, he proceeds to refer to the story of the blue-throated Siva, which has appealed to the hearts of the devotees down the ages. Sambandar, the seventh century Saiva saint "prays to Siva for the remission of the Karma of his followers, proclaiming his faith at the end of each verse of a decade that karma will not prevail against the followers of the blue-throated Siva. The lovely blue-throat of Siva is a perpetual reminder to His devotees that he would take all evil to Himself to save others."[38]

Devasenapathy concedes that the complete expression of the truth that is adumberated by the mythical image is to be found in Christianity. He, however, asks, "Could it be said that a Hindu (Saivite), who not only overcomes all sense of 'I' and 'mine', but also virtually dies while still living to become a channel of God's grace, participates in the Christian experience? Dying for the Hindu is not merely physical but also spiritual. To act in accordance with His will and become a channel of His Grace is to escape spiritual death and to become spiritually alive."[39]

Referring to the Christian claim that in Jesus Christ there is a historical manifestation of God, the Hindu *avataras* and the *bodhisattvas* being mythological and that this historical manifestation is "complete and final", Devasenapathy very modestly raises some questions: "Not that the Hindu doubts the historicity of Jesus Christ; his difficulty would be about the nature of history—especially when it is spiritual history. Could we gauge God's manifestations with our narrow measures of human history? Is the historical time-scale adequate to measure eternity? Again with the profoundest gratitude for the blessing, not only Christians but all seekers of God have in the life and teachings of Jesus Christ; a Hindu wonders whether God's revelation could be limited to one manifestation for all time?[40]

Devasenapathy then turns to Islam and seeks to win a positive meaning of Islam's opposition to idolatry. He refers to Hindu reform movements of the nineteenth century which denounced idolatry and cites the verse of a *siddha* (siva vakkiar): "Treating a (piece of) stone that is planted (somewhere) as God, adorning it with a few flowers and going round it, what are the *mantras* that you repeat by muttering a few words? Can this planted stone speak when the lord is within you? Does the pot know the taste of what is cooked in it?[41] Devasenapathy is aware of the *Śaiva Siddhānta* sense of the so-called "idols" as objects of worship: they embody the living presence of God. Idols have their value alike to persons of simple faith as well as to persons who have awakened to the presence of God. Nevertheless, in encountering the iconoclasm of Islam, the Hindu, says Devasenapathy, "could feel stimulated to direct his worship toward the Supreme Being and not allow it to become a child's play with toys or a meaningless and crude ritual".[42]

Referring to Islam's prayer "there is no God but God", Devasenapathy draws our attention to Professor Wilfred Cantwell Smith. Interpreting the first part of the Muslim prayer in a manner which may not quite meet with the official sanction of Islam, Smith says that it may not be taken to repudiate "other" Gods, but rather it stands for an ascent and growth in one's own faith from a stage of formal acceptance through a stage of doubt and denial to final recovery and stabilization of that faith, by God's grace. Devasenapathy interprets it as "a call for a vertical ascent in one's own faith, and not a horizontal repudiation of other faiths" and considers such interpretation of help to the Hindu to approach Islam and appropriate its teachings for his own benefit.

In conclusion Devasenapathy cites the celebrated prayer of a Saiva saint to God, which he would interpret to include in its scope the devotees of all faiths: "Grace dwells in you; and within Grace you live. If both of you live within me, your servant ever give me Grace to abide amidst your devotees."[43]

Notes

1. The line from the *Tevaram* "Sacred Song" of St. Sundarar (9th century) "I am the servant even of the servants from beyond, of those that abideth at the Feet". The expression "from beyond" is interpreted in *Periyapurāṇam* (11th century) to mean both from beyond the Tamil speaking terrain and also from beyond the times of the community of "servant-saints" praised in the poem, i.e., both before and after the times: '*tamil valangum nāttukkappāl. . . . tiruttondat tokaiyir kūṇm naṟṟondar kālattu mannum pinnum*', V. 4174.

2. The translation is of Isac Tambyah from his *Psalms of a Śaiva Saint*, London, Luzac & Co., 1925.

3. For *Śaiva Siddhānta* in the West, see the most recent article K. Gnanasooriyan, *Hinduism in Europe and North America, with special references to Śaiva Siddhānta in the West today* in *Śaiva Siddhānta Perumanṟam Muttuvilā malar*, ed., by P. Tirujnanasambandan, Madras, 1986.

4. *Vīraśaivism* (or *Lingāyatism*) is the name of the medieval religious movement, (the meaning of the name indicative of its "protestant" character), predominantly of the Kannada speaking parts of South India. For an account of the Lingayats as a community, as yet a caste-sect today while also originating as protestors against caste, see William Mccormack, *On Lingayat culture* in A. K. Ramanujan, *Speaking of Siva*, Penguin Classics, 1973, p. 175 ff.

5. Kamil Zvelebil describes the message of *Periyapurāaṇam* thus: "However poor, insignificant and helpless a human being may be nothing can prevent him from having an ideal. The meanest of the mean can rise to the highest spiritual level—in the life of devotion and love", *The Smile of Murugan*; on Tamil Literature of South India, Leiden, E.J. Brill, 1973, p. 187.

6. Srikaṇtha's *Bhāṣya on Brahma Sutra* 4, 1, 16. The cited *Mundaka* text is, however, missing in the printed editions of the Upanisadic text.

7. Wilfred Cantwell Smith, *Faith and Belief*, Princeton, New Jersey, 1979, p. 169, ". . . the understanding and explication for our day must be more comparitivist and historical than have served earlier times".

8. As an example at the global-spiritual level may be mentioned *World Spirituality*, An Encyclopedic History of the Religious Quest, a multi-volume series presenting the spiritual wisdom of the human race in its historical unfolding from pre-historic times, through the great religions to the meeting of traditions at the present, sponsored by the Crossroad Publishing Company, New York. The present writer is editor of the two volumes on the Spirituality of India, of the series.

9. Saivism knits together regions as far away from each other as Kashmir and South India and within South India the north-western region of Karnataka and Tamil South and Saiva "theology", likewise, ranges between the monism of the *Trika* school and of the *Vīrasaivism* which espouses the unity of *linga* "God" and *anga* "human" on the one side to a dualistically ontic "non-dualism" of *Śaiva Siddhānta* whose approach to "Śivam" is through enuniciation of the three irreducible modes of *pati, paśu* and *pāśam*. (Cf. *Śivañānacittiyār supakkam*, 8, 22.0)

10. The author of *Periyapurāṇam* cites as first among the reasons for the advent of the phenomenon of the child saint of *Saiva Siddhanta*—*Ñānacampanthar*, the "rekindled spreading of the Vedic way"—*vedaneṛi ta ḷaittonga* (V. 1604). The expression 'Vedaneri' can be translated more literally, if also more significantly, as 'the way of the Veda', where the 'of' may be understood as objective genitive, i.e. appositional.

11. '*enaturai tanaturaiyāka*' is the recurring refrain of Campanthar's Ilambayankottur decad *Campanthar Tevaram*, 1, 76.

12. *Campanthar*, the aforementioned Saiva Saint who is credited by posterity with the role as the first of the four "preceptor-founders" of Saivism, which about the same time acquired its proper name as *Śaiva Siddhānta*, is also called *nānacampanthar*, "one imbued with gnosis" named thus over the incident of his being breast-fed into a "sacred" gnosis which "mediatatively thinks but the Feet of Sivam" (*Periyapuranam*, V. 1673).

13. *Tiruvundiaār*, b.

14. G. V. Pope's translation of *Tiruvacakam* around the turn of this century printed at Oxford, is well-known. The University of Madras has brought out in recent decades two subsequent reprints. H. W. Schomerus not only published German translations of *Tiruvacakam* (1923) of *Periyapuranam* and *Tiruvatavurpuranam* (1925), but also the most comprehensive account of *Śaiva Siddhānta* based on Meykanda Sastra, *Der Caiva-Siddhānta, eine Mystik Indiens* (1912). To these must, of course, be added his book posthumously published in 1981: Arunanti's *Sivajnana Siddhiar* both *Supkkam* and *Parapakkam*, translation into German with commentary. For a detailed account of the last mentioned work, vide Luitgard Soni, *Toward an Appreciation of H. W. Schomerus with reference to his translation and Commentary of Arunanti's Sivanana Siddhiyar* in *Śaiva Siddhānta Perumanram Muttavila malar, op. cit.*

15. R. C. Zaehner, *Concordant Discord*, Oxford, 1970, p. 164.

16. *Tirumantiram*, 2372: '*tānāna vedāṅtam tānennum cittāṅtam.*'

17. Even in its atypical form the tradition, one may say, typifies certain trends of classical Hinduism, where the "particularist" strand alternates with the "universalist", where polymorphism of religious life is viewed with positive eyes along with the emphasis on unity. See Wilfred Cantwell Smith, *op. cit.*, p. 215.

18. The *Kāmika* toward the close of its *Tantrāvatārapatala* mentions *Śaiva Siddhānta* to refer to the corpus of twenty-eight Saivagamas beginning with itself. *Tantrāloka* 1, 35 refers to the "ten plus eighteen of the Agamas" and his commentator Jayaratha lists many of them and describes them as *Śiddhānta* and those accepting their authority as Śaiddhāntika.

19. *Bhagavat Gītā* 4–5, 6, 7.

20. K. Sivaraman, *Saivism in Philosophical Perspective*, Motilal Sanarsidass, Delhi, 1973, p. 519.

21. *Śivanānacittiyār*, Supakkam 2, 25.

22. Two illustrations from *Periyapuranam* accounts may be given in support. Saint Appar, after being reclaimed by the call to become a

devotee of Siva, sings refering to his days as a Jaina follower that "he never indeed ever forgot 'Thy name' in anything that his tongue ever uttered," that "he never ever overlooked offering of worship with flowers, water and sandal smoke" (in any rite that he ever performed) and that "he never ever forgot 'Thee' (in any meditation) whether in weal or woe" (*Tevaram*, 4.1.2). Likewise, Sākkiyar. a devout Buddhist "worships the *linga* form of Sivam by pelting rocks at it in apparent display of sacrilege, but was hallowed as a sanctified saint (*Periyapuranam*, 7, 1–18). Cf. *Periyapuranam*, condensed English version by G. Vanmikanthan, Sri Ramkrishna Mutt, Madras, 1985. pp. 279–280 and 512–513.

23. Cf. *Sūta Samhita*, 4, 2–6.

24. See *Buddhist Parables*, trans. from original Pali, by E. W. Barlingam, Yale University Press, New Haven, 1922, p. 75.

25. Cf. Y. J. Padmarajiah, *Jaina Theories of Knowledge and Reality*, Jaina Sahitya vikas Mandala, Bombay, 1963, Reprinted Motilal Banarsidass, Delhi, 1985.

26. The concept of a Supreme nature of the "self" as 'what was *not* unrealized before' (*na na anubhūtam)* is uniquely saivite as glimpsed and verbalized by Abhinavagupta in the opening section of his *Īśvara Pratyabhijna Vimarśini*, in in sight which the writer finds to be the operative factor also in the case of *Śaiva Siddhānta* understanding of religious pluralism. See his *Saivism in Philosophical Perspective, op. cit.*, p. 12f.

27. '*aṛuvakaiccamayattōrkkum avvavar poruḷāi*', *Śivñānacittiyār* Supakkam, 2.

28. *Faith and Belief, op. cit.*, p. 138.

29. Cf. *Study Encounter*, 1974, No. 3, World Council of Churches, Geneva, for papers presented at the Multi-lateral Dialogue held at Colombo, Sri Lanka in April 1974.

30. These remarks are offered in strictest personal capacity and may not quite reflect the standard self-understanding of the tradition. Like the generality of Hinduism, Śaiva Siddhānta affirms its faith in the 'essential unity of all religions' but not without also affirming its vantage point as intrinsically the unique and all-comprehensive and all religions deriving their intelligibility and plausibility from that perspective.

31. For the account and citations the writer draws solely from S. Ambikaipakan, *The Contribution of Sir Ponnambalam Ramanathan to the Study of Comparative Religion*, in *Śaiva Siddhānta*, Vol. XI, No. 1, April 1976.

32. *The Culture of the Soul Among Western Nations*, G. P. Putnam's and Sons, Newark and London. 1906.

33. *Śaiva Siddhānta*, Vol. XI, No. 1.

34. Ramanathan's reply is typically 'Hindu'. The following conversation between the late Chandraesekkara Bharati Swami of Sringeri *Pitha* and an American tourist in *Dialogue with the Guru: A record of talks of with the Sankaracharya*, ed., by R. Krishnaswami Aiyar, Chetana Publications, Bombay, 1938, is similar. To the tourist who expressed dissatisfaction with his Christianity,

> Indeed, it is unfortunate, was the reply, "but tell me honestly whether you have given it a real chance. Have you fully understood the religion of Christ and lived according to it? Have you been a true Christian and yet found the religion wanting?"
>
> "I am afraid I cannot say that, sir."
>
> "Then we advise you to go and be a true Christian first, live truly by the word of the Lord, and if even then you feel unfulfilled, it will be time to consider what should be done."
>
> To put the puzzled American at his ease the sage explained:
>
> "It is no freak that you were born a Christian. God ordained it that way because by the *samskara* acquired through your actions *(karma)* in previous births your soul has taken a pattern which will find its richest fulfilment in the Christian way of life. Therefore your salvation lies there and not in some other religion. What you must change is not your faith but your life," "Then, Sir," exclaimed the American, beaming with exhilaration, "your religion consists in making a Christian a better Christian, a Muslim a better Muslim and a Buddhist a better Buddhist. This day I have discovered yet another grand awpect of Hinduism, and I bow to you for having shown me this. Thank you, indeed."

35. Inge, W.R., *Christian Mysticism*, Methuen and Co. Ltd., 4th edition, 1918. pp. 112–113.

36. *Ibid.*

37. Cf. also his more recent *Keynote Address Delivered at the First International Seminar on Śaiva Siddhānta*, published in *Śaiva Siddhānta*, Vol. XIX, No. 2, November 1984.

38. Citations are from the article "Hinduism and Other Religions: in *Śiava Siddhānta*, Vols. XIII and XIV.

39. *Ibid.*

40. *Ibid.*

41. *Ibid.*

42. *Ibid.*

43. *Tiruvacakam*, 21, 1.

Chapter Nine

INDIA'S PHILOSOPHICAL RESPONSE TO RELIGIOUS PLURALISM

J.G. Arapura

Preface

Among the Indian responses to the challenging situation of religious pluralism—a response always implies a prior challenge or a question—we include the philosophical one, which is going to be considered in this essay. We will restrict ourselves to what comes under the name of academic philosophy. Further, our interest is confined to those segments of Indian philosophy (or philosophy in India) that respond to challenging historical situations, especially in our context here, those in the religious area. These we designate here by the caption "modern Indian philosophy". This "modern" Indian philosophy, while incontestibly Indian, in that the traditional is still its basis, is also a product of some constructive interactions with the powerful Western outlook and ideas.

One of the consequences of such interaction is the reappearance of even old phenomena in a new light, as matters of proper philosophical interest and even of some urgency. Forms of religious diversity were there in India throughout the ages. But the same phenomenon seen in the new light, especially with the advent of religions of foreign origin, seems to define certain challenges to religious and philosophical thought as never before in the past.

In the Indian tradition, religion had naturally been the core of the philosophical enterprises. But there was always a harmonious correspondence between a given religion and its philosophy, even when the latter entailed more than one system. It is entirely consistent with that fact that philosophy in India never found any reason to go beyond its call, thereby to reflect on the religions (in the plural), even when the ontological and other concepts within different religions were dealt with to the end chiefly, though, of proving the truth of some pre-established doctrine *(siddhānta)* or other. Modernity, or rather that aspect of it which is pertinent here, is changing it somewhat, encouraging the establishment of the concept of philosophy as more broad in base and more even-handedly open towards all members of any identifiable common phenomenon, especially the one closely linked with philosophy, namely, religion. It has very definite scientific and objectivist overtones, which, however, in the Indian world have become, as would be expected, considerably mixed with mystical, or "idealist" perceptions. These perceptions also tended to work in another direction, that is to say, of obliterating the particularities of the members of a group of religions by singling out some probably common idealist or absolutist ground, say, for example, between Vedānta and Mādhyamika Buddhism. This is especially the case in the writings of the most influential of modern Indian academic philosophers, i.e., S. Radhakrishnan, and of many others who have followed his lead. Nevertheless, there is a minority of other acute thinkers who, though idealist and absolutist themselves, seem to approach differences among philosophical systems as well as among their supporting religions in a somewhat more dialectical, less integrative way. In the following pages we shall attempt to analyze some of these. However, the impression must not be gained that tackling the pluralistic problem posed by the diversity of religions has been by any means a dominant interest in the thinking of these philosophers. On the contrary, they thought about a whole range of things which are proper to philosophers, among which, however, the pluralistic problem too finds a place, wrapped as it often is, within related metaphysical formulations.

The entry of the Western outlook and ideas, however partially assimilated, and the efforts to reformulate traditional Indian perceptions under their impact will be among our foci. We will organize the body of the essay under the following headings: the conditions and characteristics of the response in general; some specific responses.

Conditions and Characteristics of the Response in General

The Secularist Context

Since the introduction of English education, Western ideas made some inroads into India and Western intellectual situations were also transplanted to an extent. [And India was the one Eastern country that was most extensively exposed to the Western influences, and in depth.] In a significant way, the Western impact upon India—and upon the non-Western world as a whole—was made in the reverse order from the way in which developments took place in the West: the fruits first and then, gradually, the causes. However, even among the fruits there are some that are more closely dependent upon the causes than others, and accordingly, their transplantation would require that the soil has some latent capacities for naturalizing the causes which originally produced the fruits.

One of the fruits we have in our mind is the secular outlook; its causes are metaphysical, that is, those that enabled the separation of philosophy from religion, which we know to have taken place in the modern era in the West. This outlook must be defined as that which does not in principle distinguish between the religious and the non-religious, and by extension, between one religion and another, although it is not by any means anti-religious. Secularism itself is not a philosophical view of reality, although a close cousin, humanism, is.

Secularism which was spawned on the idea of freedom *from* religion has, no doubt, also an implication of a positive nature for the freedom *to be* religious and in each person's own way. Its concrete application comes within the situation of religious pluralism. It is in view of both the implication of freedom and the concrete application thereof that secularism requires the political framework of the separation of state and church. Being not a philosophical position itself, it has no definition of truth, as it has no view of reality, and hence is not an ideology, but always remains a standpoint which seeks to pull the practical aspects of a society's life out of the conflicts of whatever ideologies and religions there are, extending its regulatory capacity to the dimensions of positive principles for general governance.

This fruit, secularism, was one of Britain's greatest gifts to India. But in the colonial state of affairs which prevailed there were tragic ironies, inasmuch as great Indian products of British education like Jawaharlal Nehru, becoming true secularists, strove to lay the foundation for a genuine pan-Indian secular state, while the Britist administration placed all kinds of impediments in their path and encouraged the theocratic outlook of their opponents.[1]

While there is wide-spread acknowledgement of the association with Britain as the chief source of modern Indian secularism, some Indian scholars also try to show that the secularist principle had been embedded in the Indian tradition itself. There has been, to be sure, a certain pervasive metaphysical perception in India that removes the ground of distinction among phenomenal things, which may thus express itself as tolerance from afar, i.e., a no-contact tolerance. That is what R. C. Pandeya, a contemporary Indian philosopher–professor Delhi University witnesses to when he writes, analyzing the sources of Indian "secularism and democracy". "Religious tolerance was, in fact, a natural outcome of the famous Absolutist Philosophy which said that except Brahman everything else was an appearance."[2] There is truth in this observation, but that truth does not consist in the claim to the ground of secularism but in the pointing to the latent capacity of the Indian metaphysical soil to naturalize the causes which in the West had produced this particular fruit, i.e., secularism, as also several others. In most cases, the chain of causes is not developmentally connected link by link in the transplanted situation. There are quantum leaps and short-cuts, which make the naturalization process confused and disorderly.

But then, we also realize that secularism, modern and healthy as it is, is just one result of the deep and comprehensive processes, outlined initially as the separation of philosophy from religion. Also, there are other fruits—the technological ones especially—that are threatening and full of forebodings.

Now this separation of philosophy from religion might sound negative, but by no means need it *be* negative. For, wherever it is a genuine expression of the freedom of the human spirit it can be positive, spelling ultimate gain for both philosophy and religion. In such a truly free situation the two that were put asunder under certain circumstances might also be reunified in a deeper way, but without making a fetish of either the separation or the union (reunion). In the history of European philosophy, after the rationalist-sceptical wrench from the foundations of religion and the empiricist jolt came the deeper movement of modern idealism, especially through Kant, but a critical idealism which fully conserved the positive gains of both the former movements in a way that would be of service to religious thought also. It was carried further by Hegel and his successors. They found a new place for religion. Hegel conclusively showed that without religion "all other aspects of life will remain barren for they will not be determined by truth."[3] The Indians felt an instinctive affinity with Western idealism's main thrusts, especially concerning things spiritual, at least the way they saw it. This phase of the Indian interaction with the West drew out the inherent idealistic orientaton of Indian thought. We shall now try to see the shape of all this.

The Idealistic Orientation

Apart from the directly imbibing Western idealist writings, the Indians also profited from interpretations of the Indian systems by European scholars like Paul Deussen, who presented the Upaniṣads and Śankara as Indian parallels to Plato and Kant. Consequently, as D. M. Datta, a modern Indian philosopher, remarks: " . . . idealistic thought, specially of the type of the monistic system of Vedānta became more popular than any of the rest. Idealism of one kind or another dominates, therefore, even contemporary Indian philosophy."[4] The large number of works by modern Indian authors bearing on idealism is alone testimony to it: e.g., S. N. Dasgupta, *Indian Idealism;* S. Radhakrishnan, *An Idealist View of Life;* P. T. Raju, *Idealist Thought of India*; etc.

For the Indians, the infinite, the eternal and the absolute are the proper subject-matter of philosophy. When European idealism broke into India, the Indians took to it like ducks to water. They thought that it was speaking a language close to themselves. Hegel reached their heart as he wrote: "Essentially, every philosophy is idealism, and the question then is only how far it is actually carried through. This is as true of philosophy as of religion, for religion equally with philosophy refuses to recognize in finitude a veritable being, or something ultimate and absolute, or non-posited, uncreated or eternal."[5] The Indians saw in Western idealism a philosophy that now assures a higher vision of things spiritual. And in Hegel they were further heartened by the vision of the spiritual as the Absolute that dialectically gathers up all diversities into an ultimate unity. Vedānta had already taught them all these truths, though in a different way. The special prospect that Western idealism—especially Hegel's—held out was the ability dialectically to grasp, and deal with, the concrete diversities obtaining in the phenomenal world.

Nevertheless, further down the road, when we come to applying this ability to such a matter as concerns us here, i.e., the unitary grasp of religious diversity, we must anticipate insuperable difficulties. The Indians knew that the strength of Hegel is that he conceived a unity which exists through concrete particularities, though the unity itself is realized only at the end point. The first part of this they found helpful but the second part they could not accept. For them, the particularities, inasmuch as they are of a spiritual order, have to be placed on a horizontal plane, all of them having equal claim to the same underlying, transcendent oneness, simultaneously at the present time, or any given time. For Hegel, such spiritual principles exist in a vertical succession, i.e., progressive in stages,[6] each annulling, preserving and exalting all the previous ones (expressed by his famous concept of *aufheben*).[7] These spiritual forms appear and pass away and do not endure permanently. [Hegel assigned Indian (Vedāntic) spirituality itself to the past. Its idealism for him is only an "idealism (of its own?) existence", one of "imagination".][8] Hegel saw the unity of all successive spiritual forms from the end-point of the *Weltgeist*'s march, where stands "a religion (that) has the absolute concept of the spirit as its principle."[9] [For Hegel, that religion is Christianity, and the philosophy which corresponds to it is the absolute idealism as defined by himself.]

The first Indian to react to Hegel was Sir Brahendranath Seal (1864-1938), an eminent philosopher in the University of Calcutta. In a little known early work of his, *Comparative Studies in*

Vaishnavism and Christianity (Calcutta, 1899), (later overshadowed by his more famous work, *The Positive Sciences of the Ancient Hindus* (London, Longmans, 1915), he criticized Hegel for subordinating other traditions to the presumedly supreme, and proposed the comparative method in order to restore a "co-ordinate rank" to all.[10] More than three decades later, S. Radhakrishnan, the best known of modern Indian academic philosophers, came to closer grips with this Hegelian issue. He tried to put what was vertical for Hegel on a horizonatal plane on an idealistic basis of his own. "An idealist view", Radhakrishnan argued, "is not expressed in any one pattern. It is many-coloured and its forms are varied; yet underneath all the variations and oppositions, there are certain common fundamental assumptions that show all to be products of the same spirit."[11]

Radhakrishnan uses the same word, "spirit", as had Hegel, but in the sense of the inward *Ātman*. Thus he writes: "Spirit is something essentially and purely inward, to be known only from within, and yet when known it leaves nothing outside. In the language of religion, spirit is God, the Ultimate Reality which is one and all comprehensive."[12] Indian idealism, then, while monistic like Hegel's, is intuitive rather than speculative. And it opened itself up to the perception of unity underlying the varieties of mystical experience. Thus the Indian idealists generally felt an affinity with Western philosophers of a similar, or partially similar, position, like Josiah Royce, Hocking and even William James. On the other hand, they were deeply impressed—thanks to *māyā*—with the Appearance-Reality distinction in some forms of Western idealism—of Plato certainly, but more immediately, Kant and especially F. H. Bradley. As for the latter, while it is fundamental for the essential idealism the Indian philosophers were pursuing—and while it also accords with the classical Indian perspectives of both Vedānta and Buddhism—its importance in respect of the response to religious pluralism lies in the fact that it adds strength to the contentions that all seemingly different mystical experiences are expressions of one and the same ultimate Truth, the differences being in the Appearance only. To put together all these various things is the task of metaphysical construction with which several of the modern Indian philosophers have been engaged. How this task is performed will be examined below.

The Comparative Method in Metaphysical Construction

The comparative method is unfortunately very much misused in modern India, e.g., for trivial and pointless comparisons of some Indian thinker or doctine with some supposedly Western counterpart. "Sankara and Bradley" has been a very favorite topic. Now we see more and more of "Nāgārjuna and Wittgenstein" and such other topics. However, comparison has a proper use too, which is as an aid to philosophical construction. It is entirely the case that without some diligent use of Western metaphysics no Eastern system can seize itself as philosophy, much less as relevant to "modern" thought. In the process, the best construction might also be creative wherever new insights are generated.

In this kind of philosophical construction questions arising from the varieties of religion have also received a fair shake. [Here we shall exclusively concentrate on that aspect.] As we remarked very early on in this essay, although forms of religious diversity were there in India throughout the ages, the phenomenon they constitute appears in a new light in the context of the interaction with the West and the consequent philosophical constructions. The distinctive mark of the Indian approach to religious diversity within the characteristic metaphysical framework has been marked by the ecclectic view, which seems to appear naturally and effortlessly. The good thing about it is that far back of it stands the characteristic Indian gnosis (no relation to Gnosis of Gnosticism), which ultimately supercedes every other means of knowledge and overwhelms every critical apparatus. Here then is an absolutism of gnosis, which in the last resort is what is truly and irreproachably Indian. It is sometimes brought into play in responding to Kant's agnosticism pertaining to the thing-in-itself and to the self; at other times, to Hegel or Nietzsche or to Martin Heidegger, but the problematic thing about it is that it is often expressed in the language of mystical intuition or direct experience *(anubhava)* of the ultimate Spirit and consequently rather removed from thought as such. [Nevertheless, a different kind of response to the Western ontolog, especially to Heidegger, in the context of bringing Vedāntic gnosis to bear explicitly upon thought, is attempted by the present author in his *Gnosis and the Question of Thought in Vedānta*, Nijhoff, 1986.]

However, a besetting problem arises with many writers inasmuch as the absolutism of gnosis cannot be dissociated from the tradition to which the knowledge underlying that has been believed to be vouchsafed (originally through the *Vedas*, the impregnable fortress of the Indian tradition), meaning that a certain pre-eminence will be claimed for the latter. This is what certain Western indologists like Paul Hacker, G. Oberhammer and Wilhelm Halbfass point out—in the words of the last- named—as "inclusiveness of the heirarchic, subordinating type"—hence "an inclusivistic absolutism" that is "still clearly present in numerous works produced by representatives of modern Hinduism."[13] In these works, it is argued, the highest Indian system of Advaita Vedānta "appears as the standpoint from which a certain relative value and truth [are] assigned to other religions and the philosophies, or as the horizon and context in which they are supposed to be coexisting, reconcilable and accessible to 'comparative' and harmonizing studies."[14] True enough,but is this position necessarily more objectionable than Hegel's claiming for Christianity the status of "a religion that has the absolute concept of the spirit as its principle", thus enabling it to subordinate and complete in a vertical-historical manner the transitory realities of all other (essentially past) religions? And how about Karl Rahner's doctrine of an "anonymous Christianity" within all the world's religions? Or of so many doctrines which speak of Christ (or Christianity) as the fulfilment of all that is "true, holy and of good report" in other religions? Well, suffice it for now.

We will have to say that the Indian gnosis is not exclusively a possession of the Vedānta system, although that is where it is completely thematized with the help of the Indian logos. Actually, it is present in all the high religions of India, most certainly including Buddhism. And in the systems (like the Buddhist Mahāyāna ones) where the Vedic logos is no longer recognized, there is a radical dependence on transcendental, mystic intuitions—like *prajñāpāramitā*—in some cases accompanied by radically negative dialectics as in the Mahāyana's Mādhyamika. However, on behalf of these high religions too, as they are propelled into the modern world, among other virtues, the ability to reconcile all religions and systems is also claimed. Thus speaking of (and for) the celebrated Buddhist philosophy, T. R. V. Murti contends: "In one sense, the Mādhyamika may seem one of the most intolerant of systems, as it negates all possible views without exception. In another sense [in the manner he has shown] it can accommodate any give significance to all systems and shades of views", for as Nāgārjuna says, "All is concord indeed for him who to Śūnyatā conforms."[15]

Some Specific Responses

Having now discussed even though all but briefly, the conditions and characteristics of Indian philosophical response in general to religious pluralism, let us now examine some specific responses. There are, no doubt, a vast variety of the latter, but we can only concentrate on a few, selected largely as boundary-markers and trend-setters.

The unity of the religions, to be achieved perhaps, at any rate to be perceived as being there at some deep spiritual level, has become a characteristic Indian concern and a favorite theme for many philosophical and quasi-philosophical literary expressions. Many Christians would see this as syncretism, but in India it is regarded with much respect and as a very positive thing. [Of course, it is also being used politically, as an instrument of national integration, which naturally puts it in a different light.]

The list of even academic thinkers who have contributed to the concept of spiritual unity underneath the visible religious diversity is quite large. But we will call attention to only a few, all of them early twentieth century men, who were born, nevertheless, in the 19th. They are picked for what they possibly represent, and also for their influence as well as the quality of their ideas. They are: Bhagavan Das, A. K. Coomaraswamy, R. D. Ranade, S. Radhakrishnan and K. C. Bhattacharyya. Of these only the two last will be considered in any detail.

Bhagavan Das, who lived in Banaras, was a theosophist and a deeply respected national figure. He wrote widely in both Hindi and English, including some on his favorite theme of the reconciliation of the different religions, like the books *Samanvaya* (Hindi) and *The Essential Unity of All Religions* (English). In the last mentioned two he expounded his view of "the Truth of essential Unity in Superficial Diversity, in religious as well as scientific thought." "Such a unity," he argued, "is established by the mediation of philosophy . . . to recognize that unity in the essentials of all religions is to promote the cause of civilization."[16] His view is buttressed by his own version of idealism, a gist of which is given in his article "Adhyātma-vidyā" in *Contemporary Indian Philosophy* (1937), edited by S. Radhakrishnan. In it he tried to show how the 'I' the universal is present in all particulars and yet not needing the particulars.

Ananda Kentish Coomaraswamy was a comparative religionist and a scholar of Oriental Art. He lived in Boston as curator of the Oriental section of the Boston Museum. He counted himself in the tradition of the so-called perennial philosophy. This last, many assume, is identical with the Indian gnosis (which is not the case). Thus Louis Renou points out that some people in the West think that India is the civilization that has preserved "the one tradition which is the basis of their philosophic perennis."[17] No doubt, many latter-day writers give room for such an assumption. As a follower of the perennial philosophy, Coomaraswamy favors a metaphysical religion because metaphysics "treats of the Supreme Identity as an indisseverable unity of potentiality and act."[18] He argues that plurality itself is a complement to the truth of religion: "Religions may and must be many, each being an 'arrangement of God', and stylistically differentiated, inasmuch as the thing known can only be in the knower according to the mode of the knower."[19]

R. D. Ranade was an esteemed professor of philosophy in the University of Allahabad. His writings are many, and especially known among them are his *Constructive Survey of the Upanishadic Philosophy* and his *Pathways to God* studies in Hindi, Marathi and Kannada Literatures. Ranade believed that mysticism is the real essence of religion and that in it all religions meet. "The mystics of all ages and countries form an eternal Divine Society and there are no racial, no communal, no national prejudices among them."[20] Further, "If all men are equal before God, and if men have the same Deiform Faculty', which enables them to 'see God face to face', then there is no meaning in saying that there is a difference between *(sic)* the quality of God-realization in some, as contrasted with the quality of God-realization in others. . . . It is this element of Universality, which, as Kant contends, would confer upon mystical experience objectivity, necessity and validity [and higher than in] any other kind of human experience just because it is Deiform."[21]

Now, we will turn to the two most important modern Indian philosophers having to do with our topic: S. Radhakrishnan and K. C. Bhattacharyya. While these two persons are as different as can be—the one an outgoing leader, a public educator, an international figure and prolific writer; the other a near-hermit known only to his close colleagues and pupils, whose writings are as abstruse as they are scanty—they are both very significant in their own ways.

The Thought of Radhakrishnan

S. Radhakrishnan (1888–1973), a professor of religion and philosophy most of his long career (Mysore, Calcutta, Oxford, Banaras), ended his public life as President of the Indian Republic. The outside world knew him as modern India's most influential philosopher: he is the only Eastern philosopher to whom a volume of the *Library of Living Philosophers* has been devoted (published 1952).

Radhakrishnan's approach to the truth issue in pluralism

Radhakrishnan rightly recognizes truth as the foremost issue. The classical way in which India has approached this difficult problem is by use of the dictum "one truth, many expressions". Radhakrishnan applies this time-honored Indian solution in a way that tallies with his own philosophic construction of integral experience, wherein Spirit is viewed as growth, which, for him, is the Absolute; and all apprehensions of particular religions are held as but relative expressions of the perfect, and, accordingly, as in themselves imperfect. "No god", he writes, "seems to be final and no religion perfect. . . . The history of religion is the record of the conflicts of contradictory systems, each of them claiming dogmatic finality and absolute truth, a claim made apparently absurd by the plurality of claimants. . . . Spirit is growth, and even while we are observing one side of its life, the wheel is turning and the shadow of the past is twining itself into it."[22]

The notion of one truth permitting, nay warranting, many expressions is at the heart of Radhakrishnan's thinking. He remarks: "If religious truth is seen by different groups in different ways it is not to deny that truth is ultimately one."[23] "Every expression of truth", he observes subsequently, "is relative. It cannot possess a unique value to the exclusion of others. It cannot be the only possible expression of what it expresses."[24]

The whole position ultimately rests upon the famous statement in the Ṛg *Veda* (1.164.46): "One is the truth, the sages speak of it diversely"— *ekam sat viprāḥ bahuthā vadanti*. We also can perceive that this statement did not come out of the blue but was uttered in the context of a rudimentary theological controversy, as the rest of it says, "they speak of/call upon [him/it] as Agni, Yama or Mātariśvan"—*agniṁ yamaṁ mātariśvānam āhuḥ*. It is apparent that the Ṛg *Veda* too was resolving a pluralistic religious situation, although there only bordering between "polytheism" and its own inner, supertheistic destiny. The word *āhuḥ* (from *ā* + *hve*) has the double meaning of speaking and invocation, or worship. Various gods have been mentioned in different places as the true deity to be worshipped, for which a resolution is indicated in Ṛg *Veda* 3.55.1 in the words *mahat devānam asuratvam ekam*, which M. Hiriyanna happily translates as "the worshipful divinity of the gods is one.".[25]

Sayings bearing the same idea can be found scattered throughout old Indian religious literature, upon which Radhakrishnan draws profusely. Some of these may be cited here. The *Yogavāsiṣṭha* has the following: "Sages have called it by many names such as *Ṛta*, *Átman*, supreme *Brahman* and truth for the sake of our empirical consciousness".[26] "To the Sāṁkhyans it is the Person, to the Vedāntins it is *Brahman*, to *Vijñāna-vādins* it is the alone holy *Vijñāna*, to the *Śūnya-vādins* it is *Śūnya*, to the Worshippers of Eternal Light it is the Illuminator. It is the Speaker, the Thinker, *Ṛta*, the Enjoyer, the Seer, the Maker, all of these."[27] [We cannot fail to note that various *darśanas*, or schools of thought, are introduced here.]

The *Bhāgavata* also has something especially interesting to say: "Just as one and the same object residing in many qualities become manifold as perceived by the different senses so also is (the same) God known in different ways through different scriptures."[28] [The interesting aspect of this passage is that the notion of the different scriptures *(śāstras)* as the media of the same God/Truth is brought into play.]

There is a famous verse in the *Bhagavad Gītā* (4.11), which Radhakrishnan translates thus: "As men worship me so do I accept them; men on all sides follow my path, O Pārtha."[29] This is used by Radhakrishnan as well as several modern writers as a text for "one truth, many expressions", and also for "one spiritual goal, many paths". This is a new use of this verse which seems to have stemmed from Vivekananda. Radhakrishnan himself cites it as a text bespeaking "the (same) transcendent spiritual aim of all historical religions".[30] Actually, classical interpretations by Śaṅkara and others do not allow this wide meaning, but that is not a point to be belabored here. However, within the given tradition itself, it does have a great metaphysical bearing as to the relation between one goal and the many paths; and in a purely deductive way it could be interpreted to have a bearing on the relation between truth and its expressions. However, Radhakrishnan sees it somewhat more directly and puts it more categorically: Expressions are true only in the relative sphere *(vyavahāra)*.[31]

Reflection upon mystical experience revealing the one truth underlying the many expressions

Radhakrishnan believes that reflection upon mystical experience will show that the one truth expresses itself in many ways. Perhaps the mystics themselves do not always know that, and that is why the philosopher becomes necessary.

Accordingly, he observes: "A study of the classical types of mystical experience discloses an astonishing agreement which is almost entirely independent of race, clime or age".[32] Radhakrishnan is the leading Indian thinker who has rendered gnosis in terms of mystical experience [but questionably]. The term *anubhava* is used for such experience. [And that too is questionable.] Radhakrishnan tries to enrich the meaning of *anubhava* by rendering it by the term "integral experience", which expresses his central doctrine.[33] In his early book, *Indian Philosophy* (Vol. II), he declares his preference for *anubhava* over *jñāna*.[34] With this concept of *anubhava* Radhakrishnan moves to the unity and universality of mystical experience through the diversity of expressions, inasmuch as it is not "consciousness of this or that thing but to know and see in oneself the being of all beings, the 'Ground and the Abyss' ".[35]

However, one might, in argument against this position, suggest that mystical experience in its claimed unity and unversality can be treated as the super-solution to the problem of religious diversity only when that problem as such is under-rated and tailored in a certain way. This might actually be said of every such solution. But then, mystical experience is a witness of a different kind, though it does itself contribute to the problem, and the problem may be taken as far more existentially serious than any prescribed solvent for its stubborn elements.

The Thought of K. C. Bhattacharyya

K. C. Bhattacharyya (1875–1949), professor of philosophy at Calcutta and elsewhere, was a reclusive and abstruse thinker. His writings, though sparse, are considered very profound and seminal.[36]

Deep down he as a Vedāntin and did his thinking accordingly. But by his own declaration, his philosophy had an "orientation to Kant" which meant arguing against the Kantian agnosticism pertaining to the knowledge of the self (the self being entertained by Kant only as a necessity of thought).[37]

To Philosophy (as distinguished from Science) Bhattacharyya assigns three grades of thought, i.e., the *pure objective thought, spiritual thought* and *transcendental thought*, answering respectively to three contents—the "self-subsistent", "reality" and "truth". "The grades of thought are really grades of speaking, but speakability is a necessary character of philosophic thought" (unlike scientific thought, of which it is only a contingent, character.)[38] As such, philosophy is "self-evident elaboration of the self-evident, which is spoken but not spoken of"—i.e., spoken "in the objective, the subjective and the transcendental attitudes".[39]

In Bhattacharyya's theory, religion (which is our interest here) belongs with the spirit (and as such with spiritual thought), which corresponds to "reality". The philosophy pertaining to it is that of the spirit, whose character is subjectivity and introspection. And, "introspection, in the proper sense of the term, is to speak in the first person—actually or ideally—with the consciousness of the 'I' as what the object is not."[40] In religious experience "there is the consciousness of the over-personal reality symbolized by the 'I': this conscious symbolizing is consciously being nought."[41] Now while conscious symbolizing is set at nought, in religion consciousness of being remains as indestructible. But it is "simple" and as such "admits of no variation".[42] By "variation", one should surmise, Bhattacharyya means change or becoming. Nevertheless, this "simple" "has an infinite plurality of religious experiences." This is where Bhattacharyya comes into conflict with "the Hegelian notion of a single and exclusive gradation of religions", which he finds "unacceptable".[43] What he seems to be objecting to in Hegel is the omnipotent monism of a single process of Becoming—*a la* the vertical stages—where the Absolute at the end point has swallowed up all that, in his view, is held as merely past. What we have in Bhattacharyya is the concept of a religious experience, i.e., consciousness of being, which is simple (meaning, perhaps, ever the same), room for a simultaneously valid plurality that does not affect the sameness of being. And this concept is contrasted with the Hegelian absolutism of a single, process, wherein all grades are homogenized from the absolute standpoint of a historically envisioned end.

As for the many kinds of religious experience ("religious communion" or "worship"),[44] they cannot be externally related to one another even through re-reflection. On the contrary: "Each experience by its self-deepening gets opposed to or synthesized with other experiences. One experience may enjoy another as a stage outgrown or in absolute conflict with it, where a third experience may emerge as adjusting them to one another."[45] One very important point is the complete repudiation of the use of "secular reason" for interrelating religions.[46] Each meets up with another or the others by its own inner logic, as it goes down deep into itself. Accordingly, the religions (when they are just let be) systematize their mutual relations, and consequently "present themselves in many alternate systems."[47] The view of "alternative absolutes" is fundamental to Bhattacharyya's religious metaphysics (i.e., having to do with spiritual thought, spirit, reality) as well as to his pure metaphysics (i.e., having to do with transcendental thought and truth.) This view is systematically developed in his essay, "The concept of the absolute and its alternative forms."[48]

Self-validation of religious experience as also other validation, or other-negation, belongs to the grade of spiritual thought (hence to reality) and not *ipso facto* to transcendental thought (hence truth). There, however, is a relation between these two, which Bhattacharyya regards as symbolic. His concept of the symbolic is extremely subtle, fundamental for grasping his philosophy fully,and it involves his theory of language, i.e., of both the speakable and the unspeakable. He observes: "Within thought, the image or the word furnishes the symbolism but here the form of thought itself constitutes the symbol for the felt problem. The feeling of the problem with the unrejected active faith in its solubility is the trying to think which is beyond thought or meaning, beyond all presentation".[49] "All philosophy", he observes, "is systematic symbolism and symbolism necessarily admits of alternatives."[50]

In characteristic Indian fashion, Bhattacharyya, in order to develop his theory of alternatives, especially resorts to negation.[51] He believes that "every system of philosophical thought or religion has its own logic and is bound up with one or another of the fundamental views of negation."[52] The various types of negation "indicate certain distinctive temperaments or attitudes towards truth, certain familiar modes of handling a given content."[53] Four types of negation are listed as follows: (1) that which involves no recognition of the need to control the faculty of "introspective attention";[54] (2) that in which the negation of negation "becomes not only definite but also positive"[55] (3) [A further development of the second,] whenever "the original illusion which was pronounced subjective is turned objective, the given is taken to be the identity of the subjective and objective";[56] (4) That in which "the first three views of negation may alternate."[57]

Translated into religious terms,[58] "the first type would be the religion of *nirvāṇa*, consisting in an absolute dissatisfaction with the definite dualism of truth and untruth." "The second type would be the religion of absolute toleration, which is dissatisfaction with all negation, an absolute condemnation of the attitude in which any religion is declared to be false", for "the negation of any religion is absolute negation and the negation of this absolute negation gives the absolute truth of all particular affirmations, all particular religions". "The third type would present the faith in all religions being not only true but identical." The fourth is simply the alternation of these three. For: "The absolute negation and the particular absolute affirmation are mutual negations in identity. This identity and this mutual negation are then the terminal points of all philosophy. Either side is beyond the dualism of definite truth and definite untruth".

Now, this is as far as Bhattacharyya takes us in respect of a philosophical response to religious pluralism. He offers no real conclusion and that may be wise. What he seems to do is to present us with a new dialectic of alternatives. Now, each of the alternatives, however, is not new, but the way they are put together in a dialectical structure is.

The subject matter of this dialectic is religious truth. Religious truth is such that it always remains closed within each religion, refusing to be open to others for fear of losing its integrity—and if it does, there is the peril of cheap and meaningless syncretism, and threat to truth itself. The truth of a religion can become open to others only with a dialectical struggle, i.e., not naturally.

Bhattacharyya's alternatives seem to present precisely such a worthy struggle, which is most becoming to the enterprise of philosophy. This must be attended by the question of what makes religious truth true. To consider that is the task of what Bhattacharyya calls transcendental thought. With that the closed religious truths become open inasmuch as it is by virtue of transcendental thought (whose subject is truth itself, in principle sheer open-ness) that "philosophy is the self-evident elaboration of the self-evident". Religious truths are appropriated in the ambience of such self-elaboration. It would appear that under this principle, philosophy takes over the struggle to open what essentially is closed,without providing any ready-made solution, even of the mystical kind upon which many other modern Indian thinkers have relied so heavily. Bhattacharyya is, of course, not opposed to mysticism, but he does break new, independent ground for pursuing our topic in a way that promises to be exceptionally fruitful if carried further along the lines of his own seminal suggestions.

Notes

1. *Note:* Nehru has often commented upon the irony of Britain's discouraging secularism in India with much sorrow, for instance when he writes, "Communalism [thus] becomes another name for political and social reactions, and the British government being the citadel of this reaction naturally throws its sheltering wings upon a useful ally." Here quoted from Wm. Th. de Barry, *Sources of the Indian Tradition*, New York, Columbia University Press, 1959, p. 896.

2. R. C. Pandeya, *A Panorama of Indian Philosophy*, Delhi, Motilal Banarsidass, 1966, p. 183.

3. Hegel, *Lectures on the Philosophy of World History*, Translated by H. B. Nisbet, Cambridge University Press, 1975, p. 111.

4. D. M. Datta, *The Chief Currents of Contemporary Philosophy*, The University of Calcutta, 1961, p. 115.

5. From *Hegel's Science of Logic*, Vol. I, p. 168; quoted by P. T. Raju, *Idealist Thought of India*, London, George Allen & Unwin, 1953, p. 37.

6. For "stages", see Hegel, *Lectures on the Philosophy of World History*, pp. 129–51.

7. *Note:* The concept of *aufheben* ultimately comes from Luther's translation of the *Epistle to the Romans*, 3.33, where he used *heben . . . auf* (fulfilled, set aside) to refer to the status of the Law under the Gospel.

8. Cf. Hegel, *The Philosophy of History*, Translated by J. Sibree, New York, Dover, Copyright 1959, p. 139.

9. *Lectures on the Philosophy of World History*, p. 111.

10. Cf. Sir B. N. Seal, *Comparative Studies in Vaishnavism and Christianity*, Calcutta, 1899, p. i.

11. S. Radhakrishnan, *An Idealist View of Life*, London, George Allen & Unwin, 1932, etc., p. 16.

12. *Ibid.*, p. 303.

13. See Wilhelm Halbfass, "India and the Comparative Method", *Philosophy East and West* (Honolulu, Hawaii), Vol. XXX. No. 1, January 1985, pp. 12–13. Attention is also called to G. Oberhammer, Editor, *Inkusivismus eine indische* Denkform, Vienna, De Nobili Research Library, 1983.

14. *Loc. cit.*

15. T. R. V. Murti, *The Central Philosophy of Buddhism*, London, George Allen & Unwin, 1955. . .1970, p. 337.

16. Bhagavan Das, *The Essential Unity of All Religions*, Banaras Kashi Vidya Pitha, 1939, p. 4.

17. Cf. L. Renou, *Religions of Ancient India*, London, University of London, Athlone Press, 1953, p. 110.

18. Ananda Coomaraswamy, "On the Pertinence of Philosophy", *contemporary Indian Philosophy*, Supra, pp. 119–120.

19. *Ibid.*, p. 120.

20. R. D. Ranade, *Mysticism in Maharashtra*, here quoted from *Glory of India*, A Quarterly of Indology, Delhi, Motilal Banarsidass, Vol. V, No. 1–2, March-June, 1981, p. 45.

21. R. D. Ranade, *Pathway to God in Hindi Literature*, Bombay, Gharatiya Vidya Bhavan, 1959, Introduction, p. 8.

22. S. Radhakrishnan, *An Idealist View of Life*, p. 28.

23. S. Radhakrishnan, *Recovery of Faith*, New York, Harper (World Perspectives), 1955, p. 155.

24. *Ibid.*, p. 157.

25. M. Hiriyana, *Outlines of Indian Philosophy*, London, George Allen & Unwin, 1956, reprint, p. 39. *Note:* Other translators render these worlds

less happily, e.g., R. T. H. Griffith: "Great is the God's supreme and sole domination."

26. *ṛtam ātmā paraṁ brahma satyamityādika budhaiḥ; kalpitā vyavahārārthaṁ tasya samjnā mahātmanaḥ.*, *Yogavāsiṣṭha of Vālmīki*, with the Commentary *Tātparya prakāsa*, ed., W. L. S. Pansikar, Vol. I, 3rd edition, Bombay, Pandurang Jawaji, 1937, iii, 1.12., p. 129.

27. *yaḥ pumān sāṁkhyadṛṣṭinām, brahma vedāntavādinām; vijnānamātraṁ vijnā-nāvidām-ekānta-nirmalam. yah sūnyavādinām sūnyo bhāsako yo'rkatejasām; vaktā mantā ṛtam bhoktā draṣta kartā sadaiva ca.*, *Ibid.*, iii. 5,6,7. p. 240.

28. *yathendriyaiḥ pṛthak dvāraiḥ artho bahuguṇāsrayaḥ eko nāneyate tadvad bhavagān sāstravartmabhiḥ.*, *The Bhagavata*, iii.32.33.

29. ye yathā māṁ prapadyante tāṁs tathaiva bhajāmyaham mama vartma anuvartante manuṣyā pārtha sarvasaḥ. See S. Radhakrishnan, *The Bhagavadgītā* (text, trans. and notes) London, George Allen & Unwin, 1963, edition, p. 158.

30. *Recovery of Faith*, p. 156.

31. Cf. S. Radhakrishnan, *The Bhagavadgītā*, p. 158.

32. S. Radhakrishnan, *Eastern Religions and Western Thought*, London, Oxford University Press, 1940, p. 79.

33. See J. G. Arapura, *Radhakrishnan and Inegral Experience*, Bombay, Asia Publishing House, 1966.

34. See S. Radhakrishnan, *Indian Philosophy*, Vol. II, London, George Allen & Unwin, 1927, p. 510.

35. *Ibid.*, p. 512.

36. *Note:* K. C. Bhattacharyya's published works, including the book *The Subject as Freedom*, are collected together in two volumes, under the title *Studies in Philosophy*, edited by his son, Gopinath Bhattacharyya, Calcutta, Progressive Publishers, 1958.

37. *Studies in Philosophy*, Vol. II, pp. 100ff.

38. *Ibid.*, p. 95.

39. *Ibid.*, p. 96.

40. *Ibid.*, p. 98.

41. *Loc. Cit.*

42. *Loc. cit.*

43. *Loc. cit.*

44. *Ibid.*, p. 114.

45. *Ibid.*, p. 115.

46. *Loc. cit.*

47. *Loc. cit.*

48. See *Ibid.*, pp. 121–143. In this connection Bhattacharyya also reformulates the Jaina theory of *anekānta-vada* or pluralism of views. See *Studies in Philosophy*, Vol. II, pp. 331–343.

49. *Studies in Philosophy*, Vol. II, p. 72.

50. *Ibid.*, p. 115.

51. See *Ibid.*, pp. 207–217.

52. *Ibid.*, p. 207.

53. *Ibid.*, p. 210.

54. *Ibid.*, p. 212.

55. *Ibid.*, p. 214.

56. *Ibid.*, pp. 214–15.

57. *Ibid.*, p. 216.

58. *Ibid.*, pp. 216–17.

Part II

RESPONSES FROM OTHER RELIGIONS WITHIN INDIA

Chapter Ten

PARSI ATTITUDES TO RELIGIOUS PLURALISM

J. Hinnells

Introduction

The word 'Parsi' denotes the descendants of a group of Iranians who left Persia, or Pars, in the ninth century C.E. to escape from severe Muslim persecution and sought a new land of religious freedom in which to practice their Zorastrian religion. They settled on the north-west coast of India in 936.[1] In the following thousand years their position in Indian society has changed considerably. Prior to the seventeenth century they were essentially an insignificant caste in rural Gujarat.[2] Under British rule they flourished considerably until in the mid to late nineteenth century they were considered by others, and themselves, to represent one of the leading groups in the society of western India in general and of Bombay, the commercial capital, in particular.[3] As a result of this economic success Parsis migrated in the nineteenth century to various parts of India, notably Calcutta and Karachi, and beyond the sub continent to East Africa, Hong Kong and Britain, then in the 1960s and 70s to Canada, America and Australia.[4] In the twentieth century many Parsis consider the community's position has been eroded.[5] Nevertheless a number of Parsis have achieved considerable success in many walks of life. In commerce India's largest concern, the Tatas is a Parsi firm, as is South Asia's largest private industrial concern, Godrej Brothers. In the professions Parsis have risen to considerable heights, notably science (atomic energy research and geography), the arts (especially in music), the law, also in politics and the armed forces (Parsis have, for example, had the post of head of each branch of the armed forces since Independence).[6] The point is that the Parsis have been successful, and have been seen to be so. This has inevitable affected their image of themselves and of others. It has enhanced their sense of distinctiveness, thereby reinforcing their determination to preserve their culture. Inevitably in a community which came into existence in order to save the religion the twin aims of preserving the religion and protecting the race have merged into one. Such a merger has been strengthened in a country like India, where social divisions, specifically caste, have an important religious dimension.

Demographic trends over the last 40 years have heightened community awareness of the vital need for self-preservation. From 1951–1971 the number of Parsis in India has declined at the rate of 10% per decade, and in the following decade at the rate of 20%. Thus, whereas there were 111,791 Parsis in India in 1951, by 1981 there were only 71,630.[7] This decrease in numbers is due only in small measure to out-migration. The basic cause is a low birth rate due to delayed marriage—the average age of Parsi brides in 1982 was 29.36, resulting in smaller families (average size was 3.7). The number of never married females in the community has also increased—from a mere 3% of Parsi women in their 40s in 1901 to 21% in 1982.[8] The reason for these trends is the high expectations regarding living standards typical of Parsis. Couples delay marriage until they can attain the standards to which they aspire. Another factor is the high educational achievement of women leading to a correspondingly high level of career expectations. The consequences of these trends for the long term future of the community are emphasized in the Parsi press and are appreciated by a broad cross-section of the population. Thus the editorial of the popular magazine, *Parsiana*, reflected on the recently released 1981 census data and concluded 'We cannot reverse the trend towards extinction. No miracle can save the community. But a change in attitude could help us better cope with the inevitable.'[9] The editorial then called for greater provision of old peoples homes. Given the point already made that Parsis commonly identify religion and race a central question for this paper is how have Parsi attitudes to their own religion and that of others been affected by the community's changing fortunes, rising from obscurity to power followed by a decline which is seen as threatening the very survival of the Parsi identity?

It is, however, essential to begin this study with a consideration of traditional Zoroastrian teaching on true and false religion, particularly as expounded by the prophet Zarathuštra (Zoroaster as he is commonly known in the West). In addition it is important to consider the attitudes and practices of Zorastrians to other religions during the millenium when Zorastrianism was the official religion of a major world empire,that is from the time of Cyrus the Great in the sixth century B.C.E., to the fall of the Sasanian empire before the invading Muslim Arabs in the seventh century C.E. This is relevant not only for the broad historical principle that it is difficult to understand the present without studying the past but also because Zoroastrians have a strong sense of the authority of their prophet's words and of the importance of history both in general theological terms and as a guide for action today. An appeal to scripture and to historical prototypes are commonly made by Parsi writers—this paper must, therefore, consider them. It is also important to be clear on precisely what is relevant for this paper. It is not so much what an outside academic may consider was in fact Zarathuštra's teaching, nor what the historian considers actually happened in Zorastrian imperial history, but rather what interpretations Parsis have put on the evidence.[10]

Traditional Zoroastrian Teaching on True and False Religion

Most western acedemics would now date Zarathuštra at approximately 1,200 B.C.E.[11] (Many Parsis argue for a much earlier date, around 6,000 B.C.E.—a doctrinally relevant point which will be discussed below.) He was convinced that he had seen God (Ahura Mazdā) in visions and that the teaching thus conveyed to him carried religious authority which, if ignored, could result in the hearer going to hell: 'Then shall I speak of the foremost [doctrine] of this existence, which Mazdā the Lord. . . declared to me. Those of you who do not act upon this manthra, even as I shall think and speak it, for them there shall be woe at the end of life.'[12] On the basis of the holy word thus revealed he taught that there are two primal spirits behind existence. One, Ahura Mazdā, is associated with *aš*, order or righteousness, the other, Angra Mainyu, the Destructive Spirit, associated with chaos, violence or evil. Between these two spirits all men must choose, just as the spiritual forces have done. So in *Yasna* 30: 3ff the prophet declares: 'Truly there are two primal Spirits, twins renowned to be in conflict. In thought and word, in act they are two: the better and the bad. And those who act well have chosen rightly between these two, not so the evil doers. And when these two Spirits first came together they created life and not-life, and how at the end Worst Existence shall be for the wicked, but [the House of] Best Purpose for the just man. . . . The Daēvas [demons] indeed did not choose rightly between these two, for the Deceiver rushed upon them as they conferred. Because they chose worst purpose they then rushed to Fury, with whom they afflicted the world and mankind.' The prophet thereby asserts that the wrong religious choice results not only in the individual's damnation, but also in violence (Fury), destruction in the world and among mankind. In historical terms Zarathuštra's association of false religion with the violent destructive forces may have been due to his community of settled pastoralists' experience of violent assaults from marauding warrior nomads who had to be violently repulsed if ordered life were to continue.[13] This association of false religion with chaos and the destruction of life came to characterize traditional Zoroastrian teaching.

A central conviction of Zoroastrianism is that God is wholly good and his creation is in essence perfect, though subject to the external assaults of evil. In the myth of creation the first sin man committed, the archetypal sin, was to declare that the world was created by the forces of evil. Such a belief distorts the concept of life and duty which results in the neglect and abuse of the Good Creation. The Middle Persian text, the *Dīnkard*, sums up its attitude to 'false' religion and its effects thus: "The fruit of the harm of false religion . . . consists in their [the demons] pouring out adversity to destroy the material world and to damage creatures . . . and in Man consists in the strengthening of the vices and weakening of the virtues, in the destruction of Man's very humanity and in sowing devilry in him, in the vitiating of his actions and the damnation of his soul?'[14]. False religion is thus seen as distorting human nature, causing harm to God's creation and to the ordering of society. There is, therefore, in the prophet's teaching a clear belief in the good and right religion and in others as false, harmful and leading to damnation.

One of the crucial questions at the center of current Parsi disputes is whether this belief in true and false religions leads to the idea and practice of conversion. Did Zarathustra believe that his was the only right religion and did he therefore seek to convert non-Zoroastrians to it? Was it that only Zoroastrianism produced goodness and life, and that any other religion produced the opposite? Or was it that the good in any religion was positive and the bad in any religion evil? Was the prophet's quest to exhort the good wherever it may be found—or to convert to the Mazdayasnian (worship, *yasna*, of Masdā) religion? Many would argue that Zarathuštra and his early followers must have sought converts, otherwise his religion would not have spread. This has recently been argued strongly by Parsis who have migrated to the American continent, most extensively by Kersey Antia, the elected high priest of the Zoroastrian community in Chicago. His forty seven page document was produced as a defense against criticism he faced for his involvement in the initiation of an American into the Zoroastrian religion in New York in 1983.[15] (An event which will be discussed further below) The majority of Zoroastrians in America and Canada support the idea of conversion, arguing that it is enjoined by the prophet; that the religion has universal principles and applicability and that the community has need both of the increased numbers and of the fresh blood. This view is shared by a few in India, notably by an eminent jurist and former Indian ambassador to the United States, Nani Palkhivala. He argues that "Zarathushtra wanted his divine knowledge to be availed of all humanity. The idea of a tribal god, a god to be worshipped only by a chosen people, was wholly anathema to Zarathushtra".[16]

Mostly in India, however, the common view is that the community should not accept converts. Perhaps the figure most widely associated with this position is the high priest (Dastūr) Dr. H.D.D. Mirza. His conviction is that "There is no conversion in Zoroastrian religion." This he elaborates in a number of publications encompassing a range of issues. He disputes the interpretation of the texts used, be those texts Gāthic or later, and is convinced that historical precedent establishes the principle that Zoroastrians have never practiced conversion. This argument falls into two parts, the first is the practice of Zarathustra, the second the evidence of Zoroastrian practice under the three great Iranian empires of the Achaemenids, Parthians and Sasanians from the fifth century B.C.E. to the seventh century C.E. Each merits separate consideration.

In 1971 Mirza wrote, "If the word "conversion" means discarding one's own ancestral religion and adopting an alien religion, then there is no idea of conversion in the . . . scripture of the Zoroastrians".[17] This point is elaborated by several Parsi writers in the twentieth century. Essentially they argue that the prophet did not introduce a new religion to which he converted outsiders, but rather that he sought to reform existing religion and preached men should live up to the ideals of their own religion. Thus in 1917 P. S. Masani commented," In fact there was no prophet nor any form of established religion such as Hinduism, Buddhism etc before the advent of Zoroaster, and hence it is very improper to say that Zoroaster converted the people of primitive faith to his own faith."[18] More recently (1985) Ranina, now a trustee of the Bombay Parsi Panchayet wrote in a widely circulated memorandum: 'Zarathushtra enlightened his people, he played the role which a teacher plays towards his pupils, namely to educate them and enlighten them. When a student learns at the feet of a teacher, he is educated and enlightened; it would be absurd to say that he is converted."[19] Precisely why Parsis should want to stress the absence of the practice of conversion from the religion is a theme to which we shall return. First it is important to consider the other appeals to historical precedent.

Perceived Historical Guides on Religious Pluralism

The three Bombay high priests, Dastūrs H. D. K. Mirza, Dr. K. M. JamaspAsa and Dr. F. M. Kotwal wrote an article against conversion in the orthodox community newspaper, *Jam-e Jamshed* on June 9 and 10, 1983. They argued: 'During the long and variegated history, the Zoroastrians never adopted the policy of conversion of non-Zoroastrians. The Achaemenian kings were well-known for their liberal religious policy. They ruled over divers people professing many religions, whom they granted full freedom to practice their respective religions. They even afforded financial help to build their places of worship. . . . Similarly during the Parthian and Sasanian periods the followers of various religions were living peacefully in Iran . . .".[20] It is certainly the case that few emperors in history have had a reputation for tolerance of other races and religions equal to that of the founder of the Persian empire, Cyrus the Great, in the sixth century B.C.E. In what is known as "The Cyrus Cylinder" he presented himself to his subject peoples, specifically the Babylonians, not as an alien conqueror but as the one chosen by their own deities to rule their kingdom in peace. He stated that he became "the king of Babylon . . . whose rule [the gods] Bel and Nabu love, whom they want as king. . . . My numerous troops walked around in Babylon in peace, I did not allow anyone to terrorize any place . . . I strove for peace in Babylon, and in all other sacred cities."[21] One of the people to benefit from this religious tolerance was the Jews, whom he not only permitted to return home from exile in Babylon, but to whom he also gave funds to rebuild their temple, an act for which he is well remembered in the Hebrew Bible where he is unique among foreign rulers in being described as "the anointed", or the messiah (*Isaish* 45:1ff). Numerous Latin and Greek authors also refer to the justice and tolerance of the Achaemenid monarchs in their dealings with other races.[22]

There is less detailed evidence for the practice of the Parthians though it is clear they continued the policy of toleration. The sources are more specific for the Sasanian period (third to seventh century C.E.). Thus, for example, the Sasanian monarch, Hormizd IV, in the sixth century, decreed that Christians and other groups should not be persecuted because: "Even as our royal throne cannot stand upon its two front legs without the back ones, so also our government cannot stand and be secure, if we incense the Christians and the adherents of other religions who are not of our faith. Cease, therefore, to harass the Christians, but exert yourselves diligently in doing good works, so that the Christians and the adherents of other religions seeing that may praise you for it."[23] This royal tolerance is displayed in a Pahlavi theological work, *Dīnkard* VI: "A Jew is not wicked merely on account of his Jewish faith and followers of other bad religions are [likewise] not wicked merely on account of their bad religion."[24]

References back to such a lengthy history can, inevitably, be a two-edged sword. From a historian's perspective it is difficult to judge whether Cyrus' tolerance for other religions was due to a belief that only Aryan peoples could practice the "noble" religion; whether it was an ideal of tolerance or the enlightened self interest of a new ruler seeking to overthrow a mighty empire. Nor is it clear how much significance should be practiced, for example, by the high priest Kirdēr or certain monarchs.[25] Hormizd's proclomation quoted above itself suggests someone had been persecuting non-Zoroastrians. Some Parsi writers have used them as evidence that conversion was practiced, for example Kersey Antia referred to above.[26] Others for example the influential Persi religious teacher in Bombay, Khojesti Mistree, in his counter article to Antia argue that such acts are atypical and unZoroastrian. Dastūr Mirza argues that not even here was there any practice of conversion since the texts have been mistranslated.[27] There are, therefore, blurred features in the historical picture.

One clear and consistent practice in Zoroastrian Iran during its imperial days is the ruthless suppression of what was perceived of as heresy. From the early days of empire kingship was seen as having a religious basis. This has the corollory that opposition to the throne is considered to be provoked by evil. So, for example, declared: 'Great Ahuramazda, the greatest of gods—he created Darius the King, he bestowed on him the kingdom; by the favour of Ahuramazda Darius is King . . . Saith Darius the King: 'This country Persia which Ahuramazda bestowed upon me.'[28] Consequently Darius presented those who rebelled against him as inspired by the evil force of the Lie, and as rebelling against God's will. So in an inscription at Behistan Darius states: "These are the provinces which became rebellious. The Lie made them rebellious, so that [these] men deceived the people. Afterwards Ahuramazda put them into my hand . . .".[29] Similarly in Sasanian times the emperor Shāpur II (309–379 C.E.), when he was struggling with the social upheavals caused in his kingdom by diverse religious movements, sought a unity through an imposed orthodoxy. The priest Ádurbād in a religious disputation proved the truth of his Zoroastrian teaching by submitting successfully to the ordeal of molten metal being poured on his chest. Whereon Shāpur "issued a declaration before all those representatives of the different sects, doctrines, and schools in this wise 'Now that we have seen the Religion upon earth, we shall not tolerate false religions and we shall be exceeding jealous.' And thus he did."[30] An explicit distinction was drawn between a strict imposition of what was considered orthodoxy within Zoroastrianism on the one hand and on the other a tolerance of others' religions (and an unwillingness to propogate the royal religion) by the later Sasanian monarch Khosrau (531–579 C.E.). The *Dīnkard* describes how he vigorously imposed official orthodoxy for what he considered the beneficial unity of society and the consequent welfare of his subject: "[Khosrau] . . . after he had put down irreligion and heresy with the greatest vindictiveness, according to the revelation of the Religion in the matter of all heresy declared: The truth of the Mazdayasnian religion has been recognized. Intelligent men can with confidence establish it in the world by discussion. But effective and progressive propaganda should be based not so much on discussion as on pure thoughts, words and deeds, the inspiration of the Good Spirit, and the worship of the gods paid in absolute conformity to the word. What the chief Magians [priests] of Ohrmazd have proclaimed, do we proclaim; for among us they have been shown to possess spiritual insight . . . Fortunately for the good governance of that country the realm of Iran has gone forward relying on the doctrine of the Mazdayasnian religion . . . We have no dispute with those who have other convictions for we [ourselves] possess so much in the whole original wisdom of the Mazdayasnian religion. Whereas we have recognized that, in so far as all dubiuous doctrines, foreign to the Mazdayasnian religion, reach this place from all over the world, further examination and investigation prove that to absorb and publish abroad knowledge foreign to the Mazdayasnian religion does not contribute to the welfare and prosperity of our subjects . . ."[31]

These examples illustrate what is generally typical of official policy in Zoroastrian Iran, namely that harmony and well-being within the realm (as seen from the monarch's perspective), rather than any evangelical concern to convert aliens, may be seen as the motivation behind religious force in those comparatively few instances where it was used. As a result Zoroastrianism has consistently been harder on its heretics than it has on people of another religion. The *Dīnkard* explains this by saying, "There is no-one who is a greater enemy to religion than heretics. For apart from heretics there is no enemy who can thus come from without through the wall into religion's outermost region."[32] Just as it is important to study a religion's attitudes to other religions, so it is important to consider what its attitude is to its own heresies.

There is a further historical era to which Parsis commonly allude in their discussions of religious conversion, and that is Muslim Iran from the seventh century Arab invasion down to the twentieth century. Throughout most of these 1,300 years Zoroastrians have experienced financial penalty, social discrimination, denial of various employment possibilities, lacked equal protection in law, suffered physical abuse and even death.[33] The only way to escape from this persecution was to convert to evangelical Islam. There have, of course, been periods when a degree of tolerance has been shown but generally the lot of the *guebres* (infidels) has been extremely difficult. They have been forced to seek the security of obscurity in remote villages of the desert plain especially around Yazd and Kerman. It is little wonder their numbers have dropped to around 30,000 in the homeland,[34] and that a number set out to India to seek a land of religious freedom.

This historical lesson of the persecution which enthusiastic missionary work can produce contrasts vividly, for most Parsis, with the tolerance they have experienced from Hindus, for whom religion and race are so interwoven that conversion has never traditionally been seriously considered. In the words of a Parsi religious teacher from Karachi, Mr. F.K. Dadachanji, in a lecture in Karachi, December 1985 (and quoted with his permission): "If you study the history of the last 2,000 years you will find that more people have been murdered, butchered, and slaughtered in the name of religion and conversion than those in all the wars, in all the history put together, creating untold human misery and human sorrow". Whereas Parsis offer different interpretations of the prophet's teaching and of the significance of Zoroastrian practices during the imperial era, there is virtual unanimity in viewing the millenium of Islamic rule in Iran as illustrating beyond doubt the harm that religious intolerance, the claim of a religion to be the sole possessor truth and the consequent efforts to convert, as being harmful.

Recent Historical Developments Affecting Parsi Attitudes to Religious Pluralism

The most significant factor leading to substantial change in Parsi attitudes to religion during the last hundred years has unquestionably been the introduction of western education. Briefly, from the 1820s the Parsis began to attend western schools in Bombay in a higher proportion to their overall numbers than did any other section of western Indian society. At first they attended mostly missionary schools, but after the conversion of two boys at the school of the Revd. Dr John Wilson in the 1830s they began to build their own so that the religion of the young would not be interfered with. By 1860 Parsis occupied 40% of all places at educational institutions in Bombay, even though they represented only 6% of the city's population. They have consistently had a far higher proportion of their community educated than have other Indian races. In 1882, the first year for which such figures are available, only 26% of Bombay Parsis were illiterate compared with 73% of Hindus. This phenomenon still continues; thus, a survey published in 1985 records only a 2% illiteracy rate among the Bombay Parsi population.[35]

As for many Indian communities, western education has been perhaps the greatest influence left by British rule on Parsi religion and culture. In his famous Minute on Education, dated February 2, 1835, Macauley set out what he saw as the immediate objects of providing British Education in India. He accepted that with the limited resources available it was impossible "to educate the body of the people. We must at present do our best to form a class of people who may be interpreters between us and the millions we govern—a class of persons Indian in blood and colour but English in tastes, in opinions, in morals and in intellect."[36] Perhaps no other Indian race fulfilled this objective as much as the Parsis did. In social habits such as dress, eating, in hobbies, aspirations and not least in politics Parsis at the turn of the century identified closely with the British.[37] (Obviously this is a broad generalization requiring qualification for complete accuracy.) This resulted in many in a sense of their own intellectual and cultural distance from the mass of the Indian people. An extreme example of this anglophilia is the columnist of the glossy magazine *The Parsi* in August 1905, who wrote: "The closer union of the Europeans and Parsis is the finest thing that can happen to our race. It will mean the *lifting up* of a people who are lying *low*, though possessing all the qualities of a European race. It will make our men more of men then they are at present and will make our women better women. The complete Europeanization of the Parsis is now a mere matter of time."

What is significant in this context is that it was not simply that western education transmitted broad western values, though that is important, it was even more that Parsis studied their own religion under western scholars. A number of western academics lectured in India, two notable examples were Martin Haug, who was Professor of Sanskrit at Poona in the 1860s, and J.H. Moulton who spent the last year of his life in Bombay in 1916.[38] Some Parsi religious leaders travelled Westwards and studied their religion under western academics. The first was K. R. Cama who spent six months in Paris and Erlangen on his way back from Britain to India on a business trip in 1859.[39] There he studied

Iranian history and languages under Mohl, Oppert and Spiegel. One of the most influential western educated Parsis was M.N. Dhalla, who studied Zoroastrianism under A.V.W. Jackson at Columbia University, New York, 1905–1909.[40] Through these and other figures many educated Parsis studied various western scholarly publications on Zoroastrianism, indeed some of the community's magazines serialized academic publications. *The Journal of the Iranian Association*, for example, reproduced the work of various western authorities, notably Moulton's. Those Parsis who studied such publications themselves produced literature for internal consumption both in English and Gujarati.[41] The point is that it is not simply broad western accounts of religions in general which were being transmitted but more that detailed studies relating specifically to Zoroastrianism and its place in world religions were being consumed.

Among western educated Parsis the pressure for reform in the light of such research was considerable. The motive was to preach to co-religionists a faith which was considered acceptable to modern man with all his knowledge. An obvious illustration of this is Dhalla's explanation of pre- and early Zoroastrian religious history in the light of contemporary scholarly accounts of the evolution of religions. Thus chapter four of his *History of Zoroastrianism*, (Oxford University Press, 1938) is entitled "Towards Monotheism: Gods in evolution". A number of books were produced to present Zoroastrians in a favorable light to the West[42], favorable western accounts of Zoroastrianism were reproduced[43] and western religious vocabulary became quite widely used. Dhalla, for example, referred to man's "heavenly father" and to the prophet Zarathustra hearing "the solemn voice of the divine vicar".[44] The influence was not merely one of vocabulary, however. Some of the basic beliefs were affected. Thus, whereas Zoroastrianism traditionally teaches that death is the ultimate weapon of the forces of evil, something which destroys God-given life,[45] Dhalla, because he was influenced by current Liberal Protestant antipathy to a belief in a personal devil, referred to death as "Ahura calling men back to himself from their earthly sojourn"[46] and on the subject of the death of a loved one he writes: "If God has taken away their beloved before their time, it must be because in his infinite wisdom he must have thought this world not good enough for them. For those whom God loves most, he calls to himself sooner than others."[47] This is alien to traditional Zoroastrian thinking, but consistent with contemporary Christian piety.

It is historically significant that most of the western academics to influence Parsi thinkers, notably Haug, Jackson and Moulton, were themselves committed Protestants, hence the form of Christian influence on the Parsi community was of a distinct type and resulted in a specific typology of religions.[48] Moulton was basically a Biblical scholar, and in common with most Protestant theologians of the day contrasted two types of religion, the prophetic and the priestly. Since he greatly respected Zarathustra as a prophet, he concluded that he could not have been a priest. Moulton, in his most widely read work on Zoroastrianism, wrote: "How are we to classify Zaratushtra as between the two great categories into which men of religion naturally fall? Was he Prophet and Teacher, or was he a Priest? Is the religion of the Gathas practical and ethical, or sacerdotal?" Moulton notes that Zarathustra actually uses the term priest *zaotar*, of himself (*Yasna* 33: 6) but still concludes, "Now we can hardly understand the Gathas on the assumption that Zarathushtra himself belonged to a separate and higher priestly caste . . . That Zarathustra is teacher and prophet is written large over every page of the Gathas . . . He has a revelation . . . There is no room for sacerdotal functions as a really integral part of such a man's gospel."[49] Parsis influenced by such thought were thus encouraged to see priestly religion in general, and the rituals associated with it, as a lower superstitious level of religion.[50] Where western influenced authors did write about rituals, then the emphasis was on the scientific, hygenic benefits of Zoroastrian purity laws. The concern being not so much their importance as expressions of devotion but rather their logical consistency with modern science. The obvious example of this is work of Sir Jivanji Modi, *The Religious Ceremonies and Customs of the Parsees* (Bombay, 1922). There, for example, he explains the traditional death ceremonies in terms of the need for sanitation (pp. 49, 70). "Ritualism" became, for many western educated Parsis, a perjorative term, denoting what its users saw as a spiritually empty religion which did not meet the needs of the young generation. Those Parsis associated with such reform movements in twentieth century India have been labelled within the community as "the Protestant party". Their views on good and bad, or true and false, on meaningful and non-meaningful religions and their evaluation of religious authority lying exclusively in 'Holy Scripture', in short their general classification of religions, were akin to those of traditional western protestantism.[51] Individuals of such a persuasion typically sought to distance themselves from what they saw as Hindu accretions and superstitions. Two groups were established to eradicate such corruptions from living Zoroastrianism, the Rahnumae Mazdayasnian Sabha in 1851 and the second by K.R. Cama in 1860, the Zarthoshti Din-ni Khol-karnari Mandli.[52]

It was inevitable that such a western influenced movement within the Parsi community would provoke a reaction among others who wanted to assert the value of the traditions they feared were being swept away in a flood of change. As for many Indian communities at the turn of the century, the vehicle for this reassertion of cherished practices was Theosophy.[53] The first Theosophical Lodge founded by Madame Blawatsky and Col. Olcott in India was in Bombay in 1879. From then until the move of the Theosophical headquarters to Madras in 1907, Parsis were highly influential in the Society as office bearers and writers. Conversley Theosophical teaching was influential among many Parsis. The reasons for its popularity were its legitimation of traditional rites; the call for the preservation of the traditional sacred language (Avesta) and its elevation of eastern (occult) mysticism over western rationalism. The point is that this western-originated movement justified the use of those traditions which emotionally, and devotionally, many wanted to preserve but which were being attacked by the Parsi "Protestant Party". When its headquarters were moved to Madras, and under the new leadership of Annie Besant, the Society became more associated both with Hindus and with the Home Rule League. As a result a number of Parsis drifted away from it.

But the religious need which Theosophy had met still existed. It was now answered by what might be termed an internal Theosophical Zoroastrian movement, known as Ilm-i Khshnoom, "the Path of Knowledge". Its founder was Behramshah Shroff who claimed to have received his occult knowledge not from Tibetan Masters, as in Theosophy, but from a race of secret Zoroastrian giants in Iran. His preaching mission began in 1907 and has been continued down to the present by his followers. As there is no formal membership it is impossible to supply numbers. Khshnoomists tend to be vocal and literate so that it is possible to exaggerate their impact on the community, but their appeal to tradition carries a powerful appeal for many and they are respected by a number who would not describe themselves as Khshnoomists. As with Theosophy there is a belief in rebirth, an ascetic tendency, vegetarianism and if not an explicit teaching on the brotherhood of all religions, at least an acceptance of truth in all religions. It is a movement far removed, doctrinally, from the "Protestant Party" and the two have often been in open (verbal) conflict.[54] The issue over which they have clashed most openly is that of conversion. The Protestant party has emphasized the universal nature of the religious teaching and thereby called for the acceptance of converts. The Khshnoomists, along with those who would simple describe themselves as "orthodox", have argued that because religion and race are necessarily interwoven conversion is harmful. Before these debates can be outlined it is first necessary to provide a brief account of a series of events over the last hundred years in which the question of conversion has come to the fore.

Controversies Concerning Religion, Race and Conversion

The first of the major public outcries against the initiation of the children of intermarriages was in 1882 at Mazagon, north of Bombay, when Dastur JamaspAsa performed the intitiation of five males and four females, aged between 35 and 77. It is important for later discussions that each of the candidates was born of a Parsi father. This action was publicly and vehemently opposed by Dastur Sanjana, who in a pamphlet argued that the disasterous epidemic afflicting the community was retribution for this wrong act, which brought *juddīns* (person of another religion) into the community. The action was criticized by many Parsis, including the Panchayet.[55] Such initiations were seen by their opponents as the acceptance of converts. If the offspring of an intermarriage could be initiated, then why not anyone?

A far greater outcry arose in 1903. R. D. Tata, son of the founder of India's steel industry, married a French woman in Paris, Suzanne Brier. On their return to Bombay Dastur JamaspAsa performed Mrs. Tata's initiation and then the Parsi blessing of their wedding. In this instance, then, the query was not over the child of a mixed marriage, but concerned the spouse. The Panchayet established a sub-committee to report on the properness of such conversions. The committee was reported to be deciding in favor of their doctrinal correctness, but its report was then blocked. The Panchayet laid down that only Parsi-Zoroastrians could benefit from communal Trust Funds. Marrying into such a wealthy family Mrs. Tata was not likely to be seeking financial aid. The cause became a test case to decide whether the community could, or should, accept the conversion of aliens who would then have access to temples and, after death, be laid in a Tower of Silence.

The case eventually went to court and judgment was passed in 1906 in Suite No. 689 of the Bombay High Court by the Parsi judge, The Hon'ble Mr. Justice Davar, a noted orthodox, and the Theosophist English judge, The Hon'ble Mr. Justice Beaman. The case was complicated by two additional issues. The plaintiffs, led by Sir Dinsha Manocji Petit, argued that the Trustees of the Panchayet had not been validly appointed. The case was also linked with that of a Rajput lady whose marriage and consequent rights were similar to Mrs. Tata's. Essentially the judgment relevant to this paper was that: "even if an entire alien—a Juddin—is duly admitted into the Zoroastrian religion after satisfying all conditions and undergoing all necessary ceremonies, he or she would not, as a matter of right, be entitled to the use and benefits of the Funds and Institutions now under the Defendents' [i.e. the Panchayet's] management and control; that these were founded and endowed only for members of the Parsi community; and that the Parsi community consists of Parsis who are descended from the original Persian emigrants, and who are born of both Zoroastrian parents, and who profess the Zoroastrian religion, the Iranies from Persia professing the Zoroastrian religion, who come to India, either temporarily or permanently, and the children of Parsi fathers by alien mothers who have been duly and properly admitted into the religion."[56] In Mr. Justice Davar's opinion, although according to the tenets of the religion conversion may originally have been accepted, what had become usage must prevail. In his judgment Justice Beaman commented, "What the Defendents deny is the right of any foreign convert, in whose veins no Parsi blood runs, to become a member of the Parsi community." In his opinion there could be no doubt but that when they first settled in India Parsis would have accepted converts from among the leaders of the major communities but they dare not proselytize for fear of provoking hostility, but "it is almost certain that the caste idea must have struck a deeper and deeper root, and coloured all their relations with the indigenous Indians in their neighbourhood . . . I cannot too strongly insist upon this substitution of a caste for a religious basis of the organization of the Indian Zoroastrians . . . While theoretically adhering to their ancient religion and consistently avowing its principal tenents—including, of course, the merit of conversion as theological dogma, they erected about themselves real caste barriers.' Caste, Beaman argued, can clearly be seen to be that which saved them "from dissipating and losing themselves in the vast ocean of Hinduism about them" during their thousand year history in India.[57] The usage he felt was clear and understandable. Henceforth, Parsis have commonly appealed to this 1906 judgment as the legal directive that only the children of Parsi males can be initiated. However broad and deep the impact of western education or Protestant attitudes to true and false religion, the legal sanction based on caste has been a major factor in discussions on conversion.

The story does not end there, however. A similar issue was raised in the court of Lower Burma in 1918. In 1914 Bella, the daughter of a Parsi widow and of a non-Parsi father was adopted by a Trustee of the Rangoon temple. Her naujote was performed. Mr. Justice Davar wrote to those concerned saying the initiation was unlawful. The participants were attacked in the Parsi press, notably the orthodox newspaper *Jam-i Jamshid*. In 1915 Bella entered a fire temple and a court case began. In the 1918 judgment the court supported Bella. Repeated reference was made by the judge to the 1906 test case, specifically the comments on conversion being part of traditional Zoroastrian teaching. He concluded, "I must hold that the plaintiffs have failed to prove Bella was not duly initiated and I must hold that she is, and that no Zoroastrian can complain of her presence in the temple, unless such temple is meant not for Zoroastrians generally, but for a peculiar section of them to which she does not belong."[58] The discussions centered around the correct performance of the ceremony and the possibility of conversion. Caste in the Court of Lower Burma was not a focus of discussion. The case went on Appeal to the Privy Council who ruled that she was not entitled to Trusts designated for Parsi-Zoroastrians, though this judgment was seen as being specific to the Trust Deeds of a particular temple and not having general application.[59]A further uproar broke out in the community in 1942 when Dastur Framroze Bode, together with ten other priests, performed the initiation of seventy seven children in Bansda. In this case it was not disputed that the fathers were Parsis. The considerable outcry and the threats of violence which followed, illustrate that whatever the 1906 law case had decreed in theory about the acceptability of the initiation of children of a Parsi father much popular sentiment was strongly opposed to the initiations of the children of any mixed marriage.[60] In practice, therefore, the community was imposing stricter controls on the issue of intermarriages than was laid down in 1906 and the Rangoon judgment was ignored. Although some individuals have argued that the terms "Parsi" and "Zoroastrian" are not synonymous[61] for the majority of Parsis they are in practice and conversion to the race is not accepted.

This rigorous demand for a link between blood and religion can be seen in the Parsi protests to the proposed 1980 Adoption of Children Bill. The Bill was intended to enable Indian citizens (in India) to adopt a child from any community, race or religion and "to confer on the adopted child all rights, civil, social and religious, of the adoptive father." In a letter dated February 9, 1981, to MRs. Indhira Gandhi, the Prime Minister, the High Priest, Dastur Mirza argued that Parsis should be exempt from the bill because he considered "its application would threaten the very existence of the community". In a document issued on the proposed bill by "The Special Committee for Adoption Bill" the view was expressed that "A Parsi can be a Parsi only by birth and not by adoption or conversion or a non-Parsi adoption. Racial and genetic purity is a command of Religion. Parsis left Iran to preserve their spiritual Institutions like Sudreh-Kushti [the sacred shirt and cord], Fire Temples, Dokhmas, Death Ceremonies—and above all the genetic purity, which is the very foundation of the Parsi life." It concluded, "what is required is the preservation of the inherent genetic and racial characteristics along with all the spiritual gifts our Prophet has graciously bestowed on us."[62] The bill was eventually dropped because of protests from various communities.

In 1980 the three issues of intermarriage, communal rights and religion were again the subject of public debate. As the time for community elections to the Bombay Parsi Panchayet, (BPP) drew near a reform group, "The Committee for Electoral Reform" (CER), was established to encourage all those entitled to vote to do so in order to eject what it saw as the perpetuation of a partisan group from power the properness of whose conduct they questioned. The issues became many and involved. The important one in this context was that the BPP argued that women who had married out of the community had sacrificed their right to vote in the elections. The CER contested this in court on the grounds of sexual discrimination—since men who had married out were not so barred. On Appeal CER won their case. This fuelled suspicions that CER sought not only electoral but also religious reforms and a counter group was formed, "The Committee for United Zoroastrians" (CUZ). In a community newspaper, *Kaiser-i Hind* for Jan. 25th, 1981 the CUZ placed an advertisement (subsequently published in various papers) which illustrates the sensitivity over the question of community identity and religious allegiance. It read: "This is not a normal septennial election. This is a straight contest between two groups holding divergent views on our religious tenets, beliefs, ceremonies and practices. On your right choice will depend the future of our religion and our community. Will you choose those who hold dear our traditional values and our religious institutions and ceremonies and who fight as our forefathers did for 13 centuries, to preserve our identity as a community? OR will you choose those who decry and would destroy our religious beliefs . . . . who advocate intercommunal marriages and admission for children of non-Parsi fathers and Parsi mothers into our fold. You have to choose between the two." The CER triumphed in that particular election, but since then the more traditional party has been noticably influential. The preservation of community identity is, therefore, as powerful and emotive an issue as it was in 1903.[63] Indeed the demographic trends outlined above make it probably even more so now. Parsi attitudes to religious pluralism in the 1980s are, therefore, governed by the perceived link between religion and race.

The event which has provoked most community debate on the issue of conversion in recent times was the initiation of an all-American, Joseph Peterson, at the Zoroastrian Center (Darbe Mehr) in New York on March 5, 1983. What distinguished this event from the previous controversies was that there was not even any question of intermarriage. His wife is also a Christian American. It was widely reported in the Parsi press in India, causing a storm of protest there and in America.[64] It brought to fever pitch the debates which had been growing in the American Zoroastrian communities regarding the issue of conversion. A fundamental issue for many Zoroastrians in the "New World" is the extent to which the traditions of their Asian religion have to be changed to preserve their vitality and meaningfulness, particularly for the young, in a new setting—or must the traditions be strictly preserved in order to preserve identity? This has been reflected in the the titles and contents of the five North American congresses which have been held since 1975.[65] At the congress in Montreal in 1982, this general theme was related directly to the conversion issue by Mr. Adi Davar in a paper entitled "Non-Zoroastrians in Zoroastrian Precepts: Do They Have a Place?" (subsequently published as a separate pamphlet). He argued that the prophet had founded a universal religion; that he had envisaged it for all mankind and not just for Iranians and concluded that American Zoroastrians should allow spouses in mixed marriages, or any sincere person with a genuine interest in Zoroastrianism, to convert. In congress deliberations it was decided that a survey of community attitudes in America, and the opinions of leaders in India and elsewhere, as well as western academics, should be sought. The host Quebec Association was charged with collecting this information, which it published in September 1983. That work showed a substantial majority of American Zoroastrians in favor of accepting non-Zoroastrians into the community—though a substantial proportion would still oppose this.[66]

The debate, however, was overtaken by events. Speaking on the same congress platform at Montreal in 1982 as Adi Davar was Joseph Peterson, who declared 'Although I am not a Parsi or Irani, my interest in this subject has approached obsession.' (*Proceedings* p. 75) In his speech on the occasion of his Naujote the following year Petersen explained how he first came across Zoroastrian teaching while browsing through a library at the age of fifteen, and, after searching for all the books he could find on the subject, he made his own sudre and kusti, and had thus sought to practice the religion for the last ten years until he had made contact with the Zoroastrian Association of Greater New York. After hours of discussion with him, the New York priest, Noshir Hormuzdiar, had agreed to perform his initiation. Leading priests, the Bombay Panchayet, public meetings and various religious teachers in Bombay protested at what they described as the illegality, the divisiveness and the doctrinal impropriety of this initiation.[67] Only one Bombay newspaper, the *Bombay Samachar*, and a few leading figures, notably Nani Palkihvala, defended the action. In America the action was defended in writing mainly by one of the priests involved, Kersey Anita, whose work was quoted above. He has not, thereafter, been given the opportunity to speak on public platforms at international Zoroastrian conferences in London and Bombay. Some of his fellow priests in America have avoided "sitting with" him at ceremonies. His offer to resign as the elected high priest at Chicago was rejected by only one vote. What arguments are advanced by the community against conversions and the initiations?

The Doctrinal Debate

Probably the most widespread argument in India against converison is that it is the greatest cause of intolerance. Parsis not only argue that because of their own religion's experience of oppression in Iran, but also because they fear that if they seek converts they would be likely to provoke hostility against themselves, a hostility which could destroy such a microscopic group. Thus Homi Dhalla argues that if the Parsis proselytized they would be bound to antagonize, and he attributes the peaceful coexistence Parsis have had with Hindus to the refusal to accept converts. "If we had trampled upon the religious susceptibilities of other communities through proselytism, whether this was done through persuassion or by exerting force, this would have generated hatred, suspicion and misunderstanding."[68] The fear is not only of the masses in India, but perhaps even more the scattered oversees communities, especially the Zoroastrians in the Iranian homeland. So the three high priests, Mirza, JamaspAsa and Kotwal, wrote in the 1983 newspaper article quoted above: We are living in a free country, enjoying freedom in all spheres of life, but we must not forget that there are Zoroastrians living in non-secular countries, ruled by religious heads under religious principles. If it is established that the Zoroastrians are a proselytizing community, then what would be the position of the Zoroastrians living there? Where there is conversion by any method, force, inducement, persuation [*sic*]—trouble is certain to arise. From all practical viewpoints, conversion would prove to be a dangerous game and a disastrous play with fire for our small community."[69] It is also argued that if Zoroastrians were to accept converts the tiny community would undoubtedly be swamped by the poor and outcastes seeking to avail themselves of the many Parsi charitable Trust funds.[70] Further it has been argued, social surveys of western societies have established that intermarriages between members of different religions tends to result in marital disharmony and breakdown.[71] It has been argued that Parsi attitudes to interfaith and inter race marriages have been reinforced, if not generated, by Indian ideas of caste.[72] It is, perhaps, natural that this should be so. People often ask why the Parsis have, despite their considerable economic success, never faced the equivalent of the anti-Semitism Jews have faced in Europe. One reason is undoubtedly the caste system which by preserving the rights of diverse groups takes the heat out of various situations which might otherwise cause communal jealously and conflict. It is intelligible that Parsis should seek to remain within a system that has provided them such security for over a millenium. It might be added that the ancient Zoroastrian purity laws are commonly consistent with high caste traditions—factors due presumably to their Indo-Iranian heritage.[73]

Noting that the call for the acceptance of converts has come predominantly from the young American communities it has been argued by Khojesti Mistree that they are calling for something for which there is no communal infrastructure, by way of schools, courses; that they would produce a class of "neo-Zoroastrians" accepted perhaps in America but not in the country which is the main numerical base of Zoroastrianism. Increasing the numbers of Zoroastrians is often given as a reason for accepting converts, but since race and religion are interwoven . . . "if it is the race, and through that the religion, that we wish to safeguard and increase, then conversion of people of other ethnic backgrounds is *not* the answer. To increase the race, that is the number of Parsi and Irani Zoroastrians, we need to encourage more of our youngsters to marry within the fold and thereafter give them facilities and economic incentives to raise more children.' The need is for existing Zoroastrians to be "born again".[74]

The argument is not, however merely one of practicality, it is also theoretical. Among Indian Parsis there is an almost universal conviction that the plurality of religions is a fact of divine creation, that all people are born into a religion chosen for them by God as being appropriate for their condition. To try and change a person's religion is, therefore, opposing the divine will. As B.H. Anita expressed it: "It is the law of destiny that each man is born at a particular time in a particular family and in a particular religion according to his physical, mental and spiritual composition. In other words man has no control over birth and death, the family to be born in and the religion to be followed for the life. Once this basic fact is accepted, it will be futile for any rational human being to say that he does not like the religion of his birth or the family of his birth. To renounce one's religion is an act of defiance against the Will of God and mounts to abrogation of his will." A little later he adds: "if all human beings belong to one family, why did God not create all human beings as of one pattern, one colour and one trait?"[75] Similarly Rustom Irani argues: "A man is born of a certain family in a specific religion according to the Plan and Will of God. Any tampering with this Plan amounts to committing a Mortal sin!"[76]

Another common modern Indian teaching also taken over by Parsis is that essentially all religions say the same thing. Thus Dastur Dhalla wrote: "All religions are same and teach the same truth in their essentials. They differ in their outer forms and rituals and socio-religious customs. What differences appear on the surface are the non-essentials of religions . . . Religions seem to be many in their outward form, but in their inner, sublime, spiritual nature Religion is One. Mankind knows many religions, but God the giver of Religion, knows only One Religion."[77]

Other Parsis, however, commonly assert that theirs is the best religion. It is indeed referred to as such in the ancient literature.[78] Thus in a catechism intended for young Zoroastrians Modi explains the existence of a plurality of religions in this way: "The prophets have appeared in various countries at different times and in different circumstances; and they have revealed their religions according to divine knowledge received by them. Hence more than one religion in the world."[79] Within that plurality of religions he sees, in accord with tradition, Zoroastrianism as the best: "I put faith in good Mazdayasni Religion, which removes bondage, allays quarrels, teaches self sacrifice, which is holy, which is greatest, best and excellent among the existing ones and those that shall come into existence, which is taught by Ahura and which is revealed by Zoroaster" (p. 3). Proof of the superiority of Zoroastrianism is often seen in the fact that it is the oldest of the prophetic religions, in part this is why for some Parsis the date of 6,000 B.C. if not earlier, is important.[80] Despite its great antiquity, it is stressed, it was the first ethical monotheism.[81] Further it is stressed by a number how much influence Zoroastrianism has exercise on other religions, not least Judaism and Christianity.[82] A number of Parsis emphasize the similarities between the religion of the western rulers and their own, at least during the days of the British Empire.[83] Others stress that Zoroastrianism more than any other religion anticipated the needs of modern man; that it was the first ecological religion; it is the most logical, and is consistent with the latest discoveries of modern science such as the theory of evolution and the discovery of electricity. In which claim they often make reference to the account of Samuel Laing, a Minister of Finance in India, who wrote three popular books for the semi-scientific reader, in one of which he presented Zoroastrianism as anticipating the discovery of a duality behind all life, namely in the positive and negative forces of electricity.[84] Such expressions of (understandable) pride in their own religion, and the conviction that that religion is specifically for one race, does not, it is often argued, mean any disrespect for others. Thus Homi Dhalla wrote: "The desire to perpetuate one's own religion or to prevent its assimilation (to lose its identity) is understandable and reasonable. Just as no individual needs to explain his desire to live, in the same way neither do any ethnic or religious groups need to offer an apology for their desire to perpetuate themselves. As we are members of a minority people with a distinctive religious philosophy, a sacred literature, rituals and ceremonies, the threat of intermarriage menaces our survival. It is of course pertinent to point out that just as love of one's own family does not imply that we look down upon other families, so also the love of one's religious heritage need not produce a sense of disdain for the religious heritage of others."[85]

Some Parsi writers have faced up to the question, if men are born into a particular religion because that is the one God considers appropriate for them, why are so few born into Zoroastrianism? The writers who seek to explain this are generally followers of Ilm-i Khshnoom, that is believers in rebirth. Their answer is that Zoroastrianism is the religion appropriate only for souls who have progressed favorably through previous lives, so "a human being after many births in other religions is qualified to be born in Zoroastrian religion."[86] Birth into this particular race does, at least in the belief of some, result in a distinct spiritual "aura", evidenced by Kirlean photography.[87] The Spiritual vibrations and colors of the soul born into Zoroastrianism are said to e substantially different from those of a *juddin*. Because of this racial difference, and because of the non-Zoroastrian's non-observance of the purity laws, his or her presence in the sanctuary produces vibrations which harm the sacred fire and conversly the power of the fire would harm the *juddīn*.[88] One writer, Dr. H.R. Bana argues that simply by the act of intercourse with a non Parsi male a Parsi girl causes "Higher level of a Zoroastrian soul is lowered, the purity of our noble blood is defiled." To marry a *juddīn* is "worse than a Parsi prostitute because the latter contacts *juddin* males temporarily". He concludes that "An individual particularly a woman cannot enforce continuance of the racial traits after amalgamating the semen of Foreign racial origin into her blood and her original racial traits are injured, mixed and changed by her act of marrying out of her race and religion."[89] The argument is sometimes advanced that just as breeders of pedigree dogs and horses select mates of the same breed carefully, so one should with religions and races. Thus Adi Doctor, writing in 1979 of the calls for intercommunal marriages, says "On the one hand they clamour for pedigree dogs and horses, on the other, they don't mind rearing hybrids and bastards among their children."[90] Such strong explicit links between race and religion being in the blood tend to be typical mainly of Parsis involved in the occult. Most restrict their arguments to the practical issues and other theoretical considerations listed above.

Conclusion: Some Current Issues

The intellectual wrestling with Protestant assumptions on religion(s) diminished considerably after Indian Independence. Parsis have rarely engaged in any form of religious dialogue with Islam; in general the antipathy has been too strong. There have been the occasional papers suggesting that there is some affinity between Zoroastriansism and Sufism or that Islam was not the persecuting force often depicted,[91] but these are not representative of any group nor typical of Parsi attitudes. Since Independence the dominant element in the religious world in which Parsis have lived has been Hinduism and given the characteristic Parsi conviction that Hindus have provided a haven of security and toleration, it is natural that Parsi thinkers should be engaged in seeking to interpret their belief in terms that are meaningful and relevant, as they see it, that is in the light of contemporary Indian thought. The name most evidently associated with this is Jal Wadia, who explicitly acknowledged his indebtedness to Swami Virjananda, a disciple of Vivekananda, who gave him instruction in meditation and formally initiated him into his form of religious practice. He argued, for example, that man does not have a separate individuality, he uses the notion of *karma*, of *Sat-Chit-Ananda*, *Purusha* and *Prakriti*, he also saw Zarathustra as an *avatar* and speaks of him as his "guru".[92] Another obvious name is Framroze Bode, the Dastur who performed the Bansda naujotes. He was rather "eclectic" in his interests, active for example, in the American Mazdaznan Order which claimed to have Zoroastrian ancestry and had something of a following in Bombay in the 1930s and 40s. Bode travelled regularly to California and was interested in those aspects of modern Indian thought which had some popularity in the West, not least Aurobindo and the idea of the Supermind, and what he termed "Zarathushtra's Unique Spiritual Philslophy of Self-Unfoldment" and his "Mystical Experience of Expanded Awareness".[93]

Hindu influence is discernable at a fairly wide level in that many Parsis, be they writers or not, accept a belief in rebirth (not the Zoroastrian teaching of a resurrection of the body). Similarly many practice yoga as a physical and religious discipline without any sense of conflict with their traditional practice. The following remarks are not easily documented,but are based on personal observation of Bombay Parsis during many visits over a period of 15 years. Some are hypothetical suggestions made in the hope of stimulating further research.[94]

In the 1970s and 1980s there is a growing interest in the Babas. Meher Baba (d. 1969) was himself a Parsi, of course, but it is Sai Baba (b. 1918) and Satya Sai Baba (B. 1926) who appear to have exercised the greatest fascination for Parsis, especially for the young.[95] Alongside a growing practice of pilgrimmage to the seven great Atash Bahrams (Cathedral Fire temples) in Bombay and Gujarat is, in the 1980s, that of visiting a Catholic Church in the suburb of Mahim to say the novena for successive Wednesdays, along with a flock of people of diverse religious allegiances, in the popular belief that they will thereby receive a miraculous answer to prayer. Some, though fewer, join similar crowds for seven pilgrimmages to the tomb of Hajji Ali in Bombay. A fair number of Parsis also attend public lectures by travelling popular Hindu swamis. These practices and movements are attractive partly because they are thought to meet the yearning for a charismatic, miraculous leader, or source of inspiration, a yearning found not only in Bombay but in many cities around the globe.[96] Perhaps an important theme in attitudes to religious pluralism should not only be the teaching of the separate religions but also the contrast between rural and urban sections of those religions. At least as far as the Parsis are concerned it is my impression (though no research has ever been undertaken on this subject) that there would be a marked difference between Parsis of rural—and traditional—groups who live somewhat apart from "other" religions and rarely theorize about them. The Parsis of cosmopolitan Bombay, in contrast, live and work so close to practitioners of many religions that they can hardly fail to come into contact with, and if they think much about religion, find themselves forced to wrestle with other traditions.[97]

Few Parsis, however, would be attracted, or religiously challenged, by **any** religion. The significance of the Babas, of popular pilgrimages, yoga, Hindu thought is that they can be pursued alongside allegiance to the community. Where a religion is seen as exclusive, for example Islam or formal membership of a Christian church, then there is a substantial barrier because of the almost universal Parsi reluctance, especially in Bombay, to commit what is sometimes referred to as "tribal treason". In short, attitudes to "other" religions varies not merely with regard to individual religions, but also to types of religions according to whether they are seen as threats to the community.

Parsi responses to religious pluralism are also conditioned, I suspect, by another aspect of where one lives. The division is not only between rural and urban, but further according to where the urban setting may be. Thus Parsis living in the 'main' centre of Bombay—especially in the large community housing colonies (such as at Tardeo, or Khusrau Baug or Khareghat Colony) have the opportunity to live in a more Zoroastrian environment, and in less physical contact with other religions, than do Parsis in the much smaller communities such as those in Delhi, Calcutta, Madras etc. It is perhaps no coincidence that the writer mentioned as wrestling most with Hindu thought, Wadia, came not from Bombay but from Calcutta. Similarly the first Indian Parsi community to accept the non-Zoroastrian spouse as a member of the community was Delhi.[98] In contrast the veiws which emphasize that the religion is in the blood have been most forcefully stated (though are certainly not unique to) a volume to celebrate the Rustom Framna Agiary (temple) in Tardeo. Is it the case that religions which have the human and material resources to be self sufficient can live not only in physical but also intellectural isolation from others? That would imply that there may be a greater tendency for inter-religious activity among smaller and scattered groups, at least where these do not feel under threat.

The last remark is provoked by some extensive research on the religious beliefs and practices of Parsis who have migrated to Hong Kong, Britain, Canada and America. This is to be published in detail elsewhere (including statistics gathered from a global survey),[99] but a summary of some of the conclusions may be helpful, and, it is hoped, challenging here. The attitudes of

Parsi emigres to "other" religions appear to be conditioned by the following factors: (A) the language in which an individual thinks—those who now think in English instead of Gujarati or Persian are more 'open' to influence from, and interaction with, the religion of the host society. This links with (B) where the individual had his or her primary education—thus those who had their earliest schooling in the West appear to be more "open", as defined above. (C) If they had post-graduate education in the West (in contrast to a first degree) then these highly educated individuals again appeared more "open", especially as there appeared to be a connection with such an education and (D) Intermarriage. Almost always those who had married out of the community seemed to have this greater "openess" to western religion. It is, of course, impossible to say which comes first, the "openness", or the marriage. (E) Parsis living near to "center" (normally a community building for social and religious functions where Parsis can meet and provide mutual support and encouragement) appear to have their traditional religious ties preserved. The reverse also appears to be true, that those living in isolation from co-religionists are correspondingly more exposed to other religions (F) Recent migrants; those compelled to flee, such as Parsis from East Africa in the 1960s and 1970s and the Zoroastrians from Iran after the fall of the Shah in 1979; those who had a Zoroastrian Religious Education in childhood; those with families, especially with children, all these groups tend to keep to their Asian traditions most faithfully and involve themselves least with other religions.

The study of Indian diaspora groups merits substantially more scholarly attention than it currently receives. These groups are important partly because of the role they have in their new setting; partly because of the impact such communities have on their parent society (at least in the Parsi instance it is typically the young, able, energetic and educated who have migrated and it seems probable they will affect the religion in Bombay, as indeed they have with the Peterson Najote discussed above); partly because such groups are in a "volatile" religious state—for example, it is common to find recent migrants are more active religiously than they were in "the homeland" and at that early stage less "open" to other religions but as accultruation develops a number swing the other way. Their interpretation of their own scripture; their assessment of their past history; their sense of what constitutes determinative religious authority; their perception of what they see as priorities or what they see as important practical or theoretical issues; their understanding of their own racial identity or citizenship—all these become modified by life as a miscroscopic community in an 'alien' and new culture. This in turn affects their attitude to other religions. Despite the common assertion of the secular nature of western society, to many newly arrived Parsis it has distinct Protestant features—in such a society many of the values of those who adapt in order to settle become "protestantized". The fact that such a process occurred with some Parsis writers earlier in the century, as described above, means that there are some theological guides for those settling in the "New World". So, for example, the work of Dastur Dhalla is quite popular among many western Parsis and is often quoted in some of their newsletters, a good illustration being the newsletter of the Zoroastrian Society of Ontario, based in Toronto.

In studies of religious pluralism it is evidently necessary to consider the traditional teachings and historical example. What is being argued here is that in the study of a living religion the geographical, social and political settings are also central, since they modify or develop attitudes. Another vital balance to be achieved is an assessment of both the 'intellectual' and the 'popular' responses. Thus a study of parsis attitudes which focussed mainly on the literature and the legal judgments would not allow for the enormous groundswell of orthodox feeling that was stricter on the admission of *juddins* even than the 1906 judgment, as was shown by the violence to Dastur Bode when he performed the legally acceptable Bansda naujotes. The balanced perspective is particularly difficult with the subject of religious pluralism because it is not simply a question of theological logic, but also of deep emotion and the illogicality of sentiment. It should not be assumed that even with their undoubted sincerity some of the leading figures of the debates always pursued their arguments with life long logic. Thus the "reformist" figure of K. R. Cama towards the end of his life became actively interested first in Theosophy and then in Ilm i Khshnoom. Although Dhalla had a "Protestant" typology of religions, he himself never performed the initiation of a child of a mixed marriage. He was asked to perform Bella's initiation but declined, fearing the act would cause community harmony. What is less well-known is that while on a visit to the States, he was asked privately to perform the initiation of the American intended spouse of a Parsi in quiet, but he refused.[100] What is clear from talking to a number of his personal aquaintances is that whatever Dhalla argued logically in print, at heart he was a man of deep devotion, filled with a love of his tradition. The cold word of print rarely reflects the spirit of a burning faith.

The diverse developments of the same religion under different conditions is highlighted in modern Zoroastrian history in the meeting of Parsi and Iranian Zoroastrians in the American communities. The clashes have been so strong that, despite their small numbers, formally separate groups have been established in New York, San Francisco and Los Angeles. Conflicts have erupted over apparently trivial issues such as food at communal occasions and language, but the fundamental problem is that the two groups have been nurtured for over a millenium in two entirely different religious environments: the Iranis in a Muslim setting where religion is considered necessarily simple in that man has no need of a priestly intermediary but experiences God directly in a simple prayer ritual and where religious authority is located in the revealed word of God exclusively in scripture and where there is a conviction of the uniqueness of religious truth. Parsis, in contrast, have flourished in an environment where complex rituals are invested with profound mystical significance, where priests are men of spiritual power, where religion and race are interwoven, where truth may be found in different traditions. The two groups have clashed over numerous issues, none more so than over conversion. Irani Zoroastrians commonly have a belief in the uniqueness of religious truth and have an abhorrence of what they consider the racialism which limits the religion to the offspring of Zoroastrian parents. From the traditional Parsi perspective the Irani Zoroastrians can sometimes appear to be crypto-Muslims, destroying the qualities and the tolerance which has kept the Zoroastrian community in India not merely alive, but flourishing—and one which gave substantial help to the Irani Zoroastrians in their darkest hour at the end of the nineteenth century. Here in these tiny groups can be seen the way in which a religion develops in different cultures and how traditional teachings and historic attitudes to religious pluralism, as to much else, can be transformed by experience.

But, if there is one common theme in Zoroastrian attitudes to religious pluralism, it is perhaps a general tolerance to outsiders (though not to others within the walls considered heretics). Throughout recorded history Zoroastrians have balanced a pride in their own religion with an acceptance of religious differences between races. There has never been a doctrinal commitment to missionary activity as there has been in Christianity, Islam or Buddhism. Providing other religions have not posed a communal threat, then perhaps the words of the great Sasanian monarch, Khosrau, quoted above typify Zoroastrian, and Parsi, attitudes: "We have no dispute with those who have other convictions for we [ourselves] possess so much in the whole original wisdom of the mazdayasnian religion.

Notes

1. The story of the Parsi migration is contained in The *Zissa-i Sanjān*, a document written in 1600 C.E. The full translation is in S. H. Hodivala, *Studies in Parsi History*, Bombay, 1920, pp. 92–117. A selection of passages are included in M. Boyce's invaluable compendium of translations of Zoroastrian sources, *Sources for the Study of Zoroastrianism*, Manchester, 1984, pp. 120–22. In this article reference will normally be made to that compendium for the reader's convenience. A study of the interpretation of the *Quissa* in Parsi oral tradition is given by P. Zxelrod, 'Myth and identity in the Indian Zoroastrian community,' *Journal of Mithraic Studies*, III, 1980, pp. 150–65.

2. The two main studies are R.B. Paymaster, *Early History of the Parsis in India*, Bombay, 1954 and N.K. Firby, *European Travellers and their perceptions of Zoroastrians in the seventeenth and eighteenth centuries*, German Archaeological Institute (in press, a Manchester M. Phil Thesis, 1984.

3. See J. Masselos, *Towards Nationalism public institutions and and urban politics in the nineteenth century*, Bombay, 1974; C. Dobbin, *Urban Leadership in Western India: politics and communities in Bombay city, 1840–1885*, Oxford, 1972; J. R. Hinnels, 'Parsis and the British', *Journal of the K.R. Cama Oriental Institute*, Bombay, xlvi, 1978, pp. 1–92; G. Tyndall, *City of Gold: the biography of Bombay*, London, 1982.

4. Nothing has thus far been published on these Parsi migrations other than K.N. Vaid, *The Overseas Indian Community in Hong Kong*, Hong Kong, 1972, pp. 49–64; C. Salvadori, *Through Open Doors: a view of Asian cultures in Kenya*, Nairobi, 1983, pp. 13–24; Hinnels, *op. cit.*, pp. 65–84 (on the migration to Britain); J. Pavri, 'Contributions of Zoroastrians to the North American Society', in *The Zoroastrian Challenge in North America* (Proceedings of the Fourth North American Zoroastrian Congress, Montreal, 1982, pp. 88–94.

5. The references could be almost endless. A good example is H.K. Mirza, *Some Religious Problems Facing the Parsi Community*, Bombay, 1983.

6. A readable and thorough collection of information on recent Parsi achievement is in P. Nanavutty, *The Parsis*, 2nd Edition, Delhi, 1980.

7. A survey of literature on Parsi demography can be found in Hinnells, 'The Parsis: a bibliographical survey, *Journal of Mithraic Studies*, III, 1980, pp. 100–149. The most recent study is M. Karkal, *Survey of Parsi Population of Greater Bombay—1982*, Bombay, 1985.

8. Karkal, *op. cit.*, ch. 8.

9. *Parsiana*, August, 1986, p. 3. This magazine which probably has the widest international circulation of any Parsi magazine has carried other demographic studies, see also September 1976, p. 27.

10. For the relevant Zoroastrian teachings, see J.R. Hinnells, *Persian Mythology*, 2nd edition, London, 1985, chs. 2 and 6. In an article this size, it is impossible to give a full account of Parsi religious literature. Being such a literate and educated community, it produces a vast array of books and pamphlets out of all proportion to its numbers. A comprehensive study of the subject has been undertaken by H. Langstaff, *The Impact of Western Education and Political Changes upon Religious Teachings of Indian Parsis in the Twentieth Century*, Manchester University Ph.D. Thesis, (unpublished) 1983.

11. See, for example, M. Boyce, *History of Zoroastrianism*, Vol. II, Leiden, 1982, pp. 1–3; G. Gnoli, *Zoroaster's Time and Homeland*, Naples, 1980, ch. 5.

12. *Yasna* 45:3, E.T. Boyce, *Sources*, p. 36. See also *Yasna* 31:8.

13. For the background see M. Boyce, *History of Zoroastrianism*, Vol II, Leiden, 1975 and her *Zoroastrians: their religious beliefs and practices*, London, 1979, chs. 1 and 2.

14. *Dīnkard* (Edited D.M. Madan, Bombay, 1911 [edition hereafter referred to as DkM]) 117–119, E.T. in R.C. Zaehner, *The Teachings of the Magi*, London, 1956, pp. 88–90.

15. *The Argument for Acceptance: a reply to the three high priests*, Bombay, 1984.

16. See his speech in the *Proceedings of the Function Honouring Eniment Parsis* by the Bombay Parsi Panchayet, Dec. 21, 1982, p. 35. The event was reported in *Parsiana*, February 1983, pp. 1–6.

17. 'On Conversion', in *Golden Jubilee of the Memorial at Sanjan*, [hereafter Sanjan Volume] published by the Bombay Zoroastrian Jashan Committee, Bombay, 1971, p. 21.

18. *P.S. Masani, zoroastrianism Ancient and Modern*, Bombay, 1917, p. 54.

19. 'Didn't Zarathustra convert?', *Parsiana*, December 1983, p. 33, also circulated in extended duplicated form.

20. Also published as a separate pamphlet by the newspaper, this quotation is from p. 11.

21. E.T. in J.B. Pritchard, *Ancient Near Eastern Texts*, Princeton, 1969, pp. 315f.

22. See, for example, Herodotus III: 89; Didorus of Sicily Iv.ix.22. On the ancient Western attitudes to Iran see A. Momigliano, *Alien Wisdom*, Cambridge, 1975, ch. 6.

23. Quoted in Boyce, *Zoroastrians*, p. 141.

24. VI: 321 E.T. by S. Shaked, *Wisdom of the Sasanian Sages* [hereafter Shaked], Colorado, 1982, p. 129.

25. See Boyce, *Zoroastrians*, chs. 7–9.

26. See K. Antia pp. 28–34 and H.E. Eduljee, 'On conversion', *Parsiana*, January 1971, pp. 5–9.

27. 'Conversion: a mandate for disunity' in *Parsiana*, August 1983, pp. 53–57 revised and extended in a duplicated form for the Fifth North American Congress, Los Angeles, 1985. For Dastur Mirza's views, see his *Conversion Caucasus*, Bombay, 1971, especially ch. on Sasanian history.

28. DPd.1f., E.T. by R.G. Kent, *Old Persian Grammar, Texts and Lexicon*, New Haven, 1953, p. 136.

29. DB IV.54, Kent, p. 131. See also Boyce, *Sources*, pp. 104f.

30. *Dk.M* 412ff, E.T. by R.C. Zaehner, *Zurvan a Zoroastrian Dilemma* [hereafter *ZZD*] Oxford, 1955, p. 8.

31. *Dk.M* 413.3ff, E.T. in *ZZD*, pp. 8f.

32. *Dk* III. 216, E.T. by Shaked, p. 85.

33. See Firby Section I; E.G. Browne, *A Year Amongst the Persians*, London, 1893, especially chs. 13 and 14; A.V.W. Jackson, *Persia Past and Present*, London, 1906, pp. 354–400; M. Boyce, *A Persian Stronghold of Zoroastrianism*, Oxford, 1977, *passim* but especially chapter 1.

34. It is impossible to give precise figures in the current political situation, since no census has been conducted for twenty years. This figure is lower than a number of Irani Zoroastrians friends would accept. They estimate approximately Forty thousand.

35. See Hinnells, 'Parsis and the British', pp. 42–64 and Karkal, 8.3.

36. Quoted in *Appendix to the Education Commission Report* I, Bombay, Vol. I, Report of the Bombay Provincial Committee, Calcutta, 1884, p. 22.

37. This is illustrated in a series of books published by Parsis in the early twentieth century. By 1901 two histories of Parsi cricket (a sport indicative of the degree of westernization among subject peoples at that time) had been written: M.K. Patel, *History of Parsee Cricket*, Bombay, 1892; M.E. Payvi, *Parsi Cricket*, Bombay, 1901. Parsi involvement in diverse Anglicized sports is documented in H.D. Darukhanawala, *Parsis and sports and kindred subjects*, Bombay, 1935. On English perceptions of the westernized nature of Parsis, see Hinnells, 'Parsis and the British', pp. 20–41 and Firby, *passim*.

38. On Haug's influence see Boyce, 'Zoroastrianism', ch. 4 in Hinnells, *A Handbook of Living Religions*, Penguin, 1985. An adequate account of Moulton's work in this respect has not yet been written.

39. S.M. Edwardes, *Kharshedji Rustamji Cama: a memoir*, Oxford, 1923; J.J. Modi, *K.R. Cama*, Bombay n.d. (the work was undertaken in 1932, but the forward refers to considerable delays in publication).

40. *Dastur Dhalla: the saga of a soul* [an autobiography] E.T. by G. and B.S.H.J. Rustomji, Karachi, 1975.

41. See Hinnells, 'Social change and religious transformation among Bombay Parsis in the early twentieth century', in P. Slater and D. Wiebe, *Traditions in Contact and Change*, Ontario, 1983, pp. 105–25.

42. Perhaps the most obvious example is D.F. Karaka, *History of the Parsis*, 2 vols, London, 1884 which was dedicated to His Royal Highness the Prince of Wales. A work with a similar motive and specifically on religion is R.P. Masani, *The Religion of the Good Life: Zoroastrianism*, London, 1937.

43. See J.J. Motivala and B.N. Sahiar, *Enlightened Non-Zoroastrians on Mazdayasnism, the Excellent Religion*, Bombay, 1899.

44. *History of Zoroastrianism*, Oxford, 1938, pp. 15, 53, 63, 69.

45. Hinnells, *Persian Mythology*, ch. 2.

46. *Hommage unto Ahura Mazda*, reprinted, Karachi, 1970, p. 2, 270.

47. *History*, p. 99.

48. See Boyce, 'The Continuity of the Zoroastrian Quest', in W. Foy (Ed), *Man's Religious Quest*, London, 1978, pp. 603–619.

49. *Early Zoroastrianism*, London, 1913, pp. 116–18.

50. See, for example, M.N. Dhalla, *Our Perfecting World*, Karachi, 1950, p. 61 and P.A. Wadia, *Zoroastrianism, our spiritual heritage*, 1923 who argues that rituals are not the essence of religion.

51. Dhalla, *History*, pp. 483–85 and ch. 49 on the reform movement; *Mankind—Whither Bound?* Karachi, 1950, pp. 552–54.

52. K.R. Cama, *The Services of the Rahnumae Mazdyasnian Sabha*, Bombay, 1902 (Gujarati—I am indebted to Dastur Dr. K.M. JamaspAsa of the Anjuman Atash Bahram, Bombay, for his help with this and other Gujarati sources, and for the many years of incalculable help he has given me); J.J. Modi, *Glimpse into the History and Work of the Zathoshti Din-ni Khol-karnari Mandli*, Bombay, 1922.

53. J.E. Sanjana, *Parsis and Theosophy*, Bombay, 1954.

54. The earliest example of this is P. Masani's book, *Zoroastrianism Ancient and Modern*, which was published in 1917 as a "review", or lengthy assault, on Dhalla's *History of Zoroastrianism*, a work which is scathing in its attack on the occult, see chapter 50.

55. *Parsi Prakash*, ed., vol. III, p. 41 (Gujarati) ed., B.B. Patel.

56. The Judgment delivered on Friday, 27 November, 1908 was published in its entirety by the Panchayet in the same year. This quotation is from pp. 116f. The proceedings have been recently drawn to Parsi public attention by being published in *Parsiana*, commencing October 1981, p. 6.

57. *Judgment*, pp. 137ff.

58. The text of the judgment was reproduced in the *Journal of the Iranian Association*, December 1918, VII, no. 9, pp. 302–25. References to the 1906 case are on pp. 310, 314, 315, 317, 318.

59. Accounts of the Privy Council Appeal are in J.R. Vimadalal, *Who is a Parsee-Zoroastrian?* Poona, 1979, pp. 18–21 and Mrs. M. Master Moos in *Mazdayasnie Monasterie News Letter*, June 1983, pp. 5–7.

60. See *Parsi Prakash*, for June 26, 1942, Vol. VIII, p. 38. The violence was threatened during a congregational prayer meeting at Wadiaji Atash Bahram which Bode had been advised not to attend because of the strength of feeling. Resolutions condemning Bode's actions were passed by the Panchayets/Anjumans at Bombay, Udwada, Tarapore, Bulsar, Billimoria, Bangalore, Ahmednagar, Mhow, Sholapur, Nargol, Jamnagar, Gandevi, and Secunderbard, by the Athornan Mandal ("Priests Society") and the Navsari Bhagarsath Anjuman (a major traditional priestly body. A number of temples agreed not to employ in the future any of the priests who had been involved. The legality of the naujotes was questioned on the ground that because the weddings had been performed according to Hindu rites the children were illegitimate.

61. Vimadalal, *op cit*, pp. 22–24.

62. *Adoption of Children Bill 1980, Parsi Zoroastrian point of view*, issued by the Special Committee for Adoption Bill of the Bombay Zoroastrian Jashan Committee, for private circulation. See also *Parsiana*, July and September 1981, p. 17.

63. This episode is covered extensively in the columns of *Parsiana*, see for example, July 1978; June 1980; December 1980; February 1981; June 1981; June 1983; September 1984. The editor—Jehangir Patel—was active in the campaign, not least the case regarding the rights of the women. Later he began to distance himself a little from the issues. CER produced their own paper, *The Zoroastrian*. The daily paper *Bombay Samachar* and the *Jam-i* on the side of the traditional party.

64. All community newspapers dealt at length with the issue. The most extensive reportage (as distinct from comment) was in *Parsiana*. The subject appeared in almost every issue in 1983: March (pp. 17–31; April, pp. 1–8 (including photographs of the event); May, pp. 3f, 16f; August, pp. 3–9, 49–77; December, pp. 3–6, 33.

65. The first was in Toronto in 1975; the second in Chicago in 1977 was on 'Survival and Perpetuation of Zoroastrianism'; the third in New York in 1979; the fourth on 'The Zoroastrian Challenge in North America' in Montreal in 1982 and the fifth on 'Preservation of the Zoroastrian Identity Through Adaptation to Changing Environments', Universal City, California, 1985.

66. *Non-Zoroastrians in Zoroastrian Precepts: do they have a place?*, Montreal, 1983. The results of the survey were published in *Parsiana*, February 1984, pp. 7f.

67. See the references in n.64 above, especially the August issue of *Parsiana*.

68. "Proselytism, then what?", *Sanjan Volume*, pp. 125–38 at 128.

69. See also Vakil, *op. cit.*, p. 96.

70. H. Dhalla, *op. cit.*, pp. 131, 138; *Judgment*, p. 82.

71. H. Dhalla "A brief study of intermarriage in America with reference to the Parsi community" in N.E. Turel (ed.), *1251st Anniversary of the Installation of Sacred Iranshah Atash Bahram*, Bombay, 1972, pp. 80–93.

72. *Judgment*, pp. 81, 86, 90, 153. See also H.B.M. Homji, *O Whither Parsis*, 1978, p. 90.

73. This link has long been appreciated by Parsis, see for example, S.M. Desai, *Hindu Suktas in the Zoroastrian Scriptures*, Navsari, 1904.

74. See the reference in n.27 above.

75. *Some Thoughts for Survival of the Zoroastrian Community in the Changing World*, Bombay, 1983, pp. 13 and 20.

76. *"Acceptance"—Never Ever! Conversion in Zoroastrianism: a myth exploded*, June 1985, p. 5. See also Ranina's paper in n.19 above; the Adoption Bill pamphlet mentioned in n.62 and Adi Doctor, "The Crust and the Kernel" in *Golden Jubilee of Rustom Framna Agiary, Souvenir Volume*, [hereafter *Rustom Framna Volume*] Bombay, 1979, p. 99.

77. *Mankind—Whither Bound?* p. 561. See also P. Masani, *Zoroastrianism*, p. 50 and S.H. Jhabvala, *Catechism on Zoroastrianism*, Bombay, n.d., p. 6.

78. See, for example, the texts in Zaehner, *Teachings*, p. 24; Boyce, *Sources*, pp. 58, 100.

79. *A Catechism of the Zoroastrian Religion*, reprinted Bombay, 1962 (1st edition, 1911). See also Jhabvala, *op. cit.*, p. 17.

80. For example, J.C. Katrak, *The Age of Zarathushtra*, Bombay, 1968 who on pp. 22 and 41 interprets later dates given by western academics as attempts to denigrate Zoroastrianism. Another advocate of the earlier dating is Dastur Dr. H.D.K. Mirza, *Outlines of Parsi History*, Bombay, 1974, pp. 361–66.

81. F.A. Bode, *Sharing the Joy of Learning*, Bombay, 1978, pp. 37f; S.A. Kapadia, *The Teachings of Zoroaster*, London, 1905, p. 16.

82. See, for example, R.E.D.P. Sanjana, *Zaraṭhushtra and Zarathushtrianism in the Avesta*, Leipzig, 1906, p. 266; F. K. Dadachanji, *Philosophy of Zoroastrianism and Comparative Study of Religions*, Bombay, 1941, pp. xv, 18f. It is a thesis which meets much acceptance among western academics, see Hinnells, "Zoroastrian influence on the Judaeo-Christian tradition," in *Journal of the K.R. Cama Oriental Institute*, Bombay, 1976, xlv, pp. 1–23.

83. S.A. Kapadia, *op. cit.*, pp. 18ff; Dhalla, *Our Perfecting World*, p. 228; M. Pithawalla, *Steps to Prophet Zoroaster*, Poona, 1915, pp. 12f.

84. S. Lain, *A Modern Zorastrian*, London, 1890. For a discussion of his impact see Hinnells, 'Social Change', pp. 111f. Examples of this influence are Sir J.C. Coyajee, *The Future of Zoroastrianism*, Bombay, n.d., pp. 8f; Pithawalla, *op. cit.*, pp. 13, 174ff; F. Rustomji, *A Catechism on the Teachings of Holy Zarathushtra*, Colombo, 1959, p. 9; N.K.D. Naigamwalls, *Zarathushtra's Glorious Faith*, Poona, 1967, p. 38; R.R. Motafram, *Zoroastrianism*, Part III, Bombay, 1984, p. 128.

85. H. Dhalla, 'Brief study . . . Intermarriage', pp. 90f.

86. *Kshnaothra Ahurahe Mazdaao: the deliverance of a Zerthoshti from other religious beliefs*, (a booklet for free distribution by followers of Minocher N. Pundol), Bombay, n.d. (approximately 1984/85), pp. 22 and 54.

87. See the Sept-Dec. 1977 issue of the Khshnoomic magazine, *Dini Avaz*. It is a belief also associated with Mrs. Meher Master Moos of the Mazdayasnie Monasterie, a popular contemporary teacher in Bombay.

88. See *Mazdayasnie Monasterie Newsletter*, June 1983, pp. 9f. This is differently expressed in K. Mistree, *Zoroastrianism: an ethnic perspective*, Bombay, 1982, p. 102 where it is said that a *juddins* non-observance of the purity laws would result "in the lessening of the purity of the sacred fire."

89. *Rustom Framna Volume*, pp. 7, 18, 22. This was argued in 1917 by P.S. Masani in his book which is quite influential among Khshnoomists, see p. 97. An influential Khshnoomic writer, F.S. Chiniwalla (*Essential Origins of Zoroastrianism*, Bombay, 1942) argues simply that all religions have some truth, though they have been corrupted by their followers, since all derive ultimately from Mazdeism which is the chief of all forerunners of religion, pp. 205f, hence all religions lead to the same goal, pp. 242ff. Man should simply follow the railroad of religion onto which he was born, pp. 294f.

90. *Rustom Framna Volume*, p. 97. This, too, is an argument which Parsis interested in the occult have advanced for some time, see J.J. Vimadalal, P.D. Mahaluxmivala and C.D. Mahaluxmivala, *Racial Intermarriages: their scientific aspect*, Bombay, 1922, *passim*, but it is by no means limited to them, so for example it was used by the secular writer S.F. Desai (*A Community at the Cross Roads*, Bombay, 1948) in connection with his appeals to preserve community identity.

91. An example is M.N. Dastur, 'The Gathas and the Koran', *Journal of the Iranian Association*, Sept. 1920, pp. 129–32 and more recently Irani, *"Acceptance"—Never Ever!*, p. 47. The argument against the historicity of Muslim persecution and the story of the Qissa-i Sanjan was put by B.N. Bhathena, *Kisse-sanjan: a palpabable falsehood*, Bombay, 1943.

92. *The Inner Man*, Calcutta, 1968, see also his article in *Parsiana*, March 1972, pp. 5–11 defending the practice of Zoroastrians visiting Indian holy men.

93. *Sharing the Joy of Learning*, Nasik, 1978, especially chapter 1. A good example of a sensitive account of Zoroastrianism in terms of contemporary Indian attitudes is I.J.S. Taraporewala, *The Religion of Zarathushtra*, Bombay, 1965.

94. I wish to record my profound thanks to the University of Manchester for the research funding to make all these visits.

95. An exposition of Satya Sai Baba's teaching has been given by the Parsi, E.B. Fanibunda, *Vision of the Divine*, Bombay, 1976.

96. On modern religious movements in western societies, see J. Gordon Melton, ch. 12 in Hennells, *Handbook of Living Religions*, Penguin, 1985.

97. For a study of cosmopolitan Bombay and the interaction of religions and cultures, see, J.F. Bulsara, *Patterns of Social Life in Metropolitan Areas (with particular reference to Greater Bombay)*, Bombay, 1970.

98. It was, ostensibly at any rate, this development in 1977 which led to the recently established Federation of Zoroastrian Anjumans in India breaking up (*Parsiana*, June/July, 1977, p. 25)—though another major factor was undoubtedly a personality clash.

99. Undertaken for the Ratanbai Katrak lectures, Oxford University, 1986, to be published by O.U.P., 1987.

100. Information supplied by Mr. Rustamji Wadia, whose restaurant in New York was the meeting place for Parsis in the early decades of the twentieth century.

Chapter Eleven

MODERN INDIAN MUSLIM RESPONSES

R.E. Miller

Approaching the Issue

Before attempting to deal with this complex issue, I would like to propose some preliminary considerations. The first is that it is wise to recognize the gravity of this subject for Indian Muslims. For them it is not a merely interesting topic for discussion, but rather it is a highly critical matter that has to do with the very being of Muslims in India, and one which has in the past led to major crises in the life of the community.

It has been noted that the manner in which Indian Muslims choose to deal with this issue has significance for the larger Muslim world, and hence also for the whole of human society. Some time ago, W.C. Smith suggested that the destiny of Indian Muslims has symbolic meaning beyond itself.

> Despite its apparent isolation, the Indo-Muslim group is representative . . . All Muslims taken together are in fact in a comparable situation within mankind . . . Today we must live in collaboration. Islam like others must prove creative at this point,

> and perhaps it will learn this in India. For the Indo-Muslims are in India what the total Muslim group is in the world: an important minority.[1]

In wider perspective this may be true. For the last decades Muslims in free India have been experiencing the realities of religious pluralism in a special way, and in the process have been providing a possibly representative answer to the question of how a Muslim minority, regional or global, lives and moves and has its being. But I do not find much conscious, abstract reflection on this wider significance among Indian Muslims themselves, although occasionally it is present. For Indian Muslims the fact of religious pluralism is rather an immediate, personal reality, significant for identity and for existence itself, and therefore a reality that calls forth deep emotion. The issue, then, must be examined with the same sensitivity and empathy that is appropriate to the penetration of any particular and fundamental religious emotion.

The second consideration arises out of the use of the term "religious pluralism." The phrase does not represent common Muslim language usage. There is more at stake in this fact than the choice of vocabulary. It is the possible implications of the phrase that produce concern and hesitation on the part of Indian Muslims. One can view the term "religious pluralism" from several perspectives: as a philosophical view of the nature of truth, as a desirable state of affairs, as a description of a reality, as an inevitable and hence an acceptable state of affairs, or as a problem and a challenge. This listing, of course, does not exhaust all the possibilities. The first two of these meanings are rejected by traditional Muslims as contrary to the principle of *tauhīd* (unity), whose content and direction are made clear by the revelation of the Qur'ān. A Muslim from Bangladesh summarizes the Muslim feeling when he says: "The Deity is One. There is no plurality or division in the nature of Reality. In case there had been pluralism, the whole world would have disintegrated long ago by confliction principles . . . "[2] The reluctance of Indian Muslims to use the term "religious pluralism" is directly related to the desire to avoid connotations of relativism or the suggestion that the situation of pluralism is in itself a desirable state of affairs. The third of the possible meanings suggested above, namely, the description of religious pluralism as a reality, is only barely relevant to traditional Indian Muslims, for whom the objective empirical observation of the religious environment, in the fashion of science of religion, is not a priority concern.

The issue of religious pluralism is primarily discussed by Indian Muslims in terms of its last two meanings. The fourth option, that is, the recognition of the inevitability of religious pluralism and hence the practical necessity to accept it, is a notion that is more and more being considered. However, it is religious pluralism as a problem and a challenge that preoccupies the majority of Indian Muslims. They recognize it as a fact of life, one that must be faced, and they do strive to deal with it. But their approach to the issue is not ordinarily through a direct treatment of the topic itself, although related themes such as "inter-religious understanding" are sometimes discussed. The approach is rather through the discussion of such concepts as secularism and the secular state, nationalism, democracy, cultural integration, the relation of religion and politics, law and economics, and so forth. It is primarily in these areas that we must seek the Indian Muslim response to religious pluralism.

A third consideration has to do with the generalization "Indian Muslims." The ideological diversity within Islam is familiar to most, a variety that is intensified in India by the nation's heterogenous culture and complex history. Whose response, then, do we seek? Do we mean traditional Muslims, liberal, reform, fundamentalist, or secularized Muslims? Do we mean Muslims living in the north, east or south, each region in India differing significantly in experience and perception? Do we intend the few who still maintain a living memory of the events of 1947, or the vast majority born since that time? Do we mean urban or village folk, religious leaders or the rank and file, western educated intelligentsia writing in English or the vast and relatively unknown mass of opinion circulating in vernacular literature? When we speak of Indian Muslims whose views do we purport to represent? Ideally, the map of Indian Muslim response can be drawn only after a detailed, and region by region charting of common Muslim opinion. The practical necessity of utilizing the opinions of the few, usually the educated and those who write in English, is a narrowing and potentially misleading alternative.

Associated with the problem of "who is saying it?" is the question of "what is really being said?" There is considerable caution among Indian Muslims in expressing views about some of the delicate issues involved in religious pluralism. While that caution is part of a larger hesitation to engage in any kind of theological speculation, it is rooted in another source, namely the accentuated post-Partition minority feelings of the community. Coupled with that is the diffidence natural to a minority group that upholds an exclusive principle in the midst of a comprehensive ideal. The latter has been frequently expressed as a hope and expectation of national and Hindu leaders that Muslims would adopt a positive attitude toward religious pluralism. The President of the nation, Sri V. V. Giri, declared:

> I would like to make an appeal . . . to our Muslim brethren to participate freely and unreservedly in the mainstream of national life. All of us are Indian, and in emphasizing this basic concept in our national life there is no room for distinction between Hindus, Muslims and Christians, or any other religious group. The total obliteration of caste and communal divisions alone would bring millions into an equal and enthusiastic partnership for social and economic progress. The positive force of healthy nationalism can transcend the divisive pull of casteism, communalism and parochialism, and transform them into creative energies.[3]

This appeal from on high for the sacrificing of distinction inevitably produces a wariness among those preoccupied with the question of continuing identity. Such caution, it must be said, becomes an almost palpable concern and vigilance during the periods of communal disharmony. The results are serious for the task of penetrating to the reality. On the one hand, a kind of mantle of silence settles down over inner feelings; and, on the other hand, a distinct gap develops between public rhetoric and private opinion.[4]

A fourth consideration has to do with the term "modern." In this essay I have arbitrarily chosen to limit the period under consideration to the post-1947 years. The early period of Muslim response, from 1857 forward, has not only been well-documented, but it also represents a particular situation that no longer exists. Although there was an awareness of other faiths, the primary issue in religious pluralism—at least the issue that was most reflected upon—was the relationship between Christians and the Muslim community. For the dealing with that issue Islamic history, theology, law and long experience provided a solid array of resources. Religious pluralism, in that context, after all, had to do with *ahl al-kitāb*, the people of the book. Led by Sir Sayyid Ahmad Khan, a number of brilliant Indian Muslims drew on available resources to develop an appropriate response.

While the heritage of this early modern period carries over into contemporary Muslim discussion, the formal treatment of inter-religious relations today has taken another direction. The dominating theme in the discussion today is not how to relate to Christians in an imperial state, but rather how to relate to Hindus in a secular state. There is very little significant Indian Muslim expression today that deals with relations with Christians, with a few exceptions such as some Mappila writings in Kerala and the reports of formal dialogue events. It is not that this has become a non-issue. It is simply not *the* relevant issue of the moment. What Indian Muslims are focussing upon is their relations with Hindus in free India. Rafiq Zadaria, in his presidential address to an academic conference on the subject of "Inter-Religious Understanding" (1972), stated: "I am confining myself to Hindu-Muslim understanding because it is not only the most important but the most urgent of our problems."[5]

My final preliminary consideration is to point out that the issue of religious pluralism in Indian Muslim life is not being worked out only at the formal levels of intellectual examination. There is an articulated response and a pragmatic response. The latter is observed at the everyday levels of human interaction. Elsewhere[6] I have attempted to trace the story of Muslim interaction with Hindus and Christians in Kerala as an aspect of a long history of organic life. That interaction would be virtually untraceable through the investigation of documents containing conscious reflection on the issues of religious pluralism. It is in the matrix of common life that decisions are being taken and theory is being forged, and the shape of the Indian Muslim view of religious pluralism will largely be determined by ordinary people who live together and work together in the daily converse of Indian life. This practical and silent history is unfolding before us, and needs to be described as much as the articulated response of Muslim intellectuals and leaders.

This reality is consistent with the history of Islamic theological development. From the beginning of Islam, doctrine was a response to practical questions, many of them arising out of the expansion into new worlds. This practical orientation has remained a constant factor. While the two-nation theory was set forth in absolute terms by Muhammad 'Ali Jinnah and his colleagues, during the last decade of the freedom movement, and while *dār al-islām* (house of Islam) theory was set forth by religious leaders, it was another reality—Muslim fear of being submerged, socially, economically and politically—in other words, a practical reality, that moved the Muslim masses. So also in India today, Indian Muslims deal with religious pluralism in a practical context. Theories of cultural integration depend on the pragmatic issues of the position of Urdu, the place of Aligarh and the safety of the *shari'a* (law). Theories of inter-religious understanding are qualified by Muslim fears of assertive Hinduism. Theories of the relation between religion and politics are affected by the economic disabilities of the Muslim community. What Luther said is true of Islam—*theologia habitus practicus est*!

It is against this background that individual Indian Muslim thinkers are engaging in their constructive task of dealing with a new situation. Usually without calling it that, but in fact utilizing the principle of private interpretation *(ijtihād)*, Indian Muslims are struggling to achieve a new understanding that is Islamically valid and practically effective, one that will take the community to a new consensus, as well as to a safe and successful future. That consensus is far from being achieved. There is a broad range of response, and what we have at this stage is only a set of materials for the development of a consensus, a veritable panoply of opinion, a series of individual threads not yet woven into a common tapestry. To form and apply a frame of reference appropriate to this range of materials is difficult. For the purpose of this discussion, however, I have chosen to divide the views into two groups, which I describe as "theological extension" and "constructive reflection." By theological extension I mean two things: first, the expanding of traditional Islamic concepts that have been employed in connection with questions of religious pluralism; and second, the reinterpretation of Qur'anic motifs and their application to the issue. By constructive reflection I refer to the approach that draws freely on personal insight, experience and training to develop a reasoned understanding of the subject, often marked by distance from traditional theological interests or expression. I recognize that these are overlapping categories with a limited function.

The Context

The cultural, theological and emotional contexts are important in the consideration of the Indian Muslim response to religious pluralism.

The Culture Context

Cultural pluralism as a fact has existed for Muslims in India from the advent of Islam. How Muslims dealt with its religious aspects depended on the circumstances of time and place. From the beginning of Muslim presence in the sub-continent, the concept of "people of the book" which had been extended to Zoroastrians in Persia was *de facto* applied to Hindus in Muslim territories. In the pre-Mughul period in the north, however, the inter-religious relationship was qualified by the reality of Muslim invasion and rule, and the often militant atmosphere that it produced. In the south a different situation prevailed, and a notable model for peaceful relations developed in Kerala. Under the Mughuls "house of Islam" motifs could at least be formally recognized, but pragmatic qualifications were the norm. As noted, the British period turned Muslim attention to the relationship with Christians. After religious politics led to the division of India, Mushir ul-Haq rightly observes, "the Muslims who preferred to live in India had to take stock of the situation afresh."[7]

Various estimates have been made of the extent of the religio-cultural adaptation that occurred as the result of this long interaction between Muslims and Hindus. On the one hand, the surprise is that the mutual influence was as slight as it appears to have been. Imtiaz Ahmad, however, speaks of the double, contradicting effect of Indian Muslim experience, that is, "distancing Muslims and Hindus by creating a Muslim community, and accommodation with Muslim culture by the process of absorption and legitimization."[8] Annemarie Schimmel describes the process as "die alte Dichotomie zwischen dem 'separatistischen' Mekka-orientierten Islam und dem synkretistischen, im Subkontinent verhafteten Islam."[9] The result of the double process is a variety in the relationships in different regions that tends to defy the levelling effects of theology and law. Ahmad suggests that these theological principles really serve only as broad guidelines, the concrete relationships showing considerable deviation from the norms. What is theologically simple is culturally complex. Muslims and non-Muslims do not see each other *only* as members of religious communities, but in fact, "there are a series of identities in terms of which they see each other and interact."[10] Cultural pluralism and religious pluralism are clearly linked. For Indian Muslims attempting to respond to religious pluralism, these forces of adaptation, of which they are in part a product, present both a problem and a possibility.

The Theological Context

A number of traditional theological concepts in Islam are applicable to the questions of religious pluralism, and they provide the natural starting point for orthodox Indian Muslims. While many continue to employ the concepts in their inherited, static meanings, others attempt to extend their significance to the unique situation of Indian Muslims. They include *shirk*, associating a partner with God, the greatest of sins; and *kufr*, the attitude of unbelief, stemming from ungratefulness to God. The fact that both these terms have been used and are used today as terms of reproach within the Muslim community itself, indicates that the basic concern is for the principles involved, and hence their traditional usage with reference to non-Muslims is capable of being modified. It is in this light that Sir Muhammad Iqbal declared: "An infidel (non-Muslim) before his idol with wakeful heart, is better than the religious man (Muslim) who sleeps in the mosque." Analagous concepts are *dār al-Islām* and its opposite *dār al-harb* (house of war). Both represent formidable realities in Indian Muslim history, recalling not only the struggle for Islam, but also the vision of Islamic statehood. At the same time, both have been reinterpreted frequently and the process continues today. Similarly, *jihāh*, the effective principle of "house of war," is now widely interpreted as a spiritual effort, a meaning drawn from the original connotation of "striving."

The traditional legal consideration of the state of non-Muslims is associated with the concept of *ahl al-kitāb*, which expresses the positive Qur'anic attitude toward Jews and Christians, who have been granted the favor of divine revelation in a sacred book. This principle, in turn, gradually evolved into a set of specific regulations pertaining to a *dhimmī* (non-Muslim subject), including *jizya* (poll-tax) and *Kharāj* (land-tax). A *harbi*, that is "an enemy" outside the favorable "people of the book" provision, may become a bearer of a safe-conduct *(musta'min)* and thereby in effect enjoy the status of a *dhimmī*. The implications of these terms, and their relation to an earlier and quite different condition, do not make them helpful for the situation of Muslims in India today. The theological motifs most utilized by Indian Muslims in the discussion of the issue being considered are *tauhī*, *quam* (people) *umma* (community), and *mu'ahada* (covenant). Accompanying reflection on these concepts is a fresh examination of the "religion" *(dīn)* of the Qur'ān itself.

The Emotional Context

The emotional context was established by the Partition of India and its aftermath. It is impossible to overstate the feelings of Indian Muslims as they rebounded from that event. None expressed more poignantly the sense of disillusionment than Abul Kalam Azad, when he said:

> It was now clear to them (Muslims left in India, *ed.*) that the only result of partition was that their position as a minority was much weaker than before. In addition, they had through their foolish action created anger and resentment in the minds of the Hindus.[11]

Their leaders, their seats of power and culture, their friends and companions were gone, and they were left a truncated and defenseless minority. How was it possible to grapple positively with religious pluralism in this context? Left alone, it would have been difficult enough. In addition, the Indian Muslims had to deal with "sympathetic" condolences from Pakistan deploring Indian's policy of "de-Muslimizing those who have remained under the Hindu thumb,"[12] as well as similar sentiments from beyond South Asia attacking the idea of secularism.[13]

Indian Muslim psychological depression increased for a period after Partition when Muslim hopes for rapid socio-economic advance were disappointed, when issues important for the identity of the community failed to gain attention, and when Hindu communal movements emerged with "Indianization" platforms. Were Muslims asking too much? Were they laboring under inferiority feelings? Had they been wearing rose-colored glasses? Perhaps all of these. The disillusionment, however, was profound. K. Gauba, a Muslim who had chosen to emigrate from Pakistan-designated territory into India in support of the secular principle, is an example of that disappointment; he lists Indian Muslim grievances and then says: "For the best part of twenty-six years, the Indian Muslims have wandered shepherdless and almost friendless—misunderstood at home and misrepresented abroad."[14] Clearly the requirements of healthy existence meant that Indian Muslims would have to climb from this Slough of Despond.

Although that long climb to the peaks of emotional security is not yet over, there is evidence that the ascent is well underway. In that rise Muslims in the north have been helped by their South Indian colleagues, who had maintained a different social fabric and whose post-Partition trauma was not so intense. Whether in the north or south, however, practical issues continue to raise doubts over the success of the secular state and impede the advance of inter-religious relationships to new levels. The following grievances are most frequently cited by Indian Muslims: inadequate legislative representation; the threat of common codes of law to Muslim personal law; the lost sheep position of Urdu; concern for the preservation of the special status of Aligarh; inequities in appointments and employment; fear for the security of Muslims at times of communal violence; pressure on the managements of the religious trusts *(waqf)*; concern over the apparent Hinduization of school texts and the lack of moral education; inequities in admissions to educational institutions; and the promotion of assimilation philosophies. Impartial Hindu observers themselves have recognized the legitimacy of many of these concerns and disabilities;[15] it is the solution of some of them that will both encourage Muslims and will open the way for an improvement in positive inter-relations.

It is from within the cultural, theological and emotional context that the specific responses to the situation of religious pluralism emerge. Those responses, in turn, progressively modify the context.

Facets of Response

Theological Extension

The 'ulama are the natural interpreters of the theological issues related to religious pluralism, and more than one observer has made the point that they will continue to be the key factor in their future resolution. The attitude of these religious leaders to the issue of pluralism was greatly affected by the struggle for freedom. The division of opinion among 'ulama regarding the proposal for Pakistan has been voluminously documented. In the end, with the possible exception of Bengal,[16] the majority of the leading 'ulama associated with "nationalist" Muslims and opted for a free and united India. They disdained enténte with British power, which they regarded as the chief foe; they held in suspect the views of the Aligarh-trained leaders of the Pakistan movement, which they felt would only lead to another secularized state like Turkey; and they regarded the proposed division of India as impractical and the "death-knell" of vast numbers of Indian Muslims. Theological theory, however, was needed to buttress the position.

Extending the Idea of Social Contract

In its simplest form, the theory that was developed maintained that the concept of a multi-religious nation could be Islamically recognized. Maulana Husain Ahmad Madani, redoubtable leader of the Jam'iyat ul-'Ulama, declared:[17]

> We, the inhabitants of India, insofar as we are Indians, have one thing in common, and that is our Indianness, which remains unchanged in spite of our religious and cultic differences. As the diversities in our appearances, individual qualities and personal traits and colour and stature do not affect our common humanness, similarly our religious and cultic differences do not interfere with our common associations with our homeland.

Jinnah and his colleagues were looking for a homeland for Muslims, but these 'ulama held that they already possessed one and were liberating it. On that basis they could join with their fellow citizens in a *muttaḥuda qawmīyyāt,* that is, a united peoplehood in a united Indian nationalism. A Muslim could be loyal to Islam and to India, an India that encompassed many religions.

The fundamental basis for the position of the 'ulama was in the covenant or mutual contract *(mu'ahada)* of the Prophet Muhammad that he negotiated with the citizens of Medina, including Jews who were specifically named, and polytheists. The key phrase in his remarkable document is:

> They are one community to the exclusion of all men . . . No polytheist shall . . . intervene against a believer . . . The Jews

> are one community with the believers (the Jews have their religion and the Muslims have theirs) . . . The close friends of the Jews are as themselves . . . God is the protector of the good and God-fearing man.[18]

Many Muslims in India have followed this lead and view the Covenant as a basic historic precedent from the life of the Prophet for their participation in the plural-religious nation of India. The idea has been spelled out in greater detail by Syed Barakat Ahmad, an international civil servant.

Barakat Ahmad connects the covenant with the concept of *umma*. The constitution of Medina proves that the term *umma* was never restricted to Muslims alone. Although admittedly the Muslims were to be the dominant group, nevertheless the mutual contract lays down "the guiding principle for building a multi-cultural and multi-religious *umma*." That this was the intention of the Prophet is proved by the fact that the community remained a multi-religious entity to the end of his life. Faith in the unity of God was the only requirement for membership in that community, and within it each group was guaranteed equal political and cultural rights, the freedom of religion, and autonomy in its own affairs. "It was the concept of a plural society and an ideal type," and the Qur'ān itself (2:213; 49:13) upholds this vision of a "multi-religions, multi-cultural, plural community."[19]

Not all the elements of this contemporary interpretation would have been accepted by every member of the 'ulama as India moved toward Independence, but for most the social contract of Medina provided a rationalization for Muslim life in pluralistic India. Associated with this was the idea of *qaum* (tribe, people, nation). Madani asserted that the Qur'ān's use of *qaum* is inclusive, that is, it embraces all the people of a particular region irrespective of their religious beliefs, including non-believers have been called one people, and what could be the relation between them except race and country?"[20] Hence Madani approves the view of Sir Sayyid Ahmad Khan to the effect that "Hindu," "Muslim," and "Christian," are purely religious connotations. Not one of these independently is a nation, but rather all who are living together in one country constitute a *quam* or nation. The Treaty of Hudaibiyat is also adduced as an example of how the Prophet made a compact with unbelievers, as well providing an example of how good mutual relations serve to bring people to Islam.[21]

In short, nationalist Muslim religious leaders had a vision, at times idealized, at times formulated for public consumption, but with a basic sincerity of intention. Syed Abdulla Brelvi declared[22] that they have no fear of a Hindu majority in an independent India:

> For such a feeling of fear to them is un-Islamic. Islam teaches fearlessness. Islam teaches brotherhood. The Nationalist Muslims . . . stand for democracy, which means a rule of liberty, equality and fraternity; a rule in which the smallest minority has an equal opportunity of being heard and has never any fear of its rights being trampled on, upon and in which the majority identifies itself with the needs and hopes of the minority. They strive for Hindu-Muslim unity for its own sake, and not merely as a means to any other end, because they aspire to build a new India which will be neither a Hindu India or a Muslim India, but an India in which every Hindu, every Muslim, and in fact, every citizen will find the highest satisfaction, in politics, economics, cultural and religious spheres, that is available to a citizen in every other State in the world.

What the 'ulama also set forth with equal fervor, however, was the *sine qua non* of that social contract, namely the right to maintain the *shari'a* in its personal and religious aspects. It was this provision that enabled Muslims to view India as *dār al-islām*, despite its pluralism. The second principle maintained was that the pluralistic situation must be regarded as an essentially temporary one. Faruqi interprets the point in these words:

> An Islamic state established and run in accordance with the precepts of the *Shari'ah* is the ideal of orthodoxy—a dream which it would continue to cherish. This is the only political pattern that can be theologically aspired for and justified. All other patterns are simply historical developments and may be accepted as a matter of political convenience and expedience. That there could be a socio-politico-economic pattern where the Muslims and the non-Muslims have permanently to live and cooperate with each other on equal footing, thus collectively converting themselves into an ummat-ul-wahidah, was an idea totally unacceptable and extremely repugnant to the orthodox. And the Muslims who accept it as such on the basis of any modern political philosophies are heterodox and, to a section of the orthodox, even heretics.[23]

In short, the mission of Islam goes on within religious pluralism.

Dīn, true religion, should reach out to others by *tadhkir*, warning non-Muslims of the danger of earning God's wrath on the last day.[24]

Deepening The Idea Of Dīn

The emphasis on social contract and peoplehood has been joined by discussion of the idea of religion itself. Since the goal of Islamicizing the nation remains remote and religious pluralism is seemingly here to stay, some contemporary 'ulama are examining the question as to whether there is something deeper that Muslims should be striving for than the traditional theocratic hope and form. It is being suggested that a true *quality* of religion must be the essential goal of Muslims, and this can be achieved in a pluralistic environment as well as in an Islamic state. Maulana Abul Hasan 'Ali Nadwi, one of the most highly respected Muslim religious leaders in India, has therefore launched a major criticism against Abul Ala Mawdudi's expression of the theocratic ideal and those who share it, both within and outside his Jama'at-Islam movement. He regards this as a reductionist view of religion, which sets forth Islam as "primarily an effective sociopolitical organization," instead of a community or worship and obedience. He calls for a stronger moral emphasis, affirming that the great 'ulama of the past always stressed the importance of moral "remembrance."

> They never played down the need for developing a deep spiritual life in nearness of God, intimacy, love and wonder. If God was merely a divine Ruler, loyalty and obedience of the servant would suffice. The God of the Quran, however, is more, and thus evokes and deserves the response of love and "much remembrance."[25]

This is what will preserve the Muslims. "Neither the mightiest governments nor any political power or organization can affect by themselves the decline of the genuine Islamic temper or deviation from it."[26]

Maulavi Wahiduddin Khan, following a somewhat similar approach, also emphasizes the primacy of *dīn*, which is a focussing on God and becoming wholly a person of God, in contrast to other non-essential factors. Showing the influence of Azad, he distinguishes between essence and accidence in Islamic faith. *Al-dīn* refers to the eternal teachings that were given to all the prophets, including principles such as *tauhīd* and *ikhlās* (consecration), while the manner of prophetic action and legal details constitute non-essential factors. Included in these secondary factors are forms of government; he asserts that "the establishment of an Islamic state as such has never been enjoined by the Qur'an, nor has it ever been the overall mission of any of the prophets." To view the establishment of a state as a mission of *dīn* can only be done by a process of twisting what are personal injunctions into social ones. Therefore he advises: "It has been enjoined in the Quran: make only the first thing *(dīn)* the pivot of religion; as to other things, adopt the method of 'extension'."[27]

Even the Jama'at-Islam movement, which stood for the illegitimacy of the secular state, has moved from its earlier position, at least in its formal expression. In so doing, it reveals how a seemingly inevitable pluralism can modify attitudes and expressions of a fundamentalist group. A resolution of its Central Advisory Council (1970) states that "in the present circumstances, the Jamaat-i-Islami Hind wants that in contrast to other totalitarian and fascist modes of government, the . . . secular, democratic mode of government in India should endure."[28] The Amir of the Indian branch of the movement, Maulana Muhammad Yusuf, affirmed (1975):

> Circumstances demand that instead of mutual conflict and confrontation, our energies should be pooled and utilized for reforms in administration and in ameliorating the conditions of the common people.[29]

Thus we may conclude that even thoroughly conservative 'ulama have officially and consciously—if not always convincedly or happily—committed themselves to guiding believers within a pluralistic environment, with statehood as a necessary element in Muslim faith in retreat, while *dī* as a moral and spiritual dynamic moves forward.

This should not be taken to mean, however, that religion and politics are viewed by the majority as dissociated. Rather, the opposite is true. What we find almost everywhere is a strong sense that salvation for Muslims in a pluralistic environment may be achieved by political action.[30] Even before the Partition nationalist Muslims were contemplating a continuing political organization in free India, although Azad vigorously opposed the idea.[31] After Partition Muslim politics were temporarily paralyzed, and in 1948 at Lucknow Muslim leaders took a public position against separate political parties. "Even the Jam'iyat 'Ulama-e-Hind had to announce that it would work only for religious and cultural causes."[32] Muslim social and economic depression, communal riots, and an increasing fear of loss of identity, however, brought a rebirth of communal political activity. The Muslim League was actively reborn in Kerala, and in 1963 the all-India Muslim Majlis-e-Mushawarat was formed, as a kind of "holding company" for Muslim interests. While some Muslims opposed the development, many others were earnestly convinced that it was necessary and that it was not inherently detrimental to Hindu-Muslim relations. Ulama, who participated significantly in the rebirth of religio-political action, in the words of Mushir ul-Haq, were "of the opinion that they cannot shirk their responsibility of watching the religious interests of the community."[33] Many lay Muslim leaders of note, however, were of the same opinion. In their view, community political action and communalism are not the same.

The trend to Muslim religio-political action was an interactive development with the increase of Hindu communal political activity, involving the Hindu Mahasabha, its military wing, the Rashtriya Swayam Sevak Sangh, and Jan Sangh. The clarion call of the Jan Sangh for "Indianisation" (first resolved January 7, 1957, but publicly declared December 27, 1969) brought shivers to the Muslim spine:

> It is the duty of the Hindu state to Indianise those sections of India's national being which were shaken out of their moorings and made to look outside the country for inspiration.[34]

Prabhat Dixit traces this development to pressures for special considerations exerted by religious minorities. Muslims, however, regarded it as the appearance of feared elements that they believed would remain under control in secular India. That these fears of Hindu chauvinism were not the product of inferiority feelings or fervid imagination is illustrated by the comparative Christian reaction to the same phenomenon. Matthai Zachariah, citing the impressive statistics of the R.S.S., declared:[35]

> Suddenly an old issue has come alive again. Old fears are being voiced again . . . The minorities particularly have reason to be disturbed. In their attempt to recapture "the glory that was India"

> the RSS is projecting a purely Hindu India . . . According to the RSS, Hindu culture is coterminous with Indian culture.

Indian Muslims who criticized their community's return to a conjunction of religion and politics noted that the very concern that produces religio-political parties in turn intensifies the communal emotions, so that the net effect of such organizations is counter-productive. Normal political activities when wedded to religious feeling often become inflammatory. Those flames are frequently fed by interested parties. The distress of communal riots is used to further inflame communal passions, and thereby aggrandize political pursuits. Ali Asghar Engineer voices a widely held opinion when he says: "The shameless political opportunism of politicians has been the major contributing cause in aggravating communal conflicts."[36] Rational arguments, however, cannot prevail against the widely held conviction that religious pluralism without politics is dangerous for the Muslim community.

Extending The Principle Of Tauhīd

Underlying the concepts of *mu'ahada-umma-quam* and *dīn* is the principle of *tauhīd*. This theological principle, it is held, fundamentally determines the relationships between humans and between religions. At the core of the belief is the perception that God the Creator is One. From His unity, as necessary consequences, follow the unity of the created world, of mankind and of all of life. The first basic conclusion is that "all human beings belong to a universal brotherhood."[37] *Tauhīd*, however, also establishes the religious reality. There is one original and true religion, namely, the religion of God and His unity, and all other religions are offshoots from it. Tazimuddin Siddiqui puts it succinctly: "Many religions flowed from one religion."[38] Therefore all religions may be said to share a common divine origin,[39] and some would even say, a common divine inspiration.[40]

This positive evaluation, however, must be qualified by the recognition that the religions have experienced a distortion of the pristine truth.

> Like Islam, Christianity and Judaism and Hinduism as well in their purity proclaimed the same divine unity. The God of Christianity, the Jehova of Judaism and the Vedantic Brahma in Hinduism all stand for the unity of the divine reality. But this unity

> in divinity was later distorted at the hands of some interested people.[41]

This distortion required prophetic warning and divine guidance, culminating in the revelation of God through Muhammad. God's guidance is intended to restore to humanity the *tauhīd* of God, the *tauhīd* of the human family, and the *tauhīd* of true religion. Thereby another commonality has been added, the sharing of *hidāyat*, the guidance of the one God Who points His creation to His truth.

This understanding of *tauhīd* undergirds the Muslim ideal of toleration, which is theologically extended to the religiously pluralistic context of India. Against that background, Muslims of all persuasion are ready to point out the practical precedences for toleration to be found in Islamic history, and the guarantees for freedom of religious belief, practice and personal law under various Muslim governments are frequently cited. It is admitted that in the course of Muslim history there were departures from this ideal, but the phenomenon of oppression was inexcusable and un-Islamic behavior which affected faithful Muslims as well as non-Muslins. Although the ideal was not always attained in the past, it must now be newly apprehended and applied to interrelationships in India. The linkage of *tauhīd* and toleration is illustrated in S.Abid Husain's summary of a Muslim seminar on the subject of inter-religious understanding. The trend of the thought was

> that all faiths are of divine origin and represent a gradual realization of the religious truth culminating in Islam, with the implication that the unity among the various religions is ruled out, yet mutual tolerance and amicable co-existence is not only permitted but enjoyed by Islam.[42]

Barakat Ahmad takes the issue back to the Qur'ān. He links the matter of religious toleration with the attitude of Muhammad at the time of the first *umma*. The Prophet, he suggests, was appointed as a warner, not as a compeller, and the Qur'ān establishes the principle that there is to be no compulsion in religion (2:256). The Prophet followed this policy, even with hypocrites and recanters, leaving punishment to God, and this is the appropriate model for Muslims in India. With the exception of the duty of warfare, equality was the principle. He regards the *akhām al-dhimma*, the special provisions for the people of the book, as a later development having no basis in the Qur'ān or in the custom of the Prophet. The Qur'anic and Muslim approach, he holds is much more radically tolerant:

> A pluralistic community like the umma, which the Apostle sought to establish presupposes religious liberty. Toleration is not enough; liberty to practice and preach a dissenting religion, to retain cultural and ethnic identity, and to follow and administer personal law, must be based on the idea of rights and guaranteed by the dominant group. In the umma it was not a concession but a right established by the Quran.[43]

For most Indian Muslims it would be wrong to interpret the stress on *tauhīd*-based tolerance as implied agreement with ideas and practices defined as *shirk*. Not many therefore would be inclined to accept Zubair Siddiqui's strong statement: "The concept of divine origin of all religions, held by Islam, virtually signified the basic unity of all religions."[44] *Tauhīd* implies judgment as well as toleration. Many would therefore prefer the more measured observation of C.N. Ahmad Moulavi. The reformist Mappila theologian states:

> Because of Islam's insistence on *tauhīd* it had to oppose many practices not in tune with this belief. Muslims are not able to cooperate with others in some affairs, which causes misunderstandings among those who have not understood Islam properly.[45]

Within that fundamental restraint, however, there are few Indian Muslims who are not practically oriented to a live and let live approach in the daily affairs of life.

Constructive Reflection

We have treated some of the traditional theological themes which by extension are applied to the situation of religious pluralism. The Muslim thinkers who fall under the general head of constructive reflection represent an exceedingly diverse group with a broad range of views. It is not possible, in a short essay, to enter extensively into this vast body of material. This discussion, therefore, will be limited to three major figures: Abul Kalam Azad, Zikir Husain, and S. Abid Husain.

Abul Kalam Azad (1888–1958)

Azad represents a bridge figure between theological extension and constructive reflection. This prominent leader and thinker did two things for Indian Muslims that directly reflect on the issue of religious pluralism. He secured the concept of nationalism as a firm frame of reference for pluralistic living, and he provided fresh Qur'anic interpretations for inter-religious understanding.

Azad's leadership of nationalist Muslims and his service to the independence movement, and later to free India, need no introduction. In the following inspirational words he clearly indicated his view of the relation of being Muslim and being Indian:

> I am a Musulman and am proud of that fact. Islam's splendid traditions of 1300 years are my inheritance. The teaching and history of Islam, the arts and letters and civilization are my wealth and my fortune. It is my duty to protect them.
>
> But in addition to these sentiments, I have others also which the realities and conditions of my life have forced upon me. The spirit of Islam does not come in the way of these sentiments; it guides and helps me forward. I am proud of being an Indian. I am part of the indivisible unity that is Indian nationality. I am indispensable to this noble edifice and without me this splendid structure of India is incomplete. I am an essential element which has gone to build India. I can never surrender this dream . . .[46]

Led by Azad this became for many the conscious Indian Muslim dream. A firm hope and conviction developed that the common love of nation would be the power that would make religious pluralism work.

At the level of Qur'anic interpretation, Azad begins with the concept of the universal guidance of God. Divine revelation given to everyone without distinction inculcates universal religion, which is *al-dīn* or *al-islām*, the one religion that is appropriate to the nature and function of all humanity.

> It is the law of belief and righteous living, of belief in one supreme Lord of the universe, and of righteous living in accord with that belief. Any religion other than this or conflicting with it is not religion in the strict sense of the term.[47]

Religious history is the struggle between this primordial vision and the power for degeneration.

Azad argues that the same evolutionary process goes on in the spiritual realm as in the physical realm. By an inner law of truth, the *batīl*, the vanity in life is judged and excised. This law of truth works in conjunction with the law of mercy. God in His mercy allows humans "a time for reflection and for making amends," and thus through a gradual process, the steady movement of His mercy has effect and truth prevails. This process is taking place in all religious traditions. The Qur'ān, as an uncompromising instrument for the forward progress of God's will and truth, has a role in that development.

While this process goes on, Muslims are to maintain a twofold relation with the members of other religions. On the one hand, it is their duty to remind them of their essential truth and, as it were, to call them back to their first love.

> The first doctrinal principle of the Quran is to recognize the founders of all religions and endorse their teaching, which at the basis is one and the same, and to conform to the way shown them; as the Quran says: "We make no difference between them" (2:285).[48]

Christianity, for example, must pass through its current phase of "monotheistic polytheism"; so also Hinduism is subject to critique, for "the beauty of the Indian mind and all its great achievements have been cluttered by superstition and image worship . . . "[49] Thus Islam asks them "to return to their own religion by first discarding all the aberrations that they have heaped thereon, and strictly adhere to the original faith."[50] This return to the foundations will be effectively the same as accepting the Qur'ān and its message.

On the other hand, Muslims are also to maintain a warm and cordial relation with the people of other faiths. This is justified religiously because the spirit of these faiths is the same as the spirit of Islam. Religion, it should be understood, has two aspects. One is its inner spirit, which is *dīn*, while the other is its external manifestation (*shar'a, minhaj*: path). The outward path may vary, as is indicated by the fact that even the *qibla* (direction of prayer) was changed by the Qur'ān, when circumstances changed for believers. But this does not mean that there is not an inner congruence of spirit. "The differences which exist between one religion and another are not differences in *dīn*, the basic provision, but in the manner of giving effect to it."[51] It is the responsibility of Muslims to concentrate on this "basic provision" and make that the test of inter-religious relations. That essential is summed up in the Qur'ān (2:177) as devotion to one God and righteous living. On this basis religious pluralism will become a dynamic engagement of essentially united people in one nation.

On this basis, too, Azad calls upon Muslims to create in themselves the quality of tolerance. There will inevitably be varieties in points of view, but these must not become the grounds for conflict. He paraphrases 10:99 of the Qur'ān as follows:

> Man by disposition likes to follow a way pleasing to him. Just as you think your way is the right way, even so others think their's is the right way. Create therefore in you the quality of tolerance.

Tolerance, however, does not imply the compromise of beliefs. Without solving it, Azad states the tension that exists for Muslims in a pluralistic milieu, a tension he felt throughout his life:[52]

> Tolerance is a good thing, but strength of belief and opinion, and integrity of thought are also factors of life which we cannot discard. A line of demarcation for the expression of each quality in us needs to be drawn . . . Tolerance is to acknowledge the right of another to hold his own views and to follow his own way. Even when the way is clearly the wrong way, you cannot deny him the right to pursue it. But if tolerance is given the latitude to water down your own beliefs and affect your decisions, then it ceases to be tolerance. Compromise is a necessity of life . . . but there should be a limit to it.

An aspect of the struggle of Indian Muslims is to discern that limit.

Zakir Husain (1897–1969)

Zakir Husain and S. Abid Husain represent what Abid Husain terms "secular nationalism." No other Indian Muslims have contributed more to the intelligent leadership of their community.

Zakir Husain was a pragmatic and warm-hearted man of friendship. An economist, not a theologian, he had little regard for religious haughtiness and arrogance, and what he called "infatuation with the externals of religion."[53]

> The good Muslim cultivates friendship because it is in friendship that the true relationship between men and God is revealed, and

> to be a good friend he cultivates those social qualities which are more pleasing to his fellow man, charm of manner, ability to converse, argue, convince; participation in the enjoyments of literature, art, and in those observances which reveal deep interest in his fellow men and reverence for the divine. The practice of equality is for him not an injunction be be obeyed but an instinct, a second nature that cannot bear to be repressed. The good Muslim loves God only, but in such a way that those among whom he lives are made to feel that he loves them only.[54]

These words typify that spirit and attitude, not confined to Husain, which inspired some of the noblest examples of Hindu-Muslim relations in India.

Zakir Husain took his spirit of friendship into the arena of action. Jayaprakash Narayan remembered a great moment (November 17, 1946) when the future President of India brought together Nehru and Azad on one side, and Jinnah and Liaqat Ali Khan on the other, at the Silver Jubilee of the Jamia Millia. He spoke of the fire raging in the land:

> For God's sake, sit together and extinguish this fire of hatred. This is not the time to ask who is responsible for it and what is its cause. The fire is raging. Please extinguish it. The problem is not of this community's or that community's survival. It is the choice between civilized human life and barbarism. For God's sake,do not allow the very foundations of civilized life in this country to be destroyed.[55]

These stirring words ring with a peculiar relevance for India today.

Along with this fundamental attitude, Zakir Husain also reflected a great spirit of excitement about the developing experiment in the merging of cultures. He was one Indian Muslim who understood the remarkable implications of the experiment for Muslims everywhere. Speaking at Cairo, he said: "Muslims have either ruled exclusively in a country or been ruled by non-Muslims. Here . . . Muslim citizens of India are co-rulers with their countrymen of other faiths in a secular democracy."[56] He believed that one of the products of this new synthesis would be fresh insights into "the message of the great Prophet who was not only of the Arabs, but was a blessing for the worlds."[57]

A strong believer in Muslim indentity, Zakir Husain was deeply wounded when non-Muslims apparently failed to appreciate that reality. Yet he persisted with his own almost poetic sense of embracive homeland:

> The Himalayas and the Vindhyas, the Ganga and Jumna, the Brahmaputra, the Krishna and the Kaveri, Badranath and Rameshwaram, Dwaraka, and Jaganath Puri, Rama and Krishna, Gautama Buddha and Lord Mahavira, Sankaracarya and Ramanuja, Ashok and Akbar, Nanak and Kabir and Govind Singh, Muinuddin of Amjer and Khwaja Nizamuddin, Surdas, Tukaram and Mirabai, Kalidas and Tulsidas, Ghalib and Anis, Vallathol and Tagore, Gandhi and Abul Kalam, Jawaharlal Nehru, these and many others besides, with their names and their achievements become the home. And they give the same joy and the same warmth, the same solace and the same strength as is first found in the mother's lap.[58]

On the eve of his installation as President (May 1967), Husain called on Jagadguru Sri Sankaracarya of Srinegiri in Delhi, placed flowers and fruit at his feet, and sought and received his blessings. He felt that one cannot affirm one's own identity without allowing the same privilege to others. His colleague, M. Mujeeb, suggests that "he went to Sankaracarya . . . as an act of atonement for the narrowmindedness of his community."[59] Criticized for his action, and deeply wounded, he recited Ghalib:

> I speak the truth, the ignorant
> Laugh at me with their tongues
> O God, have judges now eschewed
> the scaffold and the noose?

Accepting the distress that accompanied his innovative approach, Zakir Husain went on to call for national advance in the comparative study of religions. "Once we start," he said, "It is certain that we shall make rapid progress. It is almost in our nature to seek unity in divesity, to reconcile opposites, to create harmony of aim."[60]

An aspect of the struggle of Indian Muslims is to discern the nature of that reconciliation.

S. Abid Husain (1896–1978)

S. Abid Husain, distinguished Muslim intellectual and founding editor of the Islam and Modern Age Society, is the most prolific Muslim scholar to reflect upon the themes of secularism, national integration and the destiny of Indian Muslims. In his more than forty books he touches on many aspects of religious pluralism, An apostle of modernism, he has called upon Indian Muslims to undertake an intellectual revolution and join the mainstream of modern life. He invited his fellow Muslims to join in the uplifting task of building a national culture, both giving and receiving as they do so, without losing the essential character and dignity of Muslim identity. "This national culture has to aim not at absolute uniformity, but at a perfect harmony of a variety of regional and sectional cultures."[61]

Abid Husain noted that the feeling of the Muslim community that "its cultural rights are not respected" is an obstacle to its members seeing their natural place in the cultural mosaic of India. This feeling fuels the growth of religious nationalism, which unfortunately is "now the prevailing trend among Muslims."[62]. Indian Muslims on their part must therefore make two things clear to their fellow citizens: first of all, that devotion to God is for Muslims the primary reality in life; and secondly, that a uniting national culture that represents a kind of civil religion drawn from the majority culture is not acceptable. Muslims, he said, have one desire, which is to view the love of nation, love of God and love of Islam in a wholistic manner.

According to Abid Husain, the proper framce of reference for Muslim thinking in this situation is that of secular nationalism. This represents neither a danger to the faith nor an impossible contradiction. Indian Muslims do not have to quail at the term "secularism," simply because Indian secularism is by no means anti-religious. Abid Husain holds that the general value system of Indian secularism is "essentially religious" and therefore it is also implicitly Islamic. While the source of the values may be viewed differently by theists and by humanists, the values themselves are objective, and a true Muslim will "regard every act which is meant for the material and social welfare of God's creatures, whether they are Muslim or non-Muslim *as a religious act*" (ed.it.).[63] This means that some of the basic Islamic values, such as freedom, brotherhood, equality and justice, are already recognized and, in fact, have become fundamental rights in the nation. Other Islamic moral values of importance also can be presented and, to the extent that they stand the test of reason and experience, they too may be accepted. Specific religious truths that are uniquely Muslim can be pursued separately within the confines of the religious community. From Abid Husain's point of view, the secret of religious pluralism lies in the overlapping and sharing of common basic values.

The options that Muslims have in India's experiment, Abid Husain suggests, should be clearly recognized. The nation's leaders are attempting to build a national life in which every religious/cultural group can express its uniqueness, and at the same time they are endeavoring to construct a secular life based on the general principles of modern culture, such as democracy, socialism and technology, and on moral values common to all. In this process,Indian Muslims have three choices: to assimilate, to remain aloof, to become part of the process. The first is not an option. The community has therefore the choice either to live as a minority which does not accept the prevailing political and social order, but is forced to submit to it; or it must live as an integral part of a secular nation, and at the same time preserve the distinctive Muslim religious and cultural life. The former, the way of religious nationalism, leads to ghettoism and dualism. The latter is the road of secular nationalism, and it is down that path that Indian Muslims must walk, engaged in a dynamic pluralism.[64]

To be successful in this venture, in the view of Abid Husain, Muslims must develop a change of approach. First of all, the spirit of dogmatism must yield to the scientific attitude toward life, which will reduce the unreasonable fears of secularism. Secondly, Indian Muslims must resist

> the reactionary forces of bigotry, revivalism, obscurantism and the disintegrating forces of casteism and communalism . . . They should look at all the common problems in the light of the larger interest of the Indian national and ultimately in the interest of the whole human brotherhood.[65]

If Louis Dumont's definition of communalism is accurate, namely, that it is "the affirmation of a religious community as a political group" and "the opposition to each other of religious communities,"[66] then Abid Husain is warning his fellow Muslims against both aspects. Thirdly, Abid Husain argues that Indian Muslims must resist the tendency to believe in salvation by politics. Political pressure groups, using the name of religion will do no Muslims good in this world or in the next. Not only must the understanding of true religion take away the concern for a theocratic state, it should remove from Indian Muslims the substitionary fetish of religious politics.

> Their religious and political salvation lies in adopting *real* Islam instead of their brand of political Islam, and in becoming a moral group which could, through its good faith, virtues, action and social service, win the love and respect of the people of their country and their world.[67]

Indian Muslims, above all, must strive to come to an understanding with the Hindu majority. This, for Abid Husain, is the crucial issue. At a practical level, these relationships are being established:

> Today we find throughout India innumerable examples of Hindus and Muslims are neighbours and colleagues, and their boys and girls who are school-fellows, behaving towards each other in a normal and in some cases friendly and affectionate way. They don't think of each other as Hindu and Muslim, but as fellow human beings.[68]

This raises a fundamental question. Why cannot the personal be translated and raised to the level of community relations? At the community level, unfortunately, there is an undercurrent of misunderstanding, mistrust and often antipathy between the two communities.

Muslims can and must take concrete steps to ease the situation. One way, Abid Husain affirms, is by making the Indian past—including the cultural life of the Hindus—their own, thereby "bringing themselves in harmony with the soul of India."[69] Of course, he notes, Hindus must also do the same. Secondly, Indian Muslims must develop a rational attitude to history. It should be understood that neither the Hindu nor the Muslim communities as a whole are responsible for the irrational and oppressive acts of their rulers in the past. There must, in fact, be a deliberate attempt at a loss of memory, for "when communities join to form a nation, they have to forgive much and forget much."[70] Finally, he commends the view that there should be a non-official but government-recognized board appointed to help protect, vindicate and monitor the fundamental rights of minorities.

S. Abid Husain, like Martin Luther King, has a dream, and in concluding his notable volume, *The Destiny of Indian Muslims*, he shares that dream. It is a dream of *tauhīd*. Muslims normally think in concentric circles: the outer circle is international life, then comes the circle of national life, and at the core is communal life. Let us think instead of two circles, he dreams. The external one is human life, and at the core is God. Human culture is one and indivisible, and some day, the walls which separate cultures from each other and the diversity of cultures will crumble. In this light, for Muslims "the whole human race is the 'clan of God', and all men are real brothers-in-God." On behalf of his brothers and the world, the Muslim cherishes and pursues the values of truth, virtue, justice, beauty and love. And at the same time,

> The Muslim considers all who accept the fundamental values and try to realize them in their lives, whatever the religious denomination or secular school of thought to which they belong, to be "Muslims in practice." He makes them comrades in the battle of life.[71]

Conclusion

There are other views[72] and other dreams, though none more gracefully portrayed. The important thing to note, in concluding, is that Indian Muslims *are* dreaming. They are looking at their situation and considering the issues of religious pluralism from many different perspectives. *This act of consideration is surely as unique as the situation itself.* Although we do not yet see its final outline, a new reality is taking shape. If the eternal can be applied to the temporal, and if the contemporary Muslim concert for *al-dunya*, life in this world, can be expressed in terms of realized eschatology, I could summarize the goal of the dream in the words of Qur'ān: "And Allah calls us to the abode of peace" (10:26).

It may well be that Indian Muslims will yet become that needed representative symbol in the life of Islam and in the life of the world.

Notes

1. W.C. Smith, *Islam in Modern History* (Princeton University Press, 1957), pp. 290ff.

2. K.A. Jamil, "Islam's Attitude towards and Relations with, other Faiths," *International Islamic Colloquium Papers, 1958* (Lahore: Punjab University Press, 1960), p. 184.

3. Quoted by Imtiaz Ahmad, *Modernization and Social Change among Muslims in India* (Delhi: Manohar, 1983), p. xx.

4. The old and respected journal of Osmania University, *Islamic Quarterly*, for example, is silent on the subject of religious pluralism. Although there are many articles dealing with such fine points as "The Chinese Origin of the Word for Garlic in Arabic and Sanskirt" (LII, 2, April 1978, pp. 93–95), in the past two decades there was no major discussion of a significant aspect of this vital contemporary issue.

5. "Presidential Address," *Islam and the Modern Age (IMA)* (III, 1, February 1972), p. 35. The *IMA* has provided a broad spectrum of opinion held by intelligentsia among Indian Muslims on the subject of religious pluralism, including: ideas of common origin coupled with the theme of evolutionary development; thoughts of a multiplicity rooted in God's order; attitudes ranging from toleration to respect and affection; goals extending from amicable co-existence and cooperation to cultural assimilation; as well as a variety of attempts to deal creatively with the tension between the universal and the particular. The purposes of the Islam and Modern Age Society, as enunicated by S. Abid Husain (*IMA*, I, 1, May 1960, pp. 1–9), reflected a multi-religious concern.

6. "Hindus, Muslims and Christians, Living Together in Kerala," an unpublished paper read at Brown University and the University of Calgary. Df. R.E. Miller, *The Mappila Muslims of Kerala, A Study in Islamic Trends* (Madras: Orient Longman, 1976), for further references.

7. "The 'Ulama and the Indian Politics," *IMA* (X, 4, November 1979), p. 90. The entire article (pp. 69–75) is an excellent sketch of Muslim-Hindu relations since 1867, from the Muslim perspective.

8. Imtiaz Ahmad, "Expulsion and Assimilation in Islam," in Attar Singh, *Socio-Cultural Impact of Islam on India* (Chandigarh: Punjab University, 1976), p. 101.

9. *Der Islam im Indischen Subkontinent* (Darmstadt: Wissenschaftliche Buchgesellschaft, 1983), p. 137.

10. Imtiaz Ahmad, in Dieter Rothermund, ed., *Islam in Southern Asia: A Survey of Current Research* (Wiesbaden: Franz Steiner Verlag, 1975), pp. 98f.

11. M.A.K. Azad, *India Wins Freedom* (London: Longmans, 1960), p. 244.

12. Quaderuddin Ahmed, *Pakistan: Facts and Fallacies* (Karachi: Rogyal Book Co., 1979), pp. 75f.

13. Cf. Some Resolutions and Recommendations of the Conference of Islamic Organizations in Mecca, April 6–10, 1974," quoted in *Al-Basheer* (III, 2, April-June 1974, pp. 61–63). Secularism is viewed as a movement to "gradually de-Islamise the Muslim society," and Muslims are urged to thwart it (p. 61).

14. K. Gauba, *Passive Voices* (New Delhi: Sterling Pub.Pvt.Ltd., 1973), p.v.

15. V.B. Kulkarni, *Problems of Indian Democracy* (Bombay: Bharatiya Vidya Bhawan, 1972), pp. 240ff.

16. Cf. Amalendu De, "Role of the Ulama in Bengal Politics (1943–1946)" in her *Islam in Modern India* (Calcutta: Marga Prakashan, 1982), pp. 215ff., where she convincingly traces the support of the Bengal 'ulama for the Muslim League.

17. Presidential Address to Jam'iyāt, June 1940, quoted by Ziya-ul-Hasan Faruqi, *The Deoband School and the Demand for Pakistan* (London: Asia Publishing House, 1963), p. 103.

18. A. Guillaume, *The Life of Muhammad: A Translation of Ishāq's Sirāt Rasūl Allāh* (London: Oxford, 1955), p. 231. Ibn Ishāq's version describes the Jews as an *umma*, a community "along with" *(ma'a)* believers; Abū 'Ubaid's version calls them a community "of" (*min*) believers; for a discussion cf. M. Hamidullah, *The First Written Constitution in the World* (Lahore: Muh.Ashraf, 1975; 2nd rev. ed.), fn. 33, p. 35.

19. Syed Barakat Ahmad, "Non-Muslims and the Umma," *Studies in Islam (SI)* (xviii, 2, April 1980), pp. 86ff.

20. A.A. Engineer, *The Islamic State* (New York: Advent Books, 1981), p. 121; quoting *Muttahida Qawmiyyat aur Islam* ("Composite Nationalism and Islam") Delhi: Qawmi Ekta Trust, n.d., p. 21.

21. Faruqi, *Deoband*, p. 114. Cf. Majid Khadduri, *War and Peace in the Law of Islam* (Baltimore: Johns Hopkins Press, 1955), p. 212.

22. Quoted in A.M. Zaidi, ed., *Evolution of Muslim Political Thought in India*, 6 vol. (New Delhi: S. Chand, 1979), VI, p. 603.

23. Z.H. Faruqi, "Orthodoxy and Heterodoxy in Muslim India," *IMA* (IX, 4, November 1978), p. 27.

24. Wahiddin Khan, "The Meaning of Dīn: Recent Views of Three Eminent Indian 'Ulama," tr. by C.W. Troll, in Troll, ed., *Islam in India: Studies and commentaries*, Vol. I (Delhi: Vikas, 1982), p. 174.

25. Abul Hasan 'Ali Nadwi, "The Meaning of Dīn," Troll, *ibid.*, p. 171.

26. *Ibid.*, p. 168.

27. *Ibid.*, p. 176.

28. T.P. Wright, Jr., "Inadvertent Modernization of Indian Muslims by Revivalists," in Ahmad, *Modernization*, p. 94; quoting M.N. Siddiqi, "Jama'at-e-Islam in Secular India," *Aligarh Law Society Review*, pp. 74–93.

29. *Ibid.*, quoting *Shamsul Islam* (1975), "Pro-Congress Shift: Jama'at-e-Islam," *Economic and Political Weekly*, p. 785.

30. Cf. Miller, *Mappila*, pp. 158–171, for a regional story of "salvation by politics."

31. Zaidi, Vol. VI, p. 609. Proceedings of the Azad Muslim Conference, Delhi, May 6-8, 1944.

32. Mushir ul-Haq, "Ulama," *IMA*, *op. cit.*, p. 20. The Jamiat is the general body of traditional 'ulama in India.

33. *Ibid.*, p. 92.

34. Prabha Dixit, *Communalism—A Struggle for Power* (New Delhi: Orient Longman, 1974) p. 209.

35. Editorial in *National Christian Council Review*, May 1979, in Zachariah, ed., *The Christian Presence in India* (Madras: Christian Literature Society, 1981), pp. 131f.

36. A.A. Engineer, *Islam-Muslims-India* (Bombay: L.V. Griha Pvt.Ltd., 1975), p. 65.

37. Abdul Jalil Mia, "The Concept of *Tauhīd* or Unity," *SI* (XVI, 2, April 1979), p. 106.

38. "*Tauhīd*—Oneness of God," *ibid.*, p. 93.

39. S. Abid Husain, "Report on a Seminar on Inter-Religious Understanding," which took place October 1971, in *IMA* (III, 1, February 1972), p. 4; citing Maulana Taqui Amini and Zubair Siddiqi.

40. *Ibid.*; citing Zainul Abidin, Maulana Abdus-Salam, and Dr. Mahmudal-Hasan.

41. Abdul Jalil Mia, "*Tauhīd*," *op. cit.*, p. 105.

42. S. Abid Husain, "Report," *IMA*, op. cit., p. 4.

43. Barakat Ahmad, "Umma," *Si*, *op. cit.*, p. 104.

44. S. Abid Husain, "Report," *IMA*, *op. cit.*, p. 3.

45. C.N. Ahmed Moulavi, *Religion of Islam: A Comprehensive Study*, tr. by V. Muhammad *et al.* (Calicut, Kerala: Azad Book Stall, 1979), p. 91.

46. Presidential Address to Indian National Congress, Ramgarh, 1940, on "The Minorities and the Political Futures in India," in Zaidi, Vol. V, p. 714. S. Radhakrishnan said of Azad: "The National spirit was the driving force in his life. He was an apostle of national unity and communal harmony." *Occasional Speeches and Writings, October 1952–January 1956* (New Delhi: Government of India, The Publications Division, 1956), pp. 278f.

47. *Tarjumān al-Qur'ān*, Vol. I, *Surāt-ul-Fātihā*, ed. and tr. by Syed Abdul Latif (Bombay: Asia Publishing House, 1965), p. 155.

48. *Ibid.*, p. 171.

49. *Ibid.*, pp. 121 and 141.

50. *Ibid.*, p. 174.

51. *Ibid.*, pp. 158f.

52. *Ibid.*, pp. 139f.

53. M. Mujeeb, *Dr. Zakir Husain* (New Delhi: National Book Trust, 1972), p. 245.

54. A.G. Noorani, *President Zakir Husain* (Bombay: Popular Prakashan, 1967), p. 88; quoting a speech at the Yusuf Meherally Centre, Bombay, in the early 1960s.

55. *Ibid.*, p.x.

56. *Ibid.*, p. 118; quoting a speech at the University of Cairo.

57. *Ibid.*

58. Mujeeb, *Husain*, p. 243.

59. *Ibid.*, p. 239.

60. *Ibid.*, pp. 242f.

61. S. Abid Husain, *The National Culture of India* (New Delhi: National Book Trust of India, 1978), p. 179.

62. S. Abid Husain, *The Destiny of Indian Muslims* (Bombay: Asia Publishing House, 1965), p. 138.

63. *Ibid.*, p. 107.

64. *Ibid.*, pp. 159f.

65. *Ibid.*, p. 169.

66. Louis Dumont, *Religion, Politics and History in India* (The Hague: Mouton, 1970), p. 89.

67. Abid Husain, *Destiny*, p. 206.

68. *Ibid.*, p. 237.

69. *Ibid.*, p. 242.

70. *Ibid.*, p. 244.

71. *Ibid.*, p. 263. Azad, *supra*, had made the same point. Cf. Mushir ul-Haq, "Inter-Religious Understanding, A Step for Realization of the Ideals of the World Community," *Al-Basheer* (Vol. II, No. 1, Jan.-Mar. 1973), p. 16, where he suggests on the basis of the Qur'ān (2:121; 23:2-11) that non-Muslims who follow their religions in their pristine form are, in fact, believers.

72. A fuller accounting of the modern Indian Muslim response to religious pluralism would take into consideration the work of the following. Philosophers like S. Alam Khundmiri view plurality of faith as something rooted in the human condition; like K.G. Saiyidain, seek the bonds of lasting unity and cooperation; and, like Jamal Khwaja, take a broad approach to the idea of salvation. Imtiaz Ahmad, cited above, represents a younger group of social scientists who detail the amazing variety of Indian Islam and call for a recognition and acceptance of the reality of religious pluralism. Moin Shakir's main works are *Muslims in Free India* (New Delhi: Kalamkar Prakashan Pvt.Ltd., 1972) and *Islam in Indian Politics* (New Delhi: Ajanta Pub., 1983). In Zafar Ahmad's fine symposium, *Muslims in India* (Orient Longman, 1975) Shakir argues that the right perception is for Muslims to recognize that they are a minority in a multi-religious society, to discard preoccupation with religious politics, to concentrate on universal themes such as democracy and socialism, and to deal with the real social economic problems of the masses (p. 174). Mushir ul-Haq's sharp analysis and liberal view may be accessed through *Muslim Politics in Modern India* (Meerut, 1970) and especially through *Islam in Secular India* (Simla: Indian Institute of Advanced Study, 1972). He ponders the rise of a new breed of 'ulama who will give deeper study to the concept of secularism, and he calls for dialogue with Hindus and other faiths, suggesting Qur'anic principles in support of his plea. A.A. Fyzee, *A Modern Approach to Islam* (Bombay: Asia, 1963), is well-known for his liberal treatment of the concept of law, and its relation to religion. M.A. Baig, once the secretary of Muhammad Ali Jinnah, in his *The Muslim Dilemma in India* (Delhi: Vikas, 1974), presents his humanist-oriented viewpoint in a manner that is vigorous, honest and provocative. He suggests that Muslims must pass through a period of enlightened communalism on their way to a modern approach. In *The Islamic State (op. cit.)* the Marxist-leaning Ali Asghar Engineer argues for a position combining composite nationalism and Islamic reform. Indian Muslims should strive for the principles of equality, social justice and practical rationalism, but to do so and thereby to become a modern living faith, "it is necessary to liberate Islam from the clutches of or-

thodoxy" (p. 205). Hasan Askari, a sociologist and dialogist, has attempted to penetrate the very nature of pluralism. In *Inter-Religion* (Aligarh: Pintwell, 1977) he suggests that multiplicity be allowed "to become a wonderful content of our religious consciousness" (p. 103), so that pluralism is not merely accepted, but leads to a deeper quality of life itself. To conclude with M. Mujeeb, *The Indian Muslims* (London: G. Allen & Unwin, 1967), is to call attention to one of the great figures of contemporary Indian Islam. The leader of the Jamia Millia foresees the birth of a new individualism in the Muslims of India, an individualism that will lead to fresh interpretations of Qur'anic truth. If he is right, the development will have great significance for the Indian Muslim response to religious pluralism. What will hold Indian Muslims together in the future, Mujeeb believes, will be their common allegiance and reverence for God. (p. 559). For documented information on Muslin-related events, and Muslim opinion and feeling, cf. *Muslim India*, a publication of the Muslim India Educational and Cultural Trust, New Delhi, edited by Syed Shahabuddin.

Chapter Twelve

THE SIKH RESPONSE

R.W. Neufeldt

Introduction

To speak of the Sikh response to religious pluralism is, of course, quite misleading. There is no single response, just as there is no single response in any of the traditions one might name. At best, one is left with various patterns of response, frequently overlapping and informing each other, rather than distinct and isolated from each other. To attempt a detailed analysis of these patterns in a single chapter is clearly impossible. My concern will be to address the issue of pluralism vis-à-vis the Sikhs through an analysis of the search for Sikh self-definition, or self-identity. Attention in this analysis will be given, not to the whole history of Sikhism, but only to major institutional and textual developments. The textual developments include the *Ādi Granth*, the *Dasam Granth*, and the *janam sākhīs*. Also included are the *rahit nāmās*, although these will be discussed under institutional developments.

For Guru Nanak and his followers, religious pluralism was a fact of life. The Sikh tradition was born in North India in the turbulent years of the fifteenth and sixteenth centuries in a religious universe that was already fairly well defined. From the beginning therefore, Guru Nanak and the tradition which developed from his teachings, was faced squarely with the problem of defining itself over against the existing and known religious paths. For the most part, these paths were of Hindu, Muslim or Nāth origins, although from the beginning there seems to be an awareness of the existence of major religious texts that are neither Hindu nor Muslim.

Throughout the history of the Sikh community, this quest for self-identity has been an important one. Given the recent nature of Sikh history one can watch, as though on a cinema screen, the vissicitudes of this quest from the start—the growth of militarism as a religious response to the threat of annihilation, the shrinking of the community in the middle of the nineteenth century, the debates over orthodoxy, the development of Sikh institutions whose chief purpose was to define Sikhism and to protect Sikhs from attraction to other religious communities. And, the process continues in the context of recent events in the Punjab in the demand for recognition of the Sikhs as a religious community distinct from the Hindus.

Ādi Granth

Certainly the basic source for understanding Sikh responses to religious pluralism is the *Ādi Granth*, which contains the writings of the early human Gurus in Sikh history beginning with Guru Nanak.[1] Because the *Ādi Granth* was designated as *guru* around the time of Gobind Singh, it is tempting to suggest that it must be viewed as providing the authoritative Sikh response to the issue of pluralism. However, this would be too simplistic for it would ignore the fact that each generation must, and does interpret or reinterpret the text for its time and and fact that the message of the *Ādi Granth* itself may be complex. A case in point is a common understanding of Nanak's attitude to Hindus and Muslims, that is, the view that Nanak was simply a bridge-builder between Hindus and Muslims, proposing a synthesis that would unify the two communities.[2] This may be a view that grows out of statements attributed to Nanak in the *janam-sākhīs* which is then read back into the *Ādi Granth* as the view expressed in the hymns of Nanak. Whether or not such a view can be supported even by the *janam sākhīs*, this does underline the problem of presenting the *Ādi Granth* as providing the authoritative Sikh understanding of pluralism. Each generation will have its own view of what that authoritative understanding is and this understanding will inevitably be concerned with the proccupations of each generation.[3]

Added to this is the issue of scholarly, or quasi-scholarly views of the relationship between Nanak and his religions milieu and therefore of Sikh response to Hindu and Islamic traditions. By now it is a well-known fact that there is considerable disagreement about that relationship. One moves from assertions that Nanak was a disciple of Kabir to a rejection of that relationship, from assertions that he leaned towards Hinduism to assertions that he was more Muslim than Hindu, from assertions that he was attempting a synthesis of Islam and Hinduism, to assertions that he rejects both, from assertions that he was essentially *sant* in outlook and from assertions that he was self-consciously attempting to establish a new tradition to assertions that he was not.

Whatever the relationship of Nanak to the religious milieu of North India may have been, a study of statements in the *Ādi Granth* making reference to beliefs, texts, and practices of other traditions serves only to underline the fact that Nanak and the succeeding Gurus made a very clear distinction between their teachings and practices and the teachings and practices of other paths. In other words, if liberation was to be had, it could be had through the path charted by Nanak, not through the paths proposed by other texts and traditions. Thus, one might want to argue that Nanak leaned in the direction of, or was influenced by the *bhaktas*, of the Muslims, or the *sants*, but this should not be used to obscure his very clear assertions that other paths were not adequate ways to a proper understanding of God and liberation. Nanak's critique of other paths is thorough, including all that might be regarded as religious—text, belief, and practice. His general rejection of other paths and the assertion of the superiority of his own path might be summed up in the following ironic description of Muslims, Hindus, and Yogis.

> The Muslims praise their law and they read and dwell upon it.
> But the Lord's bondsman is he who binds himself to see His Sight.
> The Hindus praise the Lord whose presence and form are Infinite
> (But to win Him) they bathe at the holies, and make flower offerings
> to the idols and burn perfumed incense before them.

> The Yogis who dwell on the void and name the Creator as 'Unknowable',
> (Yet) to the Absolute, the Subtle Name they give the form of a body.[4]

The paths of others simply do not lead to liberation.

Likewise, the religious texts of others are not ultimately useful. In a reference that has application beyond India Nanak states that neither the "Vedas nor the Semitic Texts know the Mystery of God."[5] In a lengthy discourse in which Hindu holy places are said to be merged in God's being, the *trimūrti* is seen as serving God, and God is referred to us *qāzī* and *mullah*, Nanak, says, "I can see naught else but in the Vedas and Puranas."[6] The futility of Hindu belief is underlined in a lengthly reference to Hindu mythology.

> If He, as Rama, cut off the head of the blind, ten-headed Ravana, it would not make Him an greater (for that). . . .
> O, how can He be any bigger for overpowering the serpent? . . .
> Brahma, born of lotus, whose companion is the Beneficient Vishnu, left on a search for the world's end;
> But he found it not; yea if He, as Krishna, chopped off Kansa's head, O, how does it make Him any the greater (for that).
> When the ocean was churned (by the angels and the demons) and the jewels came into their hands,
> They fell out as to who did it all?[7]

Not only are such stories futile but they are also misleading in that they attempt to give form to that which is essentially formless and view as incarnate that which does not incarnate itself.

External ritual observance and social practice are subjected to harsh criticism as being essentially obscuring and distracting. Both are subjected to rejection and/or radical reinterpretation. Frequently Nanak criticizes the caste pretensions of *brāhmans*, classifying a true *brāhman* as one who practices as daily routine "meditation on God and self-control," not one who is born a *brāhman*. The *kṣatriya* is described as one who practices compassion, charity and beneficence.[8] The true Muslim is not one who follows Muslim ritual, but one who adopts the path of Nanak. In a radical reinterpretation of Muslim ritual Nanak says:

> Let mercy be thy mosque, faith thy prayer-mat; and honest living thy Quran.

> Humility thy circumcision; and Good conduct thy fast. Thus dost then become a true Muslim.[9]

Similar sentiments are rejected in an extended passage in which Arjan comments at length on Muslim ritual and religious achievement

> O, he alone is a *Qazi*, who practices truth,
> And he alone is a *Haji* who disciplines his heart,
> And he alone is a *Mullah* who overcomes Evil,
> And he alone is a Darvesha whose only support is God's Praise.[10]

A true Hindu then, is not one who piously follows caste *dharma*, and adheres to Hindu texts, nor is a true Muslim one who zealously follows Islamic ritual obligations of whatever sort and adheres to the *Qur'an*. A true Hindu or a true Muslim is one who follows Nanak's path. This must be stressed lest one be tempted to suggest that one can in some sense remain a conventional Hindu or Muslim and still be liberated. The reinterpretation which Nanak gives to the terms Hindu and Muslim means that those who follow what he says must turn their backs not only on their traditional texts and beliefs but also on traditional practices which had been used for the sake of ritual definition of Hindus and Muslims. Referring to Hindu texts, worship of Hindu gods, recitation of the *Gayatri Mantra* and the application of *tīlak* marks, Nanak says, "If they knew the nature of the Lord, They would know their needs and beliefs to be vain."[11] Yogis and *saṁnyasins* who live in the woods, feed on roots, and wear the ochre robe are said to have wasted their lives.[12] Nanak radically reinterprets, Yoga, calling on the Yogi to pierce his heart not his ears, to let his body be his coat, his mind his staff, contemplation of God his food of roots and the *Guru* his Ganges.[13]

In the final analysis, without God as *Guru*, all is vain, whether belief, text, or ritual. Texts have failed to reveal the mystery of God, and a vision of Him has not been won through rites and deeds. The *yajñas*, the sacrificial fire, pious conduct, austere living, routine worship, daily prayer, the reading the study of scripture, the staff, the begging bowl, the tuft of hair, the sacred thread, the loin cloth, and pilgrimages, do not bring peace, nor liberation. This is to be had only through the contemplation of the name of God.[14] The rejection on both theological and ritual levels is clear and unequivocal. At the same time there is the assertion of the superiority of the God of Nanak, or Nanak's understanding of God.

> His word is the (Yogi's) Wordless Harmony
> His Word is the Word of the Vedas' symphony.
> In the Word doth He have His Being (The Law),
> He's Shiva, He's Vishna, He's Brahma (None other) —
> And He's Parvati, and Lakshmi, The Mother.[15]

Similar messages can be found the true writings of other Gurus. Guru Angad for example juxtaposes the teachings of Vedas and the Word of the *Guru*.

> The Vedas have given currency to the myths that make men reflect upon (human values of) good and evil;
> And also to believe that one 'taketh' (only) what one 'giveth': through this 'give and take' is man cast into heaven or hell. . . .
> But the Nectar-Word (of the Guru's) maketh one know the Quintessence.[16]

Guru Amar Das echoes Nanak's emphasis on the futility of outward religious observances pointing out that such practices cannot remove doubt and delusion and bring one to the knowledge of the transcendent.[17] Indeed, the mind is not cleansed through ritual bathings of the body nor by learning the yogic postures and disciplining sexual desires. The only discipline that works is "the Refuge of the true Guru."[18] Even the repetition of the name of God does not result in unity with God.[19] Similarly, all talk of bliss is tantamount to empty posturing, unless one keeps the company of God:

> Everyone sayeth, "I'm in Bliss," but the bliss commeth from the Guru:
> Yea, one knoweth the Bliss ever from the Guru, when the Loved Lord is in Mercy[20]

And, one who knows the bliss of union with the *Guru*, he is the true *brāhman*, not one who is born a *brāhman* and keeps caste *dharma*.[21]

Guru Arjan is unequivocal in his rejection of other texts and religious practices and his assertion of the superiority of the Sikh path:

Of all religions, this one is the purest:
Meditate on the Lord's Name and do what is holy.
Yea this is the noblest of the works:
That thou Washest the evil of thy mind associating with the Holy.
Of all efforts, this effort is the noblest:
Meditate thou on God in thy heart ever and for evermore . . . .
Of all speech this is the finest:
Listen thou to the Lord's Praise, and utter it with thy tongue.
Of all places, that one is the most blessed,
Where Nanak, one Dwelleth on the Lord's Name.[22]

None of the Hindu *Śāstras* and *Smṛtis* which Arjan has searched is equal to the Name of the Lord.[23] In a sweeping judgment of Hindu and Muslim beliefs, practices and texts Arjan states:

Some but call Thee *Rama*, while by others
Than art Known as *Khuda*,
Yea, some serve Thee as *Gosain*, others as *Allah*.
But, O Beneficient Lord, Thou art only the One Doer and the Cause.
So Bless me Thou with Thy Mercy.
Some go to the (Hindus') Pilgrim stations, others go to perform Hajj,
Some offer Thee oblations, while others bow before Thee.
Some but read the Vedas, others the Western Texts,
Yea, some are robed in white, others in blue.
Some are called Turks, others are termed Hindus,
Some seek the (Hindus') heaven, other the (Muslims') Paradise.
Sayeth Nanak: He who Realiseth the Lord's Will,
He alone knoweth the Mystery of his Lord, the God."[24]

It is Arjan who states that he is neither Hindu or Muslim, that he has settled the difference between Hindu and Muslim, not by working out some kind of synthesis of the two, nor by keeping the observances of both such as fasts, pilgrimages, prayers and worship, but by cultivating the remembrance of God within and serving that God.[25]

As in the case of the preceding Gurus we also have in Arjan a radical reinterpretation of traditional religious concerns. Thus the best light is the light of God in the heart, the best contemplation is the contemplation of God, the best renunciation is the renunciation of lust, anger, and greed, the best prayer is properly praising the Lord, the best vigil is singing God's praises, and the best attachment is attachment to God.[26]

In any discussion of pluralism with reference to the *Ādi Granth*, one cannot afford to ignore the *bhagat bānī*, the utterances (*bānī*) of past saints (*bhagats*) of *bhakti*, *sant* and *sūfī* origin. These range from twelfth century figures like Jaidev to poet saints who were contemporary with Nanak. In terms of popularity, Kabir is the most prominent, followed by Namdev and Ravidas.[27] It is tempting to suggest that the *bhagat bānī* is included in the *Ādi Granth* to demonstrate the catholic spirit of those responsible for the text. However, that is too simplistic a veiw. It is true that the hymns of the poet-saints are recorded because of a basic agreement with the beliefs of the Sikh Gurus. Indeed, a reading of the *bhagat-bānī* suggests the same critical themes as one finds in the hymns of the Gurus with respect to prevailing religiosity. If one looks at the Hymns of Kabir, it is as though one is reading the hymns of the Gurus. He criticizes outward display, religiosity such as going about naked, wrapping oneself in skins, shaving one's head, ritual bathing and insisting on continence, pointing out that deliverance is achieved through the Holy Name alone.[28] He criticizes brahmanical pretensions, pointing out that a true *brāhman* is one who meditates on God,[29] and the mullah, for climbing the minaret when he should be searching for God in his heart.[30]

While one finds in the *bhagat bānī* many of the same themes that are expressed in the hymns of the Gurus, there are perhaps two points that need to be stressed to guard against the simplistic conclusion that there is basic agreement between the *bhagat* and the Gurus. In the first instance, the agreement that one finds is there perhaps because the Gurus chose only those aspects of the *bhagat* poetry that was in basic agreement with their own teachings. The work that has been done on the *bhagat bānī* to date suggests that there may be authentic *bhagat* material that has not been included in the *Ādi Granth*. A useful study in this respect is Karine Shomer's research on Kabir in the *Adi Granth*. She attempts to make a distinction between Kabir the mystic, and Kabir of the Sikh *Panth*, pointing out that such a difference is not recognized by the Sikh tradition which simply views Kabir as one of the many *bhagats* who preached devotion to God beyond all form.[31] The questionable distinction between Kabir the mystic and the "Sikh" Kabir aside, she does point out and develop with persuasiveness the notion that the *Ādi Granth* corpus of Kabir's sayings cannot represent the total of what was accessible to the Sikhs in 1603-1604, the time of the compilation of the *Ādi Granth*.

Some selection must therefore have been made on the basis of conformity to the moods and motivations of the Sikh community.[32] Schomer argues, for example, the couplets emphasizing the ecstacy of mystical experience may have been edited out of the *Ādi Granth* by Amar Das and Arjan.[33]

Secondly, there is the fact of some comment by the Gurus on parts of the *bhagat bānī*. One has to ask for the reasons for this. A cursory reading would suggest at least three possible lines of inquiry. Are the comments there to prevent misunderstanding of the words of the *bhagats* among the faithful? Or, are the comments there to cultivate a particular Sikh view of these *bhagats*, an authoritative version in other words? This idea is supported by implication in Schomer's work in Kabir in the *Ādi Granth*. Or, are the comments there to correct views of the *bhagats* which verge on the erroneous. On the face of things this would make eminent sense if Schomer is right about an editing process exercised by Amar Das and Arjan. If full agreement is not possible at the outset, then it may be achieved by way of editing and commentary. This provides an interesting alternative to the sometimes harsh criticism, in the *Ādi Granth*, of Hindus, Muslims and Yogis. Here, rather, than criticism, because of basic agreement, there is simply editing and commentary.

Extra-Canonical Literature

Outside of the *Ādi Granth* textual developments which have exercised a great deal of influence in Sikh communities are the writings attributed to Gobind Singh, the tenth Guru and the *janam-sākhīs*, narrative and anecdotal material on the life of Guru Nanak.

Parts of the *Dasam Granth*, a work traditionally attributed to Guru Gobind Singh remain influential and popular in the devotional life of the Sikhs.[34] While different from the *Ādi Granth* in language, content, and style, on the issue of religious pluralism one finds a clear relationship to the *Ādi Granth*. In general, it calls for radical transformation or rejection of traditional religious patterns. Considerable ridicule is heaped on the claims made for outward observances. If self-inflicted wounds are the way to God, then the injured should be blessed, if repeated *mantras*, then the warbler should be blessed, if roaming the skies, then the flying bird should be blessed, if burial, then the snake should be blessed.[35] Rather than traditional asceticism, one is called to its practice within the context of life as a householder, rather than matted hair or special clothing, one's outward sign is to be continence, rather than ritual bathing, one is to wash oneself in unity with God, rather than ashes, one is to smear one's body with the love of God.[36]

In a spirit similar to that of the *Ādi Granth*, the *Dasam Granth* decries the religious divisions among people, particularly the classification into different types of Hindus and Muslims, and seeks a unity, not in a synthesis of religions, but in the transcendence of divisions through the recognition that God is the father of all, transcending our erroneous, partial, and limiting conceptions.

> God as Creator and God as Good,
> God in His Bounty and God in His Mercy,
> Is all one God. Even in our errors,
> We should not separate God from God.[37]

That much of prevailing religiosity is to be seen as wrong is clearly underlined in the discussion of Hindu *avatāras*. These are but legendary human figures who along with others were sent by God to witness to the truth but ended up forming sects committed to ritual and the worship of *avatāras*.[38]

The *Janam skhīs*, probably dating from the late sixteenth century, are, in the main anecdotal material concerning the life of Nanak derived from a number of sources—Sūfī traditions, Hindu Epics, *Purāṇas*, Nāth Yogi traditions, authentic historical incidents, suggestive references in the works of Guru Nanak, and complete hymns used as a framework for discourses.[39] The picture given of Nanak with respect to religious pluralism is, in some respects, substantially the same as in the *Ādi Granth*, and, in other respects, substantially different.

It is in the *janam sākhīs* that we find highlighted the theme of Hindu-Muslim unity, in the sense that Nanak is presented as one who attempts to reconcile the two communities. In general, he is presented as both Hindu and Muslim. In his dress he shows himself to be both *bairagi* and *faqir*.[40] In the story of the journey to Mecca he is billed as a Hindu, but comes to be recognized by the people of Mecca as a Muslim.[41] The theme of reconciliation is seen most clearly perhaps in the stories of the birth and death of Nanak. He is welcomed at birth by both Hindus and Muslims; by Hindus as god in human form, and by Muslims as a follower of divine truth.[42] At his death both communities quarrel about what to do with his remains. They are instructed to place flowers on either side of his body. The body disappears, but the flowers remain fresh. Consequently the Hindus take their flowers and cremate them while the Muslims bury theirs.[43]

The theme of reconciliation notwithstanding, as in the case of the *Ādi Granth*, the teachings or path of Nanak are shown to be superior to and distinct from other teachings or paths. While there is a recognition that other traditions do exist, and that in some ways there is a relationship to these traditions, the path of Nanak is believed to be distinct. In the B40 *Janam-sākhī* story of Nanak's meeting with God, Nanak is addressed as follows:

> "Go Nanak. Your Panth will flourish. The salutation of your followers shall be: 'In the name of the True Guru I fall at your feet'. The salutation of the Vaisnava Panth is: 'In the name of Rāma and Krisna'. The salutation of the Sanyāsī Panth is: 'In the name of Nārāyana I bow before you.' The Yogis' salutation is: 'Hail to the Primal One'. The Muslims' cry is: 'In the name of the One God peace be with you'. You are Nānak and your Panth will flourish. Your followers shall be called Nānak-panthis and their salutation shall be: 'In the name of the True Guru I fall at your feet'. Inculcate devotion towards Me and strengthen men's obedience to their *dharma*. As the Vaisnavas have their temple, the yogis their asan and the Muslims their mosque, so your followers shall have their dharmasala.[44]

The story seems to suggest that the path of Nanak is not only distinct, but is also to have exclusive claim on the lives of people. In some ways it is reminiscent of the demands of Gobind Singh's alleged sermon given at the inauguration of the initiation ceremony.

The superiority of Nanak's path is shown in the innumerable stories of his confrontation with representatives of other religions in which these representatives are consistently shown as being bested by Nanak. As a child Nanak overwhelmed *paṇḍits* and *mullahs* with his learning.[45] The colorful stories of Nanak's visits to all of the then known places of pilgrimage are consistent in their depiction of Nanak as one who is recognized as a great spiritual adept worthy of homage. He is viewed as a *Guru* to Hindus and a *pir* to Muslims.[46] Frequently these stories include episodes in which Nanak shows his disdain for and condemns the dependence on external practices such as temple and mosque worship, pilgrimage, caste, *mantras*, etc.[47] A classic example is the story of Nanak's visit to Mecca, in which he sleeps with his feet toward the *Ka'bah*, thus committing blasphemy in the eyes of Muslims.[48]

Also part of these stories and of the belief in Nanak's superiority is the emphasis on conversion to the way of Nanak. Nanak is depicted as one who corrupts Hindus and persuades Muslims to betray their faith.[49] Hindu priests are converted to his way and leave their old practices as a consequence.[50] *Paṇḍits* at Banares and Vaisnavas at Patna are converted[51] while *faqirs* and *qāzīs* recognize him as a spiritual master and offer him their submission.[52] Śaivite yogis are forced to recognize his superiority.[53] Hindus are forced to give up their idols and *Purāṇas*.[54] The superior of a Jain monastery is defeated by Nanak.[55] *Sadhus* are converted at Mathura.[56] Nanak is hailed by all the *bhagats* and recognized as the supreme *guru* by Kabir.[57]

The overwhelming emphasis of the *janam sākhī* is still, as in the case of the *Ādi Granth*, that true religion lies beyond all other systems and is to be found in Nanak's path only. Nanak is in fact, exalted by degrees to a manifestation of God, sometimes to identify with God, thus creating confrontation with any other claims to liberation. Liberation, if it was to be had, must be through the way of Nanak.[58] This surely is to be understood to indicate a struggle for identity. On the one hand there is recognition of links to the larger religious picture, particularly the Hindu and Muslim milieu. Those links are recognized in the make-up of the *janam sākhīs* as an amalgam of puranic, epic, *nāth*, and *sūfī* materials, a fact which has given rise to the view that Nanak represents simply a synthesis of Hindu and Muslim teachings.[59] On the other hand, there is also the assertion of difference from and superiority over the the traditions of that larger picture.[60]

At the same time one can see a shift towards accommodating certain religious practices of that larger picture and views which are clearly rejected by Nanak in the *Ādi Granth*. This becomes evident in at least two related issues. In the *Ādi Granth* Nanak is seen as one who counsels a disciplined worldiness which opposes both laxity and total renunciation.[61] In the *janam sākhīs* ascetisicm is seen in a much more favorable light. Nanak in varying degrees is depicted as supporting ascetics and as being himself a performer of austerities to the point of maintaining celibacy and seeking total withdrawal from the world.[62] This also means that the attitude to Nāths and their teachings is at best ambivalent. While inevitably bested by Nanak, the Nāths are shown genuine respect and aspects of their teachings which are condemned in the *Ādi Granth* are now treated with approval.

Institutional Developments

The same pattern of accommodation *and* assertion of difference, separation, or distinctiveness which is evident in the *janam sākhīs*, is also evident in major institutional developments within the history of the Sikh tradition. It is an ambivalent pattern which becomes an important ingredient in the identity crisis of the Sikhs in the eighteenth and nineteenth centuries. Further, it is a pattern which is traceable to the time of the Sikh Gurus, beginning at least as early as Amar Das.

Despite Nanak's criticism of external religious observances such as pilgrimage, under Amar Das there is established at Goindvāl a center. While this may be seen as the reintroduction of Hindu custom, at the same time there is a clear distinction from Hinduism intended. That is, the center for the Sikhs is to be Goindvāl, not Hardwar, or some other important Hindu center.[63] Further, three traditional Hindu festivals become the occasion for large gatherings at Goindvāl,[64] but, as Cole and Sambhi point out, these festivals have a distinct Sikh content reminding people of Sikh history and beliefs rather than Hinduism.[65]

A further institutional development takes place under Gobind Singh in the institution of a distinct initiation ceremony. On the one hand one can see in Gobind Singh the influence of Śaivite and Śakti elements, particularly in associating God with steel and the sword and in his references to the mother goddess.[66] On the other hand, the ceremony served to separate the Sikhs consciously from other religious paths. The ceremony meant and still means initiation into a self-consciously distinct community. The sermon attributed to Gobind Singh demands of Sikhs that they give up old scriptures, places of pilgrimage, worship of minor gods, goddesses and *avatāras*.[67] Further the code of discipline which may have been promulgated in the eighteenth century includes some quite specific anti-Islamic[68] and anti-sectarian elements, this latter probably aimed at the followers of Prithi Chand.[69]

It is evident from these early institutional developments that there was pressure for the Sikhs to be reabsorbed into the broader Hindu culture of which they were a part, a pressure which, for the most part, has been resisted, but which has called forth cries and movements for reform. That the pressure should be there is not surprising inasmuch as culturally Sikhs have and do fit into the pattern of general Indian practices and beliefs. As most Indian religion does, Sikhism too, explains life in terms of *karma* and rebirth. As in the case of general external observance, bathing before worship is emphasized, although ideally this is not to be understood as an essential ritual nor is it to be related to the notion of ritual purity. As in the case of general observance, shoes must be taken off for worship in the *gurdwara*.

Barrier, in his discussion of historical forces in the Punjab in the eighteenth and ninteenth centuries, makes the point that reabsorption was not simply a danger but a fact, that many Sikhs emerged from the period of Ranjit Singh wondering who they were and whether they really were distinct from Hinduism.[70] This uncertainty leads to re-evaluation and a process of definition which is evident in two significant developments which in some respects could be labelled anti-Hindu.

The first is the reform movement of Baba Dayal (1783–1855), the Nirankaris. In affect he was a campaigner against Hindu practices in Sikh shrines, specifically the worship of gods and goddesses and the use of the Gurbāni in the fashion of Sanskirt *mantras*; that is, repetition for the sake of acquiring merit.[71] Dayal sees this as a move by *brāhmans* to encourage superstition to satisfy their own needs and to entangle Sikhs in futile rituals and ceremonies.[72] Thus the need for reform.

A much more influential movement for reform and definition is the Singh Sabha, responsible in some respects for the slogan "Ham Hindu Nahin" (we are not Hindu), for educational institutions which helped defend and define Hinduism, and for the writing of Sikh histories and definitions of Sikh orthodoxy.[73] In Barrier's eyes these developments serve as a watershed through which Sikhism becomes a religion in the nineteenth century.[74] As in the case of the Nirankaris, here too, demands were made to cleanse Sikh shrines, particularly the Golden Temple, of Hindu images and rituals.[75] Singh Sabha cooperation in the Arya Samaj *Shuddhi* movement suggests that their concern was for definition of Sikhism vis-à-vis Islam and Christianity as well as Hinduism, for, their concern was to win back Sikhs from coversion to Islam and Christianity.[76] Cooperation with the Aryas was, however, short-lived because of the aggressive stance of the Aryas, their habit of condemning other religious leaders and doctrines[77] and the Arya practice of *Shuddhi* on the Rahtia Sikhs.[78]

The development of the *rahit nāmās* already mentioned, support the observed institutional definition of and emphasis on the distinctive and exclusive aspects of Sikhism. They are the manuals of the Panth's distinctive code of conduct and behavior, specifiying normative behavior, outward appearance, social obligation, ritual behavior, and to a certain extent, belief.[79] The early *rahit* reflects Sikh preoccupation with self-definition vis-a-vis Hindu and particularly Muslim communities. For example, part of the early *rahit* is the enunciation of a martial spirit vis-a-vis Muslims. A true member of the *Khālsā* "is one who carries arms and slays Muslims".[80] This, of course, reflects the concern for survival and defense of the faith in the face of aggressive challenge from Muslim authority. Further, to distinguish Sikhs from Hindus, a true Sikh is counselled not to wear the sacred thread or the frontal sect mark, not to cut his hair, not to be arrogant, deceitful, wanton, lustful, prone to anger, or proud, and to render service to fellow Sikhs.[81] Central theological assertions too are spelled out with some clarity. God is to be understood as manifested in three ways: as the formless spirit which dwells in the heart of all, as the word revealed in the *Ādi Granth*, and in the life of the Sikh who faithfully heeds the scripture.[82]

A more recent code is the *Sikh Rahit Maryada*, accepted as the Sikh code by the Shiromani Gurdwara Parbandhak Committee in 1945 under the influence of the Singh Sabha and Akāli movements. It reflects the need for definition of belief and practice in the face of Hindu influence in ritual and worship.[83] The definition of a Sikh in terms of both belief and practice is quite specific and exclusivistic.

A Sikh is one who believes in God, the ten Gurus, their teachings, the *Ādi Granth*, *Khālsā* initiation, and, one who does not believe in any other religion.[84] The *Khālsā* initiation, in particular, requires renunciation of all former preoccupations with caste, status, birth, country, religion, gods, goddesses, incarnations, and prophets.[85] Indeed, initiants are not to wear symbols pertaining to any other faith.[86]

What a Sikh needs to reject to remain a true Sikh is stated explicitly in the *Rahit Maryada's* understanding of *Gurmat* (the teachings of the Gurus). The rejections reflect both past and present in the larger religious environment of the Sikhs. To be a Sikh means

> To reject caste distinctions and untouchability; magical amulets, mantras, and spells; auspicious omens, days, times, planets and astrological signs; the ritual feeding of Brahmans to sanctify or propitiate the dead; oblation for the dead; the superstitious waving of lights; (traditional) obsequies; fire sacrifices; ritual feasting or libations; sacred tufts of hair or ritual shaving; fasting for particular phases of the moon; frontal marks, sacred threads and sanctified rosaries; worshipping at tombs, temples or cenotaphs; idol worship; and all other such superstitions . . . .[87]

While texts such as the *Vedas*, *Śāstras*, *Bhagavad Gītā*, *Qur'ān* and the *Bible* may be profitable, salvific faith is to be based on the *Ādi Granth*.[88]Indeed a knowledge of *Gurmukhī*, the script of the *Ādi Granth* and the commentaries by Bhai Gurdas and Bhai Nand Lal, and the *Dasam Granth* only that are to be used for *kīrtan*.[90]

The emphasis on Sikh distinctiveness and exclusivity is also seen in discussions of worship and ritual. While a *gurdwara* is open to anyone regardless of caste, religion, or nationality and, while in worship there is to be no distinction between Sikh and non-Sikh, only Sikhs who have been initiated and possess the five K's have a right to enter certain parts of the *takhts*.[91] In the case of marriage and death, rituals or practices from other religions are not to be used. In marriage, caste or status is not to play a part nor is the "tying of head bands, feigning sulking or grief, engaging professional dancers, worshipping ancestors, drinking alcohol, burning sacred fires . . . ."[92] In funeral ceremonies, "A dying person is not to be taken from his bed and placed on the ground, as is the Hindu custom. No lamps should be burned and there should be no giving of cows. Comfort should be derived from reading the Adi Granth and meditating upon God."[93]

Conclusion

What is one to make of this overview of principal textual and institutional developments of Sikh history? Minimally, such an overview suggests that there has been throughout Sikh history a process of self-definition which is traceable to the writings of Guru Nanak. Further, the emphasis must be on process, in the sense that as the religious and political situation changed for the Sikhs, new responses were called for and were made. In this respect, one might argue that the process continues, not only as the situation changes for the majority of the Sikhs in the Punjab, but as Sikhs have and continue to face new situations as immigrants in other countries.

The key issue in this process of self-definition is the emphasis on the distinctness or separateness of Sikhism whether that be distinctness from the original larger Hindu and Muslim context or, distinctness even beyond that. To a greater or lesser extent there seems always to have been the belief and the assertion that deliverance is to be had only through the cultivation of the way of Nanak, that is, through the interior discipline of meditating on the Name of god, rather than the discipline of external observance. Further, it is through the *Ādi Granth*, and meditation on the words of the text that the search for deliverance is best served, not through meditation on other scriptures. This seems to be a fairly constant refrain, the fact of accommodation notwithstanding. While the pressure for accommodation may have dulled this sensibility from time-to-time, the fact of accommodation also resulted in and gave impetus to calls for reform, calls which consistently emphasized Sikh distinctiveness and exclusiveness.

The emphasis on exclusiveness, however, must not be misunderstood. It is not an exclusiveness which denigrates or despises other traditions. Indeed, value is accorded other scriptures, inasmuch as one might read them for profit and inasmuch as one might even come to understand something of God through them. In this respect it is instructive to note that, in part, Sikhs ceased cooperating with the Aryas because of the Arya habit of condemning other religious leaders and their doctrines. Sikh exclusiveness is related specifically to the question of deliverance or liberation. With respect to this question, a true Sikh is asked to say no to other scriptures, practices, and beliefs, and is to seek deliverance through belief in the *Ādi Granth*, the teachings of the Gurus and the cultivation of meditation on the words of the *Ādi Granth* and the Gurus.

Notes

1. For a summary of the *Ādi Granth* see W. H. McLeod, *Textual Sources for the Study of Sikhism*, Manchester: University Press, 1984, pp. 1–5.

2. See Mark Juergensmeyer and N. Gerald Barrier (eds.) *Sikh Studies, Comparative Perspectives on a Changing Tradition* Berkeley: Graduate Theological Union, 1979. Juergensmeyer proposes that this view is largely dependent on the work of Khushwant Singh.

3. For example, Cole and Sambhi suggest that the view of Nānak as a bridge-builder is read back into history from later ecumenical concerns of the Sikh community. See W. Owen Cole and Piara Singh Sambhi, *The Sikhs*, London: Routledge and Kegan Paul, 1978, p. 35.

4. *Guru Granth Sahib*, Vol. 2 (translated by Gopal Singh), Delhi: Gur Das Kapur and Sons Private Ltd., 1984, p. 459. Hereafter referred to as GGS.

5. *GGS*, Vol. 4, p. 974.

6. *Ibid.*, p. 975.

7. GGS, Vol. 2, p. 340.

8. *GGS*, Vol. 4, p. 1336.

9. *GGS*, Vol. 1, p. 131.

10. GGS, Vol. 4, p. 1035.

11. GGS, Vol. 2, p. 464.

12. GGS, Vol. 1, p. 131.

13. *Ibid.*, pp. 148–9.

14. GGS, Vol. 4, pp. 1076–7.

15. GGS, Vol. 1, p. 2.

16. GGS, Vol. 4, p. 1198.

17. GGS, Vol. 3, p. 876.

18. GGS, Vol. 2, p. 546.

19. *Ibid.*, p. 485.

20. GGS, Vol. 3, p. 875.

21. GGS, Vol. 4, p. 1077.

22. GGS, Vol. 1, p. 257.

23. *Ibid.*, p. 256.

24. GGS, Vol. 3, p. 842.

25. GGS, Vol. 4, p. 1084.

26. *Ibid.*, p. 971.

27. W. H. McLeod, *The Evolution of the Sikh Community*, Oxford: Clarendon Press, 1976, p. 71.

28. *GGS*, Vol. 1, p. 314.

29. *Ibid.*

30. *GGS*, Vol. 4, p. 1307.

31. Juergensmeyer and Barrier, *Sikh Studies*, p. 75.

32. *Ibid.*, p. 77.

33. *Ibid.*, p. 86. For a discussion of the use of *bhagat bānī* by the Gurus, see Pashura Singh, "Sikh Self-Definition in Relation to *Bhagat Bānī* in the *Guru Granth Sahib*". Unpublished M.A. Thesis, University of Calgary, May, 1987.

34. For a summary discussion of the *Dasam Granth* see W. H. McLeod, *Sources*, pp. 6–7, and 55–63.

35. W. H. McLeod, *Sources*, p. 57.

36. *Selections From the Sacred Writings of the Skihs* (translated by Trilochan Singh, et. al.), New York: Samuel Weiser Inc., 1973, p. 271.

37. *Sacred Writings*, p. 268.

38. Cole and Sambhi, *The Sikhs*, pp. 97–98.

39. McLeod, *Sources*, pp. 2 and 9.

40. McLeod, *Evolution*, p. 28.

41. *Ibid.*, p. 29.

42. McLeod, *Sources*, p. 19. See also McLeod, *Evolution*, p. 28 and *Gurū Nānak and the Sikh Religion*, Oxford: Clarendon Press, 1968, p. 36.

43. McLeod, *Evolution*, p. 28. See also *Gurū Nānak and the Sikh Religion*, pp. 50–51.

44. McLeod, *Evolution*, pp. 30–31.

45. McLeod, *Gurū Nānak and the Sikh Religion*, p. 52.

46. *Ibid.*, p. 59. See also *Sources*, p. 22.

47. McLeod, *Sources*, pp. 43–44. See also *Gurū Nānak and the Sikh Religion*, pp. 55–56.

48. McLeod, *Gurū Nānak and the Sikh Religion*, p. 35. See also the story of the condemnation of brahmanical concerns for pure food and pure cooking squares on p. 45 of the same volume.

49. McLeod, *Sources*, p. 23.

50. *Ibid.*, p. 26.

51. McLeod, *Gurū Nānak and the Sikh Religion*, p. 56.

52. McLeod, *Sources*, p. 25. See also *Gurū Nānak and the Sikh Religion*, p. 38.

53. McLeod, *Gurū Nānak and the Sikh Religion*, p. 35.

54. *Ibid*, pp. 48–49.

55. *Ibid.*, p. 47.

56. *Ibid.*, p. 59.

57. *Ibid.*, pp. 56–57.

58. W. H. McLeod, *Early Sikh Tradition*, Oxford: Clarendon Press, 1980, p. 254.

59. *Ibid.*, p. 64.

60. *Ibid.*, pp. 260–261.

61. *Ibid.*, p. 79.

62. *Ibid.*, pp. 81, 94 and 251. Included is the story of Nānak existing on sand or simply on air. One can't help but to be reminded of the Jain claim that the pure can exist on air alone.

63. McLeod, *Evolution*, pp. 8–9.

64. *Ibid.*, p. 42.

65. Cole and Sambhi, *The Sikhs*, pp. 129–131.

66. McLeod, *Evolution*, p. 13.

67. *Ibid.*, p. 15.

68. *Ibid.*, pp. 51–52.

69. *Ibid.*, p. 43.

70. Juergensmeyer and Barrier, *Sikh Studies*, p. 41. For a more detailed discussion of Sikh indentity crisis see N. Gerald Barrier, *The Sikhs and Their Literature*, Delhi: Manohar Book Service, 1970.

71. McLeod, *Sources*, p. 122.

72. *Ibid.*, p. 124.

73. Juergensmeyer and Barrier, *Sikh Studies*, p. 41. *Ham Hindu Nahin* was also the title of an influential book by prominent Singh Sabha writer Kahn Singh of Nabha.

74. *Ibid.*, p. 44.
75. Kenneth Jones, *Arya Dharm*, Delhi: Manohar, 1976, p. 21.
76. *Ibid.*, pp. 134–135.
77. *Ibid.*, p. 138.
78. *Ibid.*, pp. 208–209.
79. *Sources*, p. 73.
80. *Ibid.*, p. 79.
81. *Ibid.*, p. 75.
82. *Ibid.*, p. 78.
83. Cole and Sambhi, *The Sikhs*, p. 168.
84. *Ibid.*, p. 169. See also *Sources*, p. 80.
85. *Sources*, p. 84.
86. *Ibid.*, p. 83.
87. *Ibid.*, p. 81.
88. Cole and Sambhi, *The Sikhs*, p. 175.
89. *Sources*, p. 81.
90. *Ibid.*, p. 80.
91. Cole and Sambhi, *The Sikhs*, p. 171.
92. *Ibid.*, p. 176.
93. *Ibid.*, p. 177.

Chapter Thirteen

A MODERN INDIAN CHRISTIAN RESPONSE

J. Lipner

It is only in comparatively recent times that people have begun to speak of an "Indian Christian" tradition in the sense in which I will be using this description. This tradition is yet to acquire a populist momentum; if it is to do so, its representatives will have to wrestle with some crucial issues over the next few years. I shall indicate what some of these issues are, when we are better placed to appreciate their implications.

In this essay I propose to examine work done in laying the foundation for the Indian Christian tradition so that light may be cast on its pedigree and potential. The groundwork was accomplished in the ninteenth century and at the beginning of the twentieth. Since it is generally agreed that the complex cultural and political phenomenon which we call modern India began to coalesce towards the middle of the nineteenth century, it is in

This essay is dedicated to the occasion of my father, Vojtech Lipner's, 70th birthday, July 18, 1986. To my father's example and benevolence I owe more than I could ever express.

this sense that the Indian Christian tradition may be said to have "modern" roots.

I must now explain what I mean by "Indian Christianity". I do not mean Christian life and thought as it was generally expressed in the India of the time. This was essentially an alien phenomenon for the simple reason that most practicing Christians in nineteenth-century India were either westerners who were theologically ethnocentric or native Indians who were confined to non-indigenous (viz. either western or the South Indian Syriac-based) forms of Christian allegiance. To write on such a phenomenon would be to give little if any original content to "Indian Christianity". It will be more rewarding to examine "Indian Christianity" understood as *Christian theology and commitment seeking articulation in interaction with a specifically Indian cultural component.* In effect, we shall be studying Indian Christianity (as described above) through the contributions of some of its leading pioneers.

These pioneers were, in fact, converts from Hinduism who sought to indigenize their faith with reference to their native Hindu tradition. This they did because they experienced the need to fashion new identities for themsleves by taking their old allegiances into account. Further, they saw that it was in relationship with Hinduism more than with any other native tradition that the country was being transformed. Occasionally they considered other religions in articulating their points of view, and we shall take note of this, but in the main we shall be dealing with modern Indian Christianity as it arose in and out of the encounter with Hinduism.

I shall not attempt to survey the work of all those relevant for our purposes. Rather, it will be my aim to illustrate the nature of the Indian Christian response through the contributions of chosen individuals, and to identify the chief forces which combined to produce this response in the period under consideration. Most of these individuals were Bengalis, and in this essay we shall in fact focus on Bengali pioneers of Indian Christianity.[1]

Bengali prominence in this respect derived from the fact that it was Bengal more than any other region of British India which proved susceptible with the march of the nineteenth century to the winds of cultural change blowing in from the west as British paramountcy increased. This was hardly surprising since the city of Calcutta, on the Hooghly in the heartland of Bengal's Gangetic plain, was the hub of British influence. Calcutta became the focus and symbol not only for Bengalis, but for all Indians during the nineteenth century, of the momentous cultural interaction taking place between traditional India and alien western ideas. In the wake of Lord Cornwallis' Permanent Settlement of 1793 and the resulting intricacies of the systems of land revenue, land rights and the subdivision of estates, a new pattern of mobility was emerging among certain sections of the (mainly Hindu) Bengali community. Already squeezed out of any effective role in the control of the region's trade by Europeans on the one hand and local non-Bengalis on the other, and restricted as to choice of occupation by their position in the social hierarchy, upper-caste Bengalis were coming in increasing numbers from all parts of the Presidency to settle and work in Calcutta, in a bid to "get on" under British rule. Mainly from the three upper social groupings of Bengali Hindu society—the Brahmins, the Vaidyas and the Kayasthas—they formed the backbone of a new class of Bengali which came to be called the "bhadralok" (lit. the cultured or genteel folk).[2]

Bhadralok-mindedness consisted essentially in the attempt to accommodate the new western life-style mediated and represented by the British. For this the bhadralok had to learn English. From the early nineteenth century they were the first to give sustained support to schools and institutions of higher learning patterned on the English model with special emphasis on teaching in English. English-teaching schools and Colleges were cropping up all over Bengal. They turned out a growing number of young men (hardly any women since bhadralok-mindedness was a male preserve) who sought jobs under British patronage. In particular, the bhadralok occupied various rungs of the ladder in the Civil Service (not too high up—the British saw to that) or functioned as pleaders, lawyers, doctors and teachers.

In short, by having to bring together in their lives their traditional Hindu ways and the new western patterns, the bhadralok were cultural brokers—mediators of Britain to India just as the British were mediators of the west to them. Individually, the bhadralok encounter between east and west could be more or less successful. Sometimes west and east were but juxtaposed like new wine in old wineskins, with predictable consequences. In other cases, especially among the intelligentsia, there was a genuine synthesis which was socially, religiously and later politically transformative, both for the individual concerned and for the community at large.

It is usual to characterize the period ushered in from the 1830s as a "renaissance". This description is highly misleading. It is difficult if not impossible to isolate, in the bhadralok mind, "renaissance" influences from those of the Enlightenment. It is true that a common tendency of bhadralok-mindedness was to hark back to a "glorious past" of India. But this could be done in various ways. Sometimes it was no more than a nostalgic recall of the good old days. But on the whole, for the bhadralok, it was a revisionary and even nationalizing appeal. The appeal was revisionary in the sense that some past age or character of Hindu tradition was thought to encapsulate the ideal for human living in a way the present lacked so that it became desirable to reform the decadent present by bringing to birth again something of the purity of the past. The appeal had a nationalizing effect in that educated Bengalis sought to derive from it a sense of collective dignity which would offset the humiliation of being a subject race in British eyes.

This looking to the past was inspired by the researches, by the early decades of nineteenth century, of Orientalists such as W. Jones, H.T. Colebrook, E. Burnouf and H.H. Wilson, some of whom interpreted their work as providing a glimpse into a golden age of Vedic times. A contrast was drawn between the noble simplicity of Vedic religion and subsequent idolatrous and caste-ridden Hinduism. It was common for the bhadralok intelligentsia to accept this evaluation, but often with qualifications. Sometimes later times and characters were held up as an ideal of the past, but always with the cut-off point some distance away from the present. We shall see that in coming to terms with Hinduism, most of the Indian Christians considered in this essay also looked to a past, often Vedic, ideal.[3]

But other forces were also at work. The printing press, often in furtherance of propaganda wars of one kind or another, played a leading role in developing the vernacular as a medium of sophisticated thought. Bengalis in particular, through lectures and the press, sought to define, collectivize or otherwise enhance Hindu consciousness countrywide through the medium of English, and Bengali consciousness through their own language. Some of the Bengali Christians we shall consider thought it important to contribute in some way, as Christians, to this identity-shaping process.

Further, among the intelligentsia there was a burgeoning spirit of rational inquiry. Exposure to the ideas of free-thinking, equality and liberty stemming from such thinkers as A. Smith, J. Bentham, J. Locke, D. Hume and T. Paine gave to English-educated Bengalis for the first time the confidence to challenge traditional dogmas. In the name of a reason unfettered by faith and of the fundamental equality of all human beings, they attacked what they regarded as the evils of Hinduism: discrimination against women, authoritarianism, caste and idolatry. Reason, that is, the mind's inherent power to arrive at patterns of meaning by analysis and synthesis, took on a new role. It became the arbiter of what was meaningful and true.

The autonomy thus given to reason promoted a "scientific" outlook among the bhadralok avant-garde. Imbued with the anthropocentric concern pervading Europe, they eagerly pursued, in historical perspective, the objective study of human behavior and beliefs with special reference to India. Where religious faith was concerned, it was no longer enough for reason to justify faith from *within*. Rather, faith now had to be shown to be reasonable, or at least not unreasonable. And since reason had a universal outreach, the more universally applicable to human beings the content of faith appeared, the more reasonable and therefore believable this faith became. From being for centuries the handmaid of faith, reason became faith's judge.[4]

This contrast between faith and reason as to the latter's qualities of "impartiality" and "objectivity" may appear in some respects naive to us today. But at the time the tradition of its methodological scrutiny had yet to develop. Coupled with the notions of equality, freedom, partriotism etc. then in the air, it enabled the bhadralok to devise instruments of social, religious and eventually political reform in the shape of journals, debating clubs and societies.

Perhaps the most influential society of this kind for our purposes during the greater part of the nineteenth century was the Brahmo Samaj founded in Calcutta (as the Brahmo Sabha) in 1828–9 by Ram Mohan Roy (?1772–1833). Roy based his society on rationalist, Unitarian principles with a view to transforming Hinduism from within. Caste and idol-worship were inveighed against, as was the traditional subjugation of women. Roy resisted the idea of a special divine revelation granted to a chosen people. He believed instead that every person without distinction could achieve spiritual fulfillment provided he or she responded to the illumination of Providence. Religious-minded Samajists were prone to accept his view, though not all were to agree with Roy that

Christ's life displayed in its essentials the perfect moral pattern for human living. Though in the course of time the Samaj fragmented on personal and ideological grounds, dissipating its energies, the movement it represented numbered many of the most creative minds of nineteenth-century Bengal. Nearly all the Indian Christians we shall mention viewed Brahmoism in one form or another as a serious rival to Christianity for the allegiance of Hindus willing to reform their lives, and responded to it accordingly. We shall have occasion to note one or two of these responses.

Another whose activities helped change the cultural climate of Bengal from the early 1830s was the Luso-Indian, Henry Louis Vivian Derozio (1809–1831). Derozio had been educated in an English-teaching school in Calcutta, and before he was twenty held a teaching post at Hindu College, one of the city's foremost western-orientated educational institutions for native youths. Poet and thinker, Derozio was an iconoclast who attacked the cherished Hindu idols of the day. Until his death at twenty two, he exerted enormous influence over the minds of the young men of the College. Through newly-begun journals and debating societies, he encouraged his followers, who came to be called Young Bengal, to discuss freely such topics as belief in God, freedom and patriotism, in the light of western rationalist thought. Young Bengal responded enthusiastically and outrageously. Centuries of Hindu belief and practice were cast aside overnight. The authority of tradition was dismissed and rational enquiry enthroned in its place. Part of Derozio's appeal was an evocation of India's past greatness.[5] Though unjustly accused of being an atheist, Derozio was hardly concerned to formulate a religious response to life and he may not unfairly be described as only nominally a Christian.[6]

Bhadralok-mindedness therefore expressed itself as a complex phenomenon. Among the intelligentsia it was revisionary and rationalistic, sometimes looking backwards to an ideal past, always forward-looking in its tendency towards reform. It will be interesting to see how those Hindu converts of the nineteenth century who were susceptible to the forces which we have described as shaping the bhadralok mind were more disposed to build Hindu elements into the articulation of their Christian commitment than their counterparts who were not thus susceptible. In its origins and potential it is to the former rather than to the latter kind of convert that the Indian Christian tradition is most indebted.

Here we must advert to the fact that an Indian Christian response could be significantly affected by the kind of (invariably Trinitarian) Christian allegiance of the convert. At the risk of over-simplification we may say that two doctrinal strands in particular were influential in this regard. One gave vent to the belief that human nature suffered fundamental corruption in the Fall. Consequently, human reason is a false guide in religion; other so-called revelations or scriptures are salvifically of no avail. The other strand was characterized by the assumption that because human nature was only flawed (not shattered) in the Fall, the task of grace is to perfect rather than to "recreate" nature. On this view, the revelation in Christ is requisite for the fullness of saving knowledge, yet the natural light of reason can make headway in grasping religious truth. Both views emphasized man's proneness to sin, giving to converts an articulate sense of their sinfulness, and both views stressed the need for Christ's atonement to redeem fallen humanity. Yet the first, by its uncompromising nature, was a powerful deterrent to the positive evaluation of non-Christian faiths, while the second, more tolerant of religious striving everywhere, could admit of a divine saving initiative in non-Christian contexts. In nineteenth century India, Protestant Christianity inclined to the first view and Roman Catholicism to the second, though doctrinal and other differences within both camps could create important shifts of emphasis away from the norm where the theology of non-Christian religions was concerned.

In its makings the modern Indian Christian response therefore was a many-sided one. In each case it was a combination of various forces which co-existed more or less compatibly according as individual circumstances varied. The better to understand the nature and context of the Indian Christian response, it will be necessary first to consider a somewhat contrasting form of Christian witness in the India of the time.

By the early decades of the century, the work of the British Baptist Mission in Serampore, the Danish enclave near Calcutta, provided the model and focus for a confrontational theology of non-Christian religions in general and Hinduism in particular. The Mission was headed by three remarkable men—William Carey (1761–1834), Joshua Marshman (1768–1837) and William Ward (1769–1823). All three were knowledgeable about Hindus and Hinduism, but honest though it was, their knowledge was a thing of the head not of the heart. For them, Hinduism gave false teaching: expose the errors and converts would be won to the Christian faith. Carey in particular had great learning. Later, though still based in Serampore, he was to become Professor of Sanskrit and Bengali at the (East India) Company-sponsored Fort William College in Calcutta.

Though Carey did not neglect the vernacular, he soon realized the importance of Sanskrit for evangelistic ends. Traditionally, for all Hindus Sanskrit was the perfect (=*saṃskṛta)* medium for articulating whatever was religiously or culturally worth preserving in the tradition. In translating the Bible into Sanskrit, Carey started the process of forging the linguistic tools for a modern pan-Indian, that is, Sanskritic, Indian Christianity. We cannot go into his methodology here, though later we shall assess the importance of Sanskrit in the work of the Indian Christian pioneers. Suffice it to say that his Bible translation notwithstanding, Carey himself could not or would not exploit this importance, and the mainly non-Sanskritic challenge he and the other Seramporists issued to Hinduism was ignored by orthodox Hindu pandits.

The debate in Sanskrit between orthodox Hinduism and Christianity began in earnest in 1839, with the publication of the first of three editions of a polemical treatise, the Mataparīkṣā ("Test of Doctrines")[7] written by a Scotsman, John Muir (1810–1882), then a civil servant in the East India Company. Muir, Episcopalian by background, had been required by Comapny policy to spend a year, after arrival in India, preparing for his new job by study at Fort William College. Here he must have come into contact with Carey, who was teaching in the College then without in any way disavowing his missionary commitment.

The Mataparīkṣā incorporated elements of a Paleyan rationalism and purported to identify the true religion on the basis of three criteria: (1) the ability of the religion's founder to work miracles attested by unimpeachable witnesses; (2) the superior holiness of the religion's scriptures; and (3) the religion's universally salvific character. Not surprisingly, these three criteria were applied so as to make Christianity the true religion and Hinduism, in particular, false. Behind the scenes it was really a matter of faith seeking reason, since Muir's chosen criteria were the reagents of a solution in which Christianity was the intended precipitate. But what is interesting is the role ostensibly assigned to reason in the work. Reason is set up as the impartial judge of the inquiry, and it is assumed that the application of all three criteria is rationally demonstrable. Nor is Muir's explicit starting point scriptural authority or faith. In fact the confrontational approach was being somewhat uneasily moderated by rationalist influences, and it is not irrelevant that later in life Muir's Christian stance became less confrontational.

The first two editions of the Mataparīkṣā drew interesting responses from native pandits.[8] One in particular is of special interest to us. This was entitled: Śāstratattvavinirṇaya ("Determination of the Essence of Scripture"), and was written sometime in 1844–5 by a Maharashtrian citpavana Brahmin, Nīlakaṇṭha Goreh (1825–1885), who had been brought up in Benares, the traditional stronghold of Hindu orthodoxy.

The chief target of Goreh's attack was precisely the relationship between faith and reason implied in the Mataparīkṣā.[9] The gist of Goreh's defense of the Hindu view of life (in effect, of the Vedāntic view of life) on methodological grounds was: 'Reason (*upapatti*) but conforms to scripture (*śāstra*), not scripture to reason. Scripture is self-validating while reason acts for the understanding of scripture . . . Thus those things set forth in the Vedas, Purāṇas etc. are quite true; reason only serves to make them better known'.[10]

Here reason's role is to justify scripture from within the standpoint of faith, not to judge scriptural beliefs. Scriptural authority predominates. Faith leads reason by the hand, reason grasping faith where it may. Goreh repudiates Muir's claim that the mark of the true religion is its universality, its conformability to reason. On the contrary, this is the sign of a false religion. The true religion is not based on truths susceptible to reason. "Only in scripture," he argues, "is God (*īśvara*) made known, as also the meditations, sacrifices and works relating to him."[11] He criticizes the religion advocated in the Mataparīkṣā (designedly innocent of the more recondite Christian doctrines), as "simple-minded" (*bāladhīgocara*) and therefore "man-made" (*narair iva kṛta*). In fact, on the matter of reason's relation to faith, Goreh stands squarely in the classical Vedāntic tradition, for which the nature and existence of Brahman, the supreme being, cannot be demonstrated by reason. This was affirmed on grounds which anticipate Hume's reasons by centuries.

About four years after he wrote this treatise, Goreh created a sensation by embracing Protestant Christianity. Baptised "Nehemiah", he turned his talents to upholding Christian doctrine, attacking Hindu faith as vigorously as he had defended it before.

His best-known work, written in Hindi, has a standard English translation called, *A Rational Refutation of the Hindu Philosophical Systems.*[12] Now the word "rational" in the title is misleading. For it seems to me that in converting to Christianity Goreh did not uphold his new faith by exchanging his old methodology for the new one latent in the Mataparīkṣā. On the contrary, reason was still subservient to faith, justifying it from within: only the faiths had been switched. In the *Refutation* again and again Goreh appeals to the authority of "the true word of God". All religions other than the Christian are religions of "human origin", unable to teach saving truths. Human reason, rooted in man's intrinsically sinful nature, is doomed to ignorance and illusion in matters religious. He writes: "My aim has been to show that whoever . . . undertakes to argue, in reliance on unaided reason about divine and spiritual things, must constantly fall into error, the mind of man being impotent to understand them rightly."[13] It is from the position of unquestioned faith that he seeks to refute Hinduism in particular, making it a point to argue that any similarity in the Hindu systems to Christian truths is superficial and illusory.

The nature of Goreh's Christian allegiance left very little scope for a sympathetic understanding of Hinduism. It is significant that he had never been exposed to the intellectual forces shaping the formation of the modern Hindu mind. He did not study in Benares Sanskirt College, founded and managed by the British, because, as his biographer puts it, he was convinced that "every Hindu who became acquainted with European learning, lost, in the same proportion, his respect for the shasters".[14] Certainly his writings do not intimate that he reasoned his way to Christianity, though he convinced himself that he had done so.[15] With the passage of time his inability to come to terms theologically with his native Hinduism plunged him in anguish.[16]

Goreh's contribution to the Indian Christian cause then was but an indirect one. Though the inchoate hermeneutic of his post-conversion vernacular writings lacked creative momentum, this work did help raise the prospect, as Carey and Muir had done, of a genuine indigenous Christian theology. Explicitly, however, he remained "an Indian champion of orthodox western Christianity".[17]

A more positive approach to Hinduism was shown by the Bengali, Lal Behari Day (or De; 1824–1894) who, from an early age, studied in Calcutta in the Church of Scotland's General

Assembly's Institution, a well-known English-teaching school where the redoubtable missionary and educationist Alexander Duff was Head. Largely under Duff's influence, Lal Behari became a Christian at nineteen, following Duff into the Free Church group after the 1843 split in the Church of Scotland. After serving as a respected pastor in the native Presbyterian Free Church in Cornwallis Square, Calcutta, Lal Behari left the ministry to enter Government service as a headmaster, though he retained the "Rev." before his name as an earnest of his Christian intentions. At the end of his life, Lal Behari once more attended services according to Church of England rites—an indication that he never did take the doctrinal and other divisions of western Protestant Christianity seriously.

Lal Behari lectured and wrote not a little and was involved in various journalistic enterprises. He had no scholarly pretensions and was theologically not a systematic thinker, least of all with regard to Hinduism. Thus in what follows we can but hope to give the salient features of his thinking in the context of the concerns of this essay.

We begin by noting that Lal Behari gave a rationalist dimension to his faith. Reason is God's gift to man; as such its natural religious probings—part of Providence's universal saving design—were not to be condemned out of hand. At the same time the evangelical view that natural religious striving was irredeemably vitiated was central to Lal Behari's thinking. This resulted in an inarticulate theological tension which he could not resolve. On the one hand, his rationalist predilections, coupled with his patriotism, prompted him to acknowledge the albeit limited religious viability of Hinduism. On the other hand, his evangelicalism induced him to depreciate reason, and to accept "revealed" truths not only outside reason's ken, but constitutionally repugnant to the Hindu mind.

A prime example of such a truth was the current doctrine of Christ's atonement. Simply put, this taught a substitutionary salvific act on Christ's part demanded in satisfaction of God's retributive justice towards fallen humanity. The vicarious suffering and death required of Christ here was in direct contradiction to the individualistic casual law of karma and rebirth which was the staple of Hindu morality. Yet Lal Behari swallowed it whole as part of the package of faith. In a letter to a Hindu friend contemplating baptism he wrote: "Without this doctrine (of the atonement) Christianity were a system of revealed philosophical deism, the world without a ray of hope, and man reduced to despair."[18] The uneasy balance between "philosophical deism" and the doctrine of the atonement bears ample testimony to the tension between reason and faith in his thinking.

Where Hinduism was concerned, it will be useful to distinguish between his views on the Brahmo Samaj—Hinduism's most potent modern reform movement in Bengal—and his attitude to traditional, village religion. On the Samaj he was explicitly ambivalent. Lauded as a "protest against idolatry", as "an instrument of social reform" and as "an index of that spirit of religious inquiry which has begun to manifest itself in some of our educated countrymen" it was slated as a substitute for Christianity, for it was "a very defective system of religion . . . incapable of giving everlasting happiness to its votaries, and . . . therefore . . . of no use".[19] He was particularly opposed to the claim made by Keshub Chandra Sen's faction of the Samaj then, that intuition could penetrate the divine mysteries.

But his most enduring work on Hinduism must be *Govinda Samanta or the history of a Bengal raiyat*[20]—in fact, the fictional account of a Bengali peasant. Told in fine literary style, it gives to Bengali peasant life a simple dignity without idealizing it. This is the Hinduism Lal Behari knew best—not the Sanskritized learning of a Goreh, but the everyday religion of age-old caste observances and simple teachings unquestioned for generations. We may understand Lal Behari's reasons for finding this personally inadequate, yet he does not despise it. Here a committed Christian portrays village Hinduism without apparent ulterior motive as, on the whole, a humanizing way of life. Lal Behari's rationalist and patriotic tendencies were thus allowed to exert their influence. The book was received with acclaim in India and abroad as a faithful account of its subject and is significant for the fact that while others were looking to a glorious Hindu past for inspiration, Lal Behari focused on the present, and in pioneering manner drew into that focus the ordinary folk who were neglected by the elitist reformist thinking of the age. The book gave new dignity to Hinduism in the eyes of Christians, a measure of pride to Indian Christians, and won Hindu respect for converts. These were important gains if Indian Christianity was to make progress.

In 1869, in the context of a nascent nationalism, Lal Behari delivered an address calling for the creation of a "National Church in Bengal". The organization was to incorporate not only the Protestant denominations but, remarkably for the time, the Roman

Catholic Church, provided it made some concessions.[21] The point is not the impracticability of this hope at the time, but the unitive breadth and nationalist coloring of Lal Behari's vision. He raised a banner which was to be imperfectly planted on Indian soil many generations later.

A more significant contribution to the cause of Indian Christianity was made by the Brahmin convert, Krishna Mohan Banerjea (1813–1885). Krishna Mohan had entered Hindu College as a schoolboy at eleven. Simultaneously he took the initiative of studying Sanskrit in Sanskrit College, recently established under British patronage for furthering native learning at a time when the Anglicist-Orientalist storm of the late 30s was but a cloud on the horizon. His deepening knowledge of Sanskrit was to stand him in good stead in later years.

Though never actually Derozio's pupil in Hindu College, Krishna Mohan fell under Derozio's spell. Disenchanted with his ancestral tradition, he became a leading member of Young Bengal. In the *Enquirer*, a radical journal he started in 1831, he wrote that the paper was meant to have no sectarian bias; instead, "let us all have a fair field, and adopt what reason and judgement may dictate." Before long, after dramatic personal upheavals, Krishna Mohan, now under Duff's influence, was baptized by him according to Presbyterian rites in 1832; within months he joined the Anglican Church, convinced that "Episcopacy was the form of Church Government established by the Apostles".[22] In due course Krishna Mohan studied theology at Bishop's College in Calcutta, was ordained in 1839, and became pastor of Christ Church in Cornwallis Square. He resigned this post in 1868 to become Second Professor at Bishop's College. Thence he pursued an illustrious Church and academic career, giving to his Christian witness an increasing if moderated nationalist emphasis.

From early in life he started developing perspectives of a national identity in general and of a Bengali identity in particular. An important forum for this was the Society for the Acquisition of General Knowledge (SAGK) with which he was closely associated since its inception in 1838. With Derozians in command, the Society discussed among other things Indian life and thought on a rationalist and historicist basis, tending to contrast a glorious past with the decadent present. His involvement with the SAGK helped Krishna Mohan stand back from his native tradition and assess it critically; in the process he also developed a unitive perspective of his country's history and people.

Like other English-educated Bengalis, Krishna Mohan favored British rule in India as providing the legislative climate for purging native social abuses. As a Christian he thought British rule providential, since it fostered the one religion which could regenerate his people. But with the passage of time, he became more and more dissatisfied by foreign domination of Church and State; it was time for Indians to make a stand. In 1875 he joined the Indian League, which sought native representation in Government, as its President. In 1876, the Indian Association, with similar political goals, replaced the League, again with Krishna Mohan as its President. As part of an active political career, he opposed the Vernacular Press Act of 1878, which sought to muzzle the native press. His political career continued till the formation of the Indian National Congress in 1885, the year in which he died.

But throughout Krishna Mohan remained an avowed Christian, asserting his native identity in Church affairs. In 1847 he resigned as a Canon of Calcutta's St. Paul's Cathedral, on the grounds that he was offered a stipend which, compared to the stipends of the European Canons, discriminated against him racially. Not least because he believed that western missionaries were not spokesmen for native Christian sentiment, he fought the Remarriage of Converts Bill of 1865 which proposed that converts from Hinduism married to Hindus be allowed to remarry Christians without formally divorcing their spouses. Above all he preached often in Bengali as part of a wider campaign to rehabilitate the vernacular as a means of articulating Indian pride, identity and aspirations. He was deservedly acknowledged as immensely learned. He wrote widely in English, translated Sanskrit works and edited Bengali journals as also the 13 volume Encyclopaedia Bengalensis.

After his conversion, Krishna Mohan's rationalist, bhadralok background did not allow him to reject Hinduism out of hand. Already in papers for the SAGK he looks to a glorious Hindu past, albeit with critical eye.[23] His "*wissenschaftlich*" approach to religion never left him. It was only after overcoming rationalist objections to the doctrines of the Trinity and Atonement that he embraced Christianity, and his *Dialogues on the Hindu Philosophy* (1861), in which he sets out to discredit Hindu philosophy of religion in favor eventually of Christian "truth", is itself based on rationalist principles. There it is said that though the divine mysteries transcend reason, reason is yet a reliable guide for reading the "book of nature" which "cannot contradict the book of revelation".[24] In other words, reason complements faith.

Later Krishna Mohan argues, Muir-like, that biblical faith can be verified by "strong external evidences" open to universal scrutiny. These are the "facts" (as he elsewhere calls them)[25] of (1) Christ's perfect moral example—beyond human invention—in contrast to Kṛṣṇa's immoral behavior; (2) historically verifiable prophecies of the Bible "which no human sagacity would anticipate" (e.g., the dispersal of the Jews); and (3) Christ's miracles, which, it is claimed, are compatible with rational conceptions of God's goodness and majesty (in contrast to the often unedifying marvels of the Purāṇas) and are attested by unimpeachable witnesses. Krishna Mohan affirmed that Christianity spread by "reason and evidence", while Buddhism and "Mohammedanism" did so through "speculative opinions" and the sword respectively. He regarded Buddhism as mainly a "negative" religion, i.e., a protest against Hinduism, and as a corrupting influence on pristine truths taught in the Vedas.

In a remarkable (and hitherto unquoted) Ordination sermon delivered in Bengali in 1870[26], Krishna Mohan refers to a number of Hindu themes and characters as prefiguring Christ and his true religion. Thus the central Taittirīya Upanishad description (in II.1.1) of the supreme being, viz. "reality, knowledge, infinite", refers not to "the fictitious Brahman, as unreal as flowers in the sky" *(gagaṇ-puṣpa-tulya-kālpanik brahma)* but to the Lord (Jesus) himself. Again, "the Vedic offerings and sacrifices have been propagated in the guise of the true sacrifice . . . The Lord is the true sacrifice—the Vedic offerings and sacrifices are but his copy and, in truth, hollow . . . ". Kṛṣṇa Vāsudeva "is not the true Remover (Hari) (of sins) — the one who removes our sins is the Lord alone, the true Hari. Vāsudeva has become Hari by assuming his guise."[27]

But it is in the Vedas that Krishna Mohan locates Hinduism's true center of gravity. The appeal to a glorious past, his Christian allegiance and his universalist predilections combined to produce his favorite Indian Christian theme, touched upon in the *Dialogues* and enlarged later, viz. that the Vedic notions of "saving sacrifice . . . of the double character of priest and victim, variously called Prajapati, Purusha and Viswakarma—of the Ark by which we escape the waves of this sinful world" bear witness to a primitive divine revelation vouschafed to mankind's first parents but obscured by time and fulfilled in Christ's suffering and death. "Christ is the true Prajapati," he writes, "the true Purusha begotten in the beginning before all worlds, and Himself both God and man."[28] And he asks: "On what gounds then can a Hindu advocate demand the ostracism of those who, by accepting Christianity, are only accepting a Vedic doctrine in its legitimately developed form?"[29] By thus making Hindu ideas resonate to his Christian tune, Krishna Mohan broached a fulfillment theology of a kind to be more systematically formulated not many decades later in J.N. Farquhar's famous book, *The Crown of Hinduism.*

I am not aware of others in later times taking up and developing any of Krishna Mohan's Indian Christian themes. Yet Krishna Mohan made a signal contribution to Indian Christianity. By his life and thought he showed that converts from Hinduism could be patriots and Christians at the same time, taking pride in their own culture and using this to express their Christian witness. His example gave to many Indian Christians the confidence to be truly Indian and truly Christian and to seek an effective synthesis between the two.

Less eminent but no less of a Christian patriot was Kali Charan Banerjea (1847–1907). Activist rather than scholar, Kali Charan studied for a time in the Free Church Institution under the ubiquitous Duff. Under Duff's influence he was baptized at seventeen, while still a student. After graduation he embarked on a professorial and then conspicuous political career. He joined the Indian National Congress when it was formed in 1885, and was a prominent member. He was particularly keen that Christianity should not "denationalize" or be seen to denationalize converts. Kali Charan did his share of writing and lecturing, but little of his thinking remains on record. He is noted for starting in 1887, with his friend Joy Gobind Shome, a non-denominational Protestant organization called the Christo Samaj which was to propagate Christian truth and to promote Christian union and welfare. The Samajists believed in lay baptism, lay ministry and in the ministry of women. The Christo Samaj petered out by 1895. Like Krishna Mohan, Kali Charan contributed towards the viability and respectability of Indian Christianity.

But in a class of his own for our purposes was his nephew, Bhabani Charan Banerjea (1861–1907). Variously evoked—e.g., as a "Vedantin and a Roman Catholic renunciate", as the "Father of Indian theology" and as a revolutionary nationalist[30]—he remains an enigmatic figure. He described himself as a "Hindu-Catholic", and tried to live according to this description.[31]

Motherless from infancy, Bhabani Charan spent his early childhood under the influence of his maternal grandmother, whose deep Hindu piety had a lasting effect on his self-understanding as an Indian. His father served as an Inspector in the police and had his son sent to various English-teaching schools and Colleges where he was exposed to Christianity and western thinking. However, like Krishna Mohan Banerjea, Bhabani Charan concurrently and of his own accord studied the Sanskritic tradition in a nearby native seminary or *ṭol*. His affinity for Sanskrit was to play a central role throughout his life.

Bhabani Charan was growing up at a time when the nationalist movement of Surendranath Banerjea was taking shape, and by fifteen had become militantly politicized against the British. Soon however, he fell under the sway of the great Brahmo leader, Keshub Chandra Sen, and turned his energies to social and religious pursuits. Keshub communicated to Bhabani Charan not only his vision of a harmony of all religions but a profound love for Christ. Eventually, Bhabani Charan was baptized a Roman Catholic at the age of thirty in Sindh, in north-western British India, where he had journeyed, ten years earlier, to help a friend establish and run a school on English lines. Before baptism, he read as many of the Catholic neo-Scholastic treatises as were available.

Militantly Catholic after baptism, Bhabani Charan wrote and lectured forcefully against Theosophy, the Arya Samaj, Protestant Christianity and aspects of Brahmoism and traditional Hinduism in turn. But he was proud of his cultural background and went about dressed in the traditional saffron robe of the Hindu reunciate, with only an ebony cross hanging from his neck to mark his Christian allegiance. In December 1894, in the editorial of *Sophia*, a monthly journal he was editing, he announced that he had formally adopted the life of mendicant renunciate: to mark this he was assuming a new name, Upadhyay Brahmabandu (later this became Brahmabandhab).

Upadhyay returned to Calcutta and continued his journalistic activities, treating of questions of social and religious import in both Hindu and Christian contexts. This incurred the opposition of the Papal Delegate, the Roman Church's supreme authority in the land, who became increasingly alarmed at the high profile of a convert who fostered so unconventional an image of native Catholic aspirations and who, without prior training or permission, dared to pronounce with authority on important religious matters.

But Upadhyay was not to be checked. His attitude to Hindu thought was softening in terms of a distinction, central to the rationalistic Roman Catholic philosophical-theology of the day and not incompatible with the western influences to which he had earlier been exposed, which was to become the fulcrum of his life and thought. He gives clear expression to this distinction in the January, 1895, issue of *Sophia*: "The truths in Hinduism are of pure reason illuminated in the order of nature by the light of the Holy Spirit . . . though the religion of Christ is beyond the grasp of nature and reason, still its foundation rests upon the truths of nature and reason. Destroy the religion of nature and reason, you destroy the supernatural religion of Christ. Hence a true missionary of Christ, instead of vilifying Hinduism should find out truths from it by study and research. It is on account of the close connection between the natural and the supernatural that we have taken upon ourselves the task . . . to form . . . a natural platform upon which the Hindus taking their stand may have a view of the glorious supernatural edifice of the Catholic religion of Christ'.

This distinction of complementary natural and supernatural religious truths had for Upadhyay practical and theoretical consequences. Theoretically, it enabled him to rehabilitate Hinduism from the Christian viewpoint. He began by staking a claim for "Vedic theism", viz. the Vedic belief that there is an all-powerful, all-knowing supreme being, the friend of man and the teacher of the *Rishis*, who rewards the virtuous and punishes the wicked. But gradually, Vedic theism is seen as the first step in a developing Hindu "natural" theology which reaches its high point in Śaṃkara's doctrine of non-dualism (*Advaitavāda*). In fact, this doctrine is the best expression of the natural Hindu tendency to think intuitively and unitively,[32] while Thomism expresses best the natural western tendency to think analytically and pluralistically. Both systems teach the same basic philosophical truths about the divine nature and the world's production, only their modes of expression differ culturally. On each can be superimposed the revealed truths (of the Incarnation, the Atonement and so on).

In support of his views Upadhyay proceeded to interpret the Advaitic categories of *māyā* (viz. the provisional reality of the world) and Brahman [viz. the supreme being described as *sat-cit-ānanda* (being-consciousness-bliss)] in terms of the Neo-Thomistic doctrines of creation and God respectively, claiming, not surprisingly, that both systems agree in essentials. The Hindu-Catholic should think like a Hindu in Advaitic categories where basic religious truths of reason are concerned, and superimpose upon these the Catholic system of revealed truths.

Upadhyay used the natural-supernatural distinction in other important ways: (1) to defend caste in terms of the ancient Vedic four-tiered (varṇic) ideal as a natural expression of the division of human talents and tendencies; (2) to advocate (racial) apartheid especially where marriage was concerned, so that Hindu ethnic and cultural purity could be safeguarded; (3) to justify the traditional worship of icons (*pratīkopāsana*) as a distinctive way of approaching the divine through natural (i.e., cultural) symbols; (4) to elevate Kṛṣṇa, in the light of Bankim Chatterjee's humanistic model, as the unitive and uniquely Hindu focus of natural greatness. Kṛṣṇa was to be India's natural savior-ideal, rescuing her from the social and political calamities to which she was prey; Christ was to be India's supernatural savior—rescuing her by grace from the sinful effects of the Fall. Like Krishna Mohan, Upadhyay was critical of Buddhism and Islam, which he regarded as destructive, each in its own way, of the integrity of Hindu life and thought.

From the practical point of view, the natural-supernatural divide enabled him increasingly to Hinduize his way of life. Like his uncle Kali Charan, he insisted that Christian faith must not denationalize the Hindu convert: it seemed "too . . . mixed up with beef and pork, spoon and fork, too tightly pantalooned and petticoated to manifest its universality".[33] To help indigenize the faith he proposed that a Hindu-Catholic monastery be set up, with ecclesiastical approval, for the training of native missionaries in Sanskritic thought and in accordance with Hindu ways. These itinerant missionaries would be sent out to evangelize the country, acting at the same time as a symbol of a native expression of their faith. The Papal Delegate, more alarmed than ever, quashed this proposal as it was beginning to materialize. It must also be mentioned that Upadhyay composed hymns in Sanskrit on the Trinity and the Incarnation; the former is sung in Indian Churches today.

Frustrated by misunderstanding and opposition, Upadhyay gave vent to his long-suppressed nationalist leanings with increasing virulence. In public, his Hindu profile became more and more dominant to the detriment of his Christian commitment, which he turned into a private affair. He immersed himself in the nationalist movement and took to writing crisp, usually offensive, anti-British articles in Bengali. Eventually, he was arrested for sedition. A few months before this he performed, in the public eye, the Hindu penitential rite of the outcaste returning to the fold (*prāyaścitta*). Though it can be shown, I think, that this was intended as no more than a social gesture, by and large at the time he was thought to have apostatized from the Christian faith. He died under arrest, of tetanus, at the age of forty-seven, with the word "*ṭhākur*" (his equivalent for "Lord") on his lips, and the body was disposed of according to Hindu rites.

Upadhyay's contribution to Indian Christianity is major but latent: more in the nature of banners waved and kites flown than a systematic attempt to indigenize the faith. His theology and social philosophy were bound up with a distinction between natural and supernatural which is probably passé and is certainly too naive. Some aspects of his thought are morally unacceptable, e.g., his advocacy of racial apartheid between "Aryan" Hindus and others (not excluding the tribal peoples or adivasis of India). Yet a number of his ideas are rich in potential for the development of Indian Christianity, e.g., his innovative use of Sanskrit compounds in the hymns to suggest Christian meanings; his analysis of the Hindu and western modes of thinking so that the two may be more clearly distinguished and understood. Further, his efforts to found a Hindu-Catholic monastery were not entirely in vain. They bore fruit in the establishment in 1950 by Monchanin and Abhishiktananda, with ecclesiastical approval, of the famous Hindu-Christian ashram, Shantivanam, in South India. Both founders explicitly acknowledge Upadhyay as the inspiration for their work. And a number of other Indian-Christian ashrams have been set up on this model. With Upadhyay's death in 1907, we bring to an end the period under consideration in this essay. Let us now sum up briefly, with an eye to the future of the Indian Christian movement.

We note that the pioneers we have considered located the center of gravity of their Indian Christian thinking in the Sanskritic tradition, usually focused in an ideal past. No doubt there were (and are) good reasons for regarding the Sanskritic tradition as normative, e.g., the bonding character of Sanskrit in a pan-Hindu context as the accredited repository of religious and cultural value, as the matrix of many Indian vernaculars. But the Sanskritizing tendency raises problematic questions about the continuing identities of "great" and "little" traditions, about Sanskritization riding roughshod over non-Hindu and non-Brahminical expressions of Indian Christianity deriving from e.g., Buddhism, Islam, and the adivasis. In the eyes of many, the Sanskritic tradition remains the instrument of high-caste oppression and privilege. It is significant that those we have considered in this essay showed scant respect for non-Christian religious traditions other than the Hindu. Further, what place does village Hinduism have in the indigenization of the faith? The nineteenth-century pioneers, with few exceptions, tended to dismiss village Hinduism as of little worth. Contemporary exponents of Indian Christianity have yet to tackle these issues adequately.

As our study has indicated, the indiginizing activity of the nineteenth century was uncoordinated. The lack of coordinating and ecumenical agencies resulted in the poor dissemination of insights and in much wasted effort. It was difficult if not impossible to build creatively on the labors of others. The situation has hardly improved today.

We have seen that the indigenizing process is significantly influenced by the doctrines of God, man and the world at work in the faith out of which it arises. Some Christian approaches are reluctant to tolerate the notion of saving points of contact between Christian and non-Christian faith. If Indian Christianity is to succeed the theology/-gies of non-Christian religion(s) on which it is based will be crucial. In this regard, is a theology of fulfillment to be developed, or a theology of "the complementarity of religious truths?" What is the place of Christ and the Bible in this theology? What is the theologian's attitude to modern scriptural (especially Biblical) studies?[34] What use can be made of myth—with which Hinduism is richly stocked—in the indigenizing process?[35]

Finally, nineteenth-century Indian Christianity, with one or two notable exceptions (e.g., Upadhyay) was weighted towards theory rather than practice. In recent times a shift of emphasis has been taking place. What are the dynamics of the relationship between theory and practice in this regard? Contemporary advocates of Indian Christianity will have to decide whether the best way forward is not to plunge into exploratory indigenizing activity, leaving the theory to follow as best it may.

Notes

1. Thus we shall not deal with earlier Hindu-Christian encounters such as those initiated by R. Nobili (seventeenth century) and B. Ziegenbalg (eighteenth century). The link between these earlier encounters and the subject of our study is, if anything, tenuous. Similarly, we shall not consider the doctrinally implicit religious poetry, however pregnant theologically, of such Indian Christians as the Tamil, V. Shastriar (c. 1790–1855) or the Maharashtrian, N.V. Tilak (1862–1919).

2. On the bhadralok, cf. D. Kopf's *The Brahmo Samāj and the shaping of the modern Indian mind* (Princeton, Princeton University Press, 1979) esp. ch. 3, and J.H. Broomfield, *Elite Conflict in a Plural Society: Twentieth Century Bengal* (Bombay, OUP, 1968), chs. 1 and 2. With reference to the latter, it is worth pointing out that "bhadralok" was to be contrasted with "chotolok" (lit. the vulgar or common folk) rather than with the "abhadra" (op. cit., p. 6).

3. The Indus valley civilization was then unknown.

4. The two preceding paragraphs indicate the sense in which "rationalism" is being used in this essay.

5. Cf. "My country! in thy day of glory past/A beautous halo circled round thy brow,/And worshipped as a deity thou wast./ Where is that glory, where that reverence now?" in *Sources of Indian Tradition (Vol. II)*, ed. by Wm. Theodore de Bary (New York and London, Columbia University Press, 1963) p. 19.

6. Another in this mold seems to have been the outstanding Bengali poet, Michael Madhusudan Datta (1824–1873), whose motives for conversion to Christianity have, to say the least, been doubted. Though Madhusudan may have had personal Christian convictions, for him, in effect, to "christianize" was to "civilize". Cf. " . . . believe me, it is the Solemn Mission of the Anglo-Saxon to regenerate, to civilize—or, in one word, to Christianize the Hindu" in "The Anglo-Saxon and the Hindu" (cf. *Madhusūdan Nāṭya Granthābalī*, ed. Mohammad Moniruzzaman, Dacca, Pakistan Book Corporation, 1969, p. 751).

7. Calcutta, Bishop's College Press. In 1831, William Hodge Mill's composition in verse on the life and significance of Christ—the Śrīkhr̥ṣṭasaṃgītā ("In reverent recitation of Christ")—made some impact on native pandits but did not initiate a debate.

8. R.F. Young's *Resistant Hinduism: Sanskrit sources on anti-Christian apologetics in early nineteenth-century India* (Vienna 1981, Publications of the de Nobili Research Library, vol. VIII) gives a good account of this controversy and its context.

9. Young notes: "three of six chapters of the ŚTV discussed the relation between faith (śraddhā) and reason (tarka or upapatti)"; op. cit., p. 105. See also p. 108.

10. śāstrānugaivopapattir nopapattyanugaṃ tu tat/svataḥ pramāṇakaṃ śāstram upapattis tu tadvide// . . . ato vedapurāṇādau ye ye'rthāḥ pratipāditāḥ/satyā evopapahttis tu tadbodhāya prakalpyate//. Cf. *Resistant Hinduism*, note 103, pp. 107–8. I have modified Young's translation.

11. śāstra eveśvaraḥ proktas tathaiva tadupāsanāḥ/yajñādīny atha karmāṇi tat tathā na tadanyathā// op. cit., note 103, p. 107. My translation.

12. Translated by Fitz-Edward Hall (London and Madras, The Christian Literature Society for India, 1862, 1897). The original was written in 1860, and translation began in the following year with Goreh's collaboration. Goreh appreciably modified the original in the process.

13. op. cit., p. 112.

14. *Resistant Hinduism*, p. 102.

15. Cf. "I have begun to think that it is not by going through a regular process of reason that men renounce one religion and embrace another, though such was certainly the case with me . . . " (*Resistant Hinduism*, p. 172). But note: " . . . it is demonstrably certain in my case that the [Christian] religious notions which I now entertain I never discovered by my reason or intuition", in "A Letter to the Brahmos" (Allahabad, North India Tract Society, 1868; first written in 1867).

16. He is reported as saying, with reference to his conversion, that he often "felt like a man who has taken poison" (cf. *Resistant Hinduism*, p. 171).

17. R.H.S. Boyd, *India and the Latin captivity of the Church: the cultural context of the Gospel* (CUP, 1974, p. 22).

18. Cf. G. Macpherson, *Life of Lal Behari Day: Convert, Pastor, Professor and Author* (Edinburgh, T & T Clark, 1900, p. 47).

19. *Life*, p. 87–8.

20. 2 vols., London, Macmillan, 1874.

21. viz. abandoning its stand on "the dogmas of the infallibility of the pope and the insufficiency of the holy scriptures as a rule of faith". Cf. "The Desirableness and Practicability of Organizing a National Church in Bengal" (pamphlet; Calcutta, printed by Daniel Ghose, 1870).

22. *A biographical sketch of the Rev. K.M. Banerjea* by Ramachandra Ghosha (introduced by Asis Das Gupta & Probodh Biswas, Calcutta, Progressive Publishers, 1980, p. 21).

23. Cf., e.g., "The Nature and Importance of Historical Studies" (1838) and "Reform, Civil and Social" (1840).

24. *Dialogues on the Hindu Philosophy comprising the Nyaya, the Sankhya, the Vedant, to which is added a discussion of the Authority of the Vedas* (London and Madras, The Christian Literature Society for India, 2nd. ed., 1903, p. 15).

25. In "The Claims of Christianity in British India" published in *Revelation, Christianity and the Bible*, ed. Bishop G.E.L. Cotton (Calcutta, R.C. Lepage and Co., 1864). See also *The Dialogues*, p. 386f.

26. On June 9, 1870 at Trinity Church, Amherst St., Calcutta; pamphlet, printed at Chinsurah by D.E. Rodrigues, 1870.

27. tadrūp baidik jāg jaj(ñ)ao sat(y)a jaj(ñ)er chale pracalita haiyāchila . . . prabhui sat(y)a jaj(ñ)a, baidik jāg jaj(ñ)a tā̃hā̃r anukaraṇ mātra kintu bastutaḥ asār. op. cit., p. 4; bāsudeb jathārtha hari nahen, pāp hārak āmā(r)der prabhui jathārtha hari, tā̃hā̃r beś dhāraṇ kariyā bāsudeb hari haiyāchen. op. cit., p. 6.

28. Cf. "The Relation between Christianity and Hinduism" (Calcutta, 1881), reprinted in T.V. Philip, *Krishna Mohan Banerjea: Christian apologist* (Madras, The Christian Literature Society, 1982, p. 196); see also *The Dialogues*, p. 398.

29. T.V. Philip, p. 200.

30. By Rabindranath Tagore (cf. his original Preface to *Chār Adhyāy*), by K.P. Aleaz (cf. "The theological writings of Brahmabandhav Upadhyaya reexamined" in *The Indian Journal of Theology*, vol. XXVIII, April-June, 1979, p. 77) and cf. *Upādhyāy Brahmabāndhab o bhāratīya jātīyatābād* by Haridas and Uma Mukhopadhyay (Calcutta, Firma K.L. Mukhopadhyay, 1961), respectively.

31. For the best account of his life, cf. *The Blade: Life and Work of Brahmabandhab Upadhyay* (Calcutta, Roy and Son, n.d.) by Animananda.

32. Cf. Upadhyay's "The One-centredness of the Hindu race", trans. from the Bengali by J. Lipner in *Vidyajyoti: Journal of Theological Reflection* (October 1981).

33. In *The Tablet* (Jan. 3, 1903, p. 8b). This was a familiar refrain from post-conversion days till the end of his life.

34. The Indian Christian thinkers of the nineteenth century tended to dismiss the fledgling critical Biblical studies of the time as the work of "sceptics" and "humanists".

35. The pioneers considered saw myth, not in the modern light as an enriching necessity for human living, but simply as untruth or fancy, with negative consequences for Hindu-Christian encounter.

Chapter Fourteen

THE RESPONSE OF THE DALAI LAMA AND THE TIBETAN COMMUNITY IN THE INDIAN EXILE

E.K. Dargyay

The Historical Context

To bring up the Tibetan Buddhists' response to the challenge of the plurality of religions within a volume focusing on modern India's answer to this problem may seem to be out of context and arbitrary. However, I think there are good reasons to include here a discussion of the position on religious pluralism as developed by the Tibetan Buddhist community in the Indian exile as Tibet has been a sanctuary for many aspects of ancient Indian civilization, particularly for those related to Buddhism: Statues and manuscripts, poetry and logic, rituals and the knowledge of healing, to name only a few traits, were taken from India and transplanted into the culturally virgin soil of Tibet where they adapted to the new environment and grew profusely. For this reason Tibetan studies were traditionally associated with Indian studies and for decades the study of Tibetan language was a subsidiary to the knowledge of Sanskrit. In recent times Tibetan civilization and language are considered more in their own right, but still the naval cord uniting Tibetan with Indian civilization can never be severed.

The vital linkage of Tibet with Indian civilization in general and Indian spirituality in particular was reinforced when a hundred thousand Tibetans had to leave their homeland by 1959. India welcomed the refugees despite her own full share of problems, such as overpopulation, shortage of food production, etc.

In the Indian exile, the Tibetan community had to rethink its position toward non-Buddhist communities. It was a necessity imposed on the refugees by the harsh realities of everyday life. Twenty six years have passed by since the Tibetans arrived in India, and only recently Tibetan leaders started to think about their relationship with non-Buddhist religions. Therefore only starting points for a fullfledged normative system suitable for dealing with other religions can be distinguished. But the countless contacts of everyday life in a diaspora situation forced on every Tibetan the problem of how to deal with people of other faiths. Rich anecdotal material (I shall include some of that), some tapes with public speeches given by dignitaries of the Tibetan community and several newspaper articles with interviews of their leaders are available, but only very few publications address the problem of religious pluralism in theory. Fortunately, a book has recently come out with a number of talks given by the XIVth Dalai Lama wherein he deals with this issue. This article largely reflects upon the statements of the Dalai Lama, for more than anybody else within the Tibetan refugee community, the Dalai Lama has reached out beyond the boundaries of culture and ethnicity to meet with the people of different ideological and cultural background. Bereft of his political power as King of Tibet, he demonstrated leadership in religious and philosophical matters. He traded off the role of a political and hierarchical leader for that of a spiritual leader who guides his people along a difficult path into an unknown future. Many times he departs more readily from time-honored traditions than some of his countrymen who prefer to cultivate a preservasionist attitude toward their cultural heritage. The passage dealing with the Tibetans' response to religious pluralism as formulated in exile outlines the Dalai Lama's position within Tibetan civilization and within Buddhism, but I will also try to sketch the development of his thought.

It is almost impossible to determine what the precise effects of the Indian exile were on the Tibetans' response to the phenomenon of a multiplicity of faiths and conflicting truth claims. But nobody would reject the assumption that the Tibetans' answer were different if there had not been the exile. The entire sociopolitical situation in exile is dramatically different from the one when the Tibetans still enjoyed political and cultural independence. At that time they looked at other faiths from the vantage point of strength and sovereignty; but in exile Tibetans are a minority, tolerated by followers of other faiths. This has consequences for how one addresses the problem of religious pluralism.

The Normative Context of the Past

Most people think of Tibet as a fairly isolated country which bred an enigmatic type of man who is introverted and who is shy of any contact with the outside world. Historical facts, however, show that Tibetans had multiple contacts with their neighboring countries and assimilated readily foreign cultural elements as well as lending some of their own to other nations.[1] It was inevitable that after the Tibetans had become Buddhists, they would meet people who did not share their own faith, when they travelled along the trade routes of Central Asia, bartered in the oasis cities along the Silk Road, embarked on pilgrimages to the sacred sites of Buddhism in India, or when they visited China.

Evidences of these contacts are found in rock graffiti, inscriptions, and in murals: H.J. Klimkeit demonstrated that Manichean symbols have left traces upon the murals of Alchi, a Tibetan Buddhist temple complex built during the late 11th century.[2] He even speculates that some of the people portrayed there may represent Manicheans. If his interpretation is correct, this would demonstrate a remarkable co-existence of two major religions. Nestorian crosses were found inscribed on rocks at major travel routes in West Tibet.[3]

Missionaries of various beliefs lived in Tibet, sometimes for centuries. Manicheans, Nestorians, Muslims, Jesuits, and Capucians, all stayed in Tibet for some time.[4] So far we do not know much about how the Tibetans responded to the foreign ideas promoted by these missionaries. Textual sources indicate that Tibetans, like the Buddhists in India, saw followers of other faiths mainly an unfortunate people who happened to believe into erroneous doctrines. The question of influence of other religions upon Tibetan Buddhism is separate from this issue. Western scholarship pointed at possible Manichean, Zoroastrian or Persian influences, but this does not mean that Tibetans were engaging in an exchange of ideas.[5]

There was ample opportunity for engaging in cross-religious discussion, but not dialogue, and many Tibetan texts bear testimony to this. Until 1959, when the Tibetans lost their political independence, the cross-religious discussion was conducted according to the guidelines for debating developed in ancient India for defeating one's adversaries. In such case the opponent was seen as the proponent of a faith whose truth claims were in disagreement with the claims made by one's own camp. Thus the opponent's defeat was the most desirable objective of any debate. To this end, Tibetan scholars of the past composed voluminous works discussing the deficiencies found in other belief systems.[6]

The situation changed drastically after 1959, when Tibetans came as refugees to India, Nepal, and Bhutan, and from there to many countries in Europe and North-America. Deprived of the resources of their native land, they gratefully received the aid extended to them by various Christian relief agencies. For the first time, Tibetans experienced a situation in which followers of a rival religion neither attempted to demonstrate their adversaries' heresy nor to convert them. The spiritual leaders of the Tibetan community in exile responded to this challenge with an increasing interest in non-Buddhist religions.

The Situation in the Indian Exile

In 1959 the memory of Gandhi was still fresh in India, and Nehru was a statesman whose voice was heard throughout the world. At that time the world was so optimistic to believe that non-violence was a powerful means to resolve political conflicts. When the Tibetan government sought foreign help against the increasing pressure exerted by Mao's China, India along with many Western states shied away from assisting the Tibetans in their plight in the hope to solidify a peaceful cooperation with Community China.

At this time the Tibetans could not avoid to be exposed to Gandhi's philosophy of non-violence, which was much in accordance with their Buddhist belief. Violence as a means to defend or regain the threatened or lost political independence was repeatedly rejected by the Dalai Lama and other leading dignitaries of the Tibetans. But the exile in India also provided them with an opportunity to learn more about other religions and modern ideologies, among them Communism.

When the first Tibetan monks arrived as refugees in India, many Hindu and Jaina pilgrim houses opened their doors to them, with the result that Tibetan Buddhists lived in close social contacts with followers of other beliefs. The Tibetans' dependence on a meat-containing diet became sometimes an issue which had to be addressed in order to prevent the break-out of tensions. This Tibetan habit has sometimes puzzled other Mahayana Buddhists, but it becomes understandable when considered in its historical context. When the Tibetans embraced Buddhism, they adopted in general the Mahayana *sūtras* and *tantras*, but opted for preserving the *vinaya* of the Mulasarvastivadins, a Hinayana school, which allowed meat eating under the condition that one was not involved in the slaughtering of the animal. In India, some Tibetan monks chose a vegetarian diet, others maintained their traditional diet, but avoided the cooking of meat while living together with Hindus and Jainas. If discussions touched on the issue of religious truth claims, the Tibetans, being guests in a foreign country, responded with politeness and tolerance, while looking for similarities between the two rivalling systems which would allow one to subsume the other system under one's own.

In Tibet the Dalai Lama had received the same thorough education in Buddhist philosophy and spirituality that was given to his predecessors, but we may speculate that he received very little information about the Western world. It is impossible for me to document how the Dalai Lama's thoughts were influenced through the exile in India. I learned that foreign embassies provided him with crates filled with books on western philosophies, but I do not know which books aroused his particular interest. One might also speculate that his various contacts with philosophers, artists, religious potentates, and politicians of Asian and Western descent had some impact on his own thoughts. Nevertheless, the Dalai Lama became soon the most outspoken and modern thinker among the Tibetans in exile. His authority as spiritual and political head of all Tibetans functioned like an umbrella under whose shelter he developed his own philosophy. The Tibetan youth organizations and more liberal Tibetans greeted this with enthusiasm, while the more conservatives grudgingly remained silent. In the West the Dalai Lama is seen as the most articulate representative of Mahayana Buddhism in a modern world. No other Mahayana hierarch discusses religious issues with such ease with the pope, American congressmen, academics, or writers. In a sense, the Dalai Lama became a high profile spokesman for the entirety of Mahayana Buddhism.

Scope of a Cross-religious Dialogue

A major impediment in entertaining a dialogue with members of other beliefs is the claim that the ultimate goal can only be obtained within one's own theological or doctrinal paradigms. Buddhism, although flexible in its doctrinal stand, is no exception. It is a basic understanding among Buddhists that whoever aspires to transcend this world has to pass through certain stages in his/her spiritual development and cannot fail to come to certain conclusions about reality: the non-existence of an eternal soul as an inherently existing substance or the impermanent nature of the universe, to name only a few. Whether such a person calls himself a Buddhist or not is irrelevant. This kind of insight, however, has to be acquired; otherwise this world can never be transcended: in other words, *nirvāṇa* can never be realized. Such a position does not nurture a fruitful dialogue, as it subsumes the other system under one's own.

To avoid this kind of doctrinal squabbling the Dalai Lama invites us to focus our attention on the daily practice of religion. In a talk given to the Congress of the United States His Holiness said:

> The important thing is that in your daily life you practice the essential things, and on that level there is hardly any difference between Buddhism, Christianity, or any other religion.[7]

With this statement he applies a common Buddhist rule: morality has to precede any attempt for philosophical appreciation. The contact between followers of different faiths has to be first established in the courtyard, and not in the holiest of the holy temple, i.e., the doctrine. In living a moral life, in joining our efforts to the betterment of mankind, or in loving and caring for our fellow beings (human and non-human) we may experience a unity beyond the boundaries of creeds. This is an invitation to join our efforts in helping our fellow human beings, and to coordinate the various aid campaigns, regardless of what religious group supports them. But it also implies that questions about why we do these acts of charity, compassion, and love ought to be put aside, that any attempt to use aid campaigns for missionary aims has to end; otherwise debating about the "true" reasons would reoccur immediately. Each religious group might then claim to have the "better" reasons why they support the needy, or that the "true" gift is not bread but the "right" faith.

The Dalai Lama sees compassion and love as a universal melody permeating all religions and resounding in all religious acts, which leads him to exclude those religions which advocate acts of cruelty or violence from his definition of "true" religion. He argues on the presuppositon that the many are more important than the individual I, a conviction shared by most, if not all, world religions. He compares Christian *agape* with a *bodhisattva*'s caring for all sentient beings. In a recent CBC program he called Mother Theresa working among the poor of India a bodhisattva (a Buddha to be). The context made it clear that he used the term not in a metaphorical way. From a Christian viewpoint, this statement may seem insignificant, but is a landmark for the Buddhist world. It means that a Christian nun who devotes her entire existence to improve the fate of the poor in whom she sees brothers and sisters of Christ, is identified with a Buddhist "saint" (i.e., bodhisattva) who pledges to take on the suffering of the universe as his/her sole responsibility and not to enter *nirvāṇa* before all other creatures do so. Such statement may seem to be unorthodox, and it is to some extent, although Buddhist texts say that one who takes on the suffering of sentient begins is a *bodhisattva*. But so far such statements were interpreted only within a buddhist framework. Thus the Dalai Lama interprets a given canonical statement in a more liberal manner than it was common hitherto. If we were to explore the doctrinal background assumed to be adopted by each individual, we could hardly see any similarity between a Christian loving one's neighbor for Christ's sake and a *bodhisattva* guiding others toward *nirvāṇa*. But their actual lives, the meaning of their actions and the concerns governing their day-to-day decisions are very similar. This is only possible if the doctrine does not occupy the center of religion.

The Dalai Lama goes even so far as to say that whether or not one believes in Buddha or God does not matter so much, if one only were to generate the right motivation: compassion and appreciation of our fellow human beings as brothers and sisters.

The similarity in the needs and desires cherished by all humans becomes a bridge permitting us to embrace every human as our beloved brother or sister, even if he/she may act like an enemy. From a Buddhist perspective, the universality of suffering and impermanence unites us all and makes us brothers and sisters, regardless of our individual doctrinal and philosophical stands. To include enemies and adversaries into compassion and love is stipulated by both Christianity and Buddhism. Every human being should be loved for his/her own sake, and not because our own faith assigns a certain value to the individual. This pragmatic approach toward cross-religious dialogue also affects the nature of political life.

Spiritual leaders among the Tibetan refugees consider unrestricted compassion for all living creatures a requisite for any attempt to reduce tensions among political adversaries. For this reason, Buddhists tend to emphasize the control of our aggressive mind more than the control of arms, which are considered a mere "manifestation" of an aggressive mind.[8] Buddhist ethics with its commitment to non-violence has a serious bearing on the political feelings of the Tibetans regarding the Chinese. A Tibetan Buddhist monk, who led a delegation of his peers on a tour through the United States, put it this way:

> We felt great hatred at first toward the Chinese, but then realized that their ignorance and selfishness were responsible for their actions, and now have replaced our hatred with pity and compassion.[9]

The right to political self-determination is seen within a texture of various rights mutually limiting and defining their individual boundaries. Thus, the Tibetans reason that their claim to independence is not based on the overthrow of the Chinese regime, but on the Chinese insight that the Tibetans have the same right to look after their own affairs as the Chinese have. If such basic understanding is achieved, further cooperation is not only possible, but desirable. The same paradigm rules religious dialogue.

To place the entire cross-religious dialogue on similarities found in the ethical rules of the various faiths would certainly be too shallow for a fruitful communication. After mutual respect, built upon similarities in ethics, is established, each religious community has to be open to examine and even adopt ideas and theories contained in the other's faith, but suitable to complement one's own creed. For instance, the Buddhists may learn about social engagement from their Christian brothers, and Christians may learn about disciplining and training the mind from the Buddhists. Even philosophical or theological concepts lend themselves to such a consideration. Although, for instance, the Buddhists reject the concept of an almighty Creator God, the claim that the divine is the basis and objective of not only our individual life, but also of all creatures, is an idea worthwhile for a Buddhist to study. In other words, the attempt to guide men so that they may transcend this world and realize a state beyond the limitations and pitfalls of the present one is common to all religions. That we share this fundamental orientation should make us all brothers and sisters in faith, regardless of our disagreement in philosophical and theological matters. This fundamental agreement upon how we see the world and the purpose of human life should then, according to the Dalai Lama's view, provide a framework for the sharing of philosophical and theological concepts. Debating the various, and often contradicting, philosophical and theological concepts and claims could easily result in bitter arguing, unless we are willing to rank the rationalization of religion along with the verbalization of religious experience, i.e., theology or philosophy, lower than the actual religious life. And this is what the Dalai Lama suggests. For him, all theoretical reflection upon religion is only a means for self-scrutiny, but never an end in itself. He sees in philosophical and religious theorizing a tool which sharpens our awareness for compassion and love; if it does not work toward this end—it is meaningless.

> If we go into the differences in philosophy and argue with and criticize each other, it is useless. There will be endless argument; the result will mainly be that we irritate each other—accomplishing nothing. Better to look at the purpose of the philosophies and to see what is shared—an emphasis on love, compassion, and respect for a higher force.[10]

With this statement the Dalai Lama challenges the position which Buddhist philosophy has maintained within the Tibetan tradition until the present. Perhaps there is even disagreement among some learned Tibetan monks on this matter, nevertheless I like to see it as another step taken by the Dalai Lama to leave the cocoon of scholasticism, which has enwrapped Tibetan Buddhism ever since the seventeenth and eighteenth centuries, and to invigorate its genuine creativity and dynamics.

Despite his continuous emphasis on love and compassion as *the* characteristic unifying all religions, the Dalai Lama never advocates a "universal religion" in terms of a unified theology. To the contrary, he sees in the diversity of religious claims a constant challenge which should stimulate spiritual growth. It is my impression that he sees the issue of irreconcilable truth claims more as a stimulus for constant scrutiny of one's own position rather than as a cause for judgment against a conflicting view. The Dalai Lama exemplifies this open approach to discussing apparently conflicting truth claims in a lecture about two different Buddhist traditions.[11]

The same procedure should work when Christians, Hindus, Shintoists, Jews, Buddhists, or Muslims talk to each other as religious persons, and not as exponents of certain civilizations, nations, or powers.

Tibetan Buddhists are meeting with individuals of other religions not only on ethical and philosophical grounds but also on the terrain of ritual and monasticism. The Tibetan form of Buddhism has been frequently compared with the Roman Catholic Church because of the elaborate rituals, strong monastic tradition, and exhibition of pageantry during festive seasons. Since so many Tibetan monks found asylum in the Western World after they had to leave their native land in 1959, there has been a great deal of contact between Catholic and Buddhist monks. Repeatedly, Catholic monasteries invited delegations of Tibetan monks to share temporarily with them their Christian tradition. Some years ago monks of the most renowned Upper Academy of Tantric Studies *(rGyud stod)*, relocated in South India, toured through Europe and stayed for some time in the Benedictine monastery of Niederaltaich, West Germany. In 1983 a group of three Tibetan monks visited thirteen Benedictine and Cistercian monasteries in the United States.[12] They participated in all religious services, including the recitation of the office in choir and the celebration of the Eucharist. Both sides praised the opportunity for such sharing in religous experience, which may result in a genuine feeling of unity despite some doctrinal differences. Similar meetings were arranged when outstanding spiritual masters of Tibet, such as the much venerated Kalu Rinpoche, visited Europe. On one occasion at the abbey of Sainte-Marie de la Pierre-qui-Vivre, Rinpoche participated in a stimulating dialogue with the abbot.[13]

The Naropa Institute at Boulder, Colorado, arranges annual conferences on "Christian and Buddhist Meditation", where leading representatives of Christian or Buddhist faith come together to exchange their experiences and to share with each other their individual liturgical practices.

Reflection upon the Tibetans' Response

Although the Tibetans faced the modern world, with its religious pluralism, only since 1959, they soon established a lively contact with non-Buddhist religious communities. Naturally, the first contacts were made with the Hindu and Jaina communities of India and Nepal. They have been numerous and on all levels, but are beyond the scope of this article. As early as the 1960s, several Buddhist dignitaries of Tibet met with the Pope in Rome—long before the Bishop of Rome travelled around the world. The cross-religious dialogue started seriously when the Dalai Lama visited the Western World for the first time in the early 1970s and it has continued to grow.

The Tibetan interest in cross-religious dialogue is sincere, but is is different from the avenues chosen by many academics. The Tibetans consider that debating about conflicting truth claims, reducing theoretical concepts till they fit into one's own philosophy or theology, or identifying members of other faiths as "anonymous" members of one's own does not respect the other's integrity as much as is desirable. For this reason the Tibetans focus on the humane aspects of religion, on ethical values such as compassion, love, and caring for other living beings, on liturgy, and on monasticism as fields for cross-religious contacts. This accounts for the fact that Tibetan monks are very active in ecumenical gatherings, but take little interest in academics' attempts to map out the perimeter for a cross-religious dialogue.

Given the nature of the Tibetan response to religious pluralism, there are various issues not dealt with in the cross-religious dialogue, but they may come up any time. For example, the issue of our relationship with the non-human world, i.e. animals and plants is not discussed. More than any other religion, Tibetan Buddhism developed a unique appreciation for the non-human world. As a common practice, Tibetan yogis included wild animals in their evening prayers, wishing that any hungry creature might find his adequate food. They felt responsible for the "purity" of nature, which means not to manipulate nature for the sole purpose of our economical benefits. Tibetan thinkers of the 18th century pondered upon the karmic conditions of pet dogs, whether—and if so, in what sense— was their *karma* bad, as these dogs were much loved and appreciated by their owners. Such deeply rooted respect for the animal and plant world was however balanced by the sheer necessity of human life in a cold, arid high-altitude land. Tibetans have always been meat-eaters and have depended upon their livestock as a means for transportation as well as a source for many commodities. In the Tibetans' view human life has a greater potential than animal life. But is is precisely because they belive that they also believe that humans have a responsibility for the well-being of the non-human world. Salvation or liberation, as Tibetan Buddhists see it, has to include the entire animated universe—humans, gods, ghosts, animals, and to some extent even plants.

Another issue, not sufficiently dealt with in cross-religious dialogues, is the matter of human aggression, defense, and survival. The Tibetan refugee community deliberately renounced terrorist and other acts of violence as a means for regaining their political independence. Tibetan Buddhists see the "injustice of history" from a different angle than followers of other religions might do: one's own *karma* forms this "injustice", thus leaving no room for pitying one self.

Last, but certainly not least, the Tibetans have something to contribute to the debate about the validity of truth-claims, if they would introduce Madhyamaka philosophy as a way to "evaluate" conflicting truth–claims. As a philosophical view which rejects any system of thought, because the systematization of thought restricts the universality of reality, Madhyamaka may be helpful in reconciling conflicting truth–claims without reducing them to a counterfeit of one's own position. (Although some may argue that the Madhyamaka rejection of systematization is in itself a system.) There might be a day when Buddhist Madhyamaka spirituality and Christian mysticism are unison in silence.

The Tibetans developed an original approach toward cross-religious dialogue and contacts, but there is still a huge, untapped reservoir for further fruitful sharing of ideas and views—hopefully for the betterment of this world.

Notes

1. Christopher I. Beckwith. "The Introduction of Greek Medicine into Tibet in the seventh and eighth Centuries", *Journal of the American Oriental Society*, 99.2, 1979, pp. 297–313.

2. Hans-Joachim Klimkeit. "Vairocana und das Lichtkreuz, Manichaeische Elemente in der Kunst von Alchi (West-Tibet)", *Zentralasiatische Forschungen*, 13, 1979, pp. 357–399.

3. A.H. Francke. *Antiquities of Indian Tibet* (Archeological Survey of India 38. Calcutta 1914/26, rpt. New Delhi: S. Chand, 1972, vol. 1, p. 60; —. "Some More Rock-Carvings from Lower Ladakh", *Indian Antiquary*, 32, 1903, p. 362, pl. 8 fig. 10. Giuaeppe Tucci. *Transhimalaya* (Archeologia Mundi). Delhi: Vikas Publishing House, 1973, p. 39.

4. Geza Uray. "Tibet's connection with Nestorianism and Manicheism in the 8th - 9th Centuries," *Contributions on Tibetan Language, History, and Culture* (Wiener Studien zur Tibetologie und Buddhismuskunde 10), ed. by E. Steinkellner and H. Tauscher. Vienna: Arbeitskreis fur Tibetische und Buddhistische Studien, 1983, pp. 399–429; Helmut Hoffmann. "Manichaeism and Islam in the Buddhist Kalacakra System," *Proceedings of the XIth International Congress for the History of Religions—Tokyo and Kyoto*. Tokyo: n.p., 1960, pp. 96–99; Luciano Petech. *I missionari italiani nel Tibet e nel Nepal*. 7 vols, Rome: n.p., 1952–56; H.J. Klimkeit. "Daa Kreuzsymbol in der zentralasiatischen Heilsbegegnung," *Zeitschrift fur Religions- und Geistesgeschichte*, 31, 1979, p. 99–115; G. Messina. *Christianerimo, buddhismo, manicheismo nell' Asia antica*. Rome: n.p. 1947; R.A. Stein. "Une mention du manicheisme dans le choix du bouddhisme comme religion d'etat par le roi tibetain Khri-sron lde-bcan," *Indianisme et bouddhisme* (Publications de l'Institut orientaliste de Louvain 23). Louvain-la-neuve: Institut Orientaliste, 1980, pp. 329–337.

5. Guiseppe Tucci. *The Religions of Tibet*, tr. by G. Samuel. Berkeley: University of California Press, 1980, p. 214f.

6. Lhundup Sopa / J. Hopkins, tr. *Practice and Theory of Tibetan Buddhism*. New Delhi: B.I. Publications, 1977, pp. 56–64.

7. J. Hopkins, tr. ed. *Kindness, Clarity, and Insight—The Fourteenth Dalai Lama His Holiness Tenzin Gyatso*. Ithaca, New York: Snow Lion Publications, 1984, p. 13.

8. Tinley Nyandak. "The Dalai Lama meets with U.S. Congressional Leaders", *News Tibet* 20.1. New York: Office of Tibet, 1985, p. 3.

9. Tinley Nyandak. "East-West Dialogue Phase Two is in Progress between Tibetan and Christian Monks", *News Tibet*18.2. New York: Office of Tibet, 1983, p. 5.

10. J. Hopkins, tr. ed. *Kindness* . . ., p. 47.

11. J. Hopkins, tr. ed. *Kindness* . . ., pp. 200–224.

12. Tinley Nyandak. "East-West Dialogue . . .", p. 4f.

13. *Vajradhatu Sun*, 5.5 Boulder, Colorado: Vajradhatu, 1983, p. 16.

CONTRIBUTORS

JOHN G. ARAPURA is Professor of Religion at McMaster University, Hamilton, Ontario, Canada. In addition to numerous articles, he has published *Radhakrishnan and Integral Experience* (1966), *Religion as Anxiety and Tranquility* (1972), and *Gnosis and the Question of Thought in Vedanta* (1986).

ROBERT D. BAIRD is Professor in the History of Religion, University of Iowa, Iowa City, Iowa. In addition to numerous articles, he has published *Category Formation and the History of Religion* (1971), and edited *Religion in Modern India* (1981).

HAROLD G. COWARD is Professor of Religious Studies and Director of the Humanities Institute at the University of Calgary, Calgary, Alberta. In addition to numerous articles and edited books, he has published *Bhartrhari* (1976), *The Sphota Theory of Language* (1980), *Pluralism: Challenge to World Religions* (1985), *Jung and Eastern Thought* (1985) and *Scripture in World Religions* (1987).

EVA K. DARGYAY is Professor of Religious Studies at the University of Calgary, Calgary, Alberta. She has numerous articles on Tibetan culture and Tibetan Buddhism to her credit. She has published *The Rise of Esoteric Buddhism in Tibet* (1977), *Translation of The Tibetan Book of the Dead* (into German) (1977), *Ladakh* (1980), and *Tibetan Village Communities* (1982).

JOHN R. HINNELLS is Professor of Comparative Religion at Manchester University, Manchester, England. In addition to numerous articles, he has published *Parsis and the British* (1978), *Zorastrianism and the Parsis* (1981) and edited several texts including *Hinduism*, (1972) and the MUP series *Sources for the Study of Religion*.

J.F.T. JORDENS is Reader in Asian History and Dean of the Faculty of Asian Studies, Australian National University, Canberra, Australia. In addition to numerous articles, he has published *Dayananda Sarasvati: His Life and Ideas* (1978) and *Swami Shraddhananda: His Life and Causes* (1981).

KLAUS K. KLOSTERMAIER is Professor and Chairman of the Department of Religious Studies, University of Manitoba, Winnipeg, Manitoba, Canada. In addition to numerous articles, he has published *Hinduismus* (1965), *Hindu and Christian in Vrindaban* (1970), *Mahatma Gandhi: Freiheit ohne Gewalt* (1968), *Salvation, Liberation, Self-realization* (1974), and *Mythologies and Philosophies of Salvation in the Theistic Tradition of India* (1984).

JULIUS L. LIPNER is Lecturer in the Comparative Study of Religion at the University of Cambridge and Fellow and Tutor at St. Edmund's House, Cambridge. He gave the 1981 Teape Lectures in India. In addition to his numerous articles, he recently published *The Face of Truth: A Study of Meaning and Metaphysics in the Vedantic Theology of Ramanuja* (1986).

ROLAND E. MILLER is Professor and Chairman of the Department of Religious Studies, University of Regina as well as Dean of Luther College, Regina, Saskatchewan, Canada. His publications include *The Mappila Muslims of Kerala* (1976) and *Report of the Planning Commission of the Indian Evangelical Lutheran Church* (1976).

ROBERT N. MINOR is Associate Professor of Religious Studies, University of Kansas, Lawrence, Kansas, U.S.A. In addition to many articles, he has published *The Bhagavad Gita: An Exegetical Commentary* (1981), *Sri Aurobindo: The Perfect and the Good* (1978), and edited *Modern Indian Interpreters of the "Bhagavadgita"* (1986).

RONALD W. NEUFELDT is Associate Professor of Religious Studies at the University of Calgary. In addition to various articles, he has published *F. Max Müller and the Rig Veda* (1980) and edited *Karma and Rebirth: Post Classical Developments* (1986).

JAMES N. PANKRATZ is Academic Dean and Associate Professor of Religion at the Mennonite Brethren Bible College & College of the Arts, Winnipeg, Manitoba, Canada. He has had many books and articles published including "Rannohun Roy" in *Religion in Modern India* in 1981.

KRISHNA SIVARAMAN is Professor of Religious Studies at McMaster University, Hamilton, Ontario, Canada. In addition to numerous articles he is author of *Saivism in Philosophical Perspective* (1972), *Theological Epistemology in Indian Philosophy* (1982), and *Saivism in Meykanda Sastra* (1982) (annotated translation with notes).

INDEX

grace, 157, 297

Granth Sahib, 52

guṇas, 109, 111, 113

Hare kṛṣna: *mantra*, 107, 116; movement, 65, 136; See also Bhaktivedānta, Swami

Hegel, G.F.W., 175, 176–177, 178, 179, 185–6; *aufheben*, 176

Hinduism: general, 8–10, 13, 15, 28–29, 31, 33, 34, 41–4, 45, 47, 50, 51, 55–8, 59, 90–1, 97, 109, 112, 122, 123, 137, 144, 145, 146, 155, 161, 200, 208, 211, 215, 220, 221, 239, 241, 247, 251–2, 270, 271–5, 278–80, 282–3, 284–5, 292–311, 319, 324, 325; Brāhmanical, 157; Upaniṣadic, 157

Husain, S. Abid, 252, 253, 258–62

Husain, Zikir, 253, 256–258

idealism, 175–178

idolatry (image worship), 19, 20, 21, 22, 23, 26, 30–1, 34, 165–6, 280, 295, 302, 309

ijtihād (principle of private interpretation), 240

Impermanence, 322

incarnation. *See avatār*

initiation, 209, 214–5, 219, 279, 281, 283; *See also dīkṣa, naujote*

International Society for Krishna Consciousness (ISKCON), 105, 107; "Back to Godhead," 107, 120

intuitions, 302, 308; mystical, 178, 179

Irani, Rustom, 217

Ishwara, 87

Islam (See Chapter 11), general, 31, 34, 40, 41, 45–6, 47, 49, 50–1, 54, 57, 59, 70, 90, 108, 109, 112, 118–9, 122, 144, 145, 147, 160, 165–6, 203–4, 221, 225, 270, 271–5, 278–80, 281, 282–3, 284–5, 305, 309; missionary activity, 53, 57, 58, 60, 317, 324; Sufism, 278, 280; toleration, 252–3, 256

itihāsas, 131

Jainism, 3, 4–6, 8, 40, 41, 57, 76, 109, 144, 145, 147, 156, 160, 161, 280, 319, 325; missionary activities, 57

Jama'at-Islam, 248, 249

JamaspAsa, Dr. K.M., 200, 209, 215

janam sākhīs, 269, 270, 278–280, 281

Jesus (Christ), 7, 28–29, 42, 47, 76, 77, 120–123, 139, 142–3, 164, 165, 295, 297, 300, 305, 311, 321

jihāh, 242

Jinnah, Muhammad 'Ali:, 239, 245, 257

jtva, 4, 5, 44

jñāna, 113, 162–3, 184

jñāni, 30, 143, 162–3

Jones, Dr. Stanley, 142–3

Jordens, J.F.T., 40, 41, 42, 43, 47–48

Judaism, 45, 77, 90, 145, 160, 161, 201, 216, 217, 242, 245–6, 251–2, 305, 324

juddīns, 209, 210, 218, 220

Kabir, 271, 276

Kant, I., 175, 177, 181

karuṇa, 132